Consumer Law for the Moto

Consumer Law for the Motor Trade

Fifth Edition

by

Anthea Worsdall

FIMI, Solicitor (non-practising)

Tottel Publishing
Maxwelton House
41–43 Boltro Road
Haywards Heath
West Sussex
RH16 1BJ

A CIP Catalogue record for this book is available from the British Library.

ISBN 1 84592 018 X

Typeset by Columns Design Ltd, Reading, UK
Printed and bound in Great Britain by Thomson Litho Ltd, East Kilbride, Scotland

Foreword

It gives us great pleasure to subscribe a foreword to the fifth edition of this book which explains in clear, everyday terms the law as it affects the retail motor industry and its relationships with its customers. Since the fourth edition was published in 1999, important changes to consumer law have occurred, for example, the Sale and Supply of Goods to Consumer Regulations, and these are fully covered in the new edition. In addition, the revised Block Exemption Regulation introduced in 2002; changes to the Office of Fair Trading's approach to recognised Codes of Practice, the Enterprise Act and the enhanced powers of trading standards officers under that Act in particular have been included.

The author continues to combine sound legal knowledge with extensive practical experience in advising the industry to provide a much needed work of reference. The fact the book is in its fifth edition underlines the invaluable nature of it to everyone engaged in the sale or supply of motor vehicles, accessories or parts, as well as servicing and repair, whether directly or indirectly, at all levels.

We believe that this book will prove indispensable in guiding those concerned with the distribution and retail of motor vehicles in the UK, through the complexities of the law to ensure consumer satisfaction in their day to day business operations. No motor trade professional adviser, student or users of motor vehicles can afford to be without a copy.

Sefton Samuels	David Evans
Company Secretary	Immediate Past President
The Society of Motor Manufacturers	European Council for Motor
and Traders (SMMT)	Trades and Repairs (Cecra)

Preface

The five years since the publication of the fourth edition has seen major changes in the law affecting the motor trade and its relationships with its customers, in particular the introduction of the Sale and Supply of Goods to Consumers Regulations 2002, which give consumers new rights when buying goods, and new remedies when something goes wrong. At the same time, there have been some interesting Court of Appeal cases on the interpretation of satisfactory quality, which at the time of the last edition had not yet been considered.

There have also been changes in the mechanism for enforcement of consumer law with the introduction of the Enterprise Act 2002, and a new approach to Codes of Practice. This has resulted in new Codes for the motor industry being introduced, and the two most significant, together with a new code of practice on vehicle recalls, are included as Appendices to the book.

Other new material covered in the book includes a section on the Consumer Protection (Distance Selling) Regulations 2000, and the new regulations in respect of consumer credit advertising, agreements and pre-contract information which have just been laid before Parliament.

The opportunity has been taken generally to update all the chapters, including relevant revisions to the block exemption regulations and recent cases.

I am very grateful to David Evans whose wealth of experience of the industry during his time at the RMI has made him an invaluable source of help and advice not only with this edition but with all the editions since the very first one in 1981, and to Seftton Samuels and Chris Mason at the SMMT for their continued support and assistance, and to the team at Butterworths, Etica and Tottel. Needless, to say, any errors or omissions in the text are my own.

The law is stated as at 1 September 2004.

Anthea Worsdall

September 2004

Contents

Table of statutes   *xi*

Table of statutory instruments   *xv*

Table of cases   *xix*

Chapter 1 The motor industry and the development of consumer
    protection   1

Chapter 2 Fair trading and codes of practice   14

Chapter 3 Sales promotion, advertising and pricing   24

Chapter 4 Trade descriptions   46

Chapter 5 Is there a contract?   70

Chapter 6 The impact of competition law   89

Chapter 7 Selling goods   97

Chapter 8 Financing the sale   156

Chapter 9 Credit agreements   173

Chapter 10 The manufacturer's responsibility   181

Chapter 11 Contracts for the repair and servicing of motor vehicles   197

Chapter 12 Other contracts with customers   212

Chapter 13 Safety matters   220

Chapter 14 Petrol   235

Chapter 15 Dealing with complaints   246

Appendix 1 Who's who and what's what in consumer protection   259

Appendix 2 OFT Guidance for Car Dealers   263

Appendix 3 The motor industry codes of practice   283

Appendix 4 Code of Practice on Vehicle Safety Defects 2004   309

Appendix 4A VBRA Consumer Code of Practice   315

Appendix 5 Disposal of uncollected good forms   327

Appendix 6 Code of practice for traders on price indications   329

Index   347

Table of statutes

References at the right-hand side of the column are to page numbers.

Auctions (Bidding Agreements) Act
   1969
   s 3(1).. 78
Competition Act 1980 .... 6, 9, 12
Competition Act 1998 ..... 6, 9, 12, 90
Consumer Arbitration Agreements
   Act 1988 .... 102, 252
Consumer Credit Act 1974. 8, 17, 71,
         104, 119, 156, 157, 171, 173,
              175, 212, 214, 216, 218
   s 40 160
   46 163
   57 .... 105, 177
   60 174
   75 .... 168, 170
   95, 99, 100 179
   Sch 2
      para 1–7 165
   Sch 4 118
Consumer Protection Act 1987 ... 137,
                                          151
   Pt I (ss 1–9) 152, 187, 190,
                                  200, 228
   s 2(5)....................................... 189
   Pt II (ss 10–19)............ 7, 226, 230
   s 10 232
   Pt III (ss 20–26).................. 36, 72
   s 21(1)....................................... 38
   25(1)... 39
   39(1)... 40

Consumer Safety Act 1978.......... 230
Emergency Laws (Re-Enactments
   and Repeals) Act 1964......... 180
Energy Act 1976........................... 61
   s 15 32
Enterprise Act 2002.... 7, 8, 9, 11, 12,
                             16, 18, 91
   Pt 8 (ss 210–236)...................... 12
   s 214 15
   218 16
Factors Act 1889........................ 114
   s 1 77
Fair Trading Act 1973 .... 6, 18, 89
   s 22 11
   Pt III (ss 34–43)....................... 21
Financial Services and Markets
   Act 2000
   s 23 211
Hire-Purchase Act 1964....... 119, 168
   Pt III (ss 27–29) 117, 118, 119
Minors' Contracts Act 1987 77
Misrepresentation Act 1967   105, 106
Motor Vehicles (Safety
   Equipment for Children)
   Act 1991 222
Petroleum (Consolidation) Act
   1928
   s 1 235
Police and Criminal Evidence Act
   1984...................................... 12

Powers of Criminal Courts Act 1973
s 35 57
Prices Act 1974........................ 41, 43
Proceeds of Crime Act 2002........ 113
Resale Prices Act 1976.................. 36
Restrictive Practices Court Act
1976...................................... 90
Road Traffic Act 1988 .... 30, 60
s 15a... 222
40a.. 221
41 .... 220, 221
41a, 41b.................................. 221
42 220
75 15
(1)..................................... 228
(4)(b)................................ 229
(6)(a) 229
76 .... 15, 199, 221, 229
80 224
185 230
Road Traffic Act 1991 . 220, 228, 229
Road Traffic Offenders Act
1988
s 66 218
Sale and Supply of Goods
Act 1994 .... 5, 11, 34, 44,
83, 114, 124, 125
Sale of Goods Act 1893..... 4, 83, 124
s 13 125
14(2), (3).............................. 125
Sale of Goods Act 1979. 20, 124, 129
s 3 76
11(4)...................................... 141
12 113
13 .... 122, 123
14 136
(2)-2(B)................... 134, **135**
(2C).......................... **135**, 136
(2D), (2E)........................ **137**
(3).................................. **138**
(4).................................. 138
15A(1)................................... 144
20, 23, 28 107
29(3)..................................... 108
(6)..................................... 107
34 141
35 .... 141, 143
38 109

Sale of Goods Act 1979—*contd*
s 48a... 147
48b 148
48c... 149
48d 147
48e... 149
61(1)...................................... 106
Supply of Goods and Services
Act 1982 .... 9, 198, 199,
212, 215
Supply of Goods (Implied
Terms) Act 1973 .... 5, 20, 171
s 14(6)....................................... 132
Theft Act 1968.............................. 50
Torts (Interference with Goods)
Act 1977 .... 15, 114, 120, 207
s 12, 13 209
Sch 1
Pt II
para 7 208
Trade Descriptions Act
1968................. 6, 11, 20, 29, 30,
43, 44, 47, 70, 152,
159, 223, 229,
234, 243, 244
s 1 .... **48**, 49
1(a), (b) 54, 68
2 .... 47, 52
(1)(d), (e)..............................
(f), (g)................................ 60
(j)...................................... 64
4 50
(2)..................................... 52
14 .... 31, 52, 54, 56
19(1)..................................... 58
20 48
21(1)(d), (e), (h)..................... 61
23 .... 49, 50, 57
24 .... 31, 57, 67
(1)..................................... **55**
(2), (3)............................. 55
27, 28 12
38(3)(a) 69
Trade Descriptions Act 1972... 46, 68
Trade Marks Act 1994
s 92 62
Trading Stamps Act 1964
s 7 44

Unfair Contract Terms Act
1977.......... 5, 99, 103, 125, 137,
182, 193, 204, 216, 219
s 2 .... 193, 205
3 .... 193, 204
5(1).. 193

Unfair Contract Terms Act—*contd*
s 12 125
Sch 2................................. 125, 183
Weights and Measures Act 1963 . 240
Weights and Measures Act
1985.................................... 240

Table of statutory instruments

References at the right-hand side of the column are to page numbers.

Business Advertisements (Disclosure) Order 1977, SI 1977/1918 33

Carriage of Dangerous Goods by Road Regulations 1996, SI 1996/2095 237

Consumer Credit (Advertisements) Regulations 2004, SI 2004/1484 163
reg 8, 9 165
Sch 2
para 1–7 165

Consumer Credit (Agreements) Regulations 1983, SI 1983/1553 175

Consumer Credit (Agreements) (Amendment) Regulations 1984, SI 1984/1600 175

Consumer Credit (Agreements) (Amendment) Regulations 2004, SI 2004/1482 ..... 175, 213

Consumer Credit (Agreements and Cancellation Notices and Copies of Documents) (Amendment) Regulations 1988, SI 1988/2047 175

Consumer Credit (Content of Quotations) and Consumer Credit (Advertisements) (Amendment) Regulations 1999, SI 1999/2725 166

Consumer Credit (Disclosure of Information) Regulations 2004, SI 2004/1481 166

Consumer Credit (Enforcement, Default and Termination Notices) Regulations 1983, SI 1983/1561 179

Consumer Credit (Rebate on Early Settlement) Regulations 1983, SI 1983/1562 179

Consumer Credit (Quotations) Regulations 1989, SI 1989/1126 166

Consumer Credit (Quotations) (Revocation) Regulations 1997, SI 1997/211 166

Consumer Credit (Total Charge for Credit) Regulations 1980, SI 1980/51 162

Consumer Credit (Total Charge for Credit) (Amendment) Regulations 1985, SI 1985/1192 162

Consumer Protection (Distance Selling) Regulations 2000, SI 2000/2334. 45, 71, 83, 99, 124
reg 4 107
6(2) 99, 100
7 100

Consumer Protection (Distance
    Selling) Regulations 2000,
    SI 2000/2334—*contd*
  Sch 1 101
  Sch 2 .... 100, 101
Consumer Transactions (Restrictions
    on Statements) Order 1976,
    SI 1976/1813 ...... 5, 11, 20, 137,
    .... 149, 153, 193
Consumer Transactions (Restrictions
    on Statements) (Amendment)
    Order 1978, SI 1978/127.. 5, 11,
    .... 20, 137, 149,
    .... 153, 193
Control of Hiring and Hire-Purchase
    and Credit Sale Agreements
    (Revocation) Order 1982,
    SI 1982/1034 180
Control of Misleading
    Advertisements Regulations
    1988, SI 1988/915 .... 25, 34
Control of Misleading
    Advertisements (Amendment)
    Regulations 2000,
    SI 2000/914 .... 25, 35
  reg 3(4).................................... 35
Enterprise Act 2002 (Part 8
    Domestic Infringements)
    Order 2003, SI 2003/1593 15
Filament Lamps for Vehicles
    (Safety) Regulations 1982,
    SI 1982/444 230
Financial Services and Markets
    Act 2000 (Regulated
    Activities) (Amendment)
    (No 2) Order 2003,
    SI 2003/1476 .... 155, 210
Financial Services (Distance
    Marketing) Regulations
    2004, SI 2004/2095 ...... 84, 167,
    178
  reg 3, 7 85
  8(3)... 85
  26 88
General Product Safety Regulations
    1994, SI 1994/2328. 8, 151, 232
Mail Order Transactions
    (Information) Order 1976,
    SI 1976/1812 45

Measuring Equipment (Liquid Fuel
    and Lubricants) Regulations
    1995, SI 1995/1014 240
Measuring Equipment (Liquid Fuel
    and Lubricants) (Amendment)
    Regulations 1998,
    SI 1998/2218 240
Motor Vehicle Tyres (Safety)
    Regulations 1994,
    SI 1994/3117 .... 230, 231
Motor Vehicles (Approval)
    Regulations 2001,
    SI 2001/25 223
Motor Vehicles (Designation of
    Approval Marks) Regulations
    1979, SI 1979/1088 60
Motor Vehicles (EC Type
    Approval) Regulations 1998,
    SI 1998/2051 223
Motor Vehicles Tyres (Safety)
    Regulations 1984,
    SI 1984/1233 230
Passenger Car Fuel Consumption
    Order 1983, SI 1983/1486 32
Passenger Car Fuel Consumption
    (Amendment) Order 1996,
    SI 1996/1132 32
Passenger Car (Fuel Consumption
    and CO2 Emissions
    Information) Regulations
    2001, SI 2001/3523 ... 11, 32, 64
Petroleum-Spirit (Motor Vehicles,
    etc) Regulations 1929,
    SI 1929/952 235
Petroleum-Spirit (Plastic
    Containers) Regulations
    1982, SI 1982/630 235
Price Indications (Method of
    Payment) Regulations 1991,
    SI 1991/199 40
Price Marking Order 1991,
    SI 1991/1382 240
Price Marking Order 1999,
    SI 1999/3042
  Annex 2.................................. 240
Price Marking Order 2004,
    SI 2004/102 41
  art 1(2)..................................... 42

Restriction on Agreements
(Manufacturers and Importers
of Motor Cars) Order 1982,
SI 1982/1146.......................... 90
Road Traffic (Owner Liability)
Regulations 1975,
SI 1975/324.......................... 218
Road Vehicles (Brake Linings Safety)
Regulations 1999, SI 1999/231
Road Vehicles (Construction
and Use) Regulations 1986,
SI 1986/1078........................ 220
Sale and Supply of Goods to
Consumers Regulations 2002,
SI 2002/3045...... 5, 20, 25, 153,
.... 192, 194, 249, 251
reg 2 126
3 137
Stop Now Orders (EC Directive)
Regulations 2001,
SI 2001/1422.................... 7, 14

Supply of New Cars Order 2000,
SI 2000/2088......................... 90
Three-Wheeled All-Terrain Motor
Vehicles (Safety) Regulations
1988, SI 1988/2122............. 230
Trade Descriptions (Place of
Production) (Marking) Order
1988, SI 1988/1771......... 62, 69
Unfair Arbitration Agreements
(Specified Amount) Order
1996, SI 1996/3211............. 252
Unfair Terms in Consumer Contracts
Regulations 1994, SI 1994/3159
Sch 3
para 1(b)   217
Unfair Terms in Consumer
Contracts Regulations 1999,
SI 1999/2083......................... 98
Unfair Terms in Consumer Contracts
(Amendment) Regulations 2001,
SI 2001/1186 98

Table of cases

A

Albemarle Supply Co Ltd v Hind & Co [1928] 1 KB 307, 97 LJKB 25,
　　[1927] All ER Rep 401, 71 Sol Jo 777, 138 LT 102, 43 TLR 783, CA ... 209
Alexander v Rolls Royce Motor Cars Ltd [1996] RTR 95, CA 199
Alton House Garages (Bromley) Ltd v Monk (31 July 1981, unreported) ... 123
Andrews Bros (Bournemouth) Ltd v Singer & Co Ltd [1934] 1 KB 17,
　　103 LJKB 90, [1933] All ER Rep 479, 150 LT 172, 50 TLR 33 4
Andrews v Hopkinson [1957] 1 QB 229, [1956] 3 All ER 422, [1956]
　　3 WLR 732, 100 Sol Jo 768 .... 82, 171

B

Badham v Lambs Ltd [1946] KB 45, [1945] 2 All ER 295, 115 LJKB
　　180, 89 Sol Jo 381, 173 LT 139, 61 TLR 569 152
Baldry v Marshall [1925] 1 KB 260, 94 LJKB 208, [1924] All ER Rep
　　155, 132 LT 326, CA 139
Bambury v Hounslow London Borough Council [1971] RTR 1 54
Bartlett v Sidney Marcus Ltd [1965] 2 All ER 753, [1965] 1 WLR 1013,
　　109 Sol Jo 451, CA.. 133, 140
Beale v Taylor [1967] 3 All ER 253, [1967] 1 WLR 1193, 111 Sol Jo
　　668, CA 82, 122
Beckett v Cohen [1973] 1 All ER 120, [1972] 1 WLR 1593, 71 LGR 46,
　　137 JP 116, 116 Sol Jo 882.. 53
Benerman v Association of British Travel Agents Ltd (1995) Times,
　　24 November, CA... 28
Bentley (Dick) Productions Ltd v Harold Smith (Motors) Ltd [1965]
　　2 All ER 65, [1965] 1 WLR 623, 109 Sol Jo 329, CA 81
Bernstein v Pamson Motors (Golders Green) Ltd [1987] 2 All ER 220,
　　[1987] RTR 384, [1987] BTLC 37 .... 130, 131, 132, 142, 144
Blakemore v Bellamy [1983] RTR 303, 147 JP 89, 126 Sol Jo 852 50

Bowerman v Association of British Travel Agents Ltd (1995) Times,
  24 November, CA 192
Bowmaker Ltd v Wycombe Motors Ltd [1946] KB 505, [1946] 2 All ER
  113, 115 LJKB 411, 90 Sol Jo 407, 175 LT 133, 62 TLR 437 206
Bramhill v Edwards [2004] EWCA Civ 403, [2004] All ER (D) 42 (Apr) 136,
  137
Branwhite v Worcester Works Finance Ltd [1969] 1 AC 552, [1968]
  3 All ER 104, [1968] 3 WLR 760, 112 Sol Jo 758, HL 168
Bristol Tramways etc Carriage Co Ltd v Fiat Motors Ltd [1910]
  2 KB 831, 79 LJKB 1107, 103 LT 443, 26 TLR 629, CA 140
British Car Auctions Ltd v Wright [1972] 3 All ER 462, [1972] 1 WLR
  1519, [1972] RTR 540, 116 Sol Jo 583 72
British Gas Corpn v Lubbock [1974] 1 All ER 188, [1974] 1 WLR 37,
  72 LGR 231, [1974] Crim LR 775, 117 Sol Jo 833 .... 31, 59
British Leyland plc v EC Commission: 226/84 [1986] ECR 3263,
  [1987] 1 CMLR 185, [1987] RTR 136, ECJ 223
Brogden v Metropolitan Rly Co (1877) 2 App Cas 666, HL 71
Business Application Specialists Ltd v Nationwide Credit Corpn Ltd
  (Marn Garage (Camberley) Ltd, third party) [1988] RTR 332,
  [1988] BTLC 461, [1988] CCLR 135, CA... 134
Butterworth v Kingsway Motors Ltd [1954] 2 All ER 694, [1954]
  1 WLR 1286, 98 Sol Jo 717 121

C

Carlill v Carbolic Smoke Ball Co [1892] 2 QB 484 72
Carroll v Fearon [1999] PIQR P416, Times, 26 January, CA 187
Cavendish Woodhouse Ltd v Manley 82 LGR 376, 148 JP 299, [1984]
  Crim LR 239 129
Cavendish Woodhouse Ltd v Wright (1995) 149 JP 497, [1986] BTLC 1...... 51
Century Insurance Co Ltd v Northern Ireland Road Tranport Board [1942]
  AC 509, [1942] 1 All ER 491, 111 LJPC 138, 167 LT 404, HL 200
Chapronière v Mason (1905) 21 TLR 633, CA.. 139
Charge Card Services Ltd, Re [1986] BCLC 316, 2 BCC 99, 371 172
Charnock v Liverpool Corpn [1968] 3 All ER 473, [1968] 1 WLR 1498,
  [1968] 2 Lloyd's Rep 113, 112 Sol Jo 781, CA.................................... 201
Charter v Sullivan [1957] 2 QB 117, [1957] 1 All ER 809, [1957] 2 WLR
  528, 101 Sol Jo 265, CA... 111
Charterhouse Credit Co Ltd v Tolly [1963] 2 QB 683, [1963] 2 All ER 432,
  [1963] 2 WLR 1168, 107 Sol Jo 234, CA 145
Chess (Oscar) Ltd v Williams [1957] 1 All ER 325, [1957] 1 WLR 370,
  101 Sol Jo 186, CA.. 6, 81, 82
Chidwick v Beer [1974] RTR 415, [1974] Crim LR 267 .... 52, 62
Coupe v Guyett [1973] 2 All ER 1058, [1973] 1 WLR 669, 71 LGR 355,
  [1973] RTR 518, 137 JP 694, [1973] Crim LR 386, 117 Sol Jo 415 55, 57
Cleeg v Olle Anderson (t/a Nordic Marine) (2003) Times, 14 April 144
Clode v Barnes [1974] 1 All ER 1166, [1974] 1 WLR 544, [1974]
  RTR 404, 138 JP 371, [1974] Crim LR 268, 118 Sol Jo 257 .... 49, 54

Cooper v Dempsey (1961) 105 Sol Jo 320, CA 203
Corfield v Sevenways Garage Ltd [1985] RTR 109, 148 JP 648,
    4 Tr L 172 .... 49, 51
Corfield v Starr [1981] RTR 380 67
Cottee v Douglas Seaton (Used Cars) Ltd [1972] 3 All ER 750, [1972]
    1 WLR 1408, [1972] RTR 509, 137 JP 1, [1972] Crim LR 590,
    116 Sol Jo 821 52
Crook v Howells Garages (Newport) Ltd [1980] RTR 434 65
Croshaw v Pritchard and Renwick (1899) 16 TLR 45, 2 Hudson's BC
    (4th Edn) 274, (10th Edn) 5, 8... 201
Crowther v Shannon Motor Co (a firm) [1975] 1 All ER 139, [1975]
    1 WLR 30, [1975] RTR 201, [1975] 1 Lloyd's Rep 382, 118 Sol
    Jo 714, CA.. 133

D

Daily Office Cleaning Contractors v Shefford [1977] RTR 361 146
Davies v Sumner [1984] 3 All ER 831, [1984] 1 WLR 1301, 83 LGR 123,
    [1985] RTR 95, 149 JP 110, 128 Sol Jo 814, [1985] LS Gaz R 45,
    4 Tr L 1, HL... 50
Denard v Smith and Dixons Ltd 155 JP 253, [1991] Crim LR 63, DC........... 31
Devlin v Hall [1990] RTR 320, 155 JP 20, [1990] Crim LR 879 50
Devon County Council v DB Cars [2001] EWHC Admin 521, 166 JP 38,
    [2002] Crim LR 71 .... 205, 229
Dimond v Lovell [2002] 1 AC 384, [2000] 2 All ER 897, [2000] 2 WLR
    1121, [2000] RTR 243, 22 LS Gaz R 47, 150 NLJ 740, [2000]
    CCLR 57, HL 176, 218
Dixons Ltd v Roberts (1984) 82 LGR 689, 148 JP 513 53
Donoghue v Stevenson [1932] AC 562, 101 LJPC 119, 37 Com Cas 350,
    [1932] All ER Rep 1, 76 Sol Jo 396, 147 LT 281, 48 TLR 494, 1932
    SC (HL) 31, 1932 SLT 317, HL 184
Dudley Metropolitan Borough Council v Debenhams plc (1994) 159
    JP 18, DC 12

E

Eastern Distributors Ltd v Goldring (Murphy, third party) [1957]
    2 QB 600, [1957] 2 All ER 525, [1957] 3 WLR 237, 101 Sol Jo
    553, CA... 115
Edwards v Ddin [1976] 3 All ER 705, [1976] 1 WLR 942, [1976] RTR
    508, 63 Cr App Rep 218, 141 JP 27, 120 Sol Jo 587 244
Elvin and Powell Ltd v Plummer Roddis Ltd (1933) 78 Sol Jo 48, 50
    TLR 158 204
Esso Petroleum Ltd v Customs and Excise Comrs [1976] 1 All ER 117,
    [1976] 1 WLR 1, 120 Sol Jo 49.. 29, 72
Evans v Triplex Safety Glass Co Ltd [1936] 1 All ER 283......................... 185

F

Farnworth Finance Facilities Ltd v Attryde [1970] 2 All ER 774, [1970]
    1 WLR 1053, [1970] RTR 352, 114 Sol Jo 354, CA 141, 145
Farrand v Lazarus [2002] EWHC 226 (Admin), [2002] 3 All ER 175,
    [2002] RTR 434 68
Felthouse v Bindley (1863) 1 New Rep 401, 11 WR 429, 7 LT 835 74
Financings Ltd v Stimson [1962] 3 All ER 386, [1962] 1 WLR 1184 73
Fisher v Bell [1961] 1 QB 394, [1960] 3 All ER 731, [1960] 3 WLR 919,
    125 JP 101, 104 Sol Jo 981 29
Fisher v Harrods Ltd [1966] 1 Lloyd's Rep 500, 110 Sol Jo 133 151
Fletcher v Budgen [1974] 2 All ER 1243, [1974] 1 WLR 1056, 72 LGR
    634, [1974] RTR 471, 59 Cr App Rep 234, [1974] Crim LR 489,
    118 Sol Jo 498 49
Fletcher v Sledmore 71 LGR 179, [1973] RTR 371, [1973] Crim LR 195,
    117 Sol Jo 164 49
Foakes v Beer (1884) 9 App Cas 605, 54 LJQB 130, 33 WR 233,
    [1881–5] All ER Rep 106, 51 LT 833, HL 75
Ford Credit plc v Normand 1994 SLT 318, 1993 SCCR 668 164
Forman & Co Pty Ltd v The Liddesdale [1900] AC 190, 69 LJPC 44,
    9 Asp MLC 45, 82 LT 331, PC 201
Formula One Autocentres Ltd v Birmingham City Council [1999] RTR
    195, 163 JP 234, [1998] All ER (D) 646 .... 53, 54, 55, 229
Frost v Aylesbury Dairy Co [1905] 1 KB 608, 74 LJKB 386, 53 WR 354,
    [1904–7] All ER Rep 132, 49 Sol Jo 312, 92 LT 527, 21 TLR
    300, CA 139
Furniss v Scholes [1974] RTR 133, [1974] Crim LR 199 62
Furniss v Scott [1973] RTR 314 30

G

Giles v Thompson [1994] 1 AC 142, [1993] 3 All ER 321, [1993] 2 WLR
    908, [1993] RTR 289, [1993] 27 LS Gaz R 34, 137 Sol Jo LB 151,
    HL 217
Grant v Australian Knitting Mills Ltd [1936] AC 85, 105 LJPC 6, [1935]
    All ER Rep 209, 79 Sol Jo 815, 154 LT 18, 52 TLR 38, PC 139
Green v All Motors Ltd [1917] 1 KB 625, 86 LJKB 590, [1916–17] All
    ER Rep 1039, 116 LT 189, CA 206

H

Hatton v Car Maintenance Co Ltd [1915] 1 Ch 621, 84 LJ Ch 847,
    [1911–13] All ER Rep 890, 58 Sol Jo 361, 110 LT 765, 30 TLR 275 207
Havering London Borough v Stevenson [1970] 3 All ER 609, [1970]
    1 WLR 1375, [1971] RTR 58, 134 JP 689, 114 Sol Jo 664 49
Hawkins v Smith [1978] Crim LR 578 30
Hill v James Crowe (Cases) Ltd [1978] 1 All ER 812, [1977] 2 Lloyd's
    Rep 450, [1978] ICR 298 188
Hirschler v Birch [1987] RTR 13, 151 JP 396, [1988] BTLC 27 53

Hitchens v General Guarentee Corpn Ltd (2001) Times, 13 March, CA 118
Hopkins v Tanqueray 15 CB 130, 23 LJCP 162, 18 Jur 608, 2 WR 475,
    [1843–60] All ER Rep 96, 2 CLR 842, 23 LTOS 144 3
Horner v Sherwoods of Darlington Ltd (1989) 154 JP 299 56
Howard v Harris (1884) Cab & El 253 203
Hughes v Hall [1981] RTR 430, 125 Sol Jo 255 129
Hummingbird Motors Ltd v Hobbs [1986] RTR 276, [1986] BTLC 245,
    CA 106
Hurley v Dyke [1979] RTR 265, HL 152

I

Idnani v Elisha (t/a Grafton Service Station) [1979] RTR 488, CA 202
Ingram v Little [1961] 1 QB 31, [1960] 3 All ER 332, [1960] 3 WLR
    504, 104 Sol Jo 704, CA 79, 116

J

Jackson v Chrysler Acceptances Ltd [1978] RTR 474, CA 130, 143, 146
Jackson v Rotax Cycles Ltd [1975] 38 MLR 660 131
Jenkins v Lombard North Central plc [1984] 1 All ER 828, [1984]
    1 WLR 307, [1985] RTR 21, 148 JP 280, 127 Sol Jo 782, [1984]
    LS Gaz R 124 163
Jones v Gallagher (t/a Gallery Kitchens & Bathrooms) [2004] EWCA
    Civ 10 144

K

Karsales (Harrow) Ltd v Wallis [1956] 2 All ER 866, [1956] 1 WLR 936,
    100 Sol Jo 548, CA 215
Kensington and Chelsea Royal London Borough Council v Riley [1973]
    RTR 122, [1973] Crim LR 133 52

L

Lambert v Lewis [1980] RTR 152 24
Lambert v Lewis, Larkin, B Dixon-Bate Ltd and Lexmead (Basingstoke)
    Ltd [1982] AC 225, 268, [1981] 1 All ER 1185, [1981] 2 WLR 713,
    [1981] RTR 346, [1981] 2 Lloyd's Rep 17, 125 Sol Jo 31, HL 186
Laurelgates Ltd v Lombard North Central Ltd (1983) 133 NLJ 720 142
Lazenby Garages Ltd v Wright [1976] 2 All ER 770, [1976] 1 WLR 459,
    120 Sol Jo 146, CA 109
Leaves v Wadham Stringer (Cliftons) Ltd [1980] RTR 308 143
Lee v York Coach and Marine [1977] RTR 35, CA 132, 134, 142
Lewin v Bland [1985] RTR 171, 148 JP 69 48
Lewin v Fuell 155 JP 206, [1990] Crim LR 658 67
Lewin v Rothersthorpe Road Garage Ltd (1983) 148 JP 87 56
Lewis v Averay [1972] 1 QB 198, [1971] 3 All ER 907, [1971] 3 WLR
    603, 115 Sol Jo 755 .... 79, 116

Lill (K) Holdings Ltd v White [1979] RTR 120 65
Liverpool and County Discount Co Ltd v AB Motor Co (Kilburn) Ltd
    [1963] 2 All ER 396, [1963] 1 WLR 611, 107 Sol Jo 270, CA............. 168
Long v Lloyd [1958] 2 All ER 402, [1958] 1 WLR 753, 102 Sol Jo 488,
    CA 105

M

M & T Hurst Consultants Ltd Grange Motors & Rolls Royce Motors Ltd
    (1981) unreported 132
MFI Warehouses Ltd v Nattrass [1973] 1 All ER 762, [1973] 1 WLR 307,
    137 JP 307, [1973] Crim LR 196, 117 Sol Jo 143 53
Metsoja v H Norman Pitt & Co Ltd 153 JP 485, [1989] Crim LR 560,
    [1989] COD 422, [1990] CCLR 12, 8 Tr LR 155 166
Millars of Falkirk Ltd v Turpie (1976) 1976 SLT (Notes) 66 131
Moons Motors Ltd v Kiuan Wou [1952] 2 Lloyd's Rep 80, CA................... 217
Moorgate Mercantile Co Ltd v Twitchings [1977] AC 890, [1976] 2 All
    ER 641, [1976] 3 WLR 66, [1976] RTR 437, 120 Sol Jo 470, HL... 116, 119
Morris Motors Ltd v Lilley (t/a G and L Motors) [1959] 3 All ER 737,
    [1959] 1 WLR 1184, 103 Sol Jo 1003 63
Myers (G H) & Co v Brent Cross Service Co [1934] 1 KB 46, 103 LJKB
    123, [1933] All ER Rep 9, 150 LT 96 199

N

Naish v Gore [1971] 3 All ER 737, [1972] RTR 102, 136 JP 1 55
National Employers' Mutual General Insurance Association Ltd v Jones
    [1990] 1 AC 24, [1988] 2 All ER 425, [1988] 2 WLR 952, [1988]
    RTR 289, 132 Sol Jo 658, [1988] NLJR 118, HL 115
Newell v Hicks [1984] RTR 135, 148 JP 308, [1984] Crim LR 241, 128
    Sol Jo 63, [1984] LS Gaz R 354 53
Newham London Borough v Singh [1988] RTR 359, 152 JP 239 .... 67, 68
Newtons of Wembley Ltd v Williams [1965] 1 QB 560, [1964] 3 All ER
    532, [1964] 3 WLR 888, 108 Sol Jo 619, CA 117
Nightingale v Tildsley [1980] CLY 134 202
Norman v Bennett [1974] 3 All ER 351, [1974] 1 WLR 1229, 72 LGR 676,
    [1974] RTR 441, 59 Cr App Rep 277, 138 JP 746, [1974] Crim LR
    559, 118 Sol Jo 697, [1974] CLY 3448 67
Norman (Alec) Garages Ltd v Phillips [1985] RTR 164, 148 JP 741,
    4 Tr L 21 46
North Yorkshire County Council v Rover Group Ltd (5 October 1995,
    unreported) 42

O

Olgeirsson v Kitching [1986] 1 All ER 746, [1986] 1 WLR 304, [1986]
    RTR 129, 150 JP 117, [1986] Crim LR 341, [1986] BTLC 72, 130
    Sol Jo 110, [1985] LS Gaz R 617 50

P

Pearson v Rose and Young Ltd [1951] 1 KB 275, [1950] 2 All ER 1027,
  94 Sol Jo 778, 66 (pt 2) TLR 886, CA 115
Pedrick v Morning Star Motors Ltd (14 February 1979, unreported), CA ... 203
Pharmaceutical Society of Great Britain v Boots Cash Chemists
  (Southern) Ltd [1953] 1 QB 401, [1953] 1 All ER 482, [1953]
  2 WLR 427, 117 JP 132, 97 Sol Jo 149, CA 29, 73
Phillips v Britannia Hygienic Laundry Co [1923] 2 KB 832, 21 LGR 709,
  93 LJKB 5, [1923] All ER Rep 127, 68 Sol Jo 102, 129 LT 777, 39
  TLR 530, CA 152
Phillips v Brooks Ltd [1919] 2 KB 243, 88 LJKB 953, 24 Com Cas 263,
  [1918–19] All ER Rep 246, 121 LT 249, 35 TLR 470 79

R

R v Anderson [1988] RTR 260, 152 JP 373 .... 64, 93
R v Ascot Horseboxes International Ltd (17 February 1998, unreported).... 232
R v Baldwins Garage (Warrington) Ltd [1988] Crim LR 438 163
R v Bevelectric (1992) 157 JP 323, [1992] NLJR 1342, CA 54
R v Bull [1997] RTR 123, 160 JP 240, [1996] Crim LR 438......................... 68
R v Crown Court at Shrewsbury, ex p Venables [1994] Crim LR 61 66
R v Ford Motor Co Ltd [1974] 3 All ER 489, [1974] 1 WLR 1220,
  72 LGR 655, [1974] RTR 509, 59 Cr App Rep 281, 138 JP 738,
  [1974] Crim LR 617, 118 Sol Jo 596, CA................................. 63, 64, 123
R v Haesler [1973] RTR 486, [1973] Crim LR 586, CA 61
R v Hammertons Cars Ltd [1976] 3 All ER 758, [1976] 1 WLR 1243,
  75 LGR 4, [1976] RTR 516, 63 Cr App Rep 234, [1976] Crim LR
  775, 120 Sol Jo 553, [1976] CLY 2470, CA 67, 68
R v Hewitt [1991] RTR 357, 13 Cr App Rep (S) 131, CA............................. 57
R v Holloway (1988) Times, 31 January.. 200
R v McHugh [1977] RTR 1, 64 Cr App Rep 104, [1977] Crim LR 174,
  CA 244
R v Nash (1990) 89 LGR 633, [1990] RTR 343, CA.................................... 30
R v Parking Adjudicator, ex p Wandsworth London Borough Council
  [1998] RTR 51, CA 204
R v South Western Justices and Hallcrest Garages Ltd, ex p London
  Borough of Wandsworth [1983] RTR 425, 147 JP 212 64
R v Southwood [1987] 3 All ER 556, [1987] 1 WLR 1361, [1987] RTR
  273, 85 Cr App Rep 272, 151 JP 860, [1987] Crim LR 779, [1987]
  BTLC 374, 131 Sol Jo 1038, [1987] LS Gaz R 2365, CA................ 65, 68
R v Sunair Holidays Ltd [1973] 2 All ER 1233, [1973] 1 WLR 1105,
  57 Cr App Rep 782, 137 JP 687, [1973] Crim LR 587, 117 Sol Jo
  429, CA 53
R v Warwickshire County Council, ex p Johnson [1993] AC 583, [1993]
  1 All ER 299, [1993] 2 WLR 1, 91 LGR 130, 157 JP 249, [1993]
  Crim LR 940, [1993] 6 LS Gaz R 41, [1993] NLJR 127, 137 Sol Jo
  LB 37, HL... 37

R & B Customs Brokers Co Ltd v United Dominions Trust Ltd (Saunders
    Abbott (1980) Ltd, third party) [1988] 1 All ER 847, [1988] 1 WLR
    321, [1988] RTR 134, [1988] BTLC 52, 132 Sol Jo 300, [1988] 11
    LS Gaz R 42, CA 99, 126, 139
Raynham Farm Co Ltd v Symbol Motor Corpn [1987] BTLC 157 .... 63, 123
Rees v Munday [1974] 3 All ER 506, [1974] 1 WLR 1284, [1974] RTR
    536, 60 Cr App Rep 20, 138 JP 767, [1974] Crim LR 561, 118 Sol
    Jo 697 68
Relph v Yamaha Motor Co Ltd, Yamaha Motor Co USA and Burtonwood
    Development Ltd (4 July 1996, unreported), QBD 188
Ritchie's Car Hire Ltd v Bailey (1958) 108 L Jo 348 217
Roberts v Severn Petroleum and Trading Co Ltd [1981] RTR 312 243
Robertson v Dicicco [1972] RTR 431, [1972] Crim LR 592, 116 Sol Jo
    744, 122 NLJ 680 .... 30, 52, 62
Robins & Day Ltd v Kent County Council Trading Standards Department
    [1996] CLY 1168 58
Rogers v Parish (Scarborough) Ltd [1987] QB 933, [1987] 2 All ER 232,
    [1987] 2 WLR 353, [1987] RTR 312, [1987] BTLC 51, 131 Sol Jo
    223, [1987] LS Gaz R 905, CA 132, 135, 149
Routledge v Ansa Motors (Chester le Street) Ltd [1980] RTR 1, [1980]
    Crim LR 65, 123 Sol Jo 735 61
Rover Group Ltd and Rover Finance Ltd v Sumner [1995] CCLR 1 164
Rowland v Divall [1923] 2 KB 500, 92 LJKB 1041, [1923] All ER Rep
    270, 67 Sol Jo 703, 129 LT 757, CA 121
Royscot Trust Ltd v Rogerson [1991] 2 QB 297, [1991] 3 All ER 294,
    [1991] 3 WLR 57, 135 Sol Jo 444, [1991] NLJR 493, CA 105, 168

S

Sargent (J) (Garages) Ltd v Motor Auctions (West Bromwich) Ltd [1977]
    RTR 121, CA 116
Saunders (Executrix of Will of Gallie) v Anglia Building Society [1971]
    AC 1004, [1970] 3 All ER 961, [1970] 3 WLR 1078, 22 P & CR 300,
    114 Sol Jo 885, HL 80
Scammell (G) and Nephew Ltd v Ouston [1941] AC 251, [1941] 1 All ER
    14, 110 LJKB 197, 46 Com Cas 190, 85 Sol Jo 224, 164 LT 379,
    57 TLR 280 74
Shine v General Guarantee Corpn (Reeds Motor Co (a firm), third party)
    [1988] 1 All ER 911, [1988] BTLC 1, [1987] NLJ Rep 946, CA 134
Shogun Finance Ltd v Hudson [2003] UKHL 62, [2004] 1 AC 919,[2004]
    1 All ER 215, [2003] 3 WLR 1371, [2004] 1 All ER (Comm) 332,
    [2004] RTR 153, [2004] 1 Lloyd's Rep 532, [2003] 46 LS Gaz R 25,
    [2003] NLJR 1790, Times, 20 November, 147 Sol Jo LB 1368, HL 80,
    118
Shropshire County Council Trading Standards Department v Telford
    (Vehicles) Ltd (17 August 1980, unreported) Wreckin Magistrates'
    Court 20
Simmons v Potter [1975] RTR 347, [1975] Crim LR 354 .... 55, 66

Simmons v Ravenhill [1984] RTR 412, 148 JP 109, [1983] Crim LR 749,
  3 Tr L 29 56
Southend Borough Council v White 156 LG Rev 911, 156 JP 463, [1991]
  COD 345, 11 Tr LR 65 66
Southern Industrial Trust Ltd v Brooke House Motors Ltd (t/a Starnes
  Motors) (1968) 112 Sol Jo 798, CA 169
Southern Livestock Producers Ltd, Re [1963] 3 All ER 801, [1964]
  1 WLR 24, 108 Sol Jo 15 206
Spencer v Claud Rye (Vehicles) Ltd (1972) Guardian, 19 December.......... 131
Stennett v Hancock and Peters [1939] 2 All ER 578, 83 Sol Jo 379............. 200
Stevenson v Beverley Bentinck Ltd [1976] 2 All ER 606, [1976] 1 WLR
  483, [1976] RTR 543, 120 Sol Jo 197, CA.................................. 118
Stevenson v Rogers [1999] QB 1028, [1999] 1 All ER 613, [1999] 2 WLR
  1064, [1999] 02 LS Gaz R 29, [1999] NLJR 16, 143 Sol Jo LB 21,
  CA 34, 125
Stewart v Reavell's Garage [1952] 2 QB 545, [1952] 1 All ER 1191,
  96 Sol Jo 314, [1952] 1 TLR 1266 204
Swithland Motors Ltd v Peck [1991] RTR 322, [1991] Crim LR 386 51

T

Tarleton Engineering Co Ltd v Nattrass [1973] 3 All ER 699, [1973]
  1 WLR 1261, 72 LGR 56, [1973] RTR 435, 137 JP 837, [1973]
  Crim LR 647, 117 Sol Jo 745 65
Taylor v Smith [1974] RTR 190, [1974] Crim LR 200 65
Tesco Supermarkets Ltd v Nattrass [1972] AC 153, [1971] 2 All ER 127,
  [1971] 2 WLR 1166, 69 LGR 403, 135 JP 289, 115 Sol Jo 285, HL 56
Thain v Anniesland Trade Centre 1997 SLT 102, 1997 SCLR 991 150
Thompson (W L) Ltd v Robinson (Gunmakers) Ltd [1955] Ch 177,
  [1955] 1 All ER 154, [1955] 2 WLR 185, 99 Sol Jo 76 111
Thomson Tour Operations Ltd v Birch 163 JP 465, [1999] All ER (D) 66..... 39
Toyota (GB) Ltd v North Yorkshire County Council (1998) 162
  JP 794 .... 36, 38, 43
Tweddle v Atkinson 25 JP 517, 1 B & S 393, 30 LJQB 265, 8 Jur NS 332,
  9 WR 781, [1861–73] All ER Rep 369, 4 LT 468 74

U

UCB Leasing Ltd v Holtom (t/a David Holtom & Co) [1987] RTR 362,
  [1987] NLJ Rep 614, CA... 142, 145, 146
United Dominions Trust (Commercial) Ltd v Eagle Aircraft Services Ltd
  [1968] 1 All ER 104, [1968] 1 WLR 74, 111 Sol Jo 849, CA............... 169
United Dominions Trust Ltd v Taylor 1980 SLT 28.................................... 170
United Motor Finance Co v Addison & Co Ltd [1937] 1 All ER 425, PC.... 167

V

VAG (UK) Ltd v Lancashire County Council [1997] Trading Standards
  Review 20.. 59

Vaswani v Italian Motors (Sales and Services) Ltd [1996] 1 WLR 270, [1996] RTR 115, [1996] 02 LS Gaz R 27, 140 Sol Jo LB 27, PC......... 109

W

Wadham Stringer Finance Ltd v Meaney [1980] 3 All ER 789, [1981] 1 WLR 39, [1981] RTR 152, Con LR 7, 124 Sol Jo 807 179
Walker v Simon Dudley Ltd (1997) Times, 3 January.............................. 51, 65
Waltham Forest London Borough Council v T G Wheatley (Central Garage) (No 2) [1978] RTR 333, [1977] Crim LR 761 67
Walton v British Leyland UK Ltd [1980] Product Liability International 156 .... 185, 225
Ward & Armistead Ltd v Bridgland Anca Garage (Worthing) Ltd (1976) unreported, QBD 192
Wickens Motors (Gloucester) Ltd v Hall [1972] 3 All ER 759, [1972] 1 WLR 1418, [1972] RTR 519, 137 JP 8, [1972] Crim LR 652, 116 Sol Jo 744 51
Wimpey v George Maxwell Developments Ltd (1980) unreported, Chester CC.. 12
Wings Ltd v Ellis [1985] AC 272, [1984] 3 All ER 577, [1984] 3 WLR 965, 83 LGR 193, 149 JP 33, 128 Sol Jo 766, [1984] LS Gaz R 3507, [1985] Tr L 66, HL 31
Winterbottom v Wright (1842) 11 LJ Ex 415, 10 M & W 109, 152 ER 402 3
Winward v TVR Engineering Ltd [1986] BTLC 366, CA 186
Worsley (Ben) Ltd v Harvey [1967] 2 All ER 507, [1967] 1 WLR 889, 65 LGR 373, 131 JP 376, 111 Sol Jo 541 48
Wycombe Marsh Garages Ltd v Fowler [1972] 3 All ER 248, [1972] 1 WLR 1156, [1972] RTR 503, 137 JP 138, [1972] Crim LR 456, 116 Sol Jo 467 .... 51, 60

Y

Yeoman Credit Ltd v Apps [1962] 2 QB 508, [1961] 2 All ER 281, [1961] 3 WLR 94, 105 Sol Jo 567, CA 145

Z

Zawadski v Sleigh [1975] RTR 113, [1975] Crim LR 180, 119 Sol Jo 318 ... 67

CHAPTER I

The motor industry and the development of consumer protection

A INTRODUCTION

This book is about the law as it affects the relationship between the motor industry and its customers. Although twentieth century man has often been described as having a 'love affair' with his motor car, his feelings towards the industry which makes, supplies, services and repairs the object of his affections are not so warm: indeed the relationship is often a rather uneasy one.

That this should be so is probably due to several factors. First, it has to be admitted that the industry's standards are not always as high as they should be. Whilst a great deal has been done in recent years to improve the situation with the introduction of the motor industry code of practice, and the active encouragement by many manufacturers of their franchised dealers to improve their standards of service, all too often the industry as a whole is let down by companies who do not give their customers the fair deal that they are legally and morally entitled to receive.

There is also the financial importance of the motor car to the consumer. In 1986 the Office of Fair Trading quoted, in a survey on the first Motor Code,[1] statistics that showed that something like 12.3% of the average household budget was taken up by the purchase, maintenance and running of a motor vehicle.[2] Consumers are now encouraged more

---

[1] The Motor Code – A Report on a Monitoring Survey, September 1986.
[2] Family Expenditure Survey, 1983.

than ever to look more closely to see whether they are getting value for money. The motor car is now tremendously important as the means of personal transport for the consumer who is likely to suffer not just inconvenience but real hardship if he is deprived of the use of his car. Fourth, there is the complexity of the product, and its susceptibility to poor maintenance, bad driving techniques, and other abuse and misuse by its owner.

Last, but not least, there is the emotional impact which the so-called love affair can have on otherwise perfectly rational people and turn them into the aggressive, demanding and unreasonable 'consumers' well known to any garage service receptionist.

The problems caused by the motor car to consumers are reflected in the number of complaints made about the industry. Statistics produced annually by the Office of Fair Trading show that complaints about the condition of vehicles being sold, and about standards of repair and servicing, consistently make up a large proportion of the complaints notified in relation to any one sector of industry. In addition, there are more prosecutions of motor traders under the Trade Descriptions Act than of any single group of suppliers of goods and services. Whilst this fact taken on its own paints a gloomy picture, it should also be noted that other industries have a higher ratio of complaints per million pounds of consumer expenditure (eg household appliances) and that when the number of transactions which the motor industry enters into every year with its customers in selling, servicing and repairing their cars is considered, there is a very large proportion which does not elicit any customer complaint at all.

Nevertheless, the motor car is an important consumer product and so long as it stays that way, the motor industry will come under close scrutiny from all those involved in consumer protection, from the Office of Fair Trading to the local trading standards officer, and from the Consumers Association to the Citizens Advice Bureaux. The Office of Fair Trading, for example, has stated quite clearly that it will focus a good deal of attention on the motor industry and what it is doing to improve and maintain the quality of the goods and services which it offers to consumers.

The motor industry has already been often in the forefront of legislators' minds when new consumer protection laws have been introduced or old ones amended, and as a result there is now a whole body of legislation and case law that has a direct impact on both motor manufacturers and traders. Some of it is comprised in regulations affecting specific aspects of the motor trade, for example in relation to the selling of petrol, the display of petrol prices and of fuel consumption figures; some of it in the general provisions which are aimed at protecting consumers when they acquire goods and services.

B THE DEVELOPMENT OF CONSUMER PROTECTION

Although consumer laws of one sort or another have been around for centuries, there has been an 'explosion' of new laws governing the way in which retailers and manufacturers can do business with their customers over the last fifteen to twenty years. This explosion has of course been mirrored by the twentieth century growth in the sale of consumer products, not least of which is the motor vehicle. Much of the new law introduced has been aimed, at least in part, at the motor industry.

Consumer protection laws do not just involve consumers taking action privately against retailers and manufacturers; they can also involve criminal penalties if the rules are broken. It is therefore essential that manufacturers and traders in the motor industry should be aware of their legal responsibilities, and also ensure that their staff are adequately prepared to handle the sort of day-to-day problems which may arise.

Although the modern motor industry has a poor reputation, it seems that problems with transport are not an exclusively twentieth century phenomenon. The horse and carriage could prove just as troublesome. In 1842,[3] the driver of a mail coach unsuccessfully tried to sue the manufacturer of the coach for compensation for injuries he received due to an accident caused by its defective design. In 1854,[4] the purchaser of a horse had cause to sue the seller over a statement that the horse was 'perfectly sound' in every respect and, as long ago as the sixteenth century, the author of one of the first legal textbooks used the example of the sale of a horse to illustrate the rule of 'caveat emptor', the need for the buyer to beware of what he was buying.

As the law has developed over the years, and particularly in the second half of the twentieth century, it is interesting to see how many of the

---

3   *Winterbottom v Wright* (1842) 10 M & W 109.
4   *Hopkins v Tanqueray* (1954) 15 CB 130.

leading cases have in fact involved motor cars, and in some cases have paved the way for a change in the law, for example, in relation to conditions of sale, misdescriptions of goods, unfair trading practices, consumer safety and consumer credit.

I   Conditions of sale

The Sale of Goods Act 1893 is a convenient starting point for looking at the way consumer protection laws have developed.

This Act basically stated the law as it already was being interpreted and applied, namely that in a contract for the sale of goods there were to be terms implied into the contract:
(a)   that the goods were of 'merchantable quality';
(b)   that they were fit for their purpose;
(c)   that the seller had the right to sell the goods;
(d)   that the goods corresponded to any description applied to them.

The Act then went on to provide that these terms would only apply if not 'otherwise agreed' by the parties to the contract. This was to prove to be a substantial loophole through which many sellers of shoddy goods were to escape over the years. Sellers made sure that they always did business on their own terms and conditions which would contain a clause excluding or limiting the 'implied terms', leaving the buyer with no remedies at all if the goods he had bought turned out to be faulty: a so-called 'exclusion clause'.

'Exclusion clauses' of this kind were used widely by suppliers of all kinds of goods and the motor industry was no exception. As the disputes arose the courts worked hard to avoid giving effect to these clauses where they could. For example, a firm of car dealers ordered a 'new 18 hp saloon car' from the manufacturers, Singer & Co. Their contract contained a clause which stated 'All conditions, warranties and liabilities implied by statute, common law or otherwise are excluded'. The car when delivered turned out not to be a new one, and the dealer sued the manufacturers who tried to hide behind the exclusion clause. The court held that they could not do so because the exclusion clause was not wide enough to cover the express term of the contract that the car should be a new one: it referred only to implied terms.[5]

5   *Andrew Bros (Bournemouth) Ltd v Singer & Co Ltd* [1934] 1 KB 17.

In 1973 exclusion clauses in consumer sales were outlawed with the arrival of the Supply of Goods (Implied Terms) Act. This Act made exclusion clauses used in sales of goods to consumers unenforceable (they were subsequently made illegal),[6] and exclusions used in other contracts subject to a test to see whether they are 'reasonable' or not.[7]

This change in the law did not, however, have any effect on contracts other than for the supply of goods, eg it did not apply to statements such as 'cars parked at owner's risk' in car parks. These types of statement were dealt with in 1977 when the Unfair Contract Terms Act was passed, making exclusion clauses in contracts other than for the supply of goods subject to a similar test of reasonableness. In addition, any clauses excluding liability for death or personal injury were made completely ineffective. In 1994, legal controls were expanded by the Unfair Terms in Consumer Contracts Regulations to cover all unfair contract terms in consumer contracts.

In the same year, the law covering sale of goods was updated and amended in the Sale and Supply of Goods Act. This replaced the old requirement that goods should be of 'merchantable quality' with one which referred instead to 'satisfactory quality', and also strengthened the consumer's remedies. This trend has continued with the coming into force on 31 March 2003 of the Sale and Supply of Goods to Consumers Regulations 2002. These implement an EC Directive[8] giving consumers greater legal rights in respect of the remedies available to them when buying defective goods, and reversing the burden of proof for the first six months after delivery of the goods, as well as bringing the legal definition of a 'consumer' into line with other legislation derived from Europe.

In other areas too the motor industry was to be greatly affected by developments in consumer protection legislation and was often involved in cases which illustrated a particular consumer problem, eg description of goods, unfair trading practices, consumer safety and consumer credit.

---

[6]   Consumer Transactions (Restrictions on Statements) Order 1976, SI 1976/1813 subsequently amended by SI 1978/127.

[7]   See also ch 11, below.

[8]   Directive 99/44/EC on Certain Aspects of the Sale of Consumer Goods and Associated Guarantees.

2 Misdescriptions of goods

Statements made by a seller about goods may deceive the consumer who is buying them. These statements may become terms of the contract, or they may only be representations which induce the consumer to enter into the contract.[9] Until 1967, when the Misrepresentation Act was passed, if they were representations the consumer would not be able to recover any compensation if the statement, although false, was made in innocence.

In *Oscar Chess v Williams*,[10] a customer who was trading in a car was asked the age of the car by the dealer. He said it was a 1948 model, and this was confirmed by the registration book. In fact unknown to both parties it was a 1939 model. The dealer sued for the difference in value between the two models, but he was unable to recover any damages because the age of the vehicle was held not to be a term of the contract and the representation was innocently made by the customer.

The Misrepresentation Act enabled the purchaser in this type of situation to recover damages for such an innocent misstatement even if it was too late for him to cancel the whole contract.

A year later in 1968 the criminal aspect of false statements was tackled when the Trade Descriptions Act was passed, making false descriptions as to goods or services an offence.[11]

3 Unfair trading practices

Perhaps the most significant event in the development of consumer legislation was the appointment of the Director General of Fair Trading under the provisions of the Fair Trading Act 1973. The wide powers given to the Director General include the overseeing of the legislation on restrictive practices, monopolies and mergers and, more recently, anti-competitive practices under the Competition Acts of 1980 and 1998. In addition, he is responsible for the operation of the provisions of the Consumer Credit Act 1974, the general control of 'unfair trading practices', and the encouragement of voluntary codes of practice. In the area of consumer affairs the motor industry has been considerably

---

[9]   See ch 5, below.
[10] [1957] 1 WLR 370.
[11] See ch 3, below.

affected by the work of the Office of Fair Trading: the introduction of the original motor industry code of practice in 1976; the legislation making exclusions of the implied terms in contracts for the sale of goods to consumers illegal and the legislation banning advertisements which mislead consumers by not disclosing that they are placed by businesses, are all examples.[12] In 2001, enforcement was strengthened in respect of consumer protection legislation derived from Europe[13] by the introduction of 'stop now' orders, and with the implementation of the Enterprise Act 2002 during 2003, these powers have been extended to include some aspects of civil law. Meanwhile the Office of Fair Trading has taken on a new status as a corporate body with wide-ranging powers in respect of both competition and consumer law, and the post of Director General of Fair Trading has been replaced by that of Chairman of the board of the OFT.

4 Consumer safety

Although the motor industry is controlled by the Road Traffic Acts, and construction and use regulations in the design and manufacture of motor vehicles, there is no UK legislation similar to that which exists in the USA to enable the government to force manufacturers to recall motor vehicles when safety faults are discovered. This has been frequently criticised on the grounds that the voluntary system of recalls operated by manufacturers does not provide sufficient protection for consumers. In 1978 the Consumer Safety Act was passed which, amongst other things, enabled regulations to be made banning the sale of goods which were 'unsafe'. Although this was not power to demand a recall, it was potentially even more damaging to a manufacturer. The existence of this legislation therefore gave the industry an additional incentive to agree to a voluntary Code of Practice on Vehicle Recalls in 1978 the latest version of which was issued in 2004.[14] This has been periodically revised, with the latest version issues in 2004. It should be noted, however, that this legislation has been used to ban the sale of allegedly unsafe motor accessories in the UK, as has the legislation which has now replaced it (see Chapter 13). Part II of the Consumer Protection Act 1987 now imposes a general duty to trade only in safe

[12]   See ch 2, below.
[13]   Stop Now Orders (EC Directive) Regulations 2001, SI 2001/1422.
[14]   See ch 13 and app 3, below.

goods, with criminal penalties. Motor vehicles, as defined in the Road Traffic Acts, are excluded but parts and accessories for motor vehicles are covered. The General Product Safety Regulations 1994 have also imposed more extensive obligations in respect of the supply of unsafe goods, and trading standards officers may now use their powers under these regulations in respect of used cars (see Chapter 13).

5 Consumer credit

The buying of goods on credit has always given consumers problems. The early hire-purchase legislation helped to give consumers protection, eg in relation to the form of credit contracts, and restricted the power of the owners of goods on hire purchase to repossess them. In addition, the 1965 Act recognised the special difficulties caused to consumers when buying secondhand cars which turned out to be on hire purchase. The Act provides for the first private purchaser who is ignorant of the facts to get good title to the car he has 'bought' despite an outstanding hire-purchase or conditional sale agreement.[15]

The passing of the Consumer Credit Act 1974 was another major landmark in consumer protection. One of its most important provisions relates to the setting up of a licensing system for those who supply credit or are involved in credit business. This has had a considerable effect on the motor trade, particularly because the Director General of Fair Trading (now the Office of Fair Trading)[16] can use his powers to refuse licences in cases where he believes the applicant is 'unfit' as another sanction against traders whose standards in their dealings with customers fall below a standard which is either legal or 'fair'. In addition, regulations on the way in which credit may be advertised or quoted to consumers have been introduced which have had a major impact on the trade.[17]

6 Supply of goods and services

The main thrust of the consumer protection legislation of the 1970s was to deal with contracts entered into by consumers for the purchase of

[15]   See ch 6, below.
[16]   Following the reconstitution of Office of Fair Trading under the Enterprise Act 2002.
[17]   See ch 8, below.

goods. This meant that contracts for the supply of services, for example repairing goods, and other contracts of supply but not sale, for example, hire, were not covered by the legislation. This situation was changed in 1982 with the passing of the Supply of Goods and Services Act which introduced controls over the use of exclusion clauses in these types of contracts, and also set out the terms which will be implied into such contracts. Since 1994, the provisions of the Unfair Terms in Consumer Contracts Regulations also apply to contracts to supply services.

7 Competition policy

As well as introducing direct controls over consumer contracts in various forms, attention has also been directed to general aspects of competition policy. In 1980 the Competition Act was passed which gives the Director General of Fair Trading power to identify anti-competitive practices and either seek an undertaking that those concerned will cease the practice, or refer the matter to the Monopolies and Mergers Commission which can then ban the practice by legislation.

Such an order was made in relation to the supply of spare parts for motor cars, restricting the power of manufacturers to require that their dealers buy only manufacturers' parts except for those to be fitted under warranty or during a recall campaign. The Competition Act 1998 gives the Office of Fair Trading more effective powers to control anti-competitive practices, and brings UK competition law into closer harmony with European law in this area. The Enterprise Act 2002 which came into force in June 2003 tightens controls on competition still further, and from 1 May 2004 the Office of Fair Trading has taken responsibility for the enforcement of European competition law in the UK, including the 2002 Motor Industry Block Exemption Regulation.

8 Exclusive distribution

The terms of the contracts between manufacturers and their dealers are of concern in the consumer context because of the effect that such contracts will have on the price and availability of goods. The impact of EC law on competition has been felt by the introduction in 1985 of a regulation—the so called 'block exemption'—which controls the terms of those agreements in order that they continue to operate despite the restrictions on them contained in the Treaty of Rome. The block exemption was revised and renewed in 1995, and again in 2002 the main provisions of which came fully into force in October 2003.

9 Product liability

The passing of the EC Directive on Liability for Defective Products[18] had a major impact on the civil liability of manufacturers for defects in their products by removing the need for the proof of negligence. This was introduced into UK law by Part I of the Consumer Protection Act 1987. The flood of high profile cases which some commentators expected has not materialised, as manufacturers have presumably chosen to settle cases outside court rather than expose themselves to unnecessary adverse publicity.

The consumer legislation of recent years has therefore been of considerable importance to the motor industry, and it seems certain that this will continue to be the case. Whilst the activities of the Office of Fair Trading continue to be important on a national basis, for example proposals have recently been introduced in relation to used car sales, the European dimension has assumed even greater significance with work on a range of consumer protection issues including a draft directive on 'consumer guarantees'.

C HOW CONSUMER PROTECTION WORKS

The law steps in to protect the consumer in two ways. First, by legislation which controls or modifies individual legal relationships between consumers and retailers. As already mentioned, it is now impossible to exclude liability for death or personal injury arising from negligence, or to exclude the legal rights consumers have to be sold goods which are of 'satisfactory quality' and 'fit for purpose'.[19]

Second, by establishing rules to govern the behaviour of those who do business with consumers. Where the trader breaks the rules he will be committing a criminal offence. Very often, of course, the two areas of civil and criminal law will overlap so that behaviour which gives rise to

---

[18]   EC Directive 85/874.
[19]   See ch 7, below.

a civil claim in contract or tort being made by a customer may also involve criminal proceedings brought, for example, by the local trading standards officer. For instance, the sale of a car wrongly described as new may lead to both a civil action by the customer for damages for breach of contract on the grounds that the car should have complied with the description applied to it, and to a criminal prosecution for breach of the Trade Descriptions Act 1968. Similarly an exclusion clause in a contract with a consumer which tries to avoid the trader's responsibility to sell goods which are of satisfactory quality and fit for purpose will have no legal effect under the provisions of the Sale and Supply of Goods Act 1994 and the use of such an exclusion clause is now also a criminal offence under the provisions of the Consumer Transactions (Restrictions on Statements) Orders[20] made under the Fair Trading Act 1973. Since 1973, breaches of either the civil or criminal consumer protection laws could lead to the Director General of Fair Trading using his powers under the Fair Trading Act 1973 to seek assurances from a trader that he will stop this sort of activity and mend his ways in future.[21], these powers having been strengthened and super-seded first by Stop Now orders in respect of EU consumer protection legislation, and now by the coming into force of the Enterprise Act 2002, which gives the Office of Fair Trading and other enforcement agencies powers to obtain enforcement orders from traders who do not comply with a wide range of consumer protection laws. Under the Unfair Terms in Consumer Contracts Regulations, the Office of Fair Trading may also seek changes in the offending contract terms used by a business.

The role of the trading standards officer

While the Director General of Fair Trading has very considerable over-all powers in the area of consumer protection policy, it is the trading standards officer who is responsible on a day-to-day basis for enforcing much of the criminal legislation. The Trade Descriptions Act, orders made under s 22 of the Fair Trading Act, the Passenger Car (Fuel Consumption and Co2 Emissions Information) Regulations 2004,[22] the legislation banning misleading 'bargain offers', and the control of the

---

[20]   SI 1976/1813 and SI 1978/127.
[21]   See ch 2, below.
[22]   SI 2001/3523 and see Chapter 3.

calibration and setting of petrol pumps, are all examples of consumer protection laws which come within the ambit of the local trading standards officer.

While in theory consumers can bring prosecutions privately for breaches of criminal legislation, eg the Trade Descriptions Act 1968, provided they convince a magistrate that a summons should be issued, in practice this is comparatively rare.

For example, a consumer who had taken out a private prosecution for a breach of the Trade Descriptions Act was stopped by the judge in the Crown Court from pursuing it any further unless he instructed counsel.[23]

Powers of trading standards officers

Day to day enforcement of criminal consumer protection legislation depends in the first instance on inspections by trading standards officers. Inspections are likely to be carried out with no advance warning.

Trading standards officers have various powers under several statutes, including in respect of enforcement orders under the Enterprise Act 2002. The following powers under the Trade Descriptions Act 1968, ss 27 and 28, may be exercised without a warrant, at all reasonable times on production of credentials:

— to enter business premises to see if an offence has been committed;
— if he has reasonable cause to suspect that an offence has been committed, he can require the production of documents etc, and may make copies of them. At this stage PACE[24] applies and a caution must be administered;
— if he has reasonable cause to suspect that an offence has been committed he may seize and detain any goods in order to investigate further;
— goods and documents may be seized and detained if required as evidence.

If the officer believes that permission to enter premises is likely to be refused and where there are reasonable grounds to believe that an offence has been or is about to be committed, he can apply for a warrant.

---

[23]   *Cooper v George Maxwell Developments Ltd* (1980) unreported, Chester CC.
[24]   Police and Criminal Evidence Act 1984: see *Dudley MBC v Debenhams plc* (1994) 159 JP 18, DC.

It is an offence to wilfully obstruct trading standards officers. It is also an offence to give false information.

Prosecution

The authority has a discretion as to whether to prosecute, and if the offence is a technical one may leave themselves open to criticism if a prosecution is pursued when a civil claim was the only remedy required.

Is the criminal law appropriate?

The fact that the criminal law is used to regulate the way traders conduct their businesses is something which has been frequently criticised. It is argued that in many cases a trader may be a small businessman with little access to legal advice who may quite innocently fall foul of a criminal provision.

There is no middle course between civil and criminal law however, and any injustice caused to traders by this system has to be contrasted with situations where a trader wilfully sets out to defraud his customers and where the criminal law is the most appropriate way of dealing with him. Regardless of the debate as to whether this approach is right or not the present situation is that the motor trader who is dealing with consumers faces possible prosecution as well as civil action by his customers if he does not make sure that he and his staff are aware of, and comply with, the various consumer protection measures.

We will now go on to look in more detail at the impact of the law on the relationship between the motor industry and its customers.

CHAPTER 2

Fair trading and codes of practice

In 1973 the post of Director General of Fair Trading was established by the Fair Trading Act. The Act gave the Director General wide powers in connection with consumer protection, consumer credit, monopolies, mergers and restrictive practices. Under the Competition Act 1980, uncompetitive business practices generally also came under his control, and his powers were also extended by the Competition Act 1998. The Enterprise Act 2002 has now come into force which amends, and in some cases replaces, existing law and the powers of the Office of Fair Trading in respect of both competition and consumer law. In particular, the Enterprise Act repeals and replaces Part III of the Fair Trading Act 1973 which dealt with the control of unfair 'consumer trade practices', but which had been found in practice to be slow, and largely ineffective, by a regime of enforcement orders based on the Stop Now Orders Regulations 2001 (which are now themselves repealed). Under the old regime many motor traders were required to give undertakings about unfair consumer trade practices, and it seems likely that the motor industry – or at least its fringe elements – will also be one of the main targets of the new legislation.

A ENFORCEMENT ORDERS

Part 8 of the Enterprise Act 2002 provides that enforcement action can be taken by the OFT and trading standards officers against infringements of community or domestic law. Community infringements are breaches of UK laws which gives effect to specified EC Directives on consumer protection, such as that on unfair terms in consumer contracts. Domestic infringements are breaches by businesses of UK law or contracts of a type specified[1] by the Secretary of State where the breach harms the collective interests of consumers. The Order specifies, in addition to consumer protection legislation such as the Trade Descriptions Act, breaches of s 75 of the Road Traffic Act 1988 (selling unroadworthy vehicles) and s 76 (fitting and supplying defective or unsuitable vehicle parts). Contracts to supply goods or services to consumers are included as is the power of sale of uncollected goods under the Torts (Interference with Goods) Act 1977.[2]

In addition to the enforcement powers of the OFT and trading standards, the Secretary of State may also designate sectoral regulators and consumer protection bodies as enforcers in respect of all or some infringements.

Procedure

The procedure is designed to operate swiftly. Before applying for an enforcement order the enforcer must consult[3] with the business infringing the law, and , in the case of an enforcer other than the OFT, consult with the OFT as well, with a view to getting the infringing behaviour stopped by without going to court. However, this consultation period will last for only two weeks, and in an urgent case this can be reduced to one week. In exceptional cases where urgent action is needed, application to the court can be made without any consultation at all. In this instance, if another enforcer is taking action, the OFT must give authority for action to be taken without notice. The infringing business can be required to supply information by means of a written notice, which can be enforced by court action.

During the consultation period, the enforcer may decide to accept an undertaking from the business that it will stop the infringing conduct. If no such undertaking is given within a two-week period, the enforcer can apply for an enforcement order to the High Court or county court (in England) or the Court of Session or Sheriff Court in Scotland. The court may then issue an enforcement order to the business to stop and

1   Enterprise Act 2002 (Part 8 Domestic Infringements) Order 2003, Si 2003/1593.
2   See below Chapter 11.
3   EA 2002, s 214.

not repeat the infringing conduct, with the order extending to individual company officers, or may accept undertakings that the infringing conduct has ceased. In cases where immediate action is expedient the court may issue an interim order.[4]

Breach of a court order will amount to contempt of court, punishable by fines and/or imprisonment for up to two years

B SUPER COMPLAINTS

The Enterprise Act 2002 also gives consumer bodies which have been designated by the Secretary of State the right to make a 'super complaint' where they consider that there are market features that may be significantly harming the interests of consumers. The Act lays down the criteria which must be met by any body wishing to become a designated consumer body, including being able to demonstrate considerable experience and competence in representing the interests of consumers, and the capability to put together super complaints on a range of issues.

Where a super-complaint has been made, the OFT must then respond within 90 days, stating how it proposes to deal with the complaint, and it must also issue guidance including guidance as to the way in which complaints must be made.

C THE CONTROL OF LICENSING[5]

In addition to the powers of the Office of Fair Trading described above, it can also control the actions of recalcitrant traders who indulge in unfair or illegal business practices by refusing to issue or renew their Consumer Credit Act licences. The operation of the Consumer Credit Act is one of the other responsibilities of the OFT. This enables the Director General to refuse a licence to anyone that he does not consider to be a fit person to hold such a licence. Again, details of refusals to issue or renew licences are contained in the OFT's Annual Report and a large number relate to motor traders. In fact, during 2002, the motor trade accounted for nearly one third of all licensing actions, and in February 2003 the Office of Fair Trading issued Guidance for Car

---

[4]   EA 2002, s 218.
[5]   See also ch 8, below.

Dealers.[6] The Director General has indicated particularly to the motor trade that he will not hesitate to use his Consumer Credit Act 1974 licensing powers to curtail the activities of traders who are not toeing the line. The motor industry consistently accounts for the greatest number of licence refusals and revocations. The OFT has said[7] convictions for selling clocked cars are among the most common reasons for refusing or revoking a licence, but the new Guidelines stress that a range of business practices will be taken into account when deciding the suitability of a business or individual to hold a licence. In particular, these will be where there is evidence that an applicant or licensee or any of their employees, agents or associates have:

- committed any offence involving fraud or other dishonesty or violence;
- contravened provisions of the Consumer Credit Act 1974;
- practised discrimination on grounds of sex, colour race or ethnic origin in the carrying on of a business;
- engaged in business practices appearing to the OFT to be deceitful, oppressive or improper, whether unlawful or not.

In addition, the OFT Guidelines identify a number of business practices which it regards as having a bearing on suitability to have a licence, and says that dealers must abide by the spirit as well as the letter of the Guidelines.

D CODES OF PRACTICE

One of the duties of the Director General of Fair Trading under the original Fair Trading Act was to encourage trade associations to prepare and disseminate to their members codes of practice for guidance in safeguarding and promoting the interests of consumers in the United Kingdom. Any such code of practice introduced by a trade association is, of course, voluntary although the trade association concerned may have some constitutional sanction which it can use against members who flout it, for example by expelling them or by publicising their breach of the code. There are considerable advantages in codes of

---

[6] Office of Fair Trading Guidance for Car Dealers: for consumer credit licence holders and applicants in the used and new car markets – see Appendix 2.

[7] The Purchase of Used Cars – a Consultation Paper from the Office of Fair Trading (December 1996).

practice from the point of view of industry: codes are drawn up for particular industries with very active participation by the trade associations concerned, and the contents of such a voluntary code of practice are far more likely to be flexible and geared to the needs of a particular industry than a piece of wide-ranging and necessarily generalised consumer protection legislation.

From the point of view of the consumer, although a voluntary code does not give him any legal right of action against a retailer or manufacturer who fails to comply, the fact that codes encourage compliance with the spirit rather than the letter of the provisions, means that it is arguable that he will receive in general a far better deal from companies which subscribe to codes of practice. The Enterprise Act 2002 highlights one of the key functions of the Office of Fair Trading as promoting good practice in activities which may affect consumers' interests, and marks a new stage in the development of industry codes of practice. The Office of Fair Trading has now withdrawn its support from old-style codes of practice – such as the various codes affecting the motor industry (see below) – which were originally drawn up and approved under the provisions of the Fair Trading Act 1973.

Under the new Enterprise Act regime a code will be eligible for approval by the OFT if it is intended to regulate the conduct of businesses that supply goods or services to consumers. There is a two-stage process: first, a code sponsor must draw up its code to meet core criteria published by the OFT; and then, at the second stage, provide evidence that the code works to the benefit of consumers. Once the OFT is satisfied that this second stage has been reached, it will give formal approval to the Code and promote it.

I The motor industry codes of practice

There were a number of codes of practice originally sponsored by the Office of Fair Trading under the Fair Trading Act which applied to the motor industry. These were:

(a)   the Code of Practice for the Motor Industry published jointly by the Retail Motor Industry Federation, the Scottish Motor Trade Association and the Society of Motor Manufacturers and Traders;

(b)   the Used Car Consumer Protection Plan published by the Scottish Motor Trade Association;

(c) the Code of Practice for Vehicle Body Repair published by the Vehicle Builders and Repairers Association;

(d) the Code of Practice for the Motor Cycle Industry;

(e) the Code of Practice for the Tyre and Fast Fit Trade;

(f) the Code of Conduct for the British Rental and Leasing Association.

There is also a Code of Practice published by the Society of Motor Auctions and a further Code of Practice for Vehicle Body Building and Commercial Vehicle Body Repairs.

It should be noted in passing that the Code of Practice on Action concerning Vehicle Safety Defects (Recalls) was never one of the codes sponsored by the Office of Fair Trading but was produced by the Society of Motor Manufacturers and Traders in co-operation with the Department of Transport (now operated in conjunction with the Vehicle and Operator Services Agency).[8]

Two new codes of practice for the industry have now attained Stage Two approval from the Office of Fair Trading. These Codes and the Code of Practice for the Retail Motor Industry, drawn up by the Retail Motor Industry Federation and the Scottish Motor Trade Association, are both included as appendices to this edition.[9] It is not certain, at the time of preparation of the fifth edition, what the future prospects for the retail code will now be as the RMIF and SMTA have withdrawn this Code from the approval process.

2 The legal effect of codes of practice

There has been some debate about the legal effect, if any, of codes of practice. The introduction to the original Code of Practice for the Motor Industry stated: 'the principles set out [in the Code] are not intended to interpret, qualify or supplement the law of the land, and are not intended to be applied to non-consumer sales'. The code applies therefore only to 'consumer sales'. The definition of a consumer sale which the draftsmen of the code had in mind is that contained in the Sale of

---

[8] Set out in App 4, below.
[9] See App 4.

Goods Act 1979 (first used in the 1973 Supply of Goods (Implied Terms) Act) now amended by the Sale and Supply of Goods to Consumers Regulations 2002. This has been amended in the new Retail Code to say that it does not apply to 'business sales', which is presumably intended to have the same effect.

Many of the provisions of the original Code of Practice for the Motor Industry were no more than a restatement of legal rules which already existed. For example, the code provided that a manufacturer's warranty must not adversely affect the consumer's remedies against the seller under the Sale of Goods Act and must include a statement making this clear to the consumer. This provision is now enacted in the Consumer Transactions (Restrictions on Statements) Order 1976.[10] Similarly, the code required that used cars sold to consumers should conform with legislation affecting the construction and use of cars and should, where appropriate, be accompanied by a current Department of Transport (MOT) test certificate, and these provisions have been repeated in the new Retail Code. The point has been made, however, that other provisions of codes of practice which are not restatements of the existing law may become legally binding on the members of the associations who subscribe to the codes, either through the operation of the Trade Descriptions Act 1968 or as a form of collateral contract. The first argument is put forward on the basis that a trader who holds himself out as being a member of one of the associations which support a code in applying a trade description to himself, namely that he subscribes to and complies with the association's code of practice. If he, in fact, does not comply with the code in his dealings with his customers, then it is argued that the trade description that the trader concerned subscribed to the code of practice is, in fact, a false one. A successful Trade Descriptions Act prosecution has been brought against a motor trader on this basis.[11] The possibility of codes of practice forming a sort of collateral contract rests on somewhat similar grounds. Here it is argued that if a trader is representing himself as a member of an association and in so doing impliedly supporting and subscribing to a code of practice, and the customer can show that he was induced by the trader's representation to enter into a contract, then it is possible he could have some redress against the trader if the terms of the code of practice were

---

[10]   SI 1976/1813, as amended by SI 1978/127.

[11]   *Shropshire County Council Trading Standards Department v Telford (Vehicles) Ltd* (17 August 1980, unreported, Wrekin Magistrates' Court).

not complied with. Another approach to enforcing codes of practice was illustrated in 1980 when the Office of Fair Trading sought an assurance from a shoe retailer under the provisions of the Fair Trading Act Part III.[12]

3 Impact of the codes

That the motor industry has problems with its customers not even its most ardent supporters could deny. Have those problems been improved, made worse, or simply stayed the same with the advent of the codes?

Predictably, views as to the impact of the motor industry codes differ according to the standpoint taken. Cynics in the consumer lobby would claim that the codes are nothing more than a window-dressing exercise behind which the industry carries on very much as before; that they do nothing to tackle some of the main problem areas in the industry, for example relating to quality; and that the conciliation and arbitration service provided by the codes does not give consumers as satisfactory a source of redress as taking a case before the courts.

Viewed objectively, it has to be admitted that the original codes contain few specific rules and many general statements. Where specific rules were spelt out, for example in relation to pre-delivery inspection checks, it is a fact that the Office of Fair Trading claims that its surveys have shown that these rules have not been followed by a wide section of the trade. On the credit side, it can be argued that it is not the detailed content of the code that really matters at the end of the day. The achievement of the original codes has been to create an atmosphere in which there is a far greater determination on the part of manufacturers and their dealers to give their customers a fair deal, and a recognition that to do so is commercial good sense.

The results of early surveys carried out by the Office of Fair Trading of the way in which the code operated were generally disappointing. Although the trade associations could congratulate themselves that the results showed that the performance of non-members compared very poorly with that of members, there were some areas where the picture was far from satisfactory. The 1986 survey was more encouraging

---

[12]   Reported in *The Financial Times* on 15 July 1980.

however and concluded that there were encouraging signs of better consumer awareness of the code and better compliance by the trade. Indeed in some specific areas, for example satisfaction with new cars, only 10 per cent of those surveyed were either neutral or dissatisfied overall. The Office of Fair Trading in its 1986 Report on the Monitoring Survey of the Motor Code concluded that it brought benefits to the motorist, and that if it did not exist the motorist would be significantly worse off. In its 1997 report on selling second-hand cars,[13] however, the OFT pointed out that most problem traders are not members of trade associations, and self regulation in the motor trade was not felt to be sufficient by many of those who responded to the consultation exercise.

4 Monitoring of the Codes and Disciplinary Procedures

If the new codes are to attain Stage Two approval from the OFT, it will now be necessary to demonstrate that they work more effectively than their predecessors did.

Effective monitoring of compliance is therefore seen as an integral part of the new arrangements. The New Car Code provides that members will ensure that consumers are aware of their adherence to the Code by displaying appropriate symbols, and members will maintain an analysis of complaints relating to any provisions of the Code. The Regulation and Compliance Unit of the SMMT will analyse complaints and trends or issues identified will be considered for inclusion when the Code is revised. Consumer surveys to assess compliance will also be issued from time to time.

The New Car Code also provides for the possibility of disciplinary action to be taken against manufacturers for breaches of the Code. An independent panel, the Independent Compliance Assessment Panel (ICAP) has authority to instigate an independent investigation, with which the member must cooperate, and a variety of sanctions are possible, including financial penalties or expulsion from the Code scheme.

---

[13]   A Report by the OFT – October 1997.

The Retail Motor Industry Code contains similar provisions, with the compliance regime drawn up with an Independent Scrutiny Committee and this will include periodic visits to members' premises and mystery shopping exercises, as well as analysis of consumer complaints. In the event of serious breaches of the Code, the matter may be referred to the Independent Disciplinary Committee, whose sanctions may include expulsion from membership of the association.

CHAPTER 3

Sales promotion, advertising and pricing

A INTRODUCTION

The ways in which motor manufacturers and traders try to promote the sale of their goods and services to the public have frequently got them into trouble.

Backstreet traders, persistently misdescribing the secondhand cars they are selling; motor manufacturers who use comparative advertising to extol the virtues of their own products, but choose an unfair or inaccurate comparison; some of the motor industry's advertising promotional activities can be fairly criticised.

The freedom of manufacturers and retailers to say what they like about their products and services has been gradually reduced, so that now there are numerous controls, both of a legal and a voluntary nature, which have to be taken into account. Despite these, however, there have still been a number of grey areas, where statements thought to be misleading might not be actionable either on behalf of the public through criminal procedures, or by individual consumers.

For example, the courts in the UK have in the past demonstrated a fairly relaxed attitude towards interpreting the legal status of statements made in advertisements. In one case[1] involving a defectively designed trailer coupling a statement in the manufacturer's advertising literature that it 'requires no maintenance, it is foolproof, once pin home locked absolutely' was held by the Court of Appeal not to be legally binding

---

[1] *Lambert v Lewis* [1980] RTR 152.

on the manufacturer because there was no evidence that it was intended that this statement should form part of the contract.

This attitude contrasted with the American courts which have for many years taken a rather stricter view of the manufacturer's responsibility for statements which he makes in promotional material. For example, a catalogue statement that the windscreens of Ford cars were shatterproof was held to be a statement which was intended to be relied on by prospective purchasers, and Ford were therefore liable for injuries caused when such a windscreen did in fact shatter.[2] The introduction of the Sale and Supply of Goods to Consumers Regulations 2002[3] now allows courts in the UK to take a stricter view by providing that public statements in advertising and elsewhere can be taken into account in deciding whether goods meet the contract standard.

B ADVERTISEMENTS

There are now numerous statutory requirements which regulate the content of advertisements. There are also voluntary controls which have existed for many years operated through the codes of practice of the Committee of Advertising Practice (CAP) and the Independent Television Commission (ITC) and the different industry codes sponsored by the Office of Fair Trading.

A recent development has been the introduction of an EC Directive on Misleading Advertising which was implemented in the UK by the Control of Misleading Advertisements Regulations 1988.[4-5]

These give the Director General of Fair Trading power to intervene if he considers that it would be appropriate to stop misleading advertising by applying for a court injunction. He will consider complaints made

---

[2]   SI 1988/915.
    This Directive has now been amended by a further Directive on Comparative Advertising. This has not yet been implemented in the UK, but this is required by 23 April 2000. The Directive confirms that comparative advertising is permissible in the EU, provided it conforms to the requirements in the Directive. These are broadly similar to the principles set out in the CAP Code (see below).
    [1893] 1 QB 256.
[3]   See below and Chapter 7
[4-5]   SI 1988/915 now amended by the Control of Misleading Advertisements (Amendment) Regulations 2000, SI 2000/914.

to him (other than in relation to radio, cable or television advertising where similar responsibilities are placed on the Independent Broadcasting Authority and the Cable Authority). Before taking any action however, he will wish to be satisfied that all other means of dealing with the complaint have been tried without success and bear in mind the public interest. The IBA is also given powers under the regulation to refuse to broadcast an advertisement which it thinks is misleading. An advertise-ment will be misleading if in any way, including its presentation, it deceives or is likely to deceive the persons it is addressed to or reaches, and if it is likely to affect their economic behaviour or if it injures or is likely to injure, a competitor.

I Voluntary controls

The British Codes of Advertising Sales Promotion and Direct Marketing

As the CAP Code itself points out, one of the most important distinguishing features between the law and the code is that the spirit of the code is enforced as well as the literal wording.

The CAP investigates any complaints from the public or other advertisers about advertisements which it is alleged contravene the code. It regularly publishes case reports giving the results of its investigations. If an advertiser or agency does not agree to mend or withdraw an advertisement following a complaint which has been upheld by the CAP, sanctions can be introduced. These are:

(a)   adverse publicity in the CAP case reports;
(b)   advertising space or time can be withheld from the advertiser;
(c)   the advertising agency's trading privileges may be withdrawn;
(d)   other consumer protection agencies may be notified.

Even though the codes are voluntary or self-regulating, it should be noted that if an advertiser fails to comply with an adjudication on an advertisement which contains misleading information or comparisons, this may be referred to the Office of Fair Trading for action under the regulations on misleading advertising.

The underlying principles of the code are that all advertisements should be legal, decent, honest and truthful; that all advertisements should be prepared with a sense of responsibility to the consumer and to society; and that all advertisements should conform to the principles of fair competition as generally accepted in business.

In addition, the CAP code contains a section specifically relating to motoring. This includes requirements that marketing for vehicles, fuel or accessories should not encourage or condone anti-social behaviour; that speed or acceleration claims should not be the predominant message of marketing communications, although giving general information about a vehicle's performance is legitimate; that speed should not be portrayed in a way that might encourage motorists to drive irresponsibly or break the law, and irresponsible driving should not be condoned; that vehicles should not be depicted in dangerous or unwise situations in a way that might encourage or condone irresponsible driving; that when making environmental claims for products, the rules on Environmental Claims should be conformed with; that prices quoted should correspond to the vehicles illustrated; that safety claims should not exaggerate the benefit to consumers, and claims should not be made unless they can be substantiated.[6]

Other codes of practice for example the New Car Code of Practice and the Code of Practice for the Retail Motor Industry refer to the CAP Code and require compliance with it.

The New Car Code of Practice

The New Car Code requires compliance with the CAP and ITC Codes. In addition, it makes various specific promises to consumers, for example:

(a) 'our advertisements, promotions or other publications, whether in writing or otherwise, will not contain any items which are likely to mislead you or to be misunderstood'

(b) 'Any comparison made within our advertisements with other models of different manufacturers will be based upon a similar set of criteria which will not confuse or mislead the consumer'

(c) 'where our advertisement quotes the price of one model in any model range, but depicts another, the actual price of that other model will also be clearly shown;

---

[6]   The CAP Code March 2003.

(d)   where a manufacturer advertises a rust-proofing process, information about the process and its limitations should be made
freely available.

2 Legal controls

It is possible that on occasion advertisements may be held to be some
sort of contract with the advertisers although this is comparatively rare,
and as already discussed the courts are generally reluctant to find that
statements in advertisements are contractually binding on potential customers. How a contract can come about because of an advertisement
was illustrated in a leading case at the end of the last century.

The manufacturer of a flu remedy known as a 'Carbolic Smoke Ball'[7]
was found to be liable in contract for an offer which he made in an
advertisement for the product. What happened was that he offered £100
to anyone who, having used his Carbolic Smoke Ball, contracted
influenza. The court held that this offer in the advertisement was, in
legal terms, a perfectly valid offer to the world at large and, therefore,
when customers came along who fulfilled the condition for claiming
the reward, namely they had contracted flu, despite using the remedy,
they were entitled to accept the offer and be paid the £100. Generally
speaking, however, statements in advertisements will not normally constitute the terms of a legally binding contract. The law will generally
regard the sort of statements used in advertisements as being 'mere
puffs' and will not regard them as the basis of a contract.[8]

Representations in advertisements

There does come a point, however, when a statement made in an advertisement may be a representation of fact to those reading the advertisement which has the object of inducing them to enter into a contract with
the retailer. In this situation the court might decide that the person making the representation in the advertisement should be held to it by the
legal principle that a collateral contract has been formed. This was
illustrated in a case involving Esso Petroleum Ltd, which introduced a

---

[7]   [1893] 1 QB 256.
[8]   For a modern case, see *Benerman v Association of British Travel Agents Ltd* (1995)
Times, 24 November, CA.

scheme to induce motorists to buy Esso petrol.[9] The advertisement stated 'One World Cup coin given with every 4 gallons'. The court decided that what was being said was 'if you will buy 4 gallons of my petrol I will give you one of these coins'. This meant that a collateral contract existed.

WHEN IS AN OFFER NOT AN OFFER?

What is also clear, however, is that merely indicating that you have certain goods for sale, whether in an advertisement or by displaying them in your shop or showroom, is not going to be considered to be a legal offer forming the starting-point for a contract.[10] It is well established that in these circumstances there is only 'an invitation to treat' by the advertiser or retailer and there is no liability in contract to potential purchasers to supply those goods or facilities which you have advertised or displayed for sale at the price that you indicated or at all, although as we shall see later, this would cause problems under the Trade Descriptions Act 1968 and the price marking and misleading pricing rules.

This was illustrated when a shopkeeper was cleared of a criminal prosecution for offering a flick knife for a sale which was displayed in his window (which was at the time of the case illegal) because it was held that this was not an offer for sale and, therefore, did not fall within the terms of the prohibition which stopped the offering for sale of such goods.[11]

So traditionally the consumer has not normally been able to enforce the statements in an advertisement against the advertiser by means of an individual action under a contract. Now however, as a result of the Sale and Supply of Goods to Consumers Regulations a consumer (as defined in the regulations) can rely on specific information about goods contained in advertising, labelling etc given by the retailer, the producer or his representative as part of the contract with the retailer, because it will be treated as a 'relevant circumstance' when assessing whether goods are of satisfactory quality. In other cases of dissatisfaction with adver-

---

[9]   *Esso Petroleum Ltd v Customs and Excise Comrs* [1976] 1 All ER 117.
[10] *Pharmaceutical Society of Great Britain v Boots Cash Chemists (Southern) Ltd* [1953] 1 QB 401 and see also ch 5, below.
[11] *Fisher v Bell* [1961] 1 QB 394.

tising or if the customer is a non-consumer,[12] the most effective cause
of action will be to complain to the ASA, if the advertisement breaks
the terms of the ASA Code, or to the local trading standards officer, if
the advertisement or other promotional material actually infringes the
Trade Descriptions Acts, or any of the other specific statutes controlling
the content of advertisements.

The most important of these is the Trade Descriptions Act 1968, as this
operates generally to prohibit the making of false or misleading statements whether in advertisements, brochures, or the negotiations leading
up to a sale.

The effect of the Trade Descriptions Act on advertisements

The Act is considered in more detail later on. In connection with advertisements it is only necessary to note that the Act does apply to advertisements and other marketing and promotional material such as
brochures, catalogues and so on. This means that a description in an
advertisement or sales brochure for goods which turns out to be false or
misleading raises the possibility of a prosecution under the Act. In relation to used cars this is an obvious pitfall; numerous cases have been
brought over secondhand cars which have not come up to the advertised description of them. For example, in *Furniss v Scott*,[13] a car was
advertised as being in 'really exceptional condition throughout'. In fact
the body was corroded but camouflaged and the window winders, sus-
pension and clutch plates were all faulty. The court had no hesitation in
deciding that this was clearly a false trade description. Similarly, in *R v
Nash*,[14] the Court of Appeal upheld a conviction and custodial sentence
imposed on a motor trader under the Trade Descriptions Act where an
unroadworthy car was described as being 'in excellent condition',
although it was argued that a charge under the Road Traffic Act 1988 of
selling an unroadworthy vehicle would have been more appropriate.
The court will look at the facts in each case, and assess the impact of
the words used on the ordinary man, to decide what was actually conveyed by the advertisement. For example,[15] 'beautiful' in an advertise-

---

[12]   SI 2002/2334.
[13]   [1973] RTR 314.
[14]   [1990] RTR 343, CA.
[15]   *Robertson v Dicicco* [1972] RTR 431 and see also *Hawkins v Smith* [1978] Crim LR
       578.

ment for a secondhand car was held to be capable of not only describing its external appearance, but also its mechanical condition.

The Trade Descriptions Act 1968 (s 14) provides that it is an offence for a trader to make a statement which he knows to be false. Therefore a statement in a sales brochure advertising details of 'standard' accessories which are not, in fact, fitted as standard, will be an offence if this was known about at the time that the brochure was produced. This was illustrated in a prosecution[16] brought against the British Gas Corporation where the Gas Board was convicted over a brochure which stated 'ignition by hand held battery torch supplied with cooker' when, in fact, no such torch was supplied. This incidentally was despite a disclaimer which was inserted into the brochure. It seems that a disclaimer will not offer any protection where it is established that the lack of the advertised accessory was already known at the time the brochure was produced. In *Denard v Smith and Dixons Ltd*,[17] Dixons the electrical retailers were convicted of an offence where promotional material at the point of sale referred to the inclusion of various items in a computer package offered for sale. In fact, the package was incomplete, and the retailer took no steps to bring this to the attention of customers before they purchased the goods.

In *Wings Ltd v Ellis*,[18] a holiday company which innocently issued brochures containing false information was also convicted of an offence despite the wording of s 14, as they became aware of the falsity by the time the brochure was read by the complainant.

In a situation where a prosecution is brought over a misleading statement in a brochure the trader, although he did not himself prepare the brochure, will be just as liable for prosecution as the manufacturer or importer who provided him with the brochure for advertising purposes. However, the trader would, of course, if he were ignorant of the true situation, be able to rely on the defence contained in s 24 of the Act that his act or default was due to another person.

Fuel consumption and Co2 emissions information

Anyone issuing material containing a statement about fuel consumption to the general public with a view to promoting sales of cars now has to

---

[16] *British Gas Corpn v Lubbock* [1974] 1 All ER 188.
[17] (1990) 155 JP 253.
[18] [1985] AC 272, [1984] 3 All ER 577, HL

include certain specified information as to the results of the official fuel consumption tests.[19] The introduction of this provision put an end to the frequent use of misleading comparative advertising of fuel consumption figures. All too often these were drawn from different sources which had used different methods of testing and, therefore, as a means of comparison for consumers were largely meaningless. The specified information referred to in the Act is set out in the Passenger Car Fuel Consumption (Amendment) Order 1996[20] which provides that the information to be included is the fuel consumption expressed both in miles per gallon and in litres per hundred kilometres which has been recorded in an official fuel economy certificate. This Order has now been superseded in respect of new passenger vehicles to which EC Whole Vehicle Type Approval applies by Regulations implementing an EU Directive[21] which aims to give consumers information not only about fuel consumption but also Co2 emissions.[22]

APPLICATION

The 2001 regulations apply only to new passenger cars subject to EC Whole Vehicle Type Approval. This means that they do not apply to vehicles that have been approved under the Single Vehicle Approval Scheme, or to vehicles manufactured in low volume. Other vehicles excluded are cars adapted to carry more than eight passengers (excluding the driver), van-derived passenger cars and cars built specially for export.

A new passenger car is defined for this purpose as a passenger car which has not previously been sold to a person who bought it for a purpose other than that of selling or supplying it.

Models which do not differ significantly in certain technical characteristics do not have to be tested individually, but may be grouped together into a class. The Department of Transport has expressed the view[23] that it would not expect vehicles within a model class to differ in at least the following respects:

Make; model range; engine capacity; fuel type; and transmission type.

[19]   Energy Act 1976, s 15.
[20]   SI 1996/1132 amending SI 1983/1486
[21]   EU Directive 1999/94/EC.
[22]   Passenger Car (Fuel Consumption and Co2 Emissions Information) Regulations 2001, SI 2001/3523.
[23]   DTLGR Press Release 9 April 2002.

RESPONSIBILITIES OF MANUFACTURERS, IMPORTERS AND DEALERS

The manufacturer or anyone authorised to act on his behalf within the European Community must include fuel consumption and CO_2 emissions data from the official tests[24] carried out in all brochures and printed advertisements if the literature relates to a specific model of car. He must also supply dealers on request with the relevant information.

The dealer has a duty to display a fuel economy label in a clearly visible manner on or near each new passenger car offered for sale, and also to make available on request free of charge a copy of the current edition of the fuel economy guide. A poster must also be displayed which must be updated every six months giving the official fuel consumption and CO_2 emissions information for every model. The dealer must also ensure that promotional material he uses complies with the Regulations.

The regulations lay down rules as to the design, format and some wording of the required to be included in promotional literature, labels and posters.

No other symbol or information regarding official fuel consumption or emissions information may be included in any fuel economy label, poster or promotional literature may be included if it could mislead or confuse potential end users.

OFFENCES

Failure to comply with any of these requirements is an offence, punishable by fines of up to £5000. It will be a defence in any prosecution for the defendant to show that he took all reasonable steps and exercised all due diligence to avoid committing an offence.

ADVERTISING BY BUSINESSES

The Business Advertisements (Disclosure) Order 1977[25] provides that where a person is seeking to sell goods in the course of a business it must be reasonably clear from the contents of the advertisement, its

---

[24] Measured in accordance with Directive 80/1268/EC and contained in the Certificate of Conformity for that vehicle.

[25] SI 1977/1918.

format or size or the place or manner of its publication, that the goods are being sold in the course of a business. The reason for this restriction is that the purchaser who buys goods from a private seller rather than from someone buying from a seller who sells in the course of trade or business, has fewer rights against the seller under the Sale and Supply of Goods Act 1994 if the goods turn out to be defective. The Office of Fair Trading took the view that this state of affairs was likely to deter consumers from pursuing their legal rights against the seller of the goods if, in fact, they thought that he was a private seller.

The meaning of 'trade or business' in this context was considered in *Blakemore v Bellamy*.[26] In this case the defendant was in full-time employment as a postman, and worked on cars as a hobby. He then advertised them for sale, and sold them without making any significant overall profit. His advertisements did not make it clear that he was selling in the course of a business, and he was prosecuted. It was held that the defendant's activities were merely a hobby despite the fact that over a nine-month period he acquired and sold seven vehicles.[27]

Consumer credit advertisements

Detailed regulations exist and are dealt with separately in chapter 7, below.

Misleading and Comparative Advertising

In addition to the legal controls already mentioned, Regulations[28] require the Director General of Fair Trading (now the Office of Fair Trading) to consider complaints about misleading advertisements and prohibited comparative advertising. The OFT has power to bring proceedings for an injunction to prevent the publication or continued publication of an advertisement which is misleading. An advertisement may be regarded as misleading if it deceives, or is likely to deceive, the target audience of the advertisement, and to affect their economic behaviour.

---

[26]   [1983] RTR 303.

[27]   This interpretation of the words 'in the course of a business' is different to that which will be applied in civil cases: see *Stevenson v Rogers* [1990] QB 1028, [1999] 1 All ER 613, and see ch 7, below.

[28]   Control of Misleading Advertisements Regulations 1988, 1988/915 as amended.

The original Regulations have had little direct impact on the motor industry, but following an amendment in 2000[29], the Regulations now also extend control to comparative advertising, which has traditionally been a style of advertising enthusiastically adopted by vehicle manufacturers.

A comparative advertisement is defined[30] as being an advertisement which either implicitly or explicitly identifies a competitor or goods or services offered by a competitor. The Regulations set out the conditions which must be met in order for comparative advertising to be permitted. These include: that the comparison is not misleading; that it compares like with like, and consists of verifiable and relevant features of goods and services; it does not create confusion in the market place between the advertiser and his competitor, including trade marks; it does not take unfair advantage of the reputation of a trade mark or other distinguishing features of a competitor; and does not present goods or services as imitations or replicas of goods or services bearing a protected trade mark or name.

If a comparative advertisement refers to a special offer, this will not be permitted unless it indicates in a clear and unequivocal way the date on which the offer ends or, if appropriate, that the offer is subject to availability of goods and services and/or the start date.

C PRICING

The way in which traders price their goods can of course operate as a very considerable inducement to consumers to make a purchase, and pricing policies generally can operate against the consumer's interest. The law therefore affects this aspect of a trader's activities in various ways. In addition, in respect of new car pricing, the New Car Code of Practice promises consumers that, '... in principle, a price quoted should be the "on the road" price at which you can buy the goods, in accordance with the SMMT Guide to New Car Pricing'.

I Resale price maintenance

The operation of resale price maintenance, ie agreements between supplier and retailer setting the minimum prices to be charged on the resale

---

[29] Control of Misleading Advertisements (Amendment) Regulations 2000, SI 2000/914.
[30] Reg. 3(4).

of a product, is 'unlawful', unless an exemption has been granted by the court on one of the grounds set out in the Resale Prices Act 1976. No exemptions have been made which are relevant to the motor industry.

The publishing of 'recommended resale prices' is specifically permitted by the Act, however.

The legislation does not control the setting of maximum retail prices.

2 Misleading price indications

Section 11 of the Trade Descriptions Act, which dealt with abuses arising from the way in which goods are priced for sale, and extended to prices indicated in advertisements, was repealed and replaced by the Consumer Protection Act 1987.[31]

The Consumer Protection Act 1987, Part III provides that it is an offence for a person 'in the course of a business of his' to give an indication to consumers as to the price of goods or services which is misleading (s 20(1)), and that an offence is also committed if an indication of price is given which becomes 'subsequently misleading' and the trader has failed to take reasonable steps to prevent consumers from relying on it.

It is not necessary for the prosecution to prove that any identified consumer has been misled by the price indication and paid more than the indicated price for goods or services—in other words, a prosecution need not arise from a specific consumer complaint. This point was confirmed in *Toyota (GB) Ltd v North Yorkshire County Council*.[32] Toyota appealed against conviction of an offence relating to banner prices and smaller print exclusions. The company argued that there was no evidence to show that anybody had actually purchased a vehicle at an inclusive price higher than the banner price, and produced evidence from a selection of dealers to show that, because of discounts, no vehicles had been sold at a higher price. This argument was rejected by the Divisional Court: prices paid by individual customers were irrelevant and did not alter the misleading nature of the indication given.

In order to help traders avoid giving misleading price indications, the statutory provisions are backed by a Code of Practice which may be

---

[31]   Part III.
[32]   (1998) 162 JP 794, Trading Standards Review, June 1998 CO/0110/98.

taken into account by the courts in deciding whether or not an offence has been committed.

Who is a consumer?

In relation to goods this is defined as 'any person who might wish to be supplied with the goods for his own private use or consumption'. Whether any particular customer meets this definition of a 'consumer' will therefore be as question of fact, but in situations such as a parts department where sales may be made to both retail and trade customers, price indications given to a genuine trader will not be subject to this legislation, nor presumably would price indications given to someone who purports to be a trader in order to obtain a trade discount.

In relation to services, 'consumer' means any person who might wish to be provided with the services or facilities otherwise than for the purposes of any business of his.

Who can commit an offence?

The legislation applies to indications made by someone acting 'in the course of any business of his'. This wording, which differs from that used in other legislation such as the Trade Descriptions Act, is intended to restrict prosecutions to employers. An employee will not himself be open to prosecution because he will not be acting in the course of a business of his, but of his employer.[33]

The legislation provides that anyone in the chain of supply (including the manufacturer) can commit an offence because it is made clear that it will not be relevant that the price indication is made on behalf of someone else, or that the goods and services in question are not supplied by the person making the indication. In the case of a manufacturer however, this will only apply to price indications made to the public— price indications made to retailers will not be made to consumers.

What is a 'price'?

The price is 'the aggregate of sums required to be paid by the consumer … in respect of the supply', and any method used to calculate that amount.

---

[33] *R v Warwickshire County Council, ex p Johnson* [1993] AC 583, HL.

What is 'misleading'?

Section 21(1) provides that a price will be misleading if what is conveyed by the indication, or what consumers might reasonably be expected to infer from the indication, includes any of the following:

— *'that the price is less than in fact it is'*. This would catch charging more than the price marked on the goods or on a price display such as a menu pricing list in the Service Department, although presumably it would still be open to a retailer to refuse to sell the goods in question at all at any price to any particular customer and so avoid an offence if, for example, the figure '1' became displaced from a price display on a car so that the price indicated was £5,000 instead of £15,000. A banner price for a new car with small print details of additional on the road costs such as number plates and delivery charges is misleading, even where consumers are able to buy the vehicle in question at less than the on the road price.[34]

— *'that the applicability of the price does not depend on facts or circumstances on which it does in fact depend'*. For example, a dealer advertising a free two-year parts and labour warranty and one year's road fund licence would be convicted of an offence if a customer is told the offer only operates at the weekend.

— *'that the price covers matters in respect of which an additional charge is in fact made'*. A price indicated in the showroom on a new car fitted with optional extras must therefore be the total price, or must make clear which items are not included in the displayed price. A pictured vehicle with five doors for sale at a price which relates in fact to a three door model will be misleading

— *'that a person who in fact has no such expectation expects the price to be increased or reduced, or that price to be maintained'*. The salesman who falsely suggests that the manufacturer is about to increase the recommended retail price will therefore be misleading as would an indication that prices are offered 'for this weekend only' when the same advertisement is run for several weeks.

— *'that the facts or circumstances by reference to which the consumer might be expected to judge the validity of any comparison made or implied are not in fact what they are'*. Drawing an

---

[34]   *Toyota (GB) Ltd v North Yorkshire County Council* (1998) 162 JP 794, Trading Standards Review CO/0110/98.

unfavourable comparison with a misleading high maximum retail price would fall foul of this provision as would inaccurate comparisons with prices of another trader. A dealer advertising a 'free' Mini City when a G-registered Rover was bought for £18,495 was convicted of an offence when in another edition of the same paper the Rover was offered for sale at £13,995.

Similar provisions apply to misleading information as to the method of determining prices.

The test of what is misleading is an objective one. It will not be a question of what the trader intended to convey, but the effect of the price indication on the mind of the ordinary customer. An offence will only be committed where the price indication was misleading at the time it was made, and not indications of price which subsequently become misleading.[35]

The Code of Practice for Retailers on Price Indications

The Act provides (s 25(1)) that a code of practice with statutory backing will be used to give guidance to traders on what may be regarded as 'misleading' pricing practices. The code gives advice on a number of matters including price comparisons both with traders' own previous prices and with those of other traders, as well as with recommended retail prices; and on the way actual prices are quoted. A contravention of the code does in itself give rise to a prosecution, but the provisions of the code can be taken into account by a court considering a case brought under the misleading pricing legislation. The code is set out in full in Appendix 6 and at the time of preparing the fifth edition is under review, but two extracts from the code are worth highlighting here:

— the code sets out the circumstances in which a trader may compare his current sale price with a previous price, and establishes the fact that the previous price must have been the price at which the product was available for 28 days;

— the code requires that if a 'free' offer is made, the trader must make clear to consumers exactly what they will have to buy in order to get the free offer, and any conditions which apply must be spelt out; in addition, the word 'free' must not be used if additional charges have been imposed, or the price increased of any

---

[35] *Thomson Tour Operations Ltd v Birch* [1999] ALL ER (D) 66.

other product or service the consumer must buy in order to get the 'free' offer, or if the price will be reduced for consumers who do not want to take up the 'free' offer. If the word 'free' is used in these circumstances, the price indication will be misleading.

Defences

It will be a defence to show that:

(1)   the trader took all reasonable steps and exercised all due diligence to avoid committing the offence (s 39(1)). Where this involves the trader in showing that he acted on information supplied by someone else, or that the offence was due to the act or default of someone else, he will also have to show that it was reasonable for him to rely on the information supplied having regard to the steps he took to verify it, and to whether he had any reason to disbelieve the information. In these circumstances, the 'other person' will be guilty of an offence, and may also be proceeded against. This defence, which is similar in concept to the defences in for example the Trade Descriptions Act, puts the burden on the trader to show what steps he took to try to avoid offences where he was relying on information supplied to him;

(2)   the person giving the price indication is not actually supplying the goods or services and that he is recommending a price which he had reason to assume was for the most part being followed;

(3)   the defendant is an advertiser relying on copy supplied to him;

(4)   the indication was given through the media but not in an advertisement (presumably this would allow a defence where for example a motoring magazine gave incorrect price information in a road test report on a particular vehicle);

(5)   the defendant was complying with regulations made under the Act.

Regulations

The Act provides that regulations may be made in consultation with the Director General of Fair Trading in order to regulate the way in which price indications are given. Regulations[36] which came into force on

---

[36]   The Price Indications (Method of Payment) Regulations 1991, SI 1991/199.

28 February 1991 require a trader who is giving a price indication and who is charging different prices to different classes of customers, for example cash and credit card customers, to accompany the indication of price with a statement of any method of payment to which the stated price does not apply. Unless he indicates the actual price payable by the other method, the trader must also state the difference between the two prices. Generally this information must be given at the public entrance to the business premises but there are special rules to ensure that the information reaches consumers where for example they are using a retail area which is part of a larger premises, such as a forecourt shop. Separate regulations apply to price display for fuel where differential prices are charged.[37]

3 Price marking

Since 1991 orders made under the Prices Act 1974,[38] have required that goods (subject to a very few limited exceptions) which are offered for sale by retail to consumers must be accompanied by a written indication of the selling price, or where appropriate, the unit price. The current legislation is the Price Marking Order 2004[39] The order does not apply to goods which are supplied in the course of provision of a service and does not therefore apply to parts fitted to a customer's car during repairs or servicing by a garage., nor does it apply to most advertisements for a product (although of course in the case of prices in an advertisement the rules on misleading pricing will apply).However, advertisements which encourage consumers to enter into a distance contract, for example, on the internet, are covered.

Indicating a selling price

Where a product is offered for sale by a trader to a consumer an indication of the selling price must be given, except where goods are sold from bulk (see below). This must be the final price for the product and must include VAT and any other taxes, and any non-optional extras. The price indication must be clearly legible, unambiguous and easily identifiable by a prospective purchaser as referring to the goods. It must

---

[37] See below ch 14.
[38] The Prices Act 1974 as amended,
[39] SI 2004/102.

be placed in proximity to the goods to which it relates and be placed so that it is available to consumers without the need for them to seek assistance to find it out. The price indication must be in sterling, but if the trader is willing to accept foreign currency he must also indicate the selling price in the foreign currency in question, or clearly identify the conversion rate on which the foreign currency price will be calculated, together with any commission to be charged.

Unit prices

The unit price is required for products sold loose from bulk, or where weights and measures legislation requires them to be sold in a prescribed quantity. This includes liquid fuel for cars, lubricating oil, mixtures of fuel and oil, lubricating grease and anti-freeze.

VAT

The price indicated to consumers must include VAT and the order gives a 14-day period of grace when the rate of VAT changes during which time a general notice of the fact that the price will be adjusted may be used so long as it fulfils the general requirements as to legibility, unambiguity and so on.

Application

The Order applies to traders, which is defined[40] as any person who sells or offers or exposes for sale products which fall within his commercial or professional activity. This definition will operate to exclude manufacturers in most cases from the scope of this Order, in the same way as they were excluded from the previous Price Marking Order. This may at first sight seem somewhat surprising, but prosecutions have been brought against manufacturers under these regulations for 'causing' their retailers to commit offences by supplying them with advertisments which contravene the requirements of the order.[41] It should, however, be seen in the context of the misleading price indications offences (see

---

[40]   Article 1(2).
[41]   *North Yorkshire County Council v Rover Group Ltd* (5 October 1995, unreported), Whitby Magistrates' Court.

above) under which it seems that a manufacturer could be prosecuted if it were felt that, for example, the use of exclusive banner prices without a sufficiently prominent statement of the items excluded might be 'misleading'.[42] The SMMT Guide to New Car Price Advertising states that 'In principle, any advertised or displayed price for a new car should be the 'on the road' price for that car. Accordingly Manufacturers' and Dealers' prices for new cars, whether in advertisements or displayed in show rooms, should be inclusive of the price of any extras known to be fitted to the car, number plates, any delivery charges , the appropriate VAT (quoting the rate applicable) , the cost of 12 months' government vehicle excise duty, and the first registration fee.'

Defences

Failure to comply with the Order is a strict criminal offence subject to certain statutory defences which are contained in the Prices Act 1974. These are the same as those in the Trade Descriptions Act 1968 (see Chapter 4).

Penalties

Offences are punishable by a fine of up to £5,000, or an unlimited fine, if tried in the Crown Court.

D TRADING STAMPS

I Notices

If a trader operates a trading stamp scheme he must keep:

(a)   a notice posted in a position where it can be conveniently read by customers stating the cash value of the trading stamps issued under the scheme and giving particulars which will enable customers to calculate how many stamps they are entitled to in any particular transaction;

(b)   a copy of any current catalogue published by or on behalf of the promoter of the trading stamp scheme where it can be conveniently consulted by customers.

---

[42]   On this point, now see the *Toyota* case cited above.

2 Offences

Failing to comply without 'reasonable excuse', or pulling down, or defacing a notice required by the Act is an offence.[43]

3 Trade Descriptions Act 1968

Failure to give stamps on a transaction despite an indication that a trading stamp scheme is operated will be a breach of the Trade Descriptions Act 1968.

E SUNDAY TRADING

1 Restrictions on Sunday trading

The law on Sunday trading in England and Wales has been reformed by the Sunday Trading Act 1994. The overall effect of the legislation is to control the opening hours of 'large shops' (subject to certain exceptions) and to permit unrestricted opening of all other 'shops' on Sundays.

A 'shop' for this purpose means any retail premises where the business mainly relates to the sale of goods: motor vehicle showrooms are therefore covered by the legislation. A 'large shop' is one where the display and customer serving area exceeds 280 square metres.

There is a general exemption from the restrictions for certain categories of 'large shops'. Two that are relevant are: shops selling motor supplies and accessories, and cycle supplies and accessories; and petrol filling stations. It should also be noted that the opening of premises supplying only services are not restricted.

Where restrictions apply, these are:
— no opening on Easter Sunday, or Christmas Day where this falls on a Sunday;
— Sunday opening hours are limited to a maximum period of six continuous hours between 10.00am and 6.00pm in accordance with a notice submitted to the local authority; any subsequent alteration in the hours must also be notified;

---

[43] Trading Stamps Act 1964, s 7.

— a notice specifying the permitted Sunday opening hours must be displayed in a conspicuous position inside and outside the premises during the opening hours on a Sunday.

2 Offences

Opening premises in breach of the restrictions is a summary offence carrying a maximum penalty of £50,000. Failure to display the notice specifying opening hours is also an offence carrying a maximum penalty of £500.

F MAIL ORDER TRANSACTIONS

Motor accessories and spare parts are often sold by mail order. The Mail Order Transactions (Information) Order 1976[44] used to provide that advertisements, circulars or catalogues which invite consumers to order goods by post must also contain the true name or registered business name and address of the person carrying on the mail order business. This legislation has now been revoked and superseded by the Consumer Protection (Distance Selling) Regulations 2000.[45]

---

[44]   SI 1976/1812.
[45]   SI 2000/2334, and see Chapter 5.

CHAPTER 4

Trade descriptions

A INTRODUCTION

Although the aim of this book is to treat subjects under the headings in which they are likely to crop up in the retailer's day-to-day activities, the subject of trade descriptions is so important that it has to be given a section on its own. The relevant statute is the Trade Descriptions Act 1968 which deals with false or misleading descriptions applied to goods or services and also, following the repeal of the Trade Descriptions Act 1972, with origin marking.

B TRADE DESCRIPTIONS ACT 1968

I The scope of the Act

The Act deals with descriptions of both goods and services, and to descriptions made orally and in writing.

Two types of offence arise: the first are 'absolute' offences in relation to false or misleading descriptions of goods. Here an offence can be committed even if there was no deliberate intention to mislead, if the false description was innocently applied or the trader innocently supplies goods to which someone else has applied a false description (subject to the statutory defence—see below).[1] The second category of offence arises in relation to false or misleading descriptions of services.

---

[1]   *Alec Norman Garages Ltd v Phillips* [1985] RTR 164.

Here an offence will only be committed if it is shown that there was guilty knowledge, ie that the defendant knew that he was applying a false description, or was reckless whether or not it was false.

As we have already seen in Chapter 3, the Trade Descriptions Act 1968 has an impact on the advertising and promoting of goods and it continues to apply throughout the dealings that a motor trader has with his customers, and is particularly relevant to the face-to-face negotiations carried out by the salesman.

Whilst the statements made in an advertisement or promotional literature may only rarely give rise to the customer having a legal comeback under the civil law if the statement turns out to be wrong, false or misleading, statements made during the negotiation of a sale in such a way that it is directed to the individual customer, will have much wider implications.

Not only will the Trade Descriptions Act be involved, but the customer may also have the right to take civil action for breach of contract or misrepresentation. From a practical point of view, the retailer has to appreciate that while he may be able to negotiate a settlement with an aggrieved customer and thus avoid any litigation, once a false trade description has been applied, an offence has been committed and strictly speaking, no amount of negotiation or offer of monetary compensation to the customer will help. In some cases, a trading standards officer may be prepared to drop an action if the consumer's complaint is resolved, but this cannot be relied on.

2 Trade descriptions of goods

The first point to consider is what constitutes a trade description. This is defined by s 2 of the Trade Descriptions Act 1968 as being 'an indication direct or indirect and by whatever means given of any of the following matters with respect to any goods or part of goods'. The 'following matters' set out in the Act are:

(a) quantity, size or gauge;
(b) method of manufacture, production, processing or recondition;
(c) composition;
(d) fitness for purpose, strength, performance, behaviour or accuracy;
(e) any physical characteristics not included in the preceding paragraphs;

(f)   testing by any person and the results thereof;
(g)   approval by any person or conformity with the type approved by any person;
(h)   place of date of manufacture, production, processing or reconditioning;
(i)   the person by whom manufactured, produced, processed or reconditioned; or
(j)   other history including previous ownership or use.

3 When is an offence committed?

Section 1 of the Act states that

'Any person who in the course of a trade or business:
(a)   applies a false trade description to any goods; or
(b)   supplies or offers to supply any goods to which a false trade description is applied,

commits an offence under the Act.'

Section 6 of the Act provides that a person displaying goods for supply, or having goods in his possession for supply will be deemed to be offering to supply them. This will therefore include vehicles stored in a garage awaiting display.[2]

4 Who is liable?

It should be noted that 'any person' includes limited companies who are deemed in law to have a separate legal personality. Section 20 of the Act also provides for making individual officers of a company jointly liable if it is proved that the offence was committed with their consent or by their neglect. However, where instructions have been given it is reasonable to expect they have been carried out correctly, and it is not neglect if it is not rechecked. A managing director of a garage was found not to be liable in these circumstances for the incorrect completion of a service book by his service manager, not in accordance with instructions given to him, and which was then sent by the managing director to a customer by letter.[3]

[2]   *Ben Worsley Ltd v Harvey* [1967] 2 All ER 507.
[3]   *Lewin v Bland* [1985] RTR 171.

Partners, even if ignorant of the application of a false trade description by the other, can still be prosecuted under s 1 of the Act. In the case of *Clode v Barnes*,[4] V and C were partners in a used car business. V sold the cars and C dealt with the administration. V sold a car to which he had applied a false trade description. C knew nothing of the sale or of the false trade description but nevertheless he was held to be guilty.

Section 23 of the Act allows the prosecution of someone other than the person actually committing the offence where it is found that the commission of the offence is due to the act or default of that other person. This prosecution may take place whether or not the person who actually committed the offence has been prosecuted. This section may be used to prosecute a private individual who has caused a trader to commit an offence (see below).

The Act normally applies to the seller of goods. However, in the case of *Fletcher v Budgen*,[5] a car dealer told a customer that his car was irreparable and fit only for scrap. The dealer then bought it for £2, repaired it for £56 and advertised it for sale at £135. It was held that the buyer could also be held liable for applying a false trade description to goods when buying them in the course of a trade or business.

5 'In the course of a trade or business'

It is immaterial whether the sale is part of the 'usual' business if it is clear that the sale is in the course of a business. The display for sale of a vehicle on the forecourt of a car repairer and MOT tester was held to be a sale in the course of a business.[6]

This expression has been held to extend to a car hire firm which customarily sold its cars after a certain period and who were successfully prosecuted under the Act in relation to a car sold with a false odometer reading although they were not car dealers.[7] In another case[8] a panel beater who bought and did up cars for sale made the statement that a car had 'a good little engine'. The statement was made when the dealer to whom he had disposed of the vehicle was selling it to a consumer. It

---

4   [1974] 1 All ER 1166.
5   [1974] 2 All ER 1243.
6   *Corfield v Sevenways Garage Ltd* [1985] RTR 109.
7   *Havering London Borough v Stevenson* [1970] 3 All ER 609.
8   *Fletcher v Sledmore* (1979) 71 LGR 179, [1973] RTR 371.

was held that he was guilty of applying a false trade description although he was not himself selling the goods because he knew that the statement was capable of influencing the sale.

However, these cases should be contrasted with *Blakemore v Bellamy* (see above, p 29), and it must also be shown that the sale transaction was an integral part of the defendant's business. In a case[9] where a self-employed courier who used his car almost exclusively for his business then sold it, it was held that he was not selling in the course of a trade or business, and so he had not committed an offence. A similar view was taken in *Devlin v Hall* when the Divisional Court ruled that a proprietor of a taxi firm who had clocked two of his taxis was not caught by the Act because no 'normal practice' in relation to a trade or business had been established at the time of the first offence.[10]

It will be seen that the effect of this provision is that private individuals will not be subject to prosecution under this section of the Act if they for example trade in a clocked vehicle, even if they know that the mileage is incorrect, or even if they themselves have clocked the car. It is possible however that a prosecution may be brought in these circumstances under s 23 if they have 'caused' a trader to commit an offence.[11] It is of course also possible that other criminal offences, for example, under the Theft Act 1968 could be charged in these circumstances.

6 How is a trade description applied?

This is explained in s 4 of the Trade Descriptions Act. A person 'applies' a trade description to goods if he:

(a)   affixes or annexes it to or in any manner marks it on or incorporates it with the goods themselves or anything with which the goods are supplied; or

(b)   places the goods in, on or with anything to which the trade description has been affixed or annexed or marked on or incorporated with; or

(c)   uses the trade description in any manner likely to be taken as referring to the goods.

---

[9]   *Davies v Sumner* [1985] RTR 95.
[10]   [1990] RTR 320.
[11]   *Olgeirsson v Kitching* [1986] 1 All ER 746, [1986] 1 WLR 304.

Where goods are supplied in response to a request in which a trade description is used, and in the circumstances it is reasonable to infer that the goods were supplied as corresponding to that description, this will also be treated as an application of a trade description by the person supplying the goods. In *Walker v Simon Dudley Ltd*,[12] the supply of a fire engine which did not conform to the contract specification meant that at the time of supply, the supplier had applied a false trade description to the goods. On the other hand, where goods are supplied in accordance with the contract but with some parts missing, this may be treated only as a contractual matter rather than a breach of the Trade Descriptions Act.[13] In *Swithland Motors Ltd v Peck*,[14] a part exchange vehicle had its speedometer replaced, and the vehicle records were marked accordingly. Whilst the car was being used by an employee, a customer expressed an interest in it and subsequently bought it. There was no disclaimer on the vehicle, and no one checked the records. The employee and the director who approved the sale were unaware of the incorrect mileage reading. The dealer appealed unsuccessfully against conviction of the offence of 'applying' a false description.

The description must be related in some way to the supply or intended supply of the goods. For example, in *Wickens Motors (Gloucester) Ltd v Hall*[15] car dealers sold an unroadworthy car. The purchaser complained forty days after the sale and was told there was nothing wrong. It was held that the dealer could not be convicted of an offence because no sale or supply of goods was contemplated as being affected by the sale. In another case[16] it was established that an MOT tester will not be guilty of a trade descriptions offence when issuing a certificate or invoice containing an inaccurate statement of defects because no supply of the vehicle will be affected.

Similarly, a statement of 'recorded mileage' on an MOT certificate is not a trade description,[17] although a statement that a vehicle has a valid MOT certificate will be.

[12] (1997) Times, 3 January, DC.
[13] *Cavendish Woodhouse Ltd v Wright* (1985) 149 JP 497.
[14] [1991] RTR 322, [1991] Crim LR 386, DC.
[15] [1972] 3 All ER 759.
[16] *Wycombe Marsh Garages Ltd v Fowler* [1972] 3 All ER 248.
[17] *Corfield v Sevenways Garage Ltd* [1985] RTR 109.

7 What about oral statements?

Section 4(2) of the Trade Descriptions Act provides that oral statements may also constitute trade descriptions. The six month time limit originally prescribed by the Act for bringing a prosecution for an oral false description was overridden by the Magistrates' Courts Act 1980.

8 What is a 'false' trade description?

Section 3 states that a false trade description is one that is false to a material degree. This definition includes statements which, although not false in themselves, are misleading. In addition, anything likely to be taken as an indication of one of the matters set out in s 2 of the Act although not a trade description will, if false, be covered by the Act. A car sold with smooth paintwork which concealed corrosion and filler was held to be 'likely to be taken' as an indication that the body was in sound condition.[18] In deciding whether a description is false or not, the court will consider statements in their context, to determine the effect on the ordinary consumer.[19]

For example, in *Robertson v Dicicco*[20] 'beautiful' used to describe a vehicle was held to be capable of indicating not only its external appearance, but also its running order. In another case, it was held that in ascertaining the meaning of the words 'in exceptional condition' the age, type and mileage of a vehicle may all be relevant.[21]

9 False statements about services

All the sections of the Act dealt with up to now relate to trade descriptions applied to goods. The Act also applies to trade descriptions made about services. Section 14 of the Act provides that it is an offence for any person in the course of a trade or business:

(a)   to make a statement which he knows to be false; or

(b)   recklessly to make a statement which is false about any of the matters specified.

---

[18]   *Cottee v Douglas Seaton (Used Cars) Ltd* [1972] 3 All ER 750.
[19]   *Kensington and Chelsea Royal London Borough Council v Riley* [1973] RTR 122.
[20]   [1972] RTR 431.
[21]   *Chidwick v Beer* [1974] RTR 415.

These are:

(i) the provision in the course of any trade or business of any services, accommodation or facilities;

(ii) the nature of any services, accommodation or facilities provided in the course of any trade or business;

(iii) the time at which, manner in which or persons by whom any services, accommodation or facilities are so provided;

(iv) the examination, approval or evaluation by any person of any services, accommodation or facilities so provided; or

(v) the location or amenities of any accommodation so provided.

'Services or facilities' do not include, except in exceptional circumstances, the offer of free goods with another purchase.[22]

Similar provisions as those relating to trade descriptions of goods are included dealing with statements 'likely to be taken' as a statement about any of these matters. Where the service is one of carrying out repairs, or any treatment or process, the effect of such repairs etc, is also covered.

'Recklessly' does not imply 'dishonestly'. It has been held for example that even though the chairman of a company studied an advertisement for ten minutes before approving it the advertisement contained a 'recklessly' made statement.[23] In a more recent case, the retailer was held to have been 'reckless' despite the fact that the company secretary had studied the offending advertisement, and made amendments to it.[24]

This part of the Act operates less stringently than that relating to goods, because proof of guilty knowledge or recklessness is required. It has been pointed out by the courts that the intention of this part of the Act, is not 'to make a breach of contract into a criminal offence'.[25] Where, for example, travel agents promised hotel facilities including a swimming pool, pushchairs for hire and special meals for children, and none of these were in fact provided, it was held that as these were simply promises as to the future and were not false at the time they were made, the travel agents should not be convicted.[26]

---

[22] *Newell v Hicks* [1984] RTR 135.

[23] *MFI Warehouses Ltd v Nattrass* [1973] 1 All ER 762. See also *Hirschler v Birch* [1987] RTR 13.

[24] *Dixons Ltd v Roberts* (1984) 82 LGR 689, 148 JP 513.

[25] *Beckett v Cohen* [1973] 1 All ER 120, but now see also *Formula One Autocentres Ltd v Birmingham City Council* [1999] RTR 195, below.

[26] *R v Sunair Holidays Ltd* [1973] 2 All ER 1233, CA.

So far as the motor trader is concerned this part of the Act will be mainly relevant to statements about repairs or servicing of vehicles, or application of special treatments, for example, rust proofing. In one case, it was held that the section applied to a false statement about the existence of a guarantee on a used car which would be provided by someone other than the seller.[27] It will also apply to statements made during the provision of a service, or after it has been supplied,[28] for example a statement about work which has been done during the progress of work on a customer's car.

A promise that a customer's car will be ready on a certain day or at a certain time will be a promise as to the future which will be enforceable by the customer only by bringing an action for breach of contract. It will not lay the trader open to a claim of making a false trade description about the services that he is offering. If, however, a trader were to claim that all servicing work was carried out by mechanics who had undergone appropriate training by a certain manufacturer, and this was not the case, this would clearly be a situation falling within s 14 of the Act where a false statement was being made about a service which he was offering. A statement made to a customer that certain work has been carried out on his car which has not in fact been done will again be a clear example of a false description under this part of the Act. In *Formula One Autocentres Ltd v Birmingham City Council*,[29] however, it was held that in these circumstances offences under s 1(1)(a) and (b) (strict offences) could be committed, as the return of the vehicle to the customer after work is carried out is a 'supply of goods'. The description of the work done by the repairer which is written on the invoice is therefore a 'description' applied to goods.

It has to be noted, however, that the level of liability under s14 is slightly less than in the case of offences under s 1 of the Act relating to the selling of goods. Under s 1 the offences are of strict liability and the employer will be guilty with his employees for false descriptions which they apply.[30]

In order to be convicted of an offence under s 14, however, the prosecution have to prove guilty knowledge or recklessness on the part of the

[27]   *Bambury v Hounslow London Borough Council* [1971] RTR 1, DC.
[28]   *R v Bevelectric Ltd* (1992) 157 JP 323, CA.
[29]   (1998) [1999] RTR 195.
[30]   *Clode v Barnes* [1974] 1 All ER 1166.

defendant. This was illustrated in a case involving a partnership where the sleeping partner in a business was held not liable for a false trade description made by her partner about work which he had carried out.[31] The difficulty of proving guilty knowledge or recklessness means that it is likely that the *Formula One Autocentres* case approach is increasingly likely to be seen as an attractive option to prosecutors.

10 Defences

Section 24(1) states that it shall be a defence for the accused to show that:

(a) the commission of the offence was due to a mistake or to reliance on information supplied to him or to the act or default of another person, an accident or some other cause beyond his control; and

(b) that he took all reasonable precautions and exercised all due diligence to avoid the commission of such an offence by himself or any person under his control.

Subsection 2 goes on to provide that in order for this defence to be relied on written notice must be given to the prosecution at least seven days before the hearing giving whatever information he has to identify the 'other person'.

Subsection 3 is similar to subsection 1 and provides a specific defence in relation to a charge of supply or offer to supply falsely described goods and requires that the person charged is able to prove that he could not have found out about the false description even if he had exercised 'due diligence'.

This defence has been successfully used where a dealer sold a car with a recorded mileage of 35,000 miles after having obtained an independent opinion from the AA to the effect that the car's appearance and performance were consistent with the lower mileage. In fact the original recorded mileage had been 83,060 miles.[32] This may no longer be sufficient as it has subsequently been held that the reasonable precaution of using a disclaimer should also be adopted in such cases[33] if the defence is to be relied on.

---

[31] *Coupe v Guyatt* [1973] 2 All ER 1058.
[32] *Naish v Gore* [1971] 3 All ER 737.
[33] *Simmons v Potter* [1975] RTR 347.

The extent of the 'reasonable precautions' required is a difficult issue, particularly in relation to mileage readings. Does this mean for example, as has been suggested, that a prudent dealer should check the history of every secondhand car he sells through the DVLC records? In the case of *Simmons v Ravenhill*[34] it was held that although it would be unreasonable to expect a dealer to check the whole pedigree of a used car in this way, the selling dealer should have been alerted by the fact that the recorded mileage was extremely low for a car of that age.

It certainly does mean, however, that if the trader has a fixed policy, eg to enquire of previous owners to verify the mileage, failure to follow that policy will mean that all reasonable precautions will not have been taken.[35] In *Lewin v Rothersthorpe Road Garage Ltd*,[36] the adoption of the motor industry code of practice by a dealership and evidence that the salesmen were regularly instructed about it, amounted to all reasonable precautions.

The situation sometimes arises where 'another person' may be the employee of a defendant company. In *Tesco Supermarkets Ltd v Nattrass*[37] an employee displayed a 'flash' offer on a poster relating to money off a brand of washing powder. In fact the shop had run out of packets to which the reduced price was being applied and a shopper failed to get the price of an ordinary packet reduced. This occurred because of lack of supervision by the shop manager and it was held that he was 'another person' and could be treated separately from the defendant company. The defence of act or default of another was therefore successful. This case was followed in a case involving the sale of a used car where the salesman, who was personally prosecuted, had not followed the procedure clearly laid down by his employers.[38]

In an unreported case at Coventry Magistrates' Court (5 November 1986) Lucas Autocentres Ltd were acquitted of charges brought under s 14 in relation to servicing work incorrectly carried out. They were able to convince the court that the work had been imperfectly carried out by a new mechanic, but that their system of quality control, training, random checks and supervision meant that they had exercised all due care and diligence.

---

[34] [1984] RTR 412.
[35] *Horner v Sherwoods of Darlington Ltd* (1989) 154 JP 299.
[36] (1983) 148 JP 87.
[37] [1972] AC 153, HL.
[38] *Lewin v Rothersthorpe Garage Ltd* (1983) 148 JP 87.

Section 23 of the Act allows the prosecution of someone other than the person actually committing the offence where the commission is due to the act or default of that other person. This may be so whether or not the person who actually committed the offence has been prosecuted. In *Coupe v Guyett*[39] the sleeping partner of a garage who was entirely unaware of a false statement made by her repair workshop manager was acquitted of an offence under the Act and the manager also, therefore, had to be acquitted.

The s 24 defence is extremely relevant, for example, in cases involving the clocking of odometers, where the retailer may find that he has unwittingly sold a vehicle which has been 'clocked' by someone else, including private sellers who may then be prosecuted (see above).

11 Penalties

The penalties provided by the Act are:
—   for conviction on summary trial a maximum fine of £5,000; and
—   for conviction on indictment an unlimited fine and/or imprisonment not exceeding two years.

It is worth noting that the penalties particularly for the clocking of cars have been increasing as the courts have tried to clamp down on the traders who persistently offend under the Act. In *R v Hewitt*,[40] the Court of Appeal upheld a custodial sentence and fine of £500 on each of eight counts of applying false descriptions by altering odometer readings by 30–40%. The court took the view that the Act would not work in the way parliament had intended if custodial sentences were not used in this type of case as a deterrent.

12 Compensation orders

Under the Powers of Criminal Courts Act 1973, s 35, the court has a discretionary power to make a compensation order against anyone convicted of an offence. This power is now used fairly widely in Trade Description Act cases, particularly in relation to clocked cars.

---

[39]   [1973] 2 All ER 1058.
[40]   [1991] RTR 357, CA.

13 Time limits

Under s 19(1) a prosecution must be brought within three years of the date of commission of the offence, or one year of its discovery by the prosecutor, whichever is the earlier.[41]

C TRADE DESCRIPTIONS OF MOTOR VEHICLES

In 1978–79, 1563 Trade Descriptions Act prosecutions were brought which resulted in convictions. Of that 1563, 777 related to the sale or repair of motor vehicles or accessories. Not only does this represent nearly half the convictions under the Act during that period, but also the motor industry had more convictions than any other single sector.

Trade descriptions applied to motor vehicles may relate to a variety of different aspects of a car or its performance, and may be applied in a variety of different ways, eg orally by the salesman, in writing in a sales brochure, or by the mileage reading shown on an odometer. The following are some of the most frequent problems that arise.

I Advertisements and sales literature

The effect of the Act on statements made in advertisements and sales literature has already been referred to. Any such statement, if it is false, may lead to risk of prosecution. The Act provides that a trade description in an advertisement will be taken as referring to all goods of that class, including those not yet manufactured.[42] In *Robins & Day Ltd v Kent County Council Trading Standards Department*,[43] a dealer advertised 'Peugeot 405 GTX Injection INCLUDES Air Conditioning...' by a window poster on his premises. A prospective customer was offered a vehicle without air conditioning, as the four which had been the subject of the offer had been sold. Although he bought the vehicle, he complained to trading standards six weeks later. On visiting the premises they found the posters still on display. The appeal court held that on the facts of the case, the trade description only applied to the four original vehicles, and that no offence had been committed.

---

[41]   For a detailed discussion of this section, see Butterworths Trading and Consumer Law, para 3 [192].

[42]   Section 5(2).

[43]   [1996] CLY 1168, DC.

A trader prosecuted for an incorrect statement in the manufacturer's sales literature that he hands to a customer will of course have a possible defence that the offence was due to the act or default of another (s 24).

If however he has failed to take reasonable precautions himself, for example by checking that he is using the current literature, or by affixing any amending stickers, he will not be able to rely on this defence.

It is common practice for sales literature to contain a statement such as 'specifications are liable to alteration without notice'. This amounts to a 'disclaimer' of legal liability on the part of the person making it. Whether it is effective or not would seem to depend on the precise wording and on the circumstances surrounding its use, although the use of disclaimers in the context of odometer readings has been given the stamp of respectability (see below). However, they must be bold, precise and compelling, and they will not be effective in brochures when the statement made was shown to be incorrect at the time the brochure was printed! [44]

2 Handbooks

There is some disagreement over whether a vehicle handbook contains statements which are capable of being a trade description relating to the car. As the handbook is not normally given to the customer until after the sale has been completed it seems that the Act will probably not normally apply to such statements, as it is not directly connected with the supply of the product. However in *VAG (UK) Ltd v Lancashire County Council*,[45] a prosecution was brought against a vehicle importer alleging the application of a false description under the Act in respect of a statement in the handbook about an alarm system fitted to an Audi. The description was alleged to be false in that the alarm did not activate as described in the handbook. The evidence was that the owner of the vehicle did not examine the handbook until after the vehicle had been broken into, and that the importer who was prosecuted had played no part in the production of the vehicle or the handbook or its supply to the ultimate customer. The Divisional Court upheld the appeal of the importer against conviction of an offence, and expressed doubts as to

[44] *British Gas Corpn v Lubbock* [1974] 1 All ER 188.
[45] [1997] Trading Standards Review 20.

whether the description in the handbook could in any event be false or misleading, because it was only a description of how the equipment was designed or intended to work.

3 'Current MOT Certificate'

A false statement that a vehicle has been put through an MOT test, or a false statement as to its result will be caught by s 2(1)(f) of the Act as a statement about 'testing by any person and the results thereof'. This will only be so, however, where the statement is made in relation to a vehicle which is being sold and where it is likely to affect that sale.[46]

4 'BSI approved'

This will arise mainly in relation to the sale of accessories and spare parts. An incorrect statement that a particular mirror has the 'AA seal of approval' or that a tow rope conforms to a particular BSI standard will be covered either by s 2(1)(f) or (g) of the Act.

5 Statutory approval marks and type approval[47]

The motor trader will not normally concern himself about whether a vehicle has been type approved, and whether it bears the necessary 'E' approval marks. He will rely on the manufacturer to have made sure that the vehicle conforms with these statutory requirements, and is unlikely to make statements to his customers about the existence or otherwise of a Type Approval Certificate or Certificate of Conformity, nor is a customer likely to ask.

It is worth noting however that this information is covered by s 2(1)(g) of the Act and that therefore a prosecution could be brought on this basis. It is worth noting also that designated approval marks,[48] the 'E' and 'e' marks, are specifically made trade descriptions by virtue of the Road Traffic Act 1988.

---

[46] *Wycombe Marsh Garages Ltd v Fowler* [1972] 3 All ER 248.
[47] See also ch 13, below.
[48] See the Motor Vehicles (Designation of Approval Marks) Regulations 1979, SI 1979/1088.

Unlike type approval which is only relevant when the vehicle is first put on the road, the 'E' marks will be a continuing 'trade description'. If therefore a vehicle is displayed for sale or sold secondhand with the 'E' mark still affixed but having been altered in some way from the original 'E' mark specification, the trader could be guilty of an offence under the Act. He would no doubt seek to rely on the defence that his offence was due to the act or default of another, but he would have to show that he had not made the alteration himself, and second that he had taken reasonable steps to check that the 'E' marks were still valid.

6 'Over 40 mpg'

An incorrect statement about fuel consumption will not only be a false trade description caught by s 21(1)(d) or (e), it will also be a breach of the Energy Act. This will include not only intentional false statements, but also mistakes, for example affixing the statutory fuel consumption and emissions information label to the wrong car.

7 2002 model'

False statements about the year of manufacture of a vehicle will be caught by s 2(1)(h).[49] Determining the year of manufacture can cause difficulties. The CarwiseCode of Practice for the Retail Motor Industry lays down the following rules.

In the description of a used car, any year must be either:
(a)   the year of first use, or
(b)   the year of first registration, or
(c)   the last year that the car complied with the manufacturer's specification of a model sold as new during that calendar year,

whichever is the earliest.

However, in one case[50] appearing to conflict with this provision a Ford van was manufactured in 1972 and subsequently converted to a cara-vanette before being registered and sold in 1975. It was described as a

[49]   *R v Haesler* [1973] RTR 486.
[50]   *Routledge v Ansa Motors (Chester le Street) Ltd* [1980] RTR 1, DC.

'used 1975' model. The court decided that the average customer would believe that 1975 was the date of manufacture and that an offence had been committed.

8 By whom and where manufactured

False statements about the country of origin will be caught by the Act, as will statements about the name of the manufacturer. This is now assuming more importance as the incidence of counterfeit motor components finding their way onto the UK market increases. The retailer who sells a counterfeit part bearing a false name or mark, eg FERODO, LUCAS, will be committing an offence under the Act, and the fact that he was unaware of the counterfeiting will not be a defence. In addition, the manufacture, sale or supply, or having in possession for supply, of products bearing an unauthorised trade mark will be an offence under the Trade Marks Act 1994.[51]

Regulations[52] under the Act now require corrective marking of origin in certain circumstances.

9 Statements about the condition of a vehicle

These clearly fall within the Act under s 2(1)(d) or (e) and there are numerous examples of cases where this has arisen. In *Chidwick v Beer*[53] a car which was falsely described as being in 'excellent condition throughout' brought about the prosecution of the seller even though the customer had not been deceived by the false trade description. In *Furniss v Scholes*[54] a car was advertised as being in 'really exceptional condition throughout'. The body was corroded but had been camouflaged and there were various mechanical faults. The court held that this was a clear case of a false trade description having been applied. The test is the effect of the words used on the ordinary man.[55]

---

[51]   Trade Marks Act 1994, s 92.
[52]   SI 1988/1771 and see below.
[53]   [1974] RTR 415.
[54]   [1974] RTR 133.
[55]   *Robertson v Dicicco* [1972] RTR 431.

10 A 'new car'

In the leading case of *R v Ford Motor Co Ltd*,[56] the question of what
constituted a new car was discussed at some length. The facts were that
a car was supplied to a customer in response to his order for a new car.
Unbeknown to the retailer it had been damaged before it had reached
him. It had been to a repairer approved by Ford. The damage came to
light following a complaint from the customer. In upholding Ford's
appeal against conviction by the magistrates, the Divisional Court held
that where a new car was damaged and repaired before delivery to the
retail customer the crucial question to be answered was the extent of
the damage and the quality of the repair. If the damage could be put
right in such a way that it could be said that the car was 'as good as
new', then no offence would be committed by describing it as 'new'. In
this case the repair had been well carried out and the court therefore
held that no offence was committed.

There are other issues relevant to the question of whether a car can be
described as 'new' without falling foul of the Trade Descriptions Act,
eg the amount of delivery mileage, the year of manufacture, and
whether there has been a previous retail sale that did not proceed.
Although these points were not relevant in the *Ford* case, the court
made comments about some of them. For example, the court
remarked that if a car had been the subject of a previous retail sale
then it could not be regarded as new. Whether this rule extends to a
situation where a car has been registered in a customer's name who
then decides not to proceed with the purchase is unclear. However, in
Morris Motors v Lilley[57] (not a trade descriptions case) a car was sold
by distributors to a purchaser L. It was registered in his name. The
same day L sold it to another dealer who subsequently advertised it
under the heading 'New Cars'. It was sold to P, who then brought an
action for breach of contract alleging that the car was not in fact new.
The court held that the car had ceased to be new when it was sold by
retail sale, registered, had number plates put on it and was driven
away by L. There had therefore been a breach of contract to supply a
'new' car. It has now been held, however, that a new car 'pre-regis-
tered' in the name of the dealer (typically for the purpose of achieving

---

[56] [1974] 3 All ER 489, and see also *Raynham Farm Co Ltd v Symbol Motor Corpn Ltd*
[1987] BTLC 157 referred to below, ch 7.
[57] [1959] 3 All ER 737.

manufacturers' bonuses or quotas) may not subsequently be sold as 'new'.[58]

In addition, the court in the *Ford* case went out of its way to make the point that they could not approve of an additional criterion for a new car that had been suggested, namely that the car should be in 'mint condition' meaning that it should be faultless. The court remarked that 'though it may be very desirable that new cars should be faultless it is a matter of common knowledge that frequently they are not'.

The year of manufacture has been considered in the case of a motor cycle which was manufactured in 1967, never sold, and imported into the UK where it was finally sold as 'new' in 1972. Despite the length of time which had elapsed, it was held to have been a valid description of it.

The amount of delivery mileage which is permitted is still unclear, although in the *Ford* case the court said that it must not be excessive.

It may also be helpful to consider the definition of newness in other legislation. For example, for the purposes of the requirement[59] to display fuel consumption and emissions information, a new car is now simply defined, following the implementation of an EC Directive, as '... a ... car which has not previously been sold to a person who bought it for a purpose other than that of selling or supplying it'. This is far broader than was previously the case under national fuel consumption testing rules which had referred to a figure of 500 miles as a test for newness.

11 'One lady owner';'director's car'

Statements about the previous ownership or history of a vehicle are caught by s 2(1)(j) of the Act.

In a case[60] where a motor car hired under five different leasing arrangements to different companies was then described as having 'one owner' it was ruled that this description, although technically correct, was misleading.

---

[58]   *R v Anderson* [1988] RTR 260.
[59]   The Passenger Car (Fuel Consumption and Co2 Emissions Information) Regulations 2001, SI 2001/3523.
[60]   *R v South Western Justices, ex p Wandsworth London Borough Council* [1983] RTR 425, DC.

12 Vehicle specification

An agreement to provide goods at a future date that conform to a certain specification will be treated as a trade description of the goods, and so caught by the Act if the goods fail to meet that specification when delivered.[61]

13 Odometers

It is now established law[62] that the figures on the odometer of a vehicle may amount to an indication of the distance that the vehicle has travelled, and is therefore a trade description as to the previous history or use of the vehicle. The question to be decided is the effect which this description will have on the man in the street. The courts have held that he is likely to take the odometer reading as an indication of the true mileage of the vehicle and the retailer will be guilty of an offence if it is incorrect and he has failed to take steps to warn that the reading may be incorrect.[63]

Zeroing

The practice of zeroing odometers has been held by the Court of Appeal to be applying a false trade description.[64]

Replacement odometers

In considering a case where a faulty odometer in a used car had been replaced by the defendant, who had then sold the vehicle to another trader with the words 'n/warranted' on the invoice, the Divisional Court held that the defendant had applied a false description to the vehicle. In attempting to answer the question how a trader in these circumstances could avoid criminal liability, the court suggested that one solution might be to adjust the new odometer to the correct mileage, or failing that, to display on the dashboard a clear and prominent statement show-

---

[61] *Walker v Simon Dudley Ltd* (1997) Times, 3 January DC.
[62] *Tarleton Engineering Co Ltd v Nattrass* [1973] 3 All ER 699.
[63] *Taylor v Smith* [1974] RTR 190.
[64] *R v Southwood* [1987] 3 All ER 556, overturning *K Lill Holdings v White* [1979] RTR 120.

ing the mileage covered in addition to that shown on the replacement odometer.[65] This issue was also considered in *R v Shrewsbury Crown Court, ex p Venables*,[66] where a used vehicle had been run as part of the defendant's business on trade plates, having replaced a defective odometer. The vehicle was then sold to another trader at a small loss without it having been advertised or offered for sale. The trade buyer did not rely on the mileage. The Divisional Court overturned the conviction for applying a false description, on the basis that because the odometer was replaced at a time when the vehicle was simply being used within the business, and it was never actually offered for sale to the public, the trader's activity was not 'in the course of a trade or business'.

Disclaimers

The general rule of English law is that it is not possible by means of a disclaimer to avoid liability for committing a criminal offence. However, since the introduction of the Trade Descriptions Act various decisions have now made it clear that an appropriately worded disclaimer may operate to protect the retailer who sells a vehicle to which a false description has been applied. Not only have disclaimers been given the stamp of respectability by the courts, it is now also the law that if a retailer sells a car which has been clocked and he has not used a satisfactory disclaimer, he will not be able to rely on the defence of having taken reasonable precautions and exercised 'due diligence' in checking the truthfulness of the description. In *Simmons v Potter*,[67] the defendants bought a car at auction with an odometer reading of 14,000 miles. The car's condition was not inconsistent with this figure. They made enquiries of the previous owner who referred them to the servicing garage, but got no firm information. The car was displayed for sale without a disclaimer, and the Divisional Court referred the case back to the magistrates with a direction to convict, as the use of a disclaimer was an obvious 'reasonable precaution' for a trader to take.

---

[65] *Southend Borough Council v White* (1991) 156 LG Rev 911, 156 JP 463, discussed in Butterworths Trading and Consumer Law at para 3 [267].
[66] [1994] Crim LR 61.
[67] *Simmons v Potter* [1975] RTR 347. See also *Crook v Howells Garages (Newport) Ltd* [1980] RTR 434.

Inadequate disclaimers

Various cases illustrate how strictly the courts will test the use of disclaimers. The following have all been held to be inadequate disclaimers:

—   the suppliers are not answerable for the mileage shown on the vehicle's mileometer;[68]
—   a disclaimer displayed on a wall inside an office on the retailer's premises;[69]
—   a disclaimer on documentation given to the customer at the time of delivery;[70]
—   disclaimer notices displayed round auction rooms;[71]
—   an oral disclaimer applied at the time of sale.[72]

Rules for use of disclaimers

The rules developed by the courts on the use of disclaimers may be summarised as follows:

(a)   disclaimers may provide a defence to prosecutions under the Trade Descriptions Act;

(b)   any disclaimer to be effective must be 'as bold, precise and compelling' as the original description;[73]

(c)   a disclaimer will only operate to negative the making of a trade description: it will not help once one is made;

(d)   a disclaimer is essential if a dealer is to rely on the defence of having exercised all due diligence contained in s 24 of the Act;

(e)   the disclaimer must be appropriately worded (see above for inadequate disclaimers) and must clearly convey to the customer that no reliance whatever can be placed on the odometer reading;[74]

---

[68]   *R v Hammertons Cars Ltd* [1976] 3 All ER 758.
[69]   *Waltham Forest London Borough Council v TG Wheatley (Central Garages) (No 2)* [1978] RTR 333.
[70]   *R v Hammertons Cars Ltd* [1976] 3 All ER 758.
[71]   *Zawadski v Sleigh* [1975] RTR 113.
[72]   *Lewin v Fuell* [1990] Crim LR 658, DC.
[73]   *Norman v Bennett* [1974] 3 All ER 351, [1974] 1 WLR 1229.
[74]   *Corfield v Starr* [1981] RTR 380; *Newham London Borough Council v Singh* [1988] RTR 359.

(f)   the timing of the disclaimer is vital. The false description must be disclaimed before it is applied under s l(l)(a). Under s 1(1)(b) this is before or at the same time as the offer of supply;[75]

(g)   a disclaimer cannot be a defence to a charge of actually clocking or zeroing an odometer,[76]

(h)   A disclaimer stating that the recorded mileage cannot be guaranteed when the true mileage is in fact known to the motor trader will not provide a defence.[77] Furthermore, The Office of Fair Trading has said[78] that failing to tell consumers the true mileage of a car when it is known to the trader or any of his employees will be regarded as "conduct having a bearing on the fitness of a licensee or applicant to hold a Consumer Credit Act licence". In these circumstances, the OFT says the true mileage should be disclosed, that it would be deceitful to merely disclaim the mileage reading, and that in such circumstances a disclaimer would not be a defence to a criminal charge and should not be used.

Further, it appears that a disclaimer alone may be an adequate defence to a charge of supplying a clocked vehicle without the necessity of the defendant having to show any other 'reasonable precautions' to avoid committing the offence.[79] The Court of Appeal have stressed that in considering the effectiveness of a disclaimer, the decision may ultimately turn on the positioning of the statement in relation to the odometer reading, and other relevant circumstances.[80] In *Rees v Munday*[81] it was held that goods are 'supplied' at the moment of delivery or notification of the availability for delivery and not when the property in the goods actually passes.

D ORIGIN MARKING

Following the repeal of the Trade Descriptions Act 1972, which required the country of origin to be shown on goods bearing a UK

---

[75]   *R v Hammerton Cars Ltd* [1976] 3 All ER 758.
[76]   *R v Southwood* [1987] 3 All ER 556.
[77]   *Farrand v Lazarus* [2002] EWHC 226 (Admin), [2002] 3 All ER 175.
[78]   Office of Fair Trading Guidance for Car Dealers: for consumer credit licence holders and applicants in the new and used car markets 2003 – see Appendix 2.
[79]   *Newham London Borough Council v Singh* [1988] RTR 359.
[80]   *R v Bull* [1997] RTR 123, CA.
[81]   [1974] 3 All ER 506.

name or trade mark, regulations[82] have now been introduced under the Trade Descriptions Act 1968, s 38(3)(a). These require any goods which give a misleading indication as to where they were manufactured or produced to be marked with or accompanied by a corrective statement of origin.

[82] The Trade Descriptions (Place of Production) (Marking) Order 1988, SI 1988/1771.

CHAPTER 5

Is there a contract?

A INTRODUCTION

Whether a retailer is selling a car, a tyre, a battery or a gallon of petrol, or the services of his repair workshop, he is entering into a contract with his customers.

If the contract goes wrong, and the goods or services supplied are not up to standard, the customer will be able to take action against the retailer for breach of contract. Even if a problem arises because of a false statement made before the contract was made, he may have an action for misrepresentation if he can show that the misrepresentation was one of fact which induced him to enter into the contract (see below).

He may of course also have other rights. For example, if he has had an accident caused by a defective tyre he may have a claim against the manufacturer of the tyre. Similarly, as we have already seen, a criminal offence may also have been committed, for example under the Trade Descriptions Act 1968.

Because of the importance to consumers of the terms of the contract they enter into, legislation now controls the sort of terms that may be used in consumer contracts whether they relate to buying goods (eg a motor car) or services (eg having a car repaired). The terms of these contracts are looked at in detail in Chapters 7 and 11, below. They will vary according to the type of contract, and to any specific terms agreed between the parties.

Common to all contracts, however, are certain basic elements which must be present before a legally enforceable contract can exist. The first step for any retailer faced with a customer asking for compensation, or a replacement car, therefore, is to look at the facts to find out whether or not a valid contract exists.

B FORMING THE CONTRACT

There are four basic elements which must be present in order for any contract to be a legally enforceable one. These are an offer, an acceptance of that offer, consideration and an intention to enter into legal relations. The fact that a contract is not in writing will not make any difference to whether a binding contract exists, subject to certain specific exceptions such as a finance agreement regulated under the Consumer Credit Act 1974, although it will of course make proof much easier. A contract may still exist, even if there was no specific offer and acceptance.

The courts may be prepared to imply a legally binding contract from the behaviour of the parties. For example, where one party sent a signed copy of a proposed contract to the other party's agent who altered it in a minor way and put it unsigned in his desk, and the parties then behaved as though there was a concluded contract between them, the court held that they had entered into a binding contract with one another in the terms of the unsigned document.[1] Special rules[2] now apply when a consumer enters into a contract with a business without the parties meeting face to face before the contract is made, and will apply in particular to contracts made over the Internet, by phone, fax or mail order, and these are dealt with in more detail below.

I The offer

The offer can be made to a particular person or to the world at large. It must, however, consist of a definite promise to be legally bound provided certain terms are accepted. This will mean that generally statements in advertisements and catalogues will not be 'offers' capable of being accepted by consumers.[3] It will depend on the words used how-

[1]   *Brogden v Metropolitan Rly* (1877) 2 App Cas 666.
[2]   The Consumer Protection (Distance Selling) Regulations 2000, SI 2000/2334.
[3]   See also ch 3, above.

ever. In the case of *Carlill v Carbolic Smoke Ball Co*,[4] an advertisement by the manufacturer of a flu remedy who promised to pay £100 to anyone catching flu after using the product was held to be an offer made to the whole world capable of being converted into a binding contract by an acceptance and performance of the terms by a customer. Generally speaking, however, advertisements will not be couched in those sorts of terms and statements made in them will not give rise to a legally enforceable contract.

Auctions

Special rules relating to offer and acceptance apply at auctions. A bid made is an offer which the auctioneer is free either to accept or reject.

The sale of goods by auction is complete when the auctioneer announces completion with his hammer. Until he makes that announcement the bid may be retracted.[5]

The display of goods for sale in a shop or showroom or an advertisement offering certain goods for sale is not an offer in legal terms but is known as an 'invitation to treat'. The distinction can be important: it means that as there is no contract, the retailer can refuse to sell goods at the price at which they are displayed or at all. By putting the goods on display he is not making an offer which the customer can accept by asking for the goods and tendering the price. It is an invitation to the customer to come and make an offer to buy the goods which the seller can either accept or reject. However, it must be borne in mind that this only relates to the contract of sale; refusal to sell goods at the displayed price will not only upset potential customers, it will also lay the seller open to risk of prosecution under the Consumer Protection Act, Pt III (see above).

Self-service displays

The distinction between an offer and an invitation to treat is also of importance when goods are being sold through a self-service display.

---

[4]   [1892] 2 QB 484. See also *Esso Petroleum v Customs and Excise Comrs* [1976] 1 All ER 117.
[5]   *British Car Auctions Ltd v Wright* [1972] 1 WLR 1519.

Here the contract will not be completed until the customer reaches the cash desk.[6] The act of putting goods in the basket is an offer in response to the invitation to treat which the cashier can either accept or reject.

Conditional offers

An offer may be conditional. For example, a customer's offer to buy a vehicle subject to it passing a mechanical examination can only be accepted by the retailer if the condition is satisfied.

A customer saw a car advertised for sale at £350 on a retailer's premises. He signed a form of hire-purchase agreement from a finance company. This formed an offer to the finance company to buy the car. The form stated that the agreement would only be binding on the finance company after they had signed it. The customer took the car away and paid the first instalment. He was dissatisfied and returned the car to the retailer's premises from where it was stolen and later recovered badly damaged.

The finance company signed the form in ignorance of what had happened and then tried to sue the customer for breach of the agreement. The court decided that they could not do this, because there was an implied condition that the car would remain in substantially the same state it was in when the offer was made, ie the form signed by the customer. Because it did not, the implied condition was not fulfilled and the finance company could not accept the offer. Therefore, no binding contract existed.[7] An offer may be withdrawn at any time before it is accepted, but in order to be effective this withdrawal of the offer must be notified to the other party.

2 Acceptance

Acceptance may be made orally or in writing but it must be indicated in some way and it must be communicated to the person making the offer. The acceptance must be in the precise terms of the offer otherwise it

---

[6] *Pharmaceutical Society of Great Britain v Boots Cash Chemists (Southern) Ltd* [1953] 1 QB 401, CA.
[7] *Financings Ltd v Stimson* [1962] 3 All ER 386.

will be a counter-offer and no contract will exist until acceptance of that counter-offer.

Contractual liability cannot arbitrarily be imposed by the person making the offer, for example by stating that silence will be assumed to convey acceptance of the terms offered. For example,[8] a man discussed the possibility of buying a horse which belonged to his nephew. There was some debate about the price and the nephew wrote to his uncle saying that he thought there had been a misunderstanding. The uncle believed he had bought the horse for £30 and the nephew believed he had sold it for 30 guineas. The uncle replied proposing that they should split the difference, saying: 'If I hear no more about him, I consider the horse mine at £30 15s.' The court subsequently held that the uncle could not enforce the bargain—no contract existed because there had been no acceptance of his offer of £30 15s.

Uncertainty about the terms

Even if there has been an offer and acceptance, there may still be no binding contract if it is uncertain what has been agreed. In *Scammell v Ouston*,[9] a customer gave a retailer a written order for a van containing the words 'this order is given on the understanding that the balance of the purchase price can be had on HP over 2 years'. The order was accepted by the retailer, but the HP terms never specified. The court decided that no contract had ever been concluded.

3 Consideration

Consideration is the third essential element in a binding contract. It will generally be the price that is to be paid but it can also be an action promised by one party in return for something done by the other. However, in contracts for the sale of goods the consideration has to be in money. In deciding whether or not a contract is legally enforceable, the court will not take into account whether one party has made a good bargain or not. However, the consideration must be provided by the

---

[8]   *Felthouse v Bindley* (1863) 1 New Rep 401, (1862) 11 CBNS 869.
[9]   [1941] AC 251, HL.
[10] *Tweddle v Atkinson* (1861) 1 B & S 393.

other party to the proposed contract. For example,[10] an agreement was made between two people whereby each promised the other that he would pay a sum of money to a third party. One of the two died without having paid, and the third party tried to sue his executors. He failed, because he had not provided any consideration nor was he the person to whom the promise had been made.

The rule about consideration raises an important practical point. If a person promises to pay, or pays, part of a debt which he owes to a creditor, and in return the creditor releases him from his obligation to pay the balance, the creditor will not in fact be bound to keep his part of the bargain. This is because there was no 'consideration' for his promise to release the obligation to pay the balance of the debt.[11] However, it should be noted that there are exceptions to this rule where there will be consideration and the promise of release will be enforceable. The most important examples are:

(a) where payment of a smaller sum is made before the due date at the creditor's request;

(b) payment of a smaller sum at a different place at the creditor's request;

(c) where part payment of a debt is made by a third party;

(d) where the other party has altered his position in reliance on the promise to release the rest of the debt.

4 Intention to enter into legal relations

Apart from the need for an offer, acceptance and consideration, the law will not imply an enforceable contract when it is quite clear that the parties did not intend to enter into a binding agreement. In certain cases the law will assume that the parties did not intend a legally enforceable contract, for example, an agreement between husband and wife.

Even though the basic essentials for a contract, offer, acceptance, consideration and intention to contract, are all present, there may still not be a legally enforceable contract. The parties to the contract must have legal capacity to make a contract and the subject matter of the contract must not be illegal or contrary to public policy.

[11] *Foakes v Beer* (1884) 9 App Cas 605.

C THE PARTIES TO A CONTRACT

I Limited companies

A limited company is a legal person and is able to enter into legally binding contracts provided these are made after the company has been incorporated and that the contract is within the scope of the objects clause of its Memorandum of Association. Any contracts made which are outside the scope of this clause are not binding on the company. Contracts with someone who is drunk or insane may be set aside if it is proved that they were incapable of understanding what they were doing at the time they made the contract and this condition was known to the other party at the time.

2 Minors

The capacity of minors, ie those under eighteen years of age, to enter into binding contracts is limited.

The types of contract where the motor retailer is most likely to become involved with infants are:
(a)   to sell, service or repair motor vehicles;
(b)   to finance the purchase of motor vehicles.

Other contracts, eg of employment and apprenticeship, are outside the scope of this book.

A contract to sell goods or services to an infant will be binding on the infant only if it is for 'necessaries'.[12] 'Necessary' goods are 'goods suitable to the condition in life of such infant ... and to his actual requirements at the time of sale and delivery'. This definition seems to include goods purchased for real use so long as they are not merely ornamental. Articles of mere luxury are always excluded although 'luxurious articles of utility' are in some cases allowed. This would suggest that the purchase of a racing car, for example, by an infant would not be deemed to be necessary whereas a car for use on normal roads even though a high-powered luxury model would be thought of as falling within this definition. In decided cases 'necessaries' have been held to include horses and a racing bicycle. Unfortunately, some of the cases

---

[12]   Sale of Goods Act 1979, s 3.

are rather outdated: the fact that an Oxford jury once held that champagne and wild ducks were necessaries to an infant undergraduate may seem a little anachronistic these days, to say the least.

Where a contract with a minor is unenforceable or is repudiated by him because he was a minor when it was made, he may be ordered by the court to transfer any property he acquired under the contract.[13]

3 Agents

Occasionally, the retailer will find himself in the position of entering into a contract as an agent for a third party or of contracting with somebody who is acting as an agent for someone else. Whether the contract will be binding on the third party will depend on whether the agent had his express or implied authority to contract on his behalf.

Frequently one of the parties will be a 'mercantile agent'. This is an agent who has authority in the course of his business either to sell or buy goods, or raise money on the security of goods.

Where a mercantile agent is in possession of goods with the owner's consent, he may validly sell, raise money on, or dispose of the goods as if he had the express authority of the owner to do so.[14] Where a customer enters into a hire-purchase, or similar agreement with a finance company through the medium of a retailer, the retailer will be deemed to be the agent of the finance company. This may still be so, even if there is a clause in the agreement denying that an agency exists. So far as consumer sales are concerned the consumer will now have redress against the finance company for breaches of contract by the dealer.

4 Married women

There is a presumption that a married woman living with her husband has his authority to incur bills on his behalf for the purpose of buying 'necessaries'. This presumption will not apply if, for example, the husband can show that he has stated publicly that he will not be responsible for debts incurred by his wife.

[13] Minors' Contracts Act 1987.
[14] Factors Act 1889, s 1 and see also ch 7, below.

D THE SUBJECT MATTER OF THE CONTRACT

Illegal contracts

In order for a contract to be enforceable by the courts the subject matter must not be illegal or contrary to public policy. Examples of illegal contracts will generally be outside the scope of this book, but it is worth noting in passing, for example, that the courts will not enforce a contract between two criminals as to the shareout after a robbery nor are gambling debts legally recoverable through the courts. Contracts which are contrary to public policy include agreements which contain unreasonable restrictions which are likely to operate in the restraint of trade. An example of this type of contract is a clause in an employment or service contract that the employee will not work in the same industry or for a competing company within a certain geographical area after leaving his present employer. These types of restrictions will only be enforceable by the courts if they operate on a limited basis. If they are too wide the courts will hold that they are contrary to public policy.

E OTHER UNENFORCEABLE CONTRACTS

I Fraud

Another case where the courts may rule that a binding contract does not in fact exist arises in connection with auction sales. A 'ring' of dealers, that is an agreement between dealers as to bidding which keeps the price of the goods being put up for sale lower than it would otherwise have been, is covered by the Auctions (Bidding Agreements) Act 1969.

Section 3(1) of this Act provides that where one of the parties to a bidding ring is a dealer the contract is voidable at the option of the seller. If he is not able to obtain the goods from the person who has bought them then the members of the ring will be jointly liable to make good the loss which he has suffered.

2 Mistake

Mistakes may sometimes be made by the parties to a contract which will have a fundamental effect on whether the contract will be enforced by a court. There may be a mistake as to the identity of one of the parties as to the terms being offered or the subject matter of the contract and this type of mistake may show that in fact no contract ever existed between the parties. This is particularly important where goods have been 'sold' because if the contract is void for mistake, an innocent third party who subsequently acquires the goods will stand to lose because he will be liable to restore them to the true owner.

3 Mistaken identity

If one party makes a mistake as to the identity of the other party that he is making a contract with this will not normally be relevant to the question of whether the contract is enforceable or not. The courts will take the view that he intended to contract with the party who was in front of him at the time.

For example,[15] a person calling himself Green and claiming to be a well-known actor of that name called in response to an advertisement and induced a motor retailer to sell him a car. He took the car away in exchange for a cheque which turned out to be worthless. When the seller tried to recover possession of the vehicle from a third party to whom the vehicle had then been passed on the courts held that the first transaction was not void and therefore a good title had been passed on and the seller was not able to recover the car.

However, this assumption of an intention to contract with the party who is actually present regardless of their identity can be overruled.

In another case,[16] the owners of a car who were trying to sell it refused to allow a would-be purchaser called Hutchinson to take it away against his uncleared cheque. They later agreed to let him take the car away after they had checked his name, initials and address with the details of a real Mr Hutchinson in the telephone book. The court decided that because of the check that they had made as to the identity of Mr Hutchinson, the assumption that they intended to contract with the person physically present with them was rebutted, ie they meant to contract with the real Mr Hutchinson whose details they had checked in the directory.

[15] *Lewis v Averay* [1972] 1 QB 198.
[16] *Ingram v Little* [1961] 1 QB 31 , but see also *Phillips v Brooks Ltd* [1919] 2 KB 243.

The confused state of the law in this situation was highlighted in the case of *Hudson v Shogun Finance Ltd*[17]. In this case, a man went into a dealer's showroom to buy a car on hire purchase. He produced a driving licence in the name of Durlabh Patel at an address in Leicester as proof of identity. The licence was genuine but it had been unlawfully obtained. The details were checked by the finance company which then approved the transaction. The fake Mr Patel took the car and sold it to an innocent buyer, Mr Hudson. By a majority the Court of Appeal ruled that as the debtor was not in fact the Mr Patel named in the agreement, the contract was void, and Mr Hudson was liable to return the vehicle to the finance company.

4 Documents mistakenly signed

The general rule is that someone who signs a legally binding document will be bound by it even if he misunderstood the terms of what he was signing. If, however, there is a misrepresentation or fraud which leads the party to the supposed contract to believe that he is actually signing one sort of document when he is signing another, then his signature will not be binding on him.

In addition, if it can be shown that the document signed was radically different from the one that the signer believed it was, and that he was not careless in signing it, he may be able to plead what is known as *non est factum*—'that is not my deed' and avoid liability.[18] Carelessness on the part of the signer would probably include signing a document without reading it, and signing a document in blank leaving the details to be filled in by a third party.

In addition to mistakes about a contract, there may be mis-representation either innocent or fraudulent which may affect the validity of the contract. These are dealt with in more detail in the next chapter in relation to contracts for the sale of goods.

F TERMS OF THE CONTRACT

Having found out whether or not a valid contract exists, the next consideration is 'What are its terms?'

---

[17] [2001] EWCA Civ 1000. This decision was subsequently upheld by a majority in the House of Lords 20 November 2003

[18] *Saunders v Anglia Building Society* [1971] AC 1004, HL.

I Express terms and representations

Express terms are promises made by the parties which they intended to be legally binding, or which a court assumes them to have intended to have legal effect. However, not everything said or promised by the parties during the negotiation of the contract will become contractual terms; in this instance the statement or promise may be treated as a representation which induced one party to enter into the contract with the other. A misrepresentation will not be actionable however unless it did induce one party to enter into the contract. If he did not rely on the misrepresentation, he cannot complain about it.

The distinction between terms and representations is important because breach of a term of the contract entitles the injured party to damages, and sometimes to cancellation of the whole deal. If the statement was only a representation, the injured party's rights will then depend on whether it was a misrepresentation and if so whether it was innocent or fraudulent (see Chapter 7).

The stage at which a statement stops being a representation and becomes a term of the contract is a difficult one to define clearly. There have been various cases involving the sale of cars where this problem has been discussed.

For example,[19] a private seller sold his car to a garage stating that it was a 1948 Morris which was confirmed by the registration book. In fact it was a 1939 model, and the registration book had been altered. The 1939 model was worth £115 less than the 1948 model. It was held that the seller's statement was not a term of the contract and was a mere innocent representation which meant that the retailer was able to recover no damages.

It may have been relevant in this case that the seller who made representation was a private seller who could have been expected to have had less expertise about the car than the person to whom he was selling.

In another case,[20] a Bentley was sold which was described as having been owned by a German Baron and fitted with a replacement engine and gear box and the mileage was described as 20,000. The car had various defects and the buyer brought an action for damages. He was

[19] *Oscar Chess Ltd v Williams* [1957] 1 All ER 325.
[20] *Dick Bentley Productions Ltd v Harold Smith Motors* [1965] 2 All ER 65.

awarded damages on the basis that the statement as to the mileage that the car had done was a term of the contract which had been broken because the car had actually done nearly 100,000 miles.

In yet another case,[21] a car was offered for sale by a private motorist who described it as a 'Herald convertible, white, 1961, twin carbs'. Unknown to either party the car was, in fact, the rear half of a 1961 Herald and the front half of an earlier model. Although the seller was held not to have been careless in not noticing this, the private buyer was able to recover damages for breach of a contractual term that the car was a 1961 Herald.

This case is somewhat difficult to reconcile with the *Oscar Chess* case but it illustrates the fine distinction which the courts may draw between one set of circumstances and another.

Hire-purchase sales

In the case of a sale of a motor vehicle which is being financed by a hire-purchase agreement with a finance company, the contract for the sale of the vehicle is not, of course, with the end customer but between the dealer and the finance company. Because of the legal rule that says that only parties to a contract may enforce it, the customer would not normally have any rights direct against the retailer if the car did not come up to any description which he applied to it. However, the courts have got round this by deciding that there is in addition to the hire-purchase agreement between the customer and the finance house, a 'collateral' agreement between the customer and the retailer. The consideration for this collateral agreement is the entering by the customer into the hire-purchase agreement thus enabling the retailer to sell the car to the finance company. If the retailer has made a misleading statement about the condition of the car then this will be a term of the collateral contract and the customer will be able to recover damages from the retailer direct as well as from the finance company under the provisions of the Consumer Credit Act.[22] This situation was illustrated clearly in *Andrews v Hopkinson*:[23] a retailer said to a customer, 'It's a good little bus. I would stake my life on it. You will have no trouble with it'. The

---

[21]   *Beale v Taylor* [1967] 3 All ER 253.
[22]   See also ch 8, below.
[23]   [1956] 3 All ER 422.

retailer then sold the car to a finance company which entered into a hire-purchase agreement for the car with a customer. The car was in a dangerous condition owing to defective steering and this caused an accident. It was held that the customer was entitled to recover damages for the breach of the undertaking given to him by the retailer.

Conditions and warranties

A term of a contract may be a 'condition' or a 'warranty'. A 'condition' is an important term of the contract. If one of the parties breaks a condition, the other will be able to rescind the contract (subject to the rules about 'acceptance' of goods see Chapter 7, below) and recover damages. A 'warranty' is a less important term where a breach will not affect the very basis of the contract, and here the injured party will be entitled to damages only.

2 Implied terms

Implied terms may arise because of the intentions of the parties to the contract, or perhaps through usage and custom in a particular trade. They may also arise through a statute. The most important statutory implied terms apply to contracts for the sale of goods and arise from the Sale of and Supply of Goods Act 1994 which consolidates the Sale of Goods Act 1893 with the various amendments that have been made to it. These statutory implied terms are dealt with in Chapter 7.

G DISTANCE SELLING CONTRACTS

Where a contract to supply goods or services is entered into between a business and a consumer without the parties having met face to face at any time during the negotiation of the contract, this will be categorised as a distance selling contract, and special rules will apply if the business involved is undertaking the contract as part of an 'organised process' of distance selling.[24] The Regulations do not define 'an organised process' but in its guidance on the Regulations, the DTI has said that if a business does not usually undertake distance selling, but does so in response to a one-off request from a customer, the Regulations

---

[24]   The Consumer Protection (Distance Selling) Regulations 2000, SI 2000/2334.

will not apply. However, if the business regularly handles 'one off' requests, and is organised to deal with them, then the Regulations will, in its view, apply. It should be noted, particularly in the context of the parts department which is likely to be frequently engaging in distance contracts to supply parts to other businesses, that the DTI also says that if a business has an organised scheme to enter into distance contracts with other businesses, even a one off transaction with a consumer will be covered.[25] It should also be noted however that the regulations will not apply if at any time before the consumer confirms the order there has been a face-to-face meeting between the consumer and a representative of the business. This would not have to be a meeting on the trader's premises.

Certain types of distance contract are not covered by the Regulations at all, including those for financial services although these contracts will be regulated from 31 October 2004 as a result the implementation of the EU Directive on distance marketing of consumer financial services[26]. The Regulations will potentially apply to all sales to consumers of vehicles and parts carried out over the phone, by post, fax or over the Internet, eg by email, or by a combination of any of those methods without the parties meeting face to face before the order is placed and the contract made – in other words the point at which the consumer is committed to the contract. If the consumer has placed a firm order for a vehicle, then the fact that he travels to the showroom to pick it up will not alter the fact that the distance selling rules will apply to the transaction, in particular in respect of his rights to cancel (see below).

Where a trader acts on behalf of a consumer to source a vehicle as his agent without any face-to-face contact, then this will be a distance contract to provide a service and will be covered by the Regulations. In addition, it seems that there could be circumstances in which the Regulations will apply also to servicing and repair of consumers' vehicles, for example where a garage operates a collection and delivery back service without meeting the customer. Any business undertaking regular distance selling transactions must take account of the Regulations, in particular its terms and conditions of business, in order to ensure that it complies with the Regulations.

[25]   The Consumer Protection (Distance Selling) Regulations 2000: a guide for business, DTI, October 2000, 00/1242
[26]   Directive 2002/65/EC and The Financial Services (Distance Selling) Regulations 2004, SI 2004/2095

The Office of Fair Trading has indicated in its Guidelines to Motor Traders holding or applying for consumer credit licences[27], that failure to comply with the information and cancellation requirements of the regulations will be regarded as a matter which may affect the fitness of the business to hold a consumer credit licence. At the time of going to press, it is also consulting on specific guidance for motor traders selling vehicles by distance means.[28]

Because of the nature of the rights given to consumers[29] by these Regulations businesses should review their activities in order to establish whether the Regulations are likely to apply to them and, if so, to ensure that their terms of business are amended accordingly to take account of the various requirements of the regulations. It should however be noted, that any contract term which attempts to exclude a consumer's rights will be unenforceable, as will any contract term seeking to impose any obligations on the consumer beyond what is allowed by the Regulations (see below).

Where the Regulations apply, the supplier is required to supply the consumer with information about the contract prior to its conclusion.[30] This information must then be confirmed to the consumer in writing or some other durable medium.[31] This must include information on the consumer's right to cancel, and the procedure that should be adopted in this instance.

I The right to cancel

The consumer's right to cancel will last for seven working days from delivery of the goods or, in the case of a service, seven working days from the time the contract was made, beginning with the day after the contract was concluded. In the case of a distance contract to provide a service, the Regulations require the supplier to inform the consumer that he will not be able to cancel the contract once the performance of the service has begun with his consent.[32] If the supplier fails to notify

---

[27]   See Chapter 8 and Appendix 2

[28]   Cars and other vehicles sold by distance means – Guidance on Compliance. A consultation paper February 2004

[29]   A consumer is defined as a natural person who, in contracts to which the Regulations apply, is acting for purposes which are outside his business (reg 3).

[30]   Regulation 7.

[31]   Regulation 8.

[32]   Regulation 8 (3). At the time of going to press, the Department of Trade and Industry is consulting on amendments to regs 7 and 8 in order to clarify the requirements for notification.

the consumer of his cancellation rights, the cooling-off period will be extended to a maximum of three months and seven days, or for seven days from when the information is given. The notice of cancellation must be given by the consumer in writing or other durable medium (which includes fax and email) to the seller at the address last known to the consumer.

Exceptions to the right to cancel

Unless the parties have agreed otherwise, the consumer will not have to right to cancel in a number of limited cases, for example:

(i)   where the contract is for the supply of a service, the supplier has given the consumer the requisite notice in the contract (see above), and the service has been started with the consent of the consumer;

(ii)   where the contract is for the supply of goods made to the customer's specifications or clearly personalised.

While this second point might appear to cover a consumer choosing options for a new car, the DTI in its guidance [33] states that this exception ' does not apply to options which may be selected by the consumer when placing the order – such as ... choosing alloy wheels when buying a car'.

Consequences of cancellation by the consumer

After cancellation, the consumer must receive a refund within 30 days of cancellation together with the return of any part exchanged goods. These must be returned within 10 days or, failing that, the consumer will be entitled to receive their value. The only deduction which can be made from the refund is any charge for the direct costs of recovering the goods (not to exceed the value of the goods). However this charge can be made only where there is a term in the contract providing for this charge to be made.[34]

---

[33]   Para 6.1.

[34]   It should be noted that the Office of Fair Trading has ruled that on cancellation a seller may not additionally deduct the original cost of delivering the goods to the consumer in the first place.

Where the consumer has acquired goods, and then cancelled the contract, he is under an obligation to retain possession of them, and to take reasonable care of them. He must then give them back to the seller. He is not however under any obligation, unless this is provided for in the contract, to deliver them back to the seller, but simply to make them available at his own premises. The seller must make a written request to hand the goods over within 21 days of cancellation. If, having done so, the consumer fails to return the goods, his duty of care will continue. If no written notice is given, then the consumer's duty of care ends. If the contract with the consumer imposes a duty to return the goods after cancellation, a period of six months will be substituted for the period of 21 days. Failure by the consumer to comply with his obligations under the Regulations will be actionable as a breach of statutory duty.

The effect of cancellation will be to cancel any related credit agreement and any part exchange transaction. The part-exchanged goods must be returned to the consumer in equivalent condition within 10 days, or, if this is not possible, he must receive the part exchange allowance for the goods. The Regulations contain detailed provisions as to what happens after cancellation of any related credit agreement.

2 Performing the contract

Unless agreed otherwise in the contract, the seller must perform the contract within 30 days beginning with the day after the consumer sent his order to the supplier. If the supplier cannot perform the contract within that time, he must inform the consumer and reimburse any money paid as soon as possible, and in any event within 30 days. The one relevant exception to this rule is where the supplier supplies substitute goods or services of equivalent quality, and this possibility was provided for in the contract.

3 Enforcement

Unlike the strategy adopted with other pieces of trading legislation, the government decided not to make non-compliance a criminal offence. It was apparently felt that the extended cancellation rights given to consumers would provide incentive enough for compliance. However, enforcement authorities (in respect of the motor industry, the Office of

Fair Trading and trading standards) have a duty[35] to investigate complaints unless they are thought to be frivolous or vexatious, or another enforcement authority has agreed to investigate. Undertakings or ultimately court injunctions can be sought from non-compliant businesses. The Office of Fair Trading has also warned that non-compliance with the pre-contract notification and cancellation requirements of these regulations will be regarded as conduct having a bearing on the suitability of the trader to hold a consumer credit licence.[36]

[35]   Reg 26.
[36]   Office of Fair Trading Guidance for Car Dealers: for consumer credit licence holders and applicants in the new and used car markets 2003 – see Appendix 2.

CHAPTER 6

The impact of competition law

The motor trader is not of course totally free to enter into whatever contracts he likes with his customers. Apart from the constraints imposed by the general law in relation to the quality of goods and services, methods of quoting prices, use of exclusion clauses and so on which are referred to elsewhere in this book, he will also be affected, if he is a franchised dealer in new cars, by the terms of his agreement with the manufacturer or importer. The effect of these terms on the manufacturer's liability for defects is discussed in Chapter 9.

Whilst detailed consideration of manufacturer/dealer agreements is outside the scope of this book, both national and EC law are having an increasing impact on the dealer's relationships with his customers. The changes centre on the effect on competition which exclusive distribution agreements are likely to have, and have been aimed at reducing the restrictions imposed on dealers with the objective of benefiting the consumer.

A NATIONAL LEGISLATION

I Fair Trading Act 1973

CONTROLS ON SALES OF SPARE PARTS

In 1982 the Monopolies and Mergers Commission concluded that the practice under exclusive franchise agreements, where dealers could buy spare parts only from the manufacturers from whom they hold their franchises, was against the public interest because, amongst other reasons, it led to higher prices through restricting competition and should be done away with.

Following the Commission's report, an order was made under the Fair Trading Act which came into effect on 1 November 1982.[1] This made it unlawful for any manufacturer or importer of motor cars to require its franchisees to buy car parts exclusively from itself or from sources which it had approved.

The order however allows this restriction to continue to operate where the parts are to be fitted to a car under warranty or are needed for a recall campaign. A further report under the Act, this time by the renamed Competition Commission, related to the supply of new cars and was published in April 2000.[2] This led to the Supply of New Cars Order 2000[3], aimed at bringing down the price of new cars sold in the UK.

2 Restrictive Trade Practices Act 1976

Under the Restrictive Trade Practices Act 1976, details of agreements between two or more persons carrying on business in the UK in the supply of goods or services had to be furnished to the Director General of Fair Trading for registration, if the agreements concerned imposed restrictions on the commercial freedom of the parties, for example in respect of pricing (a cartel).

This legislation has now been revoked with the coming into force of the Competition Act 1998 in March 2000, but had been used most recently to deal with cartels in respect of pricing of replacement car panels, and MOT tests in the northeast of England

3 Competition Act 1998

The prohibitions in the Act came into force on 1 March 2000. Its main effect is to introduce prohibitions, like those in EC law covering

---

[1]   The Restriction on Agreements (Manufacturers and Importers of Motor Cars) Order 1982, SI 1982/1146.
[2]   The Competition Commission Report New Cars: a report on the supply of new motor cars within the UK Cm 4660.
[3]   SI 2000/2088.

restrictive practices and abuses of dominant positions (see below). Agreements which are regarded as beneficial will still be permitted, but formal exemptions will be required. The Office of Fair Trading has increased powers to investigate breaches of the Act, and substantial fines may now be imposed automatically.

4 Enterprise Act 2002

This legislation which further changes the law on competition and consumer protection[4] came into force in June 2003. Apart from dealing with constitutional changes for dealing with fair trading and competition issues, it also introduces a new system of merger control, and permits damages actions to be brought in a special court, the Competition Appeal Tribunal.

The Act also changes the law in respect of market investigations and, given the number of market investigations already undertaken into the motor industry under other legislation (see above), it seems likely that the industry will at some point be affected by the new rules. The Competition Commission is now responsible not only for decisions on competition issues, but also on what should be done to remedy the situation, and will be allowed a longer period in which to make decisions. The Act also criminalises price- and market-fixing cartels, by creating a new offence which is committed when two or more individuals dishonestly agree to fix prices or rig bids, or to share customers or markets. This offence carries a penalty of up to five years in jail, and an unlimited fine.[5]

B THE TREATY OF ROME

I Background

Under Article 81(1)[6] of the Treaty of Rome agreements which may prevent, restrict or distort competition within the Common Market are ille-

---

4   For more detail on the impact of the Act on consumer protection, see Chapter 2.
5   For further discussion of the impact of the Act on the motor industry, see Geraldine Tickle 'The Enterprise Act 2002 – Yet more law for the Automotive Sector' 8 Motor Law Number 6.
6   Formerly Article 85 (1).

gal, but the Commission of the European Community has power to exempt any agreements if it can be shown that they improve the production or distribution of goods or promote technical or economic progress, while at the same time allowing consumers a fair share of the resulting benefit.

In applying this criterion to exclusive distribution agreements in the motor industry the Commission concluded that they should be allowed to continue for a number of reasons:
— they promote good quality pre- and after-sales service;
— there are resulting improvements in sales forecasting and therefore in production efficiency;
— they promote efficiency of distribution;
— they eliminate duplication of cost and effort.

The Commission has therefore been prepared to allow motor vehicle distribution agreements to be exempted from Article 81(3) provided that they met certain general criteria:
— they maintain competition between manufacturers;
— they maintain competition between distributors of different brands and those in the same franchise;
— they bring benefits to consumers which would not otherwise be available;
— they do not hinder free trade between member states.

Whilst various steps had been taken since 1965 to exempt categories of exclusive distribution agreements which met these criteria, in 1984 the Commission decided to introduce a new regulation[7] which would set out the criteria which motor vehicle distribution agreements must meet in future in order to be exempted from the Treaty of Rome and, at the same time, tackle an area of major public interest, the pricing of cars within different member states. It had become apparent that new car prices did vary considerably within the Community, and whilst factors such as taxation and price control legislation were clearly of importance, it seemed that the policies of the vehicle manufacturers also played a part. The Commission therefore decided to introduce as part of the block exemption a price harmonisation policy which would iron out these differences but would allow prices to fluctuate within a margin of 12–18%. It was also anxious to open up the car market so that consumers would be free to purchase their new car wherever they wished

---

[7]   Commission Regulation (EEC) No 123/85.

within the Community so as to take advantage of lower prices where available (the so-called full line availability).

After much negotiation, the Block Exemption Regulation was issued on 12 December 1984, to come into effect on 1 July 1985 for a period of ten years. Manufacturers and importers had to modify their existing agreements by 1 October 1985 in order to take advantage of the block exemption. Following a detailed review of that Regulation, it was decided that block exemption should be allowed to continue and a revised regulation came into effect on 1 July 1995,[8] becoming operative on 1 October in that year. That Regulation expired on 1 October 2002 and after an intense period of debate and speculation that the block exemption might not be renewed at all, a new Regulation intended to 'put the consumer in the driving seat'[9] came into force, with one exception, after a 12-month transitional period on 1 October 2003. The Regulation will expire on 31 May 2010, with an evaluation report expected two years before that date.[10] From 1 May 2004, the Office of Fair Trading has become responsible for national enforcement of EU competition law, including the operation of the motor industry block exemption regulation (see below).

2 The block exemption

Failure to observe the conditions of the block exemption could lead to loss of the exemption in relation to a particular agreement.

SCOPE

The block exemption applies to exclusive distribution agreements for 'motor vehicles intended for use on public roads and having three or more wheels'. This includes commercial and public service vehicles as well as passenger cars. The Regulation covers only new vehicles[11], and

---

[8]   Regulation 1475/95.

[9]   Speech by Commissioner Mario Monti 11 May 2000.

[10]   Commission Regulation (EC) No 1400/2002 of 31 July 2002, OJ L 203, 1.8.2002 p.30.

[11]   The Commission expresses the view, in a footnote in its Explanatory Brochure (see below), that 'Whether a vehicle is still new has to be decided on the basis of trade usage. For a buyer a vehicle is no longer new once it has been registered and driven on the road by another consumer. In contrast, a vehicle which has been registered by a dealer for one day without having been used is still new'. It is submitted that in the UK, this interpretation would be affected by the decision in *R v Anderson* [1988] RTR 260; and see Chapter 4 above.

does not therefore affect the used market. The new Regulation is much more flexible in the scope which it gives manufacturers and dealers when agreeing their distribution contracts. The combination of selective and exclusive distribution permitted by the previous Regulation is now banned, and manufacturers can choose which system it wishes to operate, subject to rules on market share. The overall aim however is to increase competition and improve the position of the consumer in respect of the distribution and servicing of his car. The Commission has noted[12] that the purchase price and the cost of repairing and maintaining a car each account for about 40% of the total cost of ownership, and that competition in both these markets is therefore of equal importance to consumers. Detailed consideration of the block exemption is outside the scope of this book[13], but some of the main effects of the Regulation on the dealer's and the manufacturer's relationship with the consumer are outlined below.

SALES

In order to reinforce competition between dealers in different member states, manufacturers and importers may not restrict dealers from selling to any consumer who contacts him directly, and in respect of intermediaries may only oblige dealers to ensure that an intermediary has a prior valid authorisation from a consumer. Consumers should also be able to obtain vehicles from a dealer in another member state with a specification current in the consumer's home state. The Commission gives the example[14] of allowing UK and Irish consumers to buy a new right-hand drive car in mainland Europe.

The sale of different brands from the same premises is encouraged, although manufacturers will still be able to insist on motor vehicles of different brands to be displayed in different areas of the showroom.

---

[12] Andersen, study on the impact of possible future legislative scenarios for motor vehicle distribution on all parties concerned, p 43, chapter II.2.1.B.

[13] For a detailed discussion of the 2002 Block exemption, see Peter Groves *The Motor Law Complete Guide to the 2002 Block Exemption* (2002, Motor Law Publications Ltd).

[14] European Commission – Directorate General for Competition: Distribution and Servicing of Motor Vehicles in the European Union Explanatory Brochure.

TYPE APPROVAL

Certificates of conformity should, according to the Commission[15], be made available at the time the vehicle is delivered to the consumer or his intermediary.

AFTERSALES SERVICE

The Commission is keen to allow consumers to choose between different alternatives to carry out repair and servicing. Therefore, under the Block Exemption, the consumer does not have to take the vehicle back to the dealer he bought it from in order to have warranty or servicing work carried out. Manufacturers appointing authorised repairers who conform to their qualitative standards (but who need no longer also be selling dealers) must oblige them to repair, and carry out free servicing and warranty work on all vehicles of the brand in question. Equally a consumer can choose to have his vehicle maintained or repaired outside the network, although in this instance the benefit of the warranty might be lost if the work done was faulty. Following intervention by the Office of Fair Trading in 2004, vehicle manufacturers and importers in the UK have agreed to remove requirements from new vehicle warranties that servicing during the warranty period should be carried out within its network.

Dealers must also be allowed, if they wish, to subcontract servicing and repair to other authorised repairers within the same network, and who therefore meet the same quality standards.

SPARE PARTS

A vehicle manufacturer may insist on the use of original spare parts whether made by him or by a spare parts manufacturer for supply to him, for warranty work , free servicing and recall work, but not otherwise. This means for example that a restriction in a warranty requiring only original spare parts supplied by the vehicle manufacturer to be used for routine maintenance and repair would not comply with the Regulation.

[15]   Ibid.

The vehicle manufacturer cannot restrict the supply direct to independent distributors or vehicle repairers of spare parts manufactured by a spare parts manufacturer according to the specifications and production standards supplied by the vehicle manufacturer.

CHAPTER 7

Selling goods

The type of contract which the motor retailer will probably be involved with more frequently than any other are contracts for the sale of goods. This description will cover the sales of cars, parts and accessories, of petrol and any other items sold by the retailer, for example, sweets and toys from the forecourt shop. This type of contract is a different legal animal from contracts for the sale of services such as repairs, servicing, car washes, and car parks. Different legal provisions apply in each case, although in both instances legislation now limits the freedom of the parties to agree whatever terms they wish.

The question of whether a valid contract has been formed and the type of terms it may contain has already been considered in the previous chapter.

The different stages of a sale all have particular legal problems, and we shall look in turn at:
— negotiating the sale;
— delivery payment;
— the seller's right to sell;
— whether the goods meet a description applied to them;
— the quality of the goods.

A NEGOTIATING THE SALE

This is a vital stage in the life of the contract. The statements made, and the documents signed as the deal is clinched, will constitute the basis of the contract.

As we have already seen, statements made by the salesman during the negotiation of a sale may be:

(a)   representations inducing the contract; or

(b)   express terms of the contract — either conditions or warranties; and

(c)   in either case, they may also be trade descriptions which if false may give rise to a criminal prosecution.

1 Using an order form

In the case of sales of cars, using a standard order form with your company's conditions of sale on it, makes a great deal of sense. Not only does it ensure that the essential details of the transaction, such as the price and specification of the vehicle ordered, have been recorded, but it can also cover the areas which may give rise to problems later on, such as deposits and delivery dates, and may help to cut down on arguments. Some vehicle manufacturers produce standard form contracts which their franchised dealers may use, and the RMIF also produces forms relating to used and new car sales, for use by its members.

Since the 1970s, the content of this type of contract has been subject to national legislation which controls the use of terms which limit or exclude customer's rights under the contract.[1] The use of business order forms containing standard contract terms in transactions with 'consumer' customers is also, since 1 January 1995, subject to the European Directive on Unfair Contract Terms which has been implemented in the UK most recently by the Unfair Terms in Consumer Contracts Regulations 1999.[2] The impact of this legislation on motor industry order forms will now be considered in more detail.

Is the customer a consumer?

In these Regulations, a consumer means 'a natural person who, in making a contract to which these regulations apply, is acting for purposes outside his business'. This definition means that for the purpose of these Regulations, a company can never be a consumer, even though they may be buying, for example, a vehicle which will be used for both

---

[1]   See later in this chapter, and ch 11.

[2]   SI 1999/2083 as amended by SI 2001/1186.

company and private use. This distinction has, in the past, had the confusing result that a non-consumer customer for the purpose of deciding whether these Regulations apply to a term in the contract, may be treated as a consumer for the purpose of bringing a claim, for example, that the goods are not of satisfactory quality.[3] This distinction will no longer apply in respect of contracts for the sale and supply of goods made after 31 March 2003, as the Sale and Supply of Goods to Consumers Regulations[4] now provide that a consumer is a 'natural person buying for purposes outside his trade, business or profession'. A limited company will no longer therefore be treated as a consumer for these purposes.

Scope of the regulations

The Regulations apply to all contracts between sellers or suppliers and consumers, and will control all contract terms which have not been individually negotiated. Whilst there are some certain exclusions which are not specifically relevant to the motor industry, there is one notable inclusion—these Regulations do cover insurance contracts (which were excluded from the scope of the Unfair Contract Terms Act 1977). This means that the terms of mechanical breakdown insurance policies will be subject to the Regulations (and see below).

The Regulations do not affect 'core' terms in the contract, such as the price or the main subject matter of the contract, so long as these terms are expressed in clear and intelligible language. A customer could not, for example, use these Regulations to challenge a contract with a retailer on the basis that the selling price for a vehicle was too high,[5] although a price variation clause will be covered if it is unfair. A consumer complained that the conditions of the mechanical breakdown warranty issued to him were not drawn to his attention at the time of purchase. When he did receive the policy a crucial term was hidden: this excluded liability unless the vehicle received a partial service every 3,000 miles, but appeared only on a sticker on the back of the policy. The OFT took the view that although the cover provided was a 'core' term, and therefore outside the Regulations if expressed in clear and

---

[3] See *R & B Customs Brokers Co Ltd v United Dominions Trust Ltd* [1988] 1 All ER 847 discussed at p 101.

[4] SI 2000/2334; and see below.

[5] Regulation 6(2).

intelligible language, this exemption could not apply in this case and others like it where such terms have been hidden from the consumer, or he has no chance to get to know about them. The MBI company concerned deleted the offending clause.[6]

A term covered by the Regulations is regarded as unfair which 'contrary to the requirement of good faith causes a significant imbalance in the parties' rights and duties under the contract to the detriment of the consumer'. The Regulations set out a non-exhaustive list of contract terms which may be regarded as unfair.[7] In assessing whether any particular term is unfair, it will be looked at in the context of the agreement as a whole, taking into account issues such as the nature of the goods and services for which the contract was concluded, and by referring, at the time of conclusion of the contract, to all the circumstances attending the conclusion of the contract, and all the other terms of the contract or another contract on which it is dependent.[8]

Clear and intelligible language

It is of overriding importance that, apart from the content of the contract terms, they should be expressed in clear and intelligible language. The Regulations provide that if there is any ambiguity in the wording used, the interpretation most favourable to the consumer will be adopted.[9] The Office of Fair Trading have expressed the view that, although print size is not referred to in the Regulations, this, and the way in which terms are disclosed to customers before the contract is entered into, will be regarded as key factors in assessing unfairness and good faith.[10]

Consequences of unfairness

If a term is found to be unfair, it will not be binding on the consumer, but the rest of the contract will continue in existence. Whilst the effect

---

[6]   *Olympic Warranties Ltd* Unfair Contract Terms Bulletin No 2 September 1996.
[7]   Schedule 2.
[8]   Regulation 6.
[9]   Regulation 7.
[10] Unfair Contract Terms Bulletin issued by the Office of Fair Trading, Issue No 1 May 1996.

of potentially unfair standard terms on individual customers is therefore important from the motor retailer's point of view, particularly if challenged by a customer, at a practical level the role of the Office of Fair Trading is also important. Under the Regulations, the Office of Fair Trading monitors complaints about terms of contracts and the Director General or a 'qualifying body' may act to obtain an injunction to prevent a trader using unfair terms in his consumer contracts for the purposes of the Regulations.[11] As an alternative, the Director may first seek an assurance from the trader concerned agreeing to withdraw or reword an unfair term. The OFT also disseminates information and advice about the Regulations, and in this context, has issued a series of Bulletins,[12] which are helpful in explaining its general approach and interpretation of the Regulations. Ultimately, however, it will be the courts which determine whether any particular term is unfair, and it is open to traders to disagree with the OFT's views and refuse to alter their terms.

Examples of motor industry terms challenged as unfair

There are seventeen examples of types of contract term which may be regarded as unfair contained in Sch 2 to the Regulations. This list does not however represent the only cases where terms may fall foul of the Regulations. The Office of Fair Trading has given details in its bulletins of some motor industry cases, some of which are in its view caught by Sch 2, and some of which are simply regarded by the OFT as probably failing the general test of fairness. These include:

Example 1

'Terms which have the object or effect of ... giving the seller or supplier the right to determine whether the goods or services supplied are in conformity with the contract, or giving him the exclusive right to interpret any term of the contract' (Sch 2, para 1(m)).

Under this heading the OFT objected to a term in the Rover Commitment which allowed a consumer to return a car to Rover provided that the car had suffered—in the opinion of Rover—no

---

[11] Schedule 1
[12] The Unfair Contract Terms Bulletins may be obtained from the Office of Fair Trading, PO Box 172, East Molesey, KT8 OXW.

more than £150 worth of damage. This was amended to allow for independent assessment by an RAC expert, with the costs of the assessment to be borne by the losing party.

Example 2

'Terms which have the object or effect of ... limiting the seller's or supplier's obligation to respect commitments undertaken by his agents or making his commitments subject to compliance with a particular formality' (Sch 2 , para 1(n)).

Under this heading the OFT have objected to provisions in both retailers standard terms, and terms in vehicle manufacturers' warranties.

Example 3

'Terms which have the object or effect of ... excluding or hindering the consumer's right to take legal action or exercise any other legal right, particularly by requiring the consumer to take disputes exclusively to arbitration not covered by legal provisions ...' (Sch 2, para 1 (q)).

The OFT have objected to various clauses in manufacturers' warranties and retailer's contracts requiring consumers to accept arbitration in the event of disputes.[13]

Example 4

A clause allowing a motor retailer to enter consumer's property to repossess goods not paid for in full was criticised as potentially failing the general test of fairness. The OFT felt that the retailer had more appropriate methods to recover money in case of a dispute.

Example 5

'Terms which the object or effect of ... inappropriately excluding or limiting the legal rights of the consumer vis-a-vis the seller or another party in the event of total or partial non-performance or inadequate performance by the seller or supplier of any of the contractual obligations...'

---

[13]   This type of term is in any event unenforceable against a consumer in disputes under £3,000 (the Consumer Arbitration Agreements Act 1988).

Various retailers have been criticised for attempting to exclude liability for breaches of the Sale and Supply of Goods Act implied terms requiring goods to be satisfactory and fit for purpose. As the OFT points out, these terms are in any event of no legal effect under the earlier Unfair Contract Terms Act 1977 (see below) when used in consumer contracts.

2 Part-exchange

There is some legal debate as to whether a part-exchange deal creates two separate contracts between retailer and customer, or whether in law it is one transaction. The question is not just academic, as the rights and liabilities of the parties may differ depending on which interpretation is correct. Fortunately, however, disputes over part-exchanges do not come before the courts very often, if at all.

If a part-exchange has been agreed as part of a deal, then the customer will be bound to hand over the vehicle and the retailer to accept it. The RMIF retail order forms contain terms which apply to part-exchange including:

(a) an undertaking that the vehicle belongs to the customer;
(b) an agreement that where the retailer has examined the car it will be handed over to him in the same condition;
(c) a provision for a reduction in the part-exchange allowance where delivery is delayed.[14]

Provisions of this type in a standard form contract with a consumer customer must now of course satisfy the test of reasonableness discussed above, but in principle failure by the customer to deliver a vehicle conforming to the appraisal carried out would entitle the retailer to refuse to take it. A misrepresentation by the customer about the trade in vehicle will be subject to the general law (see below).

3 Deposits

A deposit must be distinguished from a sum expressed to be a part-payment. If a customer makes a part-payment, and the event giving rise

---

[14] The Office of Fair Trading has ruled that this clause is potentially unfair when used in a consumer contract (Office of Fair Trading Bulletin 17 March 2002) and the RMI has agreed to amend its standard form contract accordingly.

to payment has not yet arisen (typically, the vehicle has not yet been delivered) then a customer will be entitled to recover his part-payment, subject to a set-off for the losses suffered by the retailer.

Non-consumer customers

The retailer and his non-consumer customer are free to agree whatever contractual terms they wish about the payment of a deposit. Having made a contract, whether or not any deposit paid by the customer will be returnable if the contract 'goes off' will then depend on the terms of the agreement. If there is nothing in the contract, then a sum paid as a deposit would not be recoverable.

Consumer customers

The position regarding deposits paid by consumer customers is now affected by the Unfair Terms in Consumer Contracts Regulations (see above), and also the Consumer Credit Act 1974. Schedule 2 to the Regulations provides that a contract term permitting the seller to retain sums paid by the consumer where the latter cancels a contract will be regarded as unfair if there is not a similar balancing term allowing the consumer to recover an equivalent amount from the trader where he cancels the agreement. At common law, if the customer breaks his part of the contract by refusing to take delivery, for example, because he has changed his mind, the deposit will not be returnable provided it only covers the trader's reasonable costs and does not amount to a penalty. If, however, the retailer is at fault, for example, by failing to deliver, the customer would be entitled to the return of his money. This suggests that the retailer may be better advised to rely on his common law rights in the event that a customer breaks the contract, rather than a contract term on his order form which might fail the test of fairness. It is however still necessary to show that the payment made was a deposit rather than a part-payment, so it should be referred to as such on the order form.

Under the Consumer Credit Act 1974, a customer entering into a regulated finance agreement is entitled to withdraw from that agreement at any time before the agreement is executed, ie signed by the finance company. In this event, the customer is entitled to recover any sums paid under a 'linked transaction'. This will include a deposit made to a retailer who has introduced the source of finance to the customer.[15]

4 Damages for misrepresentation

The basis on which an action for misrepresentation can be taken is described in Chapter 5. When a misrepresentation has been established, there are two possible remedies:

(a)   there is a limited right to rescind the contract and put the parties back in the position they were in before the contract was made. This would mean, for example, the return of the price to the purchaser and the goods to the seller. However, this may not always be permitted if it would be unfair to one or other party. This means that rescission would not be allowed where it would be impossible to put the parties back into their pre-contract position; where it would involve upsetting the rights of a third party perhaps someone to whom the goods have been sold; where there has been an unreasonable lapse of time except where the representation was fraudulent where the injured party will have a reasonable time from the time he discovered the misrepresentation; or where the injured party has confirmed the contract despite the representation.[16] This confirmation may be implied from conduct, and in this respect is rather like the limit on the right to reject goods for breach of contract once they have been accepted (see below);

(b)   the other right is to claim damages. This will not be normally available however where the representation was an innocent one, ie where the person making the representation genuinely and on reasonable grounds believed that it was true, except that the court may award damages instead of rescission in this case.[17] A motor trader innocently misrepresented to a finance company the total price for a car and the deposit to be paid by the customer in order to ensure that the customer obtained finance. It was held that the finance company was entitled to recover by way of damages the full amount of their losses under the transaction when the customer wrongfully disposed of the vehicle.[18] If a representation

15   Consumer Credit Act 1974, s 57, and see ch 9, below.
16   *Long v Lloyd* [1958] 2 All ER 402, [1958] 1 WLR 753, CA.
17   Misrepresentation Act 1967.
18   *Roycot Trust Ltd v Rogerson* [1991] 2 QB 297.

is made by someone who believes it to be true but without reasonable grounds for doing so, this will be a negligent misrepresentation and damages will be available.[19] A fraudulent misrepresentation is one made knowing it is untrue, or recklessly, careless of whether it is true or false. Damages may be claimed for deceit in this case.

Where a customer sold a secondhand car to a motor trader and signed an RMIF Used Car Purchase Invoice saying that to the best of his knowledge and belief the odometer reading was correct, it was held that in the absence of fraud or dishonesty, he was not liable to the motor trader for damages.[20]

B DELIVERY PROBLEMS

The motor retailer generally has one problem or another with supplies of the vehicles he is selling. Either he cannot obtain a particular model and the customer will have to be prepared to wait for several months, or even years to take delivery, or the retailer will have too many and will not be able to move them out of his premises quickly enough.

From a legal point of view the retailer's obligation is to deliver the goods which he has agreed to sell. Delivering the goods however is not necessarily the same thing as transferring legal ownership—that may take place before or after delivery as well as at the same time.

I What is delivery?

The Sale of Goods Act 1979 provides[21] that delivery is the 'voluntary transfer of possession from one person to another'. This does not mean that the physical handing over has to have taken place. It will be enough if the seller simply places the goods at the buyer's disposal, without any reciprocal act on the part of the buyer. This will mean that when a retailer has obtained the car which a customer has ordered he will have fulfilled his obligation to deliver it when he tells the customer that it is ready for collection and is being prepared for him. In a consumer transaction after 31 March 2003, risk passes to the customer at

---

[19] Misrepresentation Act 1967.
[20] *Humming Bird Motors Ltd v Hobbs* [1986] RTR 276.
[21] Section 61(1).

the point of delivery, not when payment is made, and delivery to a carrier is not deemed to be delivery to the consumer.[22]

2 What has to be delivered?

If the goods being sold under the contract were specific for example, where a customer makes it clear that he particularly wants to buy a car which is on display in the showroom and no other, then the seller will not be complying with his part of the contract if he tries to deliver any car to him. If, however, the contract was simply to sell a blue Ford Mondeo 2-litre, then any car which corresponds to that description will fulfil the terms of the contract.

The parties to the contract are free to make any arrangement which they wish between themselves as to how delivery and payment are to be made. In the absence of any other agreement, the Sale of Goods Act provides[23] that these two conditions go together and in order for the seller to be required to deliver, the buyer must be willing and ready to pay for the goods.

3 Delivery charges

The customer does not have to pay delivery charges unless the contract specifically provides that he will do so. If the contract has not said anything about delivery charges, the Sale of Goods Act provides[24] they must be met by the seller.

The same thing applies to the cost of putting the goods into a suitable state for delivery. The customer cannot therefore be asked to pay for the PDI unless the terms of the contract made a special reference to it, eg on the order form.

4 Failure to deliver within the time agreed

If a specific time for delivery has been agreed in the contract then in legal terms time has been made the 'essence' of the contract. This

---

[22] Sale and Supply of Goods to Consumers Regulations 2002, SI 2002/2334, reg 4 amending the Sale of Goods Act 1979, ss 20 and 23.

[23] Sale of Goods Act 1979, s 28.

[24] Sale of Goods Act 1979, s 29(6).

means that failure by the seller to deliver the goods on the agreed date will be a breach of contract. In that case the customer is entitled to reject the goods when they are offered, refuse to pay and to treat the contract as being at an end. The buyer, however, may if he wishes choose to ignore this breach of condition, treat it as a less serious breach of warranty and sue for damages only.

If, however, the customer agrees to a postponement in delivery then even if a particular date for delivery had been previously agreed he may have waived his right to insist on delivery by that date. If he agrees to a postponement without a particular period having been specified the customer can give reasonable notice requiring the retailer to deliver the goods to him within a certain time. The effect of specifying the time of the delivery means that time will again be the 'essence' of the contract and failure by the retailer to meet this new date will again be a breach of contract.

If no time has been fixed for delivery at all under the terms of the contract or if the contract says something like 'delivery to be as soon as possible' then under the Sale of Goods Act the seller has still to deliver the goods within a reasonable time[25] and failure to do so will mean that the buyer can recover damages for the delay in delivery.

If a standard type of order form is used by the retailer when taking the customer's order, specific provision may be made for delivery problems which may occur.

The forms suggested by the RMIF, for example, provide that the customer may give seven days notice to the retailer requiring delivery if the goods have not been delivered within twenty-one days of the contractual date. If the retailer still fails to deliver, the customer may cancel the contract.

5 Customer's failure to take delivery of the goods

If the customer fails to take delivery of the goods the seller's remedy is generally to sue for the price or for damages for non-acceptance of the goods.

In addition the seller may be able to resell the goods to a new buyer if there is an express term in the contract allowing him to do so. Even if

---

[25]   Sale of Goods Act 1979, s 29(3).

no such express term exists, if the original buyer fails to pay the price agreed within a reasonable time after he receives notice of the seller's intention to resell, or if the seller terminates the contract on the grounds that the buyer has repudiated his obligations under it by failing to pay him the price he will then be able to resell. It should also be noted that the right of the seller to sue for the price is independent of his right to resell, ie he can do both. In *Lazenby Garages Ltd v Wright*,[26] a retailer was not able to recover damages where he resold the car: because all secondhand cars are different it could not be said the retailer had suffered loss because he had resold the car for more than the original agreed price. Any express term in a contract with a consumer must be read in the light of the Unfair Terms in Consumer Contracts Regulations (see above). In *Vaswani v Italian Motors (Sales & Services) Ltd*,[27] a case referred to the Privy Council from Hong Kong, a customer was unable to recover a deposit of £25,000 paid for a Ferrari Testarossa when he failed to complete the purchase. He claimed that because of an excessive increase in price from £179,500 to £218,000 he was entitled to treat the contract as repudiated. The Privy Council agreed that the increase was excessive and that it should have been limited to the terms of the contract, but did not agree that this amounted to repudiation by the seller of the contract. The customer could have completed the purchase by paying the sum he felt was reasonable under the contract.

6 When is the seller unpaid?

A seller will be unpaid when the whole of the price has not been either paid or tendered by the purchaser, or when a bill of exchange or other negotiable instrument has been received as conditional payment and the condition on which it was received has not been fulfilled because it has been, for example, dishonoured. Normally a cheque will be treated as being conditional payment, ie conditional on it being honoured by the bank.[28]

Suing for the price

The remedy available to a retailer of suing for the price will in practice not normally be the most appropriate course of action. In order for the

---

[26] [1976] 2 All ER 770.
[27] [1996] 1 WLR 270, [1996] RTR 115, PC.
[28] Sale of Goods Act 1979, s 38.

seller to be able to sue for the price of the goods he has to show that not only has the buyer defaulted in paying for them but also that the property in the goods must also have passed to the buyer. The seller can only take this course of action if the contract continues in force and he is willing and able to deliver the goods to the buyer in accordance with the terms of the contract. When suing for the price the seller has to give credit for any deposit which the purchase had paid. In some cases the court may find that the buyer's failure to pay for the goods may be justified, for example, if the seller had previously broken his contractual obligation, for example, by failing to deliver the goods by the contracted date or by delivering goods which were defective.

Damages for non-acceptance

The general rule about damages will apply, namely, that the object is to compensate the innocent party for the damage he has suffered through the other's breach of contract. Occasionally a contract will contain a clause which fixes the sum to be paid in the event of a breach of contract. If the amount is such that it was obviously fixed as a deterrent this will be treated as a 'penalty' and the court will only generally award an amount to compensate for the actual loss and not the amount of the penalty. A fixed sum in a contract like this has to be a genuine estimate of likely losses in order to be enforced by the courts. In this case the retailer does not have to give credit for any deposit paid, if it is clear from the circumstances that the deposit was a security for completion of the purchase, and was intended to be forfeited if the buyer failed to complete.

Assessment of damages

Damages for non-acceptance will be assessed by reference to the estimated loss directly and naturally arising in the ordinary course of events from the buyer's breach of contract. Where there is an 'available market' for the goods, the measure of damages is calculated as the difference between the contract price and the market or current price at the time the goods should have been accepted by the buyer.

'An available market'

This is a situation where there is sufficient demand for the goods in question to absorb readily all the goods put on it. Some cases will illustrate how this operates.

In *Thompson v Robinson*[29] the plaintiff car retailers agreed to sell a new car to the defendants at the retail price fixed by the manufacturers. The defendant refused to accept the car and the plaintiff persuaded the wholesaler to take the car back. There was no difference between the current retail price and the contract price but the plaintiffs were awarded damages for loss of profit on the sale. There was no shortage of that particular car to meet the demand locally and since a subsequent buyer could not readily be found the judge held that there was no available market. If a second buyer was an additional customer of the seller and not merely a substituted customer and the seller had the ability and opportunity of making two profits on two transactions, he was entitled to damages for the loss of his first profit when the first buyer defaulted.

Another case illustrates what may happen where the demand exceeds the supply. In *Charter v Sullivan*[30] the defendant refused to accept delivery of a Hillman Minx which he had agreed to buy at a fixed retail price. Within ten days the plaintiff resold the car at the same price. It was found that the plaintiff could always find a buyer for that particular car and could not, therefore, recover more than nominal damages. The court found that he had made the same number of sales and therefore made the same amount of profit as he would have done if the defendant had performed the contract.

The extent of any 'available market' will obviously be affected by the retailer's territory under his franchise agreement. It seems that the retailer can use this point in any argument about the market 'available' to him for any particular car.

If there is no available market the seller's loss is the difference between the contract price and the value of the goods to the seller at the time and place of the breach of contract by the buyer. If the goods have some particular feature which the seller has to readapt in order to be able to resell the goods, he can carry out this work and then recover the cost from the purchaser who defaulted.

---

[29] *Thompson (WL) Ltd v Robinson (Gunmakers) Ltd* [1955] Ch 177.
[30] [1957] 2 QB 117.

Where the potential buyer indicates that he is going to break the contract, for example, where a customer tells the retailer that he has changed his mind about a purchase and does not intend to take delivery of the car when it arrives, the retailer has a choice. He can either accept this repudiation of the contract and treat it as a breach or he can wait until the goods have arrived and then sue under the contract. If he accepts repudiation he can sue the purchaser immediately for damages although where there is an available market the relevant date for the market price will be the date fixed for delivery.

The seller will of course still have a duty to reduce his loss as far as possible and this may mean that a court would treat the relevant date as being the one at which he ought reasonably to have resold the car. He will be able to recover consequential losses and expenses including reasonable expenses on resale and storage.

C PAYING FOR THE GOODS

The purchaser has to pay for the goods in accordance with the terms of the contract. Even if the seller agrees to accept a smaller sum in payment for the goods than previously agreed in the contract he can still sue the purchaser for payment of the balance because this later agreement does not discharge the purchaser's obligation under the original contract.[31] The reason for this is because there is no 'consideration' for the second promise by the seller to accept a lesser sum in settlement of the contract price. The only circumstance in which this second promise will be enforceable against the seller is where, for example, he asks for payment of this lesser sum at a different place or at an earlier time or by a different method. In this sort of situation this benefit to the seller by amending the agreement will act as consideration and he will be bound to accept the lesser sum in settlement which he has already agreed. Similarly if there is some 'consideration', eg part payment of the price by a third party in satisfaction of the debt, it will discharge the purchaser's obligation if this part payment is accepted by the seller in satisfaction of the whole debt.

Unless the parties agree otherwise between themselves, the purchaser is bound to offer the seller the price of the goods in cash at the time and place agreed in the contract. The seller does not have to accept payment

---

[31]   See also ch 5, above.

in any other form, unless it was an express part of the contract or if a term could be implied in the contract because it could be shown that the parties had always contracted on this basis before. This means that the seller is not bound to accept payment by cheque unless, for example, it can be shown that he was commonly in the habit of accepting cheques in payment and some previous course of dealing could be shown between the parties on this basis.

Dealers now have to be extremely wary about accepting payment in cash for vehicles. Not only has legislation requiring the reporting of suspected money laundering been tightened up with effect from February 2003,[32] but also since the end of 2003 motor traders accepting cash in excess of 15,000 euros (approximately £10,000) have to register with HM Customs & Excise under regulations introduced to implement the Second Money Laundering Directive. They must also appoint a Money Laundering officer to oversee registration and reporting, introduce procedures, maintain copies of documents and records of transactions and train staff.[33]

D THE SELLER'S RIGHT TO SELL

I The implied term

When buying goods, the consumer obviously needs to be assured that the seller actually has the right to sell them to him. This is the first of the implied terms contained in the Sale of Goods Act 1979.[34] This provides that in every contract for the sale of goods there is to be an implied condition on the part of the seller that he has the right to sell the goods. If he does not have this right, he will be breaking his contract with the purchaser.

In practice, cars are frequently sold by sellers who have no right to sell them because, for example, they are subject to an existing hire-purchase agreement or they are stolen. The fact that the purchaser has a right of action against the seller for breach of contract is only partial consolation to him in such a case, because the normal rule is that if the seller does not have the right to sell the goods, the buyer, even if he is

---

[32] Proceeds of Crime Act 2002.
[33] Second Money Laundering Directive 2001/97/EC.
[34] Section 12.

innocent of the true facts, will not obtain a good title to the goods because the seller had no good title to pass on.

2 Exceptions

This rule is not however an absolutely firm one and there are some important exceptions to it where even though the seller is not the owner of the goods a good title will be passed on to a third party who will then have greater rights over the goods than the true owner. The main exceptions under the Sale of Goods Act were originally:

(a)   sales in 'market overt';
(b)   sales by mercantile agents;
(c)   sales where the true owner is 'estopped' from denying the seller's right to sell;
(d)   sale under a voidable title;
(e)   sales by the seller in possession;
(f)   sales by the buyer in possession;
(g)   sale of a motor vehicle subject to a hire-purchase or conditional sale agreement;
(h)   sales by a bailee of goods.

The 'market overt' rules which dated back hundreds of years and allowed good title to be passed by non-owners of goods provided the goods were sold in certain types of market, were abolished in 1995.[35] In addition, there are certain statutory powers of sale, such as the powers under the Torts (Interference with Goods) Act (see Chapter 11, below).

Sales by mercantile agents

The retailer in the motor trade will often find himself in the position of a 'mercantile agent'. This is defined by the Factors Act 1889 as 'a mercantile agent having in the customary course of his business as such agent authority either to sell goods or to consign goods for the purpose of sale or to buy goods or to raise money on the security of goods'. The Act goes on to provide that where a mercantile agent is in possession of goods with the consent of the true owner any sale of those goods is valid as if it were expressly authorised by the owner of the goods

---

[35]   Sale of Goods (Amendment) Act 1994.

providing that the person who buys them takes them in good faith. It is worth noting in passing that this rule also applies if the agent is in possession just of the documents of title to goods; the vehicle registration document however is not legally a document of title.

This rule does not apply if the agent is holding them for some other purpose, eg a car which is being repaired. The owner must consent to the agent having the goods for a purpose which is connected in some way with his business as a mercantile agent.[36]

The effect of this rule in the Factors Act is that a retailer of a motor vehicle will be protected in a case where he is holding a car in order to sell it for the owner and, for example, the owner tries to change his mind after a contract for sale has been made by the retailer. The owner would not have any right of redress against the retailer or the new owner as the transaction will fall within the provisions of the Factors Act.

If a retailer sells a vehicle without its registration book this will not normally be a sale in the ordinary course of business. In *Pearson v Rose & Young Ltd*[37] a mercantile agent obtained possession of a secondhand car with the consent of the owner and subsequently obtained possession of the registration book without the owner's consent. The agent then sold the car with the registration book to a third party. The court held that no good title had been passed because the mercantile agent, ie the retailer, was not in possession of both the car and the registration book with the owner's consent. Both were necessary in order to constitute 'goods', therefore the buyer did not get good title.

Sales where the true owner is 'estopped' from denying the seller's right to sell

Where the true owner of goods represents that another person is the owner then any contract of sale by that other person will be enforceable against the true owner.

This rule was illustrated in *Eastern Distributors v Goldring*[38] where the owner of a van wanted to raise money on it. He agreed with the car

---

[36] The fact that the owner must consent means that this provision will not operate to confer title where the goods have been stolen: *National Employers Mutual etc Ltd v Jones* [1988] 2 All ER 425.

[37] [1951] 1 KB 275.

[38] [1957] 2 QB 600.

retailer that the retailer should represent to a finance company that he wished to take the van on hire purchase. The owner signed blank forms of a hire-purchase agreement and a delivery note stating that he had taken delivery of the van. The effect was to give the retailer documents which enabled him to represent to the finance company that the retailer was in fact the owner of the van and had the right to sell it. Because the owner had consented and was a party to this arrangement it was held that he could not deny the retailer's apparent ownership of the van. The finance company therefore got good title to the van when they purchased it from the retailer on the strength of this representation by the true owner.

A similar situation may arise if the true owner by his negligence allows someone else to appear to be the owner of the goods. However, parting with the log book and possession has been held not to debar the true owner from recovery.[39] Similarly, in *Moorgate Mercantile Co Ltd v Twitchings* the House of Lords held that the carelessness of a finance company in failing to register a hire-purchase agreement with HPI did not bar them from claiming that the car still belonged to them. This was because there was no duty to register.[40]

Sale under a voidable title

A 'voidable title' arises generally where one party has been the victim of fraud or misrepresentation by the other. In that situation, the contract will be a valid one, until the victim chooses to take steps to rescind the contract.

If when he bought the goods he did so by, for example, convincing the seller that he was someone else and passing a worthless cheque, he will not himself have got a good title but will have a title which is 'voidable'. This means that the person from whom he bought the goods would be able to get the goods back once he has discovered the fraud, provided he bought it in good faith and without notice of the true facts.[41]

---

[39]   *J Sargent (Garages) Ltd v Motor Auctions (West Bromwich) Ltd* [1977] RTR 121.

[40]   *Moorgate Mercantile Co Ltd v Twitchings* [1977] AC 890, HL.

[41]   See *Ingram v Little* [1961] 1 QB 31 and *Lewis v Averay* [1972] 1 QB 198 referred to in ch 5, above.

Sales by the seller in possession

Where a seller who has actually sold goods continues to have possession of them and he then purports to resell the goods either himself or through a mercantile agent acting on his behalf, the second sale will be valid provided the second purchaser takes the goods in good faith and without notice of the earlier transaction.

Sales by the buyer in possession

This rule is somewhat similar to sales by the seller in possession of goods and applies where a person has agreed to buy the goods but the seller still has some right over them, for example, where the purchaser has not yet paid the full price. In that situation the unpaid seller still has a lien over the goods even if he lets them out of his possession but if the purchaser purports to resell them either personally or through a mercantile agent acting on his behalf, then providing the second purchaser buys them in good faith and without notice of the unpaid seller's rights, he will get a good title to the goods.

In *Newtons of Wembley Ltd v Williams*,[42] a customer bought a car from Newtons of Wembley. The contract provided that no property should pass until the cheque was cleared. The cheque bounced and Newtons tried to trace the car. The customer resold it, and it was then resold again to Williams. Newtons sued Williams for the return of the car but their claim failed. The first sale by the customer was a sale by a 'seller in possession' and therefore, because the purchaser from him took in good faith, he acquired a good title and could pass this on to Williams.

The moral to this particular rule is obviously to ensure that goods are not released for any purpose until the bill has been paid in full.

Sale of a motor vehicle subject to a hire-purchase or conditional sale agreement

Frequently, cars are sold which are subject to outstanding credit agreements; these may be credit sale, conditional sale or hire-purchase.[43] The hirer or purchaser who is purchasing a car on credit in this way would

---

[42] *Newtons of Wembley Ltd v Williams* [1965] 1 QB 560, Hire Purchase Act 1964, Pt III.
[43] For definitions see ch 9, below.

not normally be able to pass on a good title if he tries to sell them, except in the case of credit sale where he would generally be in the position of a buyer in possession and would therefore come within exception (vi) above.

These normal rules are subject to a very important exception where motor vehicles are concerned. This is contained in Part III of the Hire Purchase Act 1964, now repeated in Sch 4 to the Consumer Credit Act 1974. This provides that where a motor vehicle which is subject to a hire-purchase or conditional sale agreement[44] is disposed of by the debtor[45] to a private purchaser and he takes it in good faith and without notice of the relevant undischarged agreement the sale will take effect as if the seller had a good title to the vehicle. The protection extends to the first private purchaser to buy the vehicle and so where a vehicle subject to an undischarged agreement is sold to a motor retailer, although he himself will not get a good title because he is not a private purchaser within the meaning of the Act, he will when he sells to a private purchaser be able to pass a good title on to him. The fact that good title has been passed on to the innocent private purchaser does not mean, of course, that the original debtor avoids his liabilities. He will still be both civilly and possibly criminally liable for his actions in selling the vehicle whilst the subject of an undischarged agreement.

What is a private purchaser?

In *Stevenson v Beverley Bentinck Ltd*[46] a purchaser bought a car which was subject to an undischarged hire-purchase agreement in good faith and without notice of the original agreement. In his spare time he

[44] In *Hitchens v General Guarantee Corpn Ltd* (2001) Times, 13 March, the Court of Appeal ruled that there is a binding contract under which title passes to the finance company when it has given oral consent to the transaction, even if at that stage it has not signed the agreement.

[45] In *Hudson v Shogun Finance Ltd* [2002] 4 All ER 572, the Court of Appeal ruled, reluctantly and by a majority, that a rogue who acquired possession of a motor vehicle after signing a hire purchase agreement using the genuine name and address of another person was not in fact the debtor under the hire purchase agreement. This meant that the subsequent private purchaser in good faith did not acquire a good title under the Act, and the finance company was able to recover possession of the vehicle. This decision has now been confirmed by the House of Lords, again by a majority (November 2003)

[46] [1976] 2 All ER 606.

carried on a part-time business of purchasing motor vehicles for resale. He bought this particular vehicle for his own private use and when the finance company repossessed the car he tried to claim that he was protected by the provisions of the Hire Purchase Act 1964, being a private purchaser. The court held that the purchaser was not a private purchaser because when he bought the car he was carrying on, even though in his spare time, the business of a motor retailer. The definition in the Act of a trade or finance purchasers refers to:

> a purchaser who ... carries on business which consists wholly or partly
> (a)   of purchasing motor vehicles for the purpose of offering or exposing them for sale ...

H P Information Ltd

Given that the trade or finance purchase as defined in the Hire Purchase Act is not protected if he mistakenly buys a vehicle which is the subject of an undischarged agreement, the prudent retailer will obviously want to take whatever steps he can to protect himself. This must include checking with Hire Purchase Information Limited and any other relevant sources to see whether a particular vehicle has a hire-purchase agreement registered in respect of it. Although HPI does not cover in its records all hire-purchase agreements relating to cars—the percentage is probably in the region of 98%—and despite the *Moorgate Mercantile Credit Co Ltd v Twitchings* case,[47] it must still be regarded as an important safeguard. The Code of Practice for the Retail Motor Industry[48] now requires members to make reasonable efforts to check that they give good title when they sell part exchange vehicles eg by obtaining a statement from a finance house) by checking and discharging finance on cars they sell.

Leased vehicles

It is important to note that the protection which Part III of the Hire Purchase Act 1964 as re-enacted by the Consumer Credit Act 1974 gives to an innocent private purchaser of a motor vehicle without

---

[47]   [1977] AC 890, HL.
[48]   See Appendix 3.

knowledge of the existence of a hire-purchase or conditional sale agreement, and in good faith, does not apply to vehicles let out under a vehicle leasing agreement. The party to whom the vehicle has been leased does not have title to the vehicle. If the vehicle is sold on by the lessee the purchaser does not obtain good title even if the buyer is a private innocent purchaser, unlike the situation which applies if the 'seller' was the hirer under a hire-purchase or conditional sale agreement. As leasing agreements in respect of vehicles do not fall within the exception as regards good title to which hire-purchase or conditional sale agreements are subject both customers and retailers are at risk. A retailer who purchases a vehicle or vehicles not knowing of the existence of an outstanding leasing contract cannot pass on good title to a customer, and the customer may have proceedings taken against him or her for re-possession on the part of the leasing company. Where this happens the customer would normally look to the retailer for recompense and the retailer in turn would go against the distributor from whom the vehicle was acquired. However, where the distributor has ceased trading or is subject to Receivership or the like, he may not recover his loss.

Sales by a bailee of goods

The final exception arises under the Torts (Interference with Goods) Act 1977 which is dealt with in more detail in the chapter on the supply of services. Briefly, the effect of the Act is to provide that where a bailee of goods sells them in certain specified circumstances and in accordance with the provisions of the Act, any purchaser of the goods will obtain a good title to them.

3 What happens if the seller does not have the right to sell the goods?

If the seller of goods does not in fact own them, and none of the exceptions already discussed apply, this will of course be a breach of the implied term as to title and the seller will be liable to the purchaser for breach of contract.

The purchaser will be able to treat the contract as if it had been brought to an end and claim damages for any loss which he has suffered. If no good title has been passed at all then the purchaser will be able to recover the whole of the purchase price because the whole basis of the contract has disappeared. In *Rowland v Divall*,[49] a purchaser bought a motor car in good faith from a thief. He resold it to a car retailer for £334 who repainted it and put it on show in his showroom for two months. He then sold it to a third party for £400 and two months later the police repossessed it on behalf of the true owner. The retailer had to refund the third party with his money and therefore sued the person who had sold the vehicle to him for return of his £334. The court held that his claim must succeed because there had been a total failure of consideration.

Similarly in *Butterworth v Kingsway Motors Ltd*,[50] a hirer sold a car to A, A then sold to B and B to the defendant. The plaintiffs bought the car from the defendant and used it for several months when they were told that it was in fact owned by the finance company. The plaintiffs wrote rescinding the contract and asking for the return of their purchase moneys and eight days later the hirer paid the balance outstanding under the hire-purchase contract and exercised the option to purchase. The effect of this was to pass a good title from the hirer to A and then on down the chain. However, as at the time the plaintiffs had demanded their money back the hirer had not paid the amount owing under the agreement, it was held that there had been a total failure of consideration and the price could be recovered.

The true owner of the goods will have an action for conversion or detinue against the purchaser. The purchaser can then take action against the thief assuming he can find him when he will be able to recover the amount he has had to pay to the true owner plus his reasonable costs. Frequently chain transactions will arise where goods are stolen and are sold many times over. In that situation each purchaser in the chain will be liable for conversion for each sale and delivery of the goods even if they are in fact innocent. If, as is likely, the thief has disappeared then the first innocent party in the chain will have to bear the loss.

If the seller has actually been fraudulent in representing that he has good title to the goods this does not make any difference to his liability under the contract but if he made an express representation as to the ownership of the goods he may also be liable to the purchaser for the damages in tort for deceit.

---

49 [1923] 2 KB 500.
50 [1954] 2 All ER 694.

4 Can the seller limit his responsibility?

Unlike the other implied terms in the Sale of Goods Act, the implied term as to title may be partially limited. Where the seller is uncertain about his right to sell, he may use a term in the contract by which he agrees to sell only as good a title as he may have. Alternatively, the court may be prepared to infer an intention from the circumstances that this limitation should be read into the contract.

E ARE THE GOODS AS DESCRIBED?

Where the seller sells goods by description, eg 'a new car', a 'reconditioned engine', the purchaser will have a remedy if the goods do not meet that description. This is provided for in s 13 of the Sale of Goods Act which states that:

> 'where there is a contract for the sale of goods by description there is an implied condition that the goods shall correspond with the description; and if the sale be by sample as well as by description it is not sufficient that the bulk of the goods corresponds with the sample if the goods do not also correspond with the description.'

A contract for the sale of goods will be a sale by description even where the customer has had the opportunity of examining the goods, as will sales in self-service shops.

Where the description applied relates to the quality of the goods, satisfactory quality or fitness for purpose will generally be involved and s 13 will no longer be relevant. However, it is important to note that sales by description also extend to private sales not just sales in the course of a business as in the case of the conditions of satisfactory quality and fitness for purpose. This may, therefore, provide a valuable right of redress against a private seller where other possibilities of action are limited.

For example, in the case of the half-and-half Herald convertible referred to earlier,[51] the private seller was held to be liable to the purchaser for breach of the condition implied by s 13 that the goods should comply with the description applied to them.

---

[51]   *Beale v Taylor* [1967] 3 All ER 253, [1967] 1 WLR 1193, CA.

Failure to comply with this implied condition may vary in degree. For example, the goods may not be exactly in accordance with the description, or there may be a complete failure to supply the goods contracted to be sold, eg by supplying a secondhand car instead of the new one ordered.[52] The key element in considering whether a car complies with its description is whether the purchaser got what he bargained for, and therefore it will be a question of fact in each case. In *Raynham Farm Co Ltd v Symbol Motor Corpn*,[53] the sale of a Range Rover described as 'new' when in fact it had been previously severely damaged by fire and written off by the manufacturer before being repaired and sold, did not pass this test. It was not possible to be certain in the circumstances that other parts of the car had not been distorted or affected by the fire, and therefore it could be distinguished from the Trade Descriptions Act case of *R v Ford*,[54] where a car which had been perfectly repaired could legitimately be described as 'new'.

In *Alton House Garages (Bromley) Ltd v Monk*,[55] a secondhand Rolls Royce Corniche was advertised for sale with a 'full service history'. In fact it was supplied with a service record relating to another car. It was held that the seller had contracted to sell the car with its service record. This was a sale by description and as the service record was not delivered the seller was liable for damages.

Words with a special meaning in the trade

If a particular word has acquired a particular meaning through trade usage, eg reconditioned, reworked, then the court will take that meaning into account when deciding whether there has been a breach of s 13. In any particular case, the question of what meaning a word has in the trade will be determined by evidence.

F QUALITY OF THE GOODS

Complaints about the quality of goods supplied to customers probably cause the motor trade more headaches than any others. Given that that

---

[52]   *Morris Motors Ltd v Lilley* [1959] 3 All ER 737.
[53]   [1987] BTLC 157.
[54]   Above see ch 4.
[55]   31 July 1981, unreported.

is the case, it is at first sight surprising that the law is still so unclear about what exactly a consumer is entitled to expect in terms of quality from a car, or replacement part. In practice it seems that in cases involving new cars in particular where legal action might seem worthwhile, many customers are content to rely on manufacturers' warranties or media pressure to provide a remedy. It has also been suggested[56] that one reason for the longevity of the original quality provisions of the Sale of Goods Act 1893 was because in many cases it was not relied on—for example many High Street retailers will allow customers to return goods for a refund even when they are not defective. It is ironic that the two remedies of most interest to customers and most used in practice in the motor industry as elsewhere—repair or replacement of the defective goods—are not covered in the Sale of Goods Act at all.

The sellers' obligations with regard to quality may also arise from an express term of the contract or a representation which has become a term of the contract, eg 'it's a good little bus; I will stake my life on it; you will have no trouble with it' which has been held to be a term of the contract (*Andrews v Hopkinson*): contrast 'as far as I know this vehicle is mechanically sound' which was held not to be part of the contract.

In practice, the most important terms are those which arise as a result of implication under the provisions of sale of goods legislation. Originally enshrined in the Sale of Goods Act 1893 and its consolidating statute the Sale of Goods Act 1979, the most recent legislation is the Sale and Supply of Goods Act 1994 which applies to contracts entered into after 3 January 1995, and The Sale and Supply of Goods to Consumers Regulations 2002[57] which applies to contracts made after 31 March 2003. Both pieces of legislation introduced changes to the implied term of satisfactory quality and to the customer's legal remedies.

It should be noted that the commission of a criminal offence in connection with the sale or supply of an unroadworthy vehicle (see Chapter 13, below) does not of itself entitle the buyer to treat the contract as discharged, although evidence of its condition will clearly be material in determining satisfactory quality and fitness for purpose.

[56]   By the Law Commission in their Report No 24.
[57]   SI 2000/2334.

I The implied terms as to quality

Two terms as to quality were implied into sale of goods contracts by the original Sale of Goods Act 1893. Section 14(2) provided that goods supplied under a contract of sale should be of merchantable quality, and s 14(3) provided that they should be fit for purpose. The merchantable quality term has now been replaced by a requirement that the goods should be of 'satisfactory quality'.[58]

Sale in the course of a business

Both these terms apply only to contracts made by the seller who sells in the course of a business. This means that in a private sale by someone not selling in the course of a business, a purchaser complaining about the quality of goods has to rely on an express term as to quality in the contract (if any) or if the circumstances are suitable a claim under s 13 that the goods did not meet the description applied to them. It is worth noting that a sale in the course of a business includes situations where the goods are sold as ancillary to some other business carried on by the seller. If, for example, a coal merchant sells his lorry he will probably be making a sale in the course of a business although his main business is not that of selling motor vehicles but of being a coal merchant.[59]

Consumer and non-consumer sales

Where goods are sold in the course of business to a consumer, the implied terms as to quality, fitness and description cannot be excluded from the contract.[60] Where the customer does not buy as a consumer, any clause limiting or excluding these terms will be subject to a reasonableness test. The guidelines as to what may be regarded as reasonable are set out in the Unfair Contract Terms Act 1977.[61] These include:

---

[58]   Sale and Supply of Goods Act 1994.
[59]   This was confirmed in *Stevenson v Rogers* [1999] 1 All ER 613. The Court of Appeal made it clear that the interpretation of the words 'in the course of a business' will depend on the legislative context in which they are used. For example, the same words when used in a criminal statute, eg the Trade Descriptions Act 1968, will not be interpreted in the same way: see Chapter 4.
[60]   Unfair Contract Terms Act 1977, s 12.
[61]   Schedule 2.

—   the relative bargaining strength of the parties;
—   whether the customer received an inducement to agree to the term;
—   whether the customer knew or ought to have known of the existence of the term—for example because of a previous course of dealing between the parties;
—   where the term excludes liability for non-compliance with a particular condition, whether it was reasonable at the time of the contract to expect that condition would be practicable;
—   whether the goods were manufactured, processed or adapted to the special order of the customer.

It seems likely that in many of the borderline cases where there may be uncertainty whether a customer is a consumer or not (see below), for example where a sole trader buys a car for mixed business and private use, any exclusion in the contract might well fail the test of reasonableness, particularly in relation to the bargaining strength test.

For contracts concluded before 31 March 2003, the definition of a consumer is: someone who does not buy or hold himself out as buying in the course of a business, and the goods sold are of a type ordinarily sold for private use or consumption. After 31 March, the definition is brought into line with other EU-derived legislation and provides that a consumer is 'any natural person who, in the contracts covered by these Regulations, is acting for purposes which are outside his trade profession or business'.[62] This change has the principal effect of, first, preventing limited companies from taking advantage of the new legal remedies that these Regulations (see below) provide for consumers, as well as removing the protection they would have in some cases previously been given from exclusion and limitation clauses (see for example the *R & B Customs Brokers Ltd* case referred to below); secondly, the nature of the goods being purchased is no longer to be treated as relevant. This means that a person buying a van or other commercial vehicle for private purposes will now be able to take advantage of legal status as a consumer.

Buying in the course of a business

Buying in the course of a business prior to 31 March 2003 did not necessarily mean that any business customer of the motor industry was

---

[62]   Sale and Supply of Goods to Consumers Regulations 2002, SI 2002/3045, reg.2

treated as a non-consumer. In *R & B Customs Brokers Co Ltd v United Dominions Trust Ltd*,[63] it was held that a firm of shipping brokers buying a company car for the use of one of their directors was buying as a consumer, as in order for them to be treated as buying in the course of a business, some regularity of that type of transaction as an integral part of the business would be needed. The result was that they were therefore not subject to the exclusion clause which applied to non-consumer sales contained in the standard form contract they had signed.[64] Had they been buying a van rather than a car, presumably this would not be 'goods of a type ordinarily bought for private use' and the exclusion clause would have applied, subject to its 'reasonableness' in a non-consumer transaction (see below). The streamlining of the various definitions of a 'consumer' is undoubtedly helpful, but the retailer may still be left with the dilemma that the same customer may be a consumer for the purposes of one transaction and a non-consumer for others. How does he know when a customer is a consumer? The European Court of Justice has expressed the view that only contracts concluded for the purpose of satisfying an individual's needs in terms of private consumption are consumer contracts for the purposes of the convention on enforcement of judgments.[65]

To sum up, for transactions entered into after 31 March, the following will not be regarded as consumer transactions for the purposes of the Sale of Goods Act:

— sales of new goods by auction or competitive tender, even where the buyer is a private individual;
— sales of used goods at an auction which a consumer has the possibility of attending in person;
— sales of goods to an individual buying for purposes of his trade profession or business; this would presumably include transactions where a sale is made to an individual claiming to be a business, eg placing an order on business letter head in order to take advantage of a trade discount, or other trade terms.
— a sale to a limited company.

63 [1988] 1 All ER 847.
64 It is interesting to note that R & B Customs Brokers Ltd as a limited company would not meet the definition of a consumer for the purpose of deciding whether the standard contract terms were 'unfair' within the meaning of the Unfair Terms in Consumer Contracts Regulations 1994 (see above).
65 *Francesco Beninsca v Dentalkit Srl* Case C-269/95 ECJ/CFI Bulletin No 20/97, 0, interpreting the Brussels Convention on the Enforcement of Judgments in Civil and Commercial matters.

In some cases, there may be still areas of uncertainty, for example where a person is buying a vehicle for mixed business and private use, but the retailer must bear in mind that for this purpose, it is up to him to prove that a customer is not a consumer.

Exclusion clauses

The effect of the prohibition of exclusion clauses was to make them ineffective when used in relation to consumer sales. It did not however stop retailers from continuing to use these types of clauses in their contracts. It was felt by the Office of Fair Trading that whilst these clauses would have no validity, consumers would be misled as to their rights. An order was therefore made under the Fair Trading Act which makes clauses in a consumer contract appearing to exclude liability in relation to the implied terms as to quality, fitness, or description under the Sale of Goods Act, illegal and their use a criminal offence.

An offence will be committed by displaying a notice containing an exclusion clause, by including it in any contract or in any other documents, or by including it in advertisements or sales literature. It is also an offence to supply goods bearing a statement about the seller's liability without also making it clear that the statement does not affect the consumers' rights under the Sale of Goods Act.

The test of any wording used is whether a reasonable person is likely to conclude that he would not be able to pursue a claim against the retailer, or if he does that the retailer will attempt to rely on the notice in rejecting the claim.

There have been a number of prosecutions of motor traders under this order, and apart from convictions in respect of complete exclusion clauses the following have all led to conviction:

— a receipt marked 'Sold as scrap—no warranty given or implied' (Blyth Magistrates' Court, 23 November 1982);
— a receipt endorsed 'As seen, tried and approved' (Tottenham Magistrates' Court, 11 January 1983);
— a rubber stamp on a used car sales invoice 'This vehicle sold without any warranty' (Derby Magistrates' Court, 1979);
— a statement 'Sold for spares or repair. No warranty whatsoever' (Grimsby Magistrates' Court, 1979).

In *Hughes v Hall*,[66] motor dealers sold secondhand cars giving purchasers documents which included the phrase 'sold as seen and inspected'. The court held that this phrase would exclude the implied term that the goods would comply with any description applied to them, and the dealers were convicted. In a more recent case,[67] however, the court distinguished where the sale is not by description, and it can be said that the customer was simply buying specific goods which he had inspected. In that case, the phrase meant that the purchaser was buying what he had seen, and no offence had been committed.

Merchantable and satisfactory quality

The definition of merchantable quality contained in the Sale of Goods Act 1979 was as follows—

goods of any kind are of merchantable quality ... if they are as fit for the purpose or purposes for which goods of that kind are commonly bought as it is reasonable to expect having regard to any description applied to them, the price (if relevant) and all the other relevant circumstances.

It is quite obvious from this definition that what is merchantable is going to depend on the facts in any particular case. However, it seems that in general a product, in order to be merchantable, must be fit for the purpose to which such a product might normally be expected to be put.

The implied condition of merchantable quality would not apply:
(a) as regards defects specifically drawn to the buyer's attention before the contract is made; or
(b) if the buyer examines the goods before the contract is made, as regards defects which that examination ought to reveal.

Merchantable quality has now been replaced by 'satisfactory quality' (see below), but it is still relevant to consider the ways in which the courts dealt with merchantability cases involving cars, as it seems likely that the more recent cases will still be relevant in determining the standard for 'satisfactory' quality.

---

[66] *Hughes v Hall* [1981] RTR 430, DC.
[67] *Cavendish Woodhouse Ltd v Manley* (1984) 148 JP 299, DC.

2 Merchantability and cars

The application of this principle to motor vehicles had been a major area of difficulty for both the trade and the consumer, and was undoubtedly one of the reasons for the amendment of the law in 1994. Some years ago, the Consumers' Association sought the views of a number of leading lawyers as to what constituted an 'unmerchantable' car.[68] It is salutary to discover that there was no unanimous agreement between them as to whether, in what at the time was a fairly typical situation of a new car with numerous minor faults, the car could be said to be unmerchantable, and as to the extent of the buyer's right to reject the goods.

New cars

Where a car had a serious fault or a number of serious faults, the situation was relatively clear cut. It would be unmerchantable, and the customer will be entitled to damages,[69] or to reject the car and get his money back from the seller.

For example, in *Bernstein v Pamsons Motors (Golders Green) Ltd*,[70] a new car whose engine seized within three weeks and 140 miles due to a manufacturing defect was held to be clearly unmerchantable, because although as the judge said, the purchaser of a new car must expect some teething troubles, this went far beyond what a purchaser should be expected to put up with.

Similarly, in *Jackson v Chrysler Acceptances Ltd*,[71] a new cam shaft, a new exhaust, a new radiator and a new clutch assembly together with other more minor faults, which required rectification during the first few months after purchase were held to make the car unmerchantable.

It is in the area of numerous minor faults, eg badly fitting trim, tear in the roof lining, squeaks and rattles, minor bodywork scratches, that the concept of merchantability was in particular criticised as being quite unsuited to the latter part of the twentieth century at all, let alone to a complex product such as a motor car.

---

[68]   Merchantable Quality: What does it Mean? published by the Consumer's Association.
[69]   The question of remedies is discussed in more detail later.
[70]   [1987] 2 All ER 220.
[71]   [1978] RTR 474.

There were two ways of looking at the problem:

(a)   that consumers should expect that cars they buy should have teething troubles: that a modern motor car is a highly complex piece of machinery and with modern methods of mass production aimed at producing goods which a customer can afford, some minor defects are inevitable. This point of view can be linked with the definition of merchantable quality in the Sale of Goods Act, namely that they are as fit for the purpose or purposes for which goods of that kind are commonly bought as it is *reasonable* to expect ...' (my italics). This view was given support in the unreported case of *Spencer v Claud Rye (Vehicles) Ltd*,[72] where it was suggested that the buyer must be prepared to accept some minor faults, and has now been confirmed and strengthened by the *Bernstein* case (above);

(b)   the second, conflicting view is that any defect however minor (unless so small that it can be called *de minimis* eg, possibly if it would not affect the resale value of the vehicle at all in its defective state) will make the car unmerchantable. In the case of *Jackson v Rotax Cycles Ltd*,[73] 600 motor horns were sold and delivered. 364 of them were found to be scratched and dented, and although this could have been put right easily, the court held they were all unmerchantable. Although there is some disagreement as to the precise effect of this case, it does seem to confirm that a retailer cannot avoid the legal consequences of defects by offering to put them right, which is of course the normal practice in the motor industry.

The view that purchasers of new cars must expect some faults as confirmed in the *Bernstein* case above could lead on, as the Law Commission had pointed out earlier, to the situation where any general decline in the manufactured quality of goods of a certain kind would be accompanied by a general decline in the standard of merchantable quality.

The concept of minor faults not being actionable became further confused when a Scottish case *Millars of Falkirk v Turpie*[74] was decided. In this case a new car was supplied which the day after delivery was

---

72   Reported in the Guardian 19 December 1972 and referred to by M Whincup in 'The Reasonable Fitness of Cars' [1975] 38 MLR 660.

73   [1975] 38 MLR 660.

74   1976 SLT (Notes) 66.

found to have a leak in the power-assisted steering system. The dealers made an adjustment, but it leaked again the following day. The buyer then refused to pay the balance and purported to reject the car on the ground that it was not of merchantable quality. The court unanimously upheld the sheriff's decision that the car was indeed merchantable, and held that the relevant circumstances referred to in the definition of merchantable quality included in this case the following:

— the defect was minor and could be rectified at small cost;
— the dealer was willing and anxious to cure the problem;
— many new cars have defects on delivery and the problem was not exceptional.

They may also have taken into account the fact that the car had been sold with the benefit of the vehicle manufacturer's warranty, although in the later *Bernstein* case it was held that free repair under the warranty was not relevant to the issue of merchantablity.

Later cases[75] have, however, now made it clear that the possibility of rectification at low cost was not the only criterion to apply when considering the nature of the defect. If it creates a danger—even if potential rather than actual—then it must make the vehicle unmerchantable despite the possibility of rectification at low cost.

The *Bernstein* case applied these criteria and also made it clear that any danger caused by the defect would be relevant, as would the possibility of a knock-on effect from the defect even if it had been rectified.

In addition, the price of the car would be relevant, and the standard expected from a high-value car would be greater than that in a cheaper model.

This test was confirmed by the Court of Appeal in *Rogers v Parish (Scarborough) Ltd.*[76] Here the court stated that cases decided before the Supply of Goods (Implied Terms) Act 1973 could not any longer be relied on, as the broad test of merchantable quality adopted in s 14(6) which relates merchantable quality to fitness for purpose must mean that it was not sufficient just to be able to drive the vehicle from one place to another. In addition it was necessary that the vehicle could be driven with the 'appropriate degree of, comfort, ease of handling, relia-

---

[75]   See *Lee v York Coach and Marine* [1977] RTR 35 and *M & T Hurst Consultants Ltd v Grange Motors & Rolls Royce Motors Ltd* (1981) (unreported).
[76]   [1987] QB 933.

bility and pride in the vehicle's outward and interior appearance'.

Of course, from the buyer's point of view the consequences, if minor faults are not considered to make the car unmerchantable, are extremely unfortunate. If the car was in law merchantable, the buyer has no redress at all in law for the defects, and would have to rely on the warranty or guarantee (if any) offered by the manufacturer or retailer, or on their goodwill in order to get a remedy. Therefore not only will he not have any right to reject the car, but he will not be able to claim damages either.

This problem was reviewed by the Law Commission[77] which recommended that the law should be changed so as to replace the concept of 'merchantable' quality with 'acceptable' quality.

Used cars

The question of merchantability in relation to secondhand vehicles was easier to assess as it depends more on such matters as the price, and various cases have come before the courts where this has been considered.[78]

The test suggested by Lord Denning in *Bartlett v Sidney Marcus Ltd* [79] was that a secondhand car was merchantable if it was capable of being driven and driven in safety.

Later cases, however, have made it clear, as we have seen above, that the requirement that the car should be capable of being driven safely does not just mean that there should be no actual danger from the defect, if the danger is only potential then this may be sufficient to make the vehicle unmerchantable.

In *Crowther v Shannon Motor Co*[80] an eight-year-old Jaguar with 82,165 miles on the clock sold for £390, broke down completely after another 2,300 miles and three weeks use. The court here had no difficulty in finding that the car was not reasonably fit for its normal purpose at the time of sale and was therefore unmerchantable.

---

[77] Report on Sale and Supply of Goods May 1987 (Cmnd 137).
[78] See 'The Reasonable Fitness of Cars' [1975] 38 MLR 660.
[79] [1965] 2 All ER 753.
[80] [1975] 1 All ER 139, [1975] 1 WLR 30.

In *Lee v York Coach and Marine*,[81] a consumer bought a secondhand car for £355. It was potentially dangerous because of corrosion to the subframe and the brake pipes. The court decided that the car was not merchantable because it was not fit for the purpose of being driven safely on the roads, even though it was capable of being rectified.

Needless to say the car must also be capable of lawfully being driven on the roads. It is therefore arguable if there is any fault which in fact constitutes a breach of the construction and use requirements,[82] that the car must be unmerchantable because it is not fit for the purpose of being driven on the road.

The relevance of the price when selling a secondhand car was under-lined in the case of *Shine v General Guarantee Corpn*[83] where the Court of Appeal held that in considering whether a car was merchantable a subjective test should be applied to assess what the purchaser was entitled to think he was buying. In this case, a car sold as a 'superb Bertoni-bodied sports' was in fact, the judge found, 'a car which no member of the public, knowing the facts, would touch with a bargepole unless they could get it at a substantially reduced price to reflect the risk they were taking.'

The Court of Appeal has held[84] that the standard of merchantability for a used car, whilst it should reflect 'value for money' is not the same as for a new car. A buyer must expect that sooner or later there will be defects. The purchaser of a secondhand Mercedes which cost £15,000 was not able to claim it was unmerchantable when its engine failed due to burnt out valves 800 miles later.

3 Satisfactory quality

In 1994, four years after the Law Commission's report recommended the replacement of merchantable quality by 'acceptable quality', Parliament finally produced the Sale and Supply of Goods Act which replaced s 14(2) of the Sale of Goods Act 1979 with the following provisions:

---

[81]   [1977] RTR 35.
[82]   Road Traffic Act 1988, and the Motor Vehicles (Construction and Use) Regulations 1986, SI 1986/1078.
[83]   [1988] 1 All ER 911.
[84]   *Business Applications Specialists Ltd v Nationwide Credit Corpn Ltd* [1988] RTR 332.

'(2) Where the seller sells goods in the course of a business there is an implied term that the goods supplied under the contract are of satisfactory quality;

(2A) For the purposes of this Act goods are of satisfactory quality if they meet the standard that a reasonable person would regard as satisfactory, taking account of any description of the goods, the price (if relevant) and all other relevant circumstances.

(2B) For the purposes of this Act the quality of the goods includes their state or condition and the following (among others) are in appropriate cases aspects of the quality of goods:
(a)   fitness for all the purposes for which goods of the kind in question are commonly supplied;
(b)   appearance and finish;
(c)   freedom from minor defects;
(d)   safety; and
(e)   durability.

(2C) The term implied by subsection (2) above does not extend to any matter making the quality of the goods unsatisfactory:
       which is drawn to the buyer's attention before the contract is made,
       where the buyer examines the goods before the contract is made, which that examination ought to reveal, or
       in the case of a contract for sale by sample, which would have been apparent on a reasonable examination of the sample.'

Point 2B(a) undoubtedly reflects the reasoning adopted in the Court of Appeal in the *Rogers* case (see above), and ensures that it is no longer possible for a retailer to argue that because a vehicle is driveable it must also necessarily be of satisfactory quality despite the existence of other defects. The extent to which the specific inclusion of minor defects, and the appearance and finish of goods as part of the assessment of overall quality, really helps customers is perhaps questionable, as the test still turns not on the subjective view of an individual customer, but on that of the 'reasonable person'. On the other hand, the 'reasonableness' test might enable a customer to bring an action against a retailer to challenge a manufacturer's view that a particular feature of a new car which the customer perceives to be unsatisfactory is actually a 'characteristic' of the vehicle which cannot be changed or rectified.

The fact that durability is also specifically included as an aspect of quality will also help customers, but again 'reasonableness' will be a question that will have to be proved, and in the case of a latent fault which becomes apparent later on in a vehicle's life it may be difficult for the customer to prove, as he would have to in a sale of goods contract, that the defect was present at the time of delivery of the vehicle.

In the case of *Bramhill v Edwards*[85], the Court of Appeal had to consider the question of whether an American motorhome which was, at 102 inches wide, technically too wide to be driven on the road in the UK, was not of satisfactory quality within the meaning of s 14. It stressed that the test was an objective one and the reasonable buyer had to be attributed as being in possession of all the relevant facts. In this case, the fact that the evidence showed that there was general awareness among motorhome enthusiasts that the vehicles were technically illegal, but that the UK authorities turned a blind eye to their use on the roads here, meant that the motorhome could still be regarded as being of satisfactory quality.

Inspection by the buyer

The provisions of s 14 (2C) highlight the legal significance of the retailer making sure that if he knows of any defects, he draws them to the customer's attention before he buys the vehicle. Similarly, offering customers facilities to have inspections carried out by their own engineer, eg AA or RAC, is clearly in his own interests, as if there are problems with the car which the engineer should have spotted, the customer will not have a claim against the seller afterwards.

There will obviously be cases where an examination is not going to reveal a latent defect. In that case, it seems that this will not fall within the exception and the retailer will still be liable provided, of course, that the customer can still prove that the defect, although latent, existed at the time of sale. It should be noted that the order form suggested by the RMIF for used car sales contains a condition that the buyer will carry out a pre-sale inspection of his vehicle. However, if the customer signs a statement that he has examined a vehicle this will not help if he has not actually carried out such an examination and might be said to

---

[85]   [2004] EWCA Civ 403, [2004] All ER (D) 42 (Apr).

be an exclusion clause which would therefore be both void[86] and illegal.[87]

In the *Bramhill v Edwards* case discussed above, the importance of this defence was highlighted. The lower court, although finding that the motorhome was not of satisfactory quality, dismissed the case on the ground that the buyer had had ample opportunity to examine the motorhome and measure it, as he had had discussions with the vendor about the spacious nature of the accommodation the vehicle offered and this should have alerted him to the fact that the vehicle might be over - width. This view was upheld by the Court of Appeal.

Satisfactory quality in consumer transactions

The Sale and Supply of Goods to Consumers Regulations 2002 further amend this section by providing[88] that a new relevant circumstance can be taken into account when determining satisfactory quality of goods in consumer transactions:

'(2D) If the buyer deals as a consumer, or , in Scotland , if a con-tract is a consumer contract, the relevant circumstances mentioned in subsection (2A) above include any public statements on the spe-cific characteristics of the goods made about them by the seller, the producer or his representative, particularly in advertising or on labelling.

'Producer' in this context has the same meaning as under other consumer legislation[89], and is defined as the manufacturer of goods, the importer of goods into the EEA, or anyone purporting to be the producer by putting his name or mark on the goods. The retailer is therefore now in the posi-tion that a mistake in an advertisement or sales literature issued by the manufacturer will be taken into account in assessing the retailer's liability to the consumer under the contract of sale, subject to the proviso that:

'(2E) A public statement is not by virtue of subsection (2D) above a relevant circumstance for the purposes of subsection (2A) above in the case of a contract of sale if the seller shows that:

---

86   Unfair Contract Terms Act 1977.
87   Consumer Transactions (Restrictions on Statements) Order 1976, SI 1976/1813 as amended by SI 1978/127.
88   SI 2002/3045, reg 3.
89   For example, the Consumer Protection Act 1987.

(a)   at the time the contract was made, he was not, and could not reasonably have been, aware of the statement;
(b)   before the contract was made, the statement had been withdrawn in public, or , to the extent that it contained anything which was incorrect or misleading, it had been corrected in public;
(c)   the decision to buy the goods could not have been influenced by the statement.'

This proviso will not be of assistance if the public statement in question would have treated as a relevant factor in any case, whether or not the buyer was a consumer.

4 Fitness for purpose

The provisions relating to fitness for purpose overlap with satisfactory quality but may also in practice impose a higher standard. Goods may be satisfactory but not fit for the particular purpose for which they were sold.

Section 14(3) provides:

> Where the seller sells goods in the course of a business, expressly or by implication, makes known:
> (a)   to the seller; or
> (b)   where the purchase price or part of it is payable by instalments and the goods were previously sold by a credit-broker to the seller, to that credit-broker,
>
> any particular purpose for which the goods are being bought, there is an implied condition that the goods supplied under the contract are reasonably fit for that purpose, whether or not it is a purpose for which the goods are commonly supplied, except where the circumstances show that the buyer does not rely, or that it is unreasonable for him to rely, on the skill or judgment of the seller or credit-broker.

Section 14(4) then goes on to provide that 'An implied condition or warranty about quality or fitness for a particular purpose may be annexed to a contract of sale by usage'.

The overlap between the two sections was illustrated in a case involving excess sulphites in underpants which caused extreme discomfort to the wearer. The court held that because the goods were unfit for purpose, ie being worn as underpants, they were clearly unmerchantable.[90] It should be noted that there is no provision for exclusion of the implied term of fitness where an examination of the goods has taken place. This means that although a customer may have lost his right to sue for a breach of satisfactory quality through having examined the goods, he may still have a claim because the car was not fit for purpose.[91] What is fit for purpose?

A bun with a stone in it,[92] on which a solicitor broke a tooth, was not fit for its purpose, ie of being eaten, nor was milk infected with typhoid.[93] It is worth noting that the seller will not be liable for breaches of the implied conditions of quality where the buyer had some part to play to make the goods safe. For example, where a pork chop was sold which contained harmful parasites which would have been killed had the chop been cooked properly, the customer could not recover damages from the seller.

Is a car fit for purpose?

As already mentioned this condition is often used as an alternative to a claim being made for a breach of merchantable quality. The purpose made known by the buyer does not have to be an express statement to the seller. The courts will normally readily accept that the buyer implicitly made known his purpose. For example, in the case of a motor car it will obviously be implied that the customer wished to purchase it for the purpose of driving it on the roads unless, of course, he specifically made known that he was buying it for scrap.

In *Baldry v Marshall*[94] the buyer claimed to reject an 8-cylinder Bugatti car because it was not fit for purpose when he had specified the purpose as being to acquire a fast, flexible and easily managed car which would be comfortable and suitable for ordinary touring purposes which the Bugatti was not.

---

[90] *Grant v Australian Knitting Mills Ltd* [1936] AC 85.
[91] See for example *R & B Customs Brokers v United Dominions Trust* [1988] 1 All ER 847 where a car with water leaks was held to be unfit for the implied purpose of being driven on English roads in English weather.
[92] *Chaponière v Mason* (1905) 21 TLR 633.
[93] *Frost v Aylesbury Dairy Co* [1905] 1 KB 608, CA.
[94] [1925] 1 KB 260.

So far as secondhand cars are concerned, they may be reasonably fit for purpose, although needing some repair.[95] When consumers are buying goods they are entitled to rely on the seller as an expert to a much greater degree than where two businesses are contracting with each other.

The area of fitness for purpose is one where the retailer can probably do much to help himself particularly in relation to the sales of new vehicles. The customer who is relying on the retailer to recommend a vehicle that is going to be really suitable for his purpose, for example, a large amount of motorway use, would seem to have a very good claim if he is in fact sold a vehicle which is not suitable for being driven at sustained high speeds.

In *Bristol Tramways Carriage Co Ltd v Fiat Motors Ltd*,[96] which involved two businesses rather than a sale to a consumer, buses were ordered which were known to be wanted for heavy passenger work. They were unsuitable for that purpose and it was held that the seller was liable.

Whilst in general satisfactory quality and fitness for purpose will very often coincide and mean in effect the same thing, it seems that a purchaser who makes a particular special purpose known to the seller will be able to demand a higher standard under the fitness for purpose condition.

G THE CUSTOMERS' REMEDIES

Where there has been:
(a)   a breach of one of the terms of the contract whether an express or an implied term; or
(b)   a misrepresentation which has become a part of the contract; or
(c)   even if a misrepresentation has not become a term of the contract, but was merely one of the factors which induced the customer to buy the goods,

the customer will have a remedy. Following the implementation of the Directive on Consumer Guarantees and Related Rights[97] by the Sale and Supply of Goods to Consumers Regulations 2002[98], the remedies

---

[95]   *Barlett v Sidney Marcus Ltd* [1965] 2 All ER 753.
[96]   [1910] 2 KB 831.
[97]   1999/44/EC.

available to a customer will depend on whether he is a consumer or non-consumer (see above). While all customers will be able to take advantage of the historic remedies in the Sale of Goods Act of rejection of the goods and compensation for breach of contract, consumers will now as an alternative be able to take advantage of the more extensive remedies provided by the Directive.

I Rejection

The main remedy for breach of a term of the contract is for the buyer to reject the goods and claim the price he paid for them as well as additional damages for losses which were reasonably foreseeable. Alternatively the buyer can treat the breach as being less serious and retain the goods he has bought but claim damages for the breach of contract. However, if the purchaser has 'accepted' the goods then he will only have the right to sue for damages and he will have lost his right to reject the goods altogether. The right to reject the goods has never therefore been as automatic as customers sometimes appear to assume, but the position about acceptance has now been altered in the consumer buyer's favour as a result of the Sale and Supply of Goods Act 1994.

Under the Sale of Goods Act, the buyer has the right to be given a reasonable opportunity to examine the goods he is buying (s 34) to check whether the goods conform to the contract. The Act goes on to provide that where the goods are delivered to the buyer and he has not previously examined them, he has a right to do so (s 35).

Acceptance takes place when '[the buyer] intimates to the seller that he has accepted them or ... when the goods have been delivered to him and he does any act in relation to them which is inconsistent with the ownership of the seller, or when after the lapse of a reasonable time he retains the goods without intimating to the seller that he has rejected them'.[99] Historically, the concept of a 'reasonable time' has always given rise to problems in sale of goods contracts which the courts have been able to avoid in hire purchase cases. For example, in *Farnworth Finance Facilities v Attryde*,[100] a customer entered into a hire-purchase agreement for a new motor cycle. He subsequently returned it to the retailer and the manufacturer when he found it was faulty. Although

---

[98]   SI 2002/3045.
[99]   Sale of Goods Act 1979, s 11(4).
[100]   [1970] 2 All ER 774, [1970] 1 WLR 1053.

they had it for a substantial period not all the faults were remedied. Finally, after paying four instalments, the customer repudiated the contract and the finance company repossessed the motor cycle. The court found that the customer was entitled to repudiate the contract because the condition of the motor cycle was so bad that it constituted a fundamental breach of contract. Lord Denning commented:

> 'A man only affirms a contract when he knows of the defects and by his conduct elects to go on with the contract despite them. In this case the [customer] complained from the beginning of the defects and sent the machine back for them to be remedied. He did not elect to accept it unless they were remedied. But the defects were never very satisfactorily remedied.'

Similarly, in the case of *Laurelgates Ltd v Lombard North Central Ltd* [101] the judge pointed out that the concept of acceptance linked to the discovery of defects only applies where goods are sold on hire purchase. Similar rules will apply in leasing agreements or sales made on hire purchase. In *UCB Leasing Ltd v Holtom* [102] a car leased on an agreement for 37 months from August 1980 had a serious defect in its electrical system and suffered three complete electrical failures between August and December. The hirer complained but continued to pay instalments until November. The car was not, however, returned until March 1981. It was held that by this time the hirer had lost the right to reject. Under an ordinary sale contract the test is whether the buyer has had the goods for a 'reasonable' time, and all the cases confirm that in order for a customer to be able to reject a car and claim the return of money paid he needs to act very quickly.

In the case of a sale of goods contract, the *Bernstein* case held that a period of three weeks and 140 miles from delivery of a new car did constitute a 'reasonable' time, and that by then the purchaser had accepted the car and was entitled only to damages. [103]

In another case, *Lee v York Coach and Marine*, [104] a consumer purchased a car on 7 March and immediately complained about its condition. The retailers made two attempts to put it right but refused to do anything after the third complaint. On 26 April and again on 10 May

---

[101]   (1983) 133 NLJ 720.
[102]   [1987] RTR 362.
[103]   But this is no longer to be regarded as good law – see the 2003 case of *Clegg v Olle Andersson* (below)
[104]   [1977] RTR 35.

the customer's solicitors wrote to the retailer asking that the defects be remedied or a refund given. The court decided that the consumer had by then lost the right to reject the car, and was only entitled to damages. They held that the solicitor's letters did not constitute unequivocal rejection and that it was too late to reject in the statement of claim.

In *Jackson v Chrysler Acceptances Ltd*,[105] Mr Jackson had sought to claim to reject his new car because of the serious nature of the defects which made it unmerchantable and unfit for the purpose. It was held, however, that the using of the car for 6,000 miles between April and November, paying instalments between May and November, and allowing the car to be repaired free of charge under the warranty by the selling retailer and continuing to keep and use the vehicle despite its defective condition, were all matters which meant that Mr Jackson was no longer able to rescind the contract. In *Leaves v Wadham Stringer (Cliftons) Ltd*,[106] the purchaser of a new car which had various minor faults, and a more serious problem with the brakes, claimed the return of the money he had paid for the vehicle. The minor faults had been put right, and his claim was on the basis that the brakes were still defective and rendered the car unmerchantable. The court found that the brakes were not in fact defective when he sought to reject the car and that it was therefore merchantable at that time and he was not entitled to his money back.

The amendment inserted into s 35 provides that determining whether a reasonable time has elapsed may now take into account whether the buyer has had a reasonable opportunity to examine the goods, and he will not now be deemed to have accepted the goods simply because he asks for or agrees to their repair, or where he has already disposed of the goods. Whilst this amendment certainly reflects the commonsense approach which encourages sellers and buyers to resolve problems if they can by repairing the goods, rather than encouraging the buyer to immediately reject them, there is still no clear picture of what amounts to a 'reasonable time' in which to discover faults. Does this mean that in the case of a latent defect which takes months to become apparent a car buyer may still be entitled to reject and get all his money back even though he has had extensive use of the vehicle in the meantime? The difficulty of assessing the extent of the so-called 'short term' right to reject in the light of these amendments in any particular case has been highlighted by the case of *Clegg v Olle Andersson (t/a Nordic Marine)*.[107]

---

[105]   [1978] RTR 474.
[106]   [1980] RTR 308.

The case involved the purchase of a new yacht, which was rejected as being of unsatisfactory quality by the purchasers who sought to recover the price paid and damages for breach of contract. The lower court decided they were not entitled to a refund of the purchase price, because more than a reasonable time – some seven months – had elapsed before rejection took place. The Court of Appeal overturned this decision, ruling that *Bernstein* was no longer good law in the light of the later amendments, which it interpreted as meaning that the time required to see what would be required to effect a repair should be taken into account in assessing the 'reasonable time'. Given that this 'short term' right to reject allows the purchaser to recover all the money paid, the potential extension of the right to cover such a long period is alarming, and must provide an incentive for retailers to resolve disputes with customers as quickly as possible, particularly when repairs are being carried out. In the later case of *Jones v Gallagher*[108], however, the Court of Appeal distinguished the *Clegg* case on its facts and stated that it was not a correct interpretation of the Act to argue that while a repair or complaint was in progress the right to reject could not be lost, and stressed that such delays were simply one factor to be taken into account when the court assesses whether the buyer has accepted the goods. In *Cruickshank v Specialist Cars (Aberdeen) Ltd* it was stressed that there was no hard and fast rule as to what constituted a reasonable time to reject. In this case, rejection after five months was not unreasonable, as the alleged defect related to the vehicle's towing performance which the consumer did not test until he attached his caravan to the car when he went on holiday.

Non-consumer buyers' rights

Whilst the potential impact of the *Clegg* case on the motor industry has been reduced by the introduction of the new remedies for consumers (see below), non-consumers will undoubtedly benefit from the more relaxed approach to assessing what constitutes as reasonable time. However, this benefit has to be seen in the context that where the buyer is a non-consumer, his rights to reject are different. The 1994 Act inserts a new s 15A(1) into the Sale of Goods Act which provides that where a buyer would have a right to reject for breach of one of the implied terms, but the breach is so slight that it would not be reasonable to allow him to do so, then the condition may be treated as a warranty only, and so no right to reject will apply.

---

[107]   (2003) Times, 14 April.
[108]   *Jones v Gallagher (t/a Gallery Kitchens & Bathrooms)* [2004] EWCA Civ 10.
[10aa]   Aberdeen Sheriff Court, 10 July 2002, (2002) GWD 858.

2 Damages

The customer may have a claim for damages in addition to having rejected the car, or he may only be entitled to damages under the rules just discussed. Generally speaking when the customer is claiming damages for breach of one of the conditions of quality in the contract, the amount of the damages which he can recover will be the difference between the value of the goods at the time of delivery to the buyer and the value that they would have had if they had been in the promised condition.

In practice this will normally be the difference between the contract price and the diminished value of the defective goods. Because the value must be taken 'at the time of delivery' this means that the customer cannot increase his claim by taking account of inflationary rises in the cost of repairing or replacing the goods since the time of delivery.

Where a vehicle is hired under a hire-purchase or leasing contract, the customer may not be able to recover all the money previously paid under the contract,[109] unless the defect and its consequences were so serious as to amount to a total failure of consideration—in other words going to the very root of the contract. In some cases, however, the courts have been readier to allow a claim for amounts already paid less a deduction for use of the vehicle[110] although in one case where the inconvenience was substantial, no deduction for use was made.[111] In the case of *UCB Leasing v Holtom*,[112] a hirer was able to recover damages equal to the amount of the instalments due under the agreement less the value of the use actually obtained.

Consequential losses

The customer can also claim damages for consequential loss arising from a defective product so long as the loss is not too 'remote'. This means that there must have been a strong possibility of the losses being claimed arising from the particular defect. These losses would include physical injury to the consumer or damage to his property or indeed

---

109   *Yeoman Credit Ltd v Apps* [1962] 2 QB 508.
110   *Charterhouse Credit Co Ltd v Tolley* [1963] 2 QB 683.
111   *Farnworth Facilities Ltd v Attridge* [1970] 2 All ER 774, [1970] 1 WLR 1053.
112   [1987] RTR 362.

damage to other property, for example, as where the brakes of a car fail and cause it to be involved in an accident. He will also be entitled to recover the cost of alternative transport, of recovery charges in getting a vehicle back to the repairing garage, etc. In one case, a customer who had planned to take a car on holiday, was awarded damages for the spoilt holiday.[113] The customer is under a duty to mitigate his loss and so, for example, a customer who is claiming damages for loss of use of his defective car must have used his second one if it was available or where he has to hire alternative transport he must do so at the most reasonable rate. The question frequently comes up as to whether he is entitled to a complete replacement for the vehicle which is off the road.

There are no helpful cases directly on this point but in *Daily Office Cleaning Contractors Ltd v Shefford*,[114] the plaintiffs provided prestige motor cars for use by their directors. One of them had an American Rambler Ambassador motor car. In an accident caused by the negligent driving of the defendant, the car was badly damaged and needed replacement parts. While the car was being repaired the plaintiffs hired a substitute Jaguar XJ6. The repairs took twenty-five weeks to complete because of a delay by suppliers and the defendant argued that the plaintiff was not justified in hiring an XJ6 for so long. The court held that this claim was perfectly reasonable and that despite the delay the hire charges were recoverable.

The courts have in some cases allowed damages for less concrete claims, such as disappointment. For example, in *Jackson v Chrysler Acceptances*,[115] a consumer told a dealer that he wanted a car for a holiday. When it turned out to be defective he was able to recover £75 for a spoilt holiday. Mr Bernstein was awarded £150 for a spoilt day 'comprising nothing but vexation'! In *UCB Leasing v Holtom*,[116] a consumer was awarded £500 for distress where a hire car had three complete electrical failures in three months.

3 Remedies for consumers

The Sale and Supply of Goods to Consumers Regulations 2002 amend the Sale of Goods Act 1979 by providing that in the case of contracts

---

113   *Jackson v Chrysler Acceptances Ltd* [1978] RTR 474.
114   [1977] RTR 361.
115   [1978] RTR 474.
116   [1987] RTR 362.

for the sale of goods to a consumer made after 31 March 2003, he will now have additional remedies available to him if the goods do not conform to the contract at the time of delivery, and also the advantage of a partial reversal in the burden of proof. The new remedies can be used as an alternative to the right to reject and the right to compensation, but cannot be pursued at the same time, and if the buyer has opted for repair or replacement of the goods he must allow a reasonable time before pursuing an alternative remedy.[117] These rights extend to breaches of express terms of the contract as well as the statutory implied terms. The new remedies do not extend to consumers acquiring goods under other types of supply contracts, for example hire purchase or lease[118], but they will be able to take any public statements into account in assessing whether goods are of satisfactory quality (see above).

Reversal of the burden of proof

The regulations amend the Sale of Goods Act[119] with the practical effect that where the buyer is a consumer, if a defect is found in the first six months it will be assumed that it was there at the time of delivery. It will of course still be necessary for it to be established that the defect complained of meant that the goods did not conform to the contract, i.e. that the goods were not of the quality that a reasonable person would regard as satisfactory, or were not fit for purpose, did not meet description or did not conform to an express term of the contract. In practice however this provision does put a burden on the retailer to consider how he might prove that the goods did conform to the contract when they were delivered. How easy or problematic this will be will undoubtedly depend on the nature of the defect alleged, but the need for keeping evidence of pre-delivery inspections of new vehicles, and checks carried out on used vehicles, will be of particular importance.

Repair or replacement of the goods

The Regulations put into place an alternative sequence of remedies for consumers to pursue if they wish. This involves first a right to require a

---

[117] Sale of Goods Act 1979, s 48D.
[118] The remedies in respect of these contracts are assessed in accordance with common law rules (see above), and are unchanged by these Regulations.
[119] Sale of Goods Act 1979, s 48A.

repair or replacement, followed by a right to a full or partial refund of the price if the other remedies are impossible, disproportionate or cannot be effected within a reasonable time. While this sequence reflects what happens as a matter of practice in many cases, the shift in emphasis from, for example, replacing a vehicle as a matter of goodwill, to a situation where a consumer can 'require' that this should happen, will undoubtedly cause retailers some concern.

The Sale of Goods Act is amended so that a consumer buyer may now require the seller to either repair or replace the goods if they do not conform to the contract.[120] The wording here makes it quite clear that it is the intention that it should be the consumer who calls the shots when trying to resolve a dispute over a defective product. A retailer can no longer resist a claim from a consumer for a replacement vehicle on the grounds that he is not legally entitled to this particular remedy. The repair or replacement must be done within a reasonable time, and without significant inconvenience to the buyer, and the seller must bear any necessary costs.

The right to 'require' the chosen remedy is balanced by the fact that the buyer cannot require a remedy that is impossible, disproportionate in comparison to the other of the two remedies, or disproportionate in comparison to a full or partial refund of the price. The question of what is a proportionate remedy is to be assessed by considering whether the costs on the seller of one remedy are unreasonable compared with the other, taking into account the value of the goods, the significance of the defect, and whether the other remedy could be effected without significant inconvenience to the buyer.

In deciding what is a reasonable time, or what is significant inconvenience to the buyer, the regulations provide that the nature of the goods and the purpose of acquisition must be taken into account.

In respect of the motor industry, this could mean for example that if the retailer is unable or unwilling to provide alternative transport for the customer if his car is off the road awaiting parts to fix a fault, this might be regarded as constituting significant inconvenience to the buyer, and entitle him to require the alternative of a replacement vehicle. If on the other hand, a customer were to require a replacement of a model that was no longer available, this would clearly be impossible

---

[120]   Sale of Goods Act 1979, s 48B.

for the retailer to provide and he could not therefore be forced to do so.

Full or partial refund

If the remedies of repair or replacement are either impossible or disproportionate, or cannot be effected within a reasonable time without significant inconvenience to the consumer, then the buyer can require the seller to give a partial refund of the purchase price, or rescind the contract and refund the purchase price. In this latter case, the reimbursement to the buyer can be reduced to take account of use of the goods.[121]

Powers of the court

A court can order a different remedy to the one requested, and has power to reduce reimbursement of the purchase price to take account of any use of the goods since delivery.[122]

Relevance of a manufacturer's or retailer's warranty

In practice of course, the purchaser of a new vehicle will very often make a claim under a vehicle manufacturer's or retailer's warranty as a way of achieving a resolution to his problem as an alternative to pursuing his legal rights , and a guarantee or warranty may not exclude a consumer's legal rights.[123]

The fact that repairs have been carried out under warranty are not relevant for the purposes of deciding whether the vehicle conformed to the contract at the time of delivery (see above) but it may inevitably have some impact on the amount of compensation to which the customer is entitled, if he chooses to pursue this as a claim under his 'old' rights. The courts have shown a somewhat equivocal approach to the effect that the existence or otherwise of a warranty may have on the customer's rights. For example, in the case of *Rogers v Parish*

[121] Sale of Goods Act 1979, s 48C.
[122] Sale of Goods Act 1979, s 48E.
[123] Consumer Transactions (Restrictions on Statements) Order 1976, SI 1976/1813 as amended by SI 1978/127.

(Scarborough) Ltd [124], the court rejected an argument that the existence of a manufacturer's warranty under which defects could be remedied free of charge effectively meant that a new car was merchantable. On the other hand, in a Scottish case in 1997 the decision by the consumer not to buy a retailer's warranty when purchasing a used car was regarded by the appeal court as an indication that the consumer was, given that a reasonable person would accept that with a five-year-old vehicle durability was a matter of luck, prepared to 'take the risk' that the vehicle might develop defects [125]. While failure to purchase an additional retailer's warranty should not affect a consumer's legal rights, this comment seems to come perilously close to that proposition. In the event, however, the court ruled as that the consumer could not prove that the vehicle was faulty at the time of sale, she lost her case anyway. Given that the car in this case developed a major fault with the gearbox after only a matter of weeks, a similar case arising now might well be decided differently given that burden of proof would now rest with the retailer on this point rather than with the consumer.

The legal aspects of the enforceability of the manufacturer's warranty are dealt with in more detail in Chapter 10.

In some cases, for example if the repairing dealer did not sell the vehicle, there may be reluctance to carry out work under warranty. If, however, the vehicle was sold within the EC, European law requires that the manufacturer should honour his warranty throughout the Community even if the consumer has purchased the vehicle through unofficial channels. This will mean that the manufacturer will normally require his dealers in their agreements to carry out such work.

H ADDITIONAL LIABILITY OF THE RETAILER

I Criminal liability

The Road Traffic Acts deal with the responsibility of the retailer to sell vehicles that are roadworthy and conform to construction and use requirements. In addition the Consumer Safety Act 1978 established a procedure whereby an order can be made prohibiting the sale of 'unsafe' products. This legislation, as has already been noted, has been

---

[124]   [1987] QB 933.
[125]   *Thain v Anniesland Trade Centre* 1997 ALT 102, 1997 SCLR 991.

applied to motor accessories. The Consumer Protection Act creates a general duty to sell only safe goods breach of which will be a criminal offence. Motor vehicles are expressly excluded, but motor components and accessories are covered. In addition, the General Product Safety Regulations[126] were introduced on 3 October 1994 to implement the European Directive. This legislation is dealt with in more detail in Chapter 13.

2 Non-contractual civil liability

Negligence

Although generally a retailer will be sued in contract if there are problems with defective goods, it should be noted that in some circumstances a retailer may find that a claim is brought against him also in tort for alleged negligence. In *Fisher v Harrods Ltd*,[127] a Mrs Fisher was awarded damages against Harrods when she was injured by a bottle of cleaning fluid that her husband had purchased for her. It was held that Harrods had been negligent in selling an untested product that they had obtained from an unreliable source. The manufacturers of the product might also have been liable, of course, but in this instance they were not sued by the plaintiff. This could be relevant, eg where someone other than the purchaser is injured by a defect in the car in which they were a passenger.

This does highlight the fact that the retailer is under a duty to take care that the goods that he sells are safe. If, for example, a motor retailer sells replacement parts which are defective in design or unsuitable for a particular car to which they are subsequently fitted, he may well be held to be liable for any damage that results. The prudent retailer should therefore make sure that any products he is selling are bought from reputable sources and that, as far as possible, he has ensured that they are in fact safe and fit for the purpose of which he is going to sell them. In the case, for example, of parts for cars which have been counterfeited, the retailer may well find himself in the unfortunate position of being held liable for damage caused either in tort or under the contract of sale, without being able to identify the true manufacturer himself.

[126] SI 1994/2328.
[127] [1966] 1 Lloyd's Rep 500.

Where however the retailer of a used car warns that the vehicle may be defective, and the buyer fails to have it inspected, the retailer may not be liable in negligence to someone injured in a subsequent accident.[128]

Strict liability under the Consumer Protection Act, Pt I

In addition the retailer of defective goods will be liable as 'producer' under the provisions of the Consumer Protection Act 1987, Pt I (see Chapter 10) unless he can identify his supplier within a reasonable time of being asked to do so. Furthermore, he will take on liability for items which bear his name—for example promotional give-away goods, unless he can identify the actual producer.

Breach of statutory duty

It seems that it will not normally be possible for a claim to be brought for damages in civil law arising from a breach of a statutory duty, for example under the Trade Descriptions Act 1968, or under safety legislation unless the legislation specifically provides for that possibility.[129] Two fairly old motor industry cases illustrate this point. In neither case were the plaintiffs able to recover damages from defendants who had not complied with statutory motor vehicle safety requirements.[130]

I RETAILERS' WARRANTIES

In addition to the terms of the contract which are implied by statute, eg Sale of Goods Act, when selling goods, and to express or implied terms that may arise through discussion or course of dealing between the parties (as previously discussed) there may also be situations where the retailer voluntarily extends his liability under a contract of sale, particularly of a used car, by offering his own warranty or guarantee with the vehicle.

The first point that should be made is that there is no legal duty to offer his own specific warranty with a used car. The retailer may, if he

---

[128]   *Hurley v Dyke* [1979] RTR 265, HL.
[129]   As for example under the Consumer Protection Act 1987.
[130]   *Phillips v Britannia Hygienic Laundry Co* [1923] 2 KB 832 and *Badham v Lambs Ltd* [1946] KB 45.

wishes, simply sell a vehicle which must, of course, comply with the satisfactory quality and fitness for purpose requirements under the Sale of Goods Act, and also the Road Traffic Acts, but without any further sort of guarantee at all.

If the retailer offers a warranty or guarantee then he will be bound by the terms of what he offers, as it will form part of the contract of sale. So, for example, if he agrees to supply parts free of charge for a period of three months he will be bound to do just that and if he fails to do so the consumer will have a right of action against him. Under the Consumer Transaction (Restrictions on Statements) Order,[131] the warranty or guarantee offered by a retailer cannot take away or diminish any rights which the consumer would otherwise have under the Sale of Goods Act, and the warranty document must also include a statement advising the consumer that the warranty is in addition to his statutory or common law rights. The Sale and Supply of Goods to Consumers Regulations 2002[132] now confirm that where a consumer guarantee[133] is given free of charge, this will be enforceable against the guarantor as a contract. The terms of the contract will be the conditions expressed in the warranty document, and also any related advertising. A retailer advertising a '12-month comprehensive warranty' which in fact contains restrictions as to fair wear and tear, or in respect of certain items, could therefore find that his legal liability to be more extensive than intended as any ambiguity would presumably be interpreted in favour of the consumer.

The same regulations provide that where a consumer guarantee is given, the terms must be made available to the consumer before the goods are purchased, it must be expressed in English, in clear language, and state that it does not affect the consumer's legal rights.

J EXTENDED WARRANTIES

It has become common in recent years for retailers to offer their customers who buy a secondhand car the opportunity of buying a so-called 'extended warranty'. This will commonly give the customer, in return for payment, a guarantee that the cost of repairs will be covered for a certain period of time or mileage.

---

[131] SI 1976/1813, as amended by SI 1978/127.
[132] SI 2002/3045.
[133] As defined in the Regulations.

Although these types of schemes are often called 'warranties' they are in fact a sort of insurance against mechanical breakdown, and this is the better way of describing them.

The way such a scheme commonly operates is that the retailer will be associated with a company offering mechanical breakdown insurance. If he has a franchise from a vehicle manufacturer, it may be with a company with which the manufacturer has an arrangement, or if he is a member of the RMIF, it may be through the scheme operated by them, or it may be through the retailer's own contacts.

In each case, the role of the retailer will generally be as an agent for the company operating the scheme, although the actual contract of 'insurance' will be between the consumer and the operating company or insurer, which means that usually a retailer will not be liable himself under the 'insurance' contract.

In any event of course the retailer cannot use the mechanical breakdown insurance scheme to avoid any of his own liabilities under the contract of sale.

The terms on which these schemes are offered to consumers, and their financial stability, has caused a number of problems. All too frequently, the terms of the 'insurance' are extremely unfair to consumers, and have been used by disreputable companies to avoid having to make payments to consumers whose cars have broken down. For example, requirements have been made that the vehicle covered must be serviced at intervals of 3,000 miles when the manufacturer's recommendation is 6,000, or that the vehicle must not have been moved after the breakdown even to be taken to a repairing garage. The fact that these insurance contracts are now subject to the Unfair Terms in Consumer Contracts Regulations (see above) will be of assistance to consumers faced with terms which are unreasonably being used to exclude their rights under the contract.

In other cases, companies have collapsed leaving thousands of consumers without the protection they have paid for.

A number of efforts are being made to clean up this sector of the motor trade. Mechanical breakdown insurance schemes have been launched by the AA and the Retail Motor Industry Federation and several of the vehicle manufacturers now have links with the larger, reputable companies. With effect from 14 January 2005 all motor vehicle warranties which are contracts of insurance will be within the scope of regulation by the Financial Services Agency (FSA).[134] The broad effect of the Regulations is that businesses involved in the selling of insurance, claims handling and some administrative activities with an insurance element will be regulated by the FSA and will have to seek authorisation either on their own account or as an Appointed Representative of another company unless their activities are restricted to simply providing information about insurance products, and comply with FSA requirements in respect of matters such as the training and competency of staff, provision of information to customers and complaint handling.

[134] The Financial Markets Act 2000 (Regulated Activities) (Amendment) (No 2) Order 2003, SI 2003/1476.

CHAPTER 8

Financing the sale

A INTRODUCTION

Frequently the customer who comes to buy a car will not be purchasing it with his own cash. If he is buying a car for his own private use the money will often be supplied by a third party or more rarely by the retailer himself. The source which supplies the money may either be one introduced by the retailer, eg a finance company with which the retailer has a business arrangement or one privately arranged by the customer, eg a loan from his own bank direct to him. The form of credit used may be a loan, or a credit or conditional sale, or hire purchase. These are defined in the next chapter.

All these forms of credit are controlled to a greater or less extent by legislation. Until 1974 there were several different statutes and the resulting confusion of legislation became inadequate to match the growing number of credit transactions being entered into. In 1974 however, the Consumer Credit Act was passed which had the aim of getting rid of this variety of approaches to credit and bringing together all the law relating to consumer credit in one statute and at the same time introducing further safeguards for consumers.

Although the Consumer Credit Act reached the statute book in 1974, it took some eleven years to be brought fully into effect. There are two main aspects of the Act, the first dealing with the control of those involved in consumer credit business, and the second with the content of consumer credit agreements. This latter aspect is dealt with in more detail in the next chapter.

B THE CONSUMER CREDIT ACT

The main features of the 1974 Consumer Credit Act are:
(a) the creation of a system of licensing of credit businesses;
(b) regulation of the way in which consumer credit business is to be conducted;
(c) the extension of the protection available to consumers who enter into credit agreements.

The Act is mainly a framework on which various regulations and orders are hung dealing in detail with various aspects of consumer credit.

The Office of Fair Trading (formerly the Director General of Fair Trading) is responsible for the administration of the Act and in particular for the handling of the licensing scheme. At the time of preparing the fifth edition, the government is conducting an extensive review of consumer credit legislation, and a draft EU directive has been approved and is also now under consideration. It contains a number of controversial proposals, including one that a 14-day cooling-off period be applied to all consumer credit agreements.

At the time of preparing the fifth edition, the Government has stated that a Consumer Credit Bill is being drafted and will be brought forward when Parliamentary time is available. The major provisions are stated to deal with:

- the reform of the licensing regime to strengthen the 'fitness' test for lenders to hold a consumer credit licence, and strengthen the powers of the Office of Fair Trading;
- the introduction of an 'unfair credit' test to replace the current extortionate credit test;
- the introduction of alternative dispute resolution into consumer credit disputes;
- the removal of the limit of £25,000 on regulated credit agreements with consumers;
- new requirements for clearer information during the currency of the agreement;
- new provisions relating to default.

C AGREEMENTS COVERED BY THE ACT

Any business that relates to the provision of credit under regulated consumer credit agreements will be a consumer credit business so far as the Act is concerned. In general terms a regulated consumer credit agreement is any agreement providing an individual with credit not exceeding £25,000. An individual includes partnerships, one-man businesses and any other unincorporated body. The government has announced[1] its intention to remove the upper limit altogether, so that all consumer credit agreements made with consumers will become regulated. However, it is expected that the exemption from the Act of agreements with limited companies will continue, and agreements with partnerships of over three people will also lose the protection of the Act.

In calculating the amount of credit to see whether the agreement falls within the Act the charge for credit and any deposit taken must be excluded. For example, if a self-employed trader buys a truck for £30,000 which carries a credit charge of £2,000 and pays a deposit of £6,000, with the balance to be financed by equal instalments this would still be a consumer credit agreement. This is because both the deposit and the charge for credit must be deducted from the total price of £30,000 which in this example would bring the total to £22,000 and therefore be within the scope of the Act.

An agreement made before 1 April 1977 will not be a regulated agreement unless it was varied on or after that date.

D LICENSING

Licensing is one of the most important features of the Act and has been described as being its 'teeth'. Because a licence is required before consumer credit business can be undertaken it is an effective way of ensuring that undesirable credit businesses are weeded out.

I Types of licence

The types of licence which may be issued under the Act are:
(a)   standard, and
(b)   group.

Contrary to what one would expect group licences are not for groups of companies but for categories of creditors where the Office of Fair

---

[1]   Statement by Consumer and Competition Minister Gerry Sutcliffe, 22 July 2003.

Trading feels that individual examination as to their fitness is not necessary. For example, solicitors have been issued a group licence through the Law Society.

2 Who needs a licence?

A licence is needed for all the following categories of business:
(a)   consumer credit business;
(b)   consumer hire business;
(c)   credit brokerage;
(d)   debt adjusting and debt counselling;
(e)   debt collection;
(f)   credit reference agency operation.

Whether or not a retailer is going to be considered to be carrying on a business falling within one of these categories will obviously be an important issue. The Act provides that a person is not to be treated as carrying on a particular business merely because he occasionally enters into transactions related to that type of business although a licence will be needed even where a credit business forms only a small part of a retailer's activities. Unfortunately the Act does not define what is 'occasional' but it seems that this is intended to cover the exceptional case where credit is granted outside the normal course of a retailer's business.

The Act provides that a licence must be granted if the applicant satisfies the Office of Fair Trading that:
(a)   he is a fit person to engage in activities covered by the licence; and
(b)   the name or names under which he applies to be licensed are not either misleading or otherwise undesirable.

However, it is up to the applicant to satisfy him that this is so. The Office of Fair Trading can take various matters into account, eg unfair business practices and offences of dishonesty, when deciding whether or not an applicant is a fit person. So, for example, a motor retailer who is convicted of offences under the Trade Descriptions Act relating to the clocking of cars or who persistently sells unsatisfactory vehicles will be at risk of not being granted a licence or of having his existing licence revoked, suspended or varied. It should be noted that it is not necessary for an actual offence or offences to have been committed.

If the Office of Fair Trading has it in mind to refuse, revoke or suspend a licence he must invite the applicant to make representations. An appeal may be made to the Secretary of State.

3 Applications for a standard licence

Applications for a standard licence must be in writing on prescribed forms obtainable from the Office of Fair Trading, Consumer Credit Licensing Bureau, Craven House, 40 Uxbridge Road, Ealing, London, W5 2BS or from local authority trading standards departments. When submitted it must be accompanied by the specified fee. The licence when issued will last for fifteen years unless revoked or suspended.

4 Unlicensed activities

Anyone carrying on an activity which is covered by the licensing provisions of the Act without first obtaining a licence is committing an offence for which the maximum fine on summary conviction is £5,000. If convicted on indictment the maximum penalty is two years' imprisonment or a fine or both. In addition any agreements made by unlicensed credit business are unenforceable unless covered by an order made by the Office of Fair Trading under s 40 of the Act. Agreements made as a result of an introduction by an unlicensed credit broker will also be unenforceable, and finance companies will not normally deal with an unlicensed retailer.

5 Duty to notify changes

The licensee has a duty to inform the OFT of changes affecting them. Failure to do so is a criminal offence. Notifiable events include changes in officers of a licensed or controlling company and changes in control of a licensed company.

6 Licensing and the motor trade

The licensing provisions of the Consumer Credit Act are of great importance to those in the motor trade.

The categories of business for which a motor retailer is likely to find he may need a licence are:

(a)   consumer credit if he lends money, offers credit or gives customers time to pay;

(b)   consumer hire if he wants to let or hire or lease a motor vehicle under transactions which may last more than three months and where the total payments do not exceed £25,000;

(c)   credit brokerage if he introduces customers to a source of credit or hire if the amount involved does not exceed £25,000;

(d)   debt adjusting and debt counselling if he negotiates terms of settlement on existing hire-purchase agreements when vehicles are given in part exchange.

Not only will most motor retailers require a standard licence for at least one of these activities listed in the Act but, as already mentioned, the Office of Fair Trading sees the licensing system as a way of helping to regulate the activities of those businesses that do not meet the standard which the Office of Fair Trading believes that they should in their dealings with consumers. The Director General may refuse to grant a licence if he is not satisfied that the applicant is a fit person and he may refuse to renew a licence for the same reason. The number of cases where the Director General has refused a licence has been increasing steadily over the last year or so and inevitably many of those who have had their licences refused or taken away have been motor retailers.

Reports of the Office of Fair Trading highlight certain activities of the motor trade in connection with the fitness of applicants to hold a Consumer Credit Act licence. Inevitably the problem of clocking cars is mentioned as is the sale of unroadworthy vehicles and vehicles of unmerchantable (or unsatisfactory) quality. In connection with this last category the Director General particularly mentions cases where the cash price of a car bought on credit is not clearly stated; where copies of hire-purchase or credit sale agreements have not been given to the customer; where vehicles are illegally repossessed; and where retailers have not always ensured that customers have clearly understood the nature of the transaction and the extent of their statutory rights.

In February 2003, the Office of Fair Trading underlined for the motor industry the standards that are expected by producing guidelines for motor dealers holding or applying for consumer credit licences, and these make it clear that a wide range of matters can be taken into account, and that retailers are expected to comply not only with the law, but also to refrain from business activities which in the opinion of the Office of Fair Trading are in any way 'deceitful or oppressive'. In addition, motor dealers are expected to comply with the spirit as well as the letter of the guidelines.[2]

E THE TOTAL CHARGE FOR CREDIT

One of the main principles of the Act is that consumers should be made aware of all the costs of credit, stated in terms of a true annual rate, enabling them to compare the cost of borrowing from different lenders and make sensible judgments about relative costs of different types of credit agreement. The Act implements this principle by regulations[3] which prescribe the method of calculation of the amount and rate of the cost of credit and requires this figure, the annual percentage rate (APR), to be disclosed in advertisements, quotations and contract documents.

F CONSUMER CREDIT ADVERTISEMENTS

One of the most important parts of the Act is aimed at ensuring that consumers have full information as to the relative costs of credit that is being offered to them so that they can make the best choice—the so-called 'truth in lending' provisions. The regulations implementing this part of the Act are extremely complicated, but as part of the Government's current review of the Consumer Credit Act new regulations aimed at simplifying the rules have been laid before Parliament and will come into force on 31 October 2004. These regulations also lay down new rules for the calculation of the APR, and provide that where the interest rate for the product varies according to the type of loan an individual borrower's circumstances 66% of borrowers must be reasonably expected to receive either the quoted typical APR or a lower APR.

---

2   OFT Guidelines for Consumer Credit Licence Holders and Applicants in the New and Used Car Markets, February 2003. These are set out in full in Appendix 2.
3   Consumer Credit (Total Charge for Credit) Regulations 1980, SI 1980/51 as amended by SI 1985/1192.

1 Application

The provisions of the Act apply to any advertisement published for the purposes of a business carried on by the advertiser, indicating that he is willing:

(a)   to provide credit; or
(b)   to enter into an agreement for the bailment of goods by him.

'Advertisement' is interpreted very widely: it includes any form of advertisement, eg on television or radio, the internet, displays of notices as well as advertisements contained in newspapers and magazines.

It seems likely that the definition of 'advertiser' means that there may be more than one in relation to a particular advertisement. If a motor trader publishes an advertisement stating that hire-purchase facilities are available from a particular finance company, then both are advertisers.

'Indicating he is willing' means that there must be a specific statement to that effect. Corporate advertising not stating willingness to grant credit is not caught, so that the mere use of a finance company's name or logo is not covered even if it is associated with a sticker displaying the 'cash price'.[4]

A person who causes a credit or hire advertisement to be published has a duty to ensure that the advertisement complies with the requirements of the Regulations.[5]

2 Requirements

Advertisements to which the Act applies:

(a)   must not give false or misleading information[6];
(b)   must not offer to supply goods or services on credit if they are not also available for cash;
(c)   must comply with the Consumer Credit (Advertisements) Regulations 2004.[7] An advertisement can be misleading even though it conforms with the requirements of the Regulations; see for example the case of *R v Baldwins Garage (Warrington) Ltd*[8]. In

---

[4]   *Jenkins v Lombard North Central plc* [1984] 1 All ER 828.
[5]   Regulation 2
[6]   Consumer Credit Act 1974, s 46.
[7]   SI 2004/1484 which came into force on 31 October 2004
[8]   [1988] Crim LR 438.

an advertised example the cash price was calculated on the Manufacturer's List Price without a discount for cash. Had the discounted price been used, the APR would have been 46.8 rather than the advertised 'Up to 20% discount or 4.6% finance (APR 8.9%)'. It was held that the cash price is the price at which a person indicated that he was willing to sell to cash customers which was not in fact the MLP but that price subject to a discount. The dealer had therefore committed an offence.

By contrast, an offence may be committed if the Regulations are not complied with even if the advertisement is not misleading. An offence was committed by an advertisement offering '0% finance or 10% discount'. Even though this was not misleading, it was in breach of the regulation which restricts the use of the words 'interest free' or any words having like effect in any case where credit buyers are paying more than cash buyers.[9]

The three categories of advertisements defined by the previous regulations have been replaced with a general requirement that all credit and hire advertisements shall use plain and intelligible language, be easily legible (or, if the information is given orally, clearly audible) and specify the name of the advertiser.

Credit advertisements which contain no more than contact details, general information about the products on offer, including general statements about the types of loans available will only have to comply with these requirements. In addition some information as listed in the Regulations may also be included in the advertisement without including further detailed information, eg as to the APR, provided that the advertiser does not make any subjective claims about the credit available, eg 'cheapest loans', in which case the typical APR will have to be shown as well. The permissible additional items of information which may be included are listed in Sch 2 to the Regulations:

- the amount of credit which may be provided under a consumer credit agreement, or an indication of the minimum or maximum which may be provided;
- a statement of any requirement to place on deposit any sum of money;

---

[9] *Ford Credit plc v Normand* 1994 SLT 318. For an example of a case where a credit advertisement was found to be misleading because of small print exclusions from the headline price, see *Rover Group Ltd v Sumner* [1995] CCLR 1.

- the cash price of goods which may be financed;
- a statement as to whether any advance payment is required and if so the amount or minimum amount of the payment expressed as a sum of money or a percentage.[10]

In cases where a credit advertisement includes specified key information about the cost of a loan, ie:

- the frequency, amount and number of payments;
- notification of other charges and fees associated with the credit, or
- the total amount payable[11]

then more details will be required to be shown together with this information and with equal prominence. These are:

- the amount of credit
- the amount of any deposit required
- (where appropriate) the cash price of the goods
- any advance payment if required.

In addition, the typical APR must also be shown where any of the key information is shown, or where any other interest rate is included, or where the advertisement suggests that credit is available to those who might have difficulty getting credit, or where favourable reference is made about the credit or nature of the repayments or interest eg 'low interest' or where any incentive is offered to enter into a credit agreement, and in this case must be shown more prominently.[12]

Only one typical APR may be shown in each advertisement, and must always be located with and be more prominent than any of the other types of information listed in Sch 2, and must be at least one and a half times the size of those items. The typical APR must also be more prominent than any other rate of charge, or any of the items listed in Sch 2.

CERTAIN STATEMENTS ARE RESTRICTED

Where the expression 'interest free' or similar are used the total amount payable must not exceed that paid by a cash customer;[13] and see also

---

[10] Sch 2, paras 1–4.
[11] Sch 2, paras 5–7.
[12] Regulation 8.
[13] Regulation 9.

the case of *Metsoja v Norman Pitt & Co Ltd* [14] where the Divisional Court ruled that an advertisement stating '0% APR' is an indication that the debtor is liable to pay no greater amount under a transaction financed by credit than he would be liable to pay as a cash purchaser.

Where the words 'no deposit' or similar are used no advance payments must be required.

The expression 'weekly equivalent' or similar may not be used unless such payments are provided for in the agreement.

G PRE-CONTRACT INFORMATION

The Consumer Credit (Quotations) Regulations 1989[15] have now been revoked, and replaced by a less onerous requirement relating to 'health warnings' where loans are secured on property, or where a loan repayment may be subject to currency fluctuations.[16] Where a customer asks for a quotation for a regular finance agreement, this must be given, but at present the onus is on the individual trader, so long as information given is not misleading.

At the time of preparing the fifth edition, Regulations[17], due to come into force on 31 May 2005, have been laid before Parliament which will require specified information in respect of regulated agreements (except distance contracts – see below) to be disclosed before an agreement is made,

The pre-contract information will mimic the information found at the start of the credit or hire agreement, and will allow the consumer to have a summary of the key features that they can use to help them compare products. This may be estimated information if it is not known at the time of disclosure. The information must be contained in a document headed 'Pre-contract Information' that can be taken away by the consumer and it must be separate from the agreement document, but they may be delivered together to the consumer. There are legibility

[14]   (1989) 153 JP 485, [1989] Crim LR 560.
[15]   SI 1989/1126, revoked by the Consumer Credit (Quotations) (Revocation) Regulations 1997, SI 1997/211.
[16]   Consumer Credit (Content of Quotations) and Consumer Credit (Advertisements) (Amendment) Regulations 1999, SI 1999/2725.
[17]   Consumer Credit (Disclosure of Information) Regulations 2004, SI 2004/1481.

and equal prominence requirements, and the APR may not be more prominent than any other interest rate or other financial information.

Where a credit agreement is concluded with a consumer at a distance, ie as part of an organised process of distance selling and without the parties coming face to face before the contract is concluded, the pre-contract information requirements of the Financial Services (Distance Marketing) Regulations 2004 will apply as from 31 May 2005.[18] For non-regulated agreements, the requirement operates from 31 October 2004. The definition of consumer in this context excludes sole traders, partnerships and unincorporated associations.

H CANVASSING

The soliciting of trade premises of a customer to make a regulated agreement is prohibited. No offence will be committed, however, if the visit was made in response to a prior written request signed by or on behalf of the person making it.

I THE RETAILER AND THE FINANCE COMPANY

Where the retailer sells goods to a finance company to be let on hire purchase the terms of the contract will be governed by the Sale of Goods Act and by any express terms incorporated into the contract. There may be express warranties or representations by the retailer. For example in the information which he sets out in the retailer's offer for sale to the finance company. These may relate to whether he has good title, whether the car is fit for purpose or whether it is of satisfactory quality. If the statement made by the retailer falls short of the term of the contract and is only a misrepresentation the finance company can recover the loss they have suffered but not the loss of profit as a result of being unable to enforce the agreement.[19] It will depend on the facts as to whether a statement made by the retailer is a misrepresentation or a warranty. For example a retailer completed a hire-purchase proposal form and signed a sales note which indicated that he expressly warranted that the statements in the proposal were true. In fact the hirer's address was wrong and when he defaulted and disappeared the finance

---

[18] SI 2004/2095.
[19] *United Motor Finance Co Ltd v Addiston Co Ltd* [1937] 1 All ER 425.

company took action against the retailer. It was held that the retailer's statement was not a mere representation, but was a warranty and therefore part of the contract and he had to pay the finance company.[20] In another case, a trader who misrepresented to the finance company the amount of deposit paid by a customer taking out a hire purchase agreement was found liable to pay all the losses incurred by the finance company when the customer wrongfully disposed of the vehicle.[21]

1 Retailer as agent of the finance company

The Hire Purchase Act 1964 provided that any representations made by the retailer about the goods during the negotiations leading up to the contract were deemed to have been made by him as agent for the finance company. This has been repeated in the Consumer Credit Act. This means that the finance company is liable to the customer for the representations the retailer makes, eg to refund an initial deposit paid to the retailer if the retailer defaults,[22] or for a misrepresentation, eg as to the recorded mileage of a particular vehicle.

2 Recourse agreements

Frequently the finance house will have the right through the terms of his contract with the retailer to look to the retailer for any loss suffered on transactions put through by him. This right will either arise as a general one imposed by a master agreement or in a specific case relating to a particular transaction. In addition, there is a statutory indemnity in relation to liability arising under s 75 of the Consumer Credit Act (see below).

The terms of a recourse agreement will generally take one of two forms. Either there will be an obligation on the part of the retailer to repurchase the goods from the finance house on the occurrence of certain stated events, for example, default by the hirer or loss or damage to the goods before the payment of the hire-purchase price has been completed. The disadvantage for the finance company in having this type of

---

[20]   *Liverpool & County Discount Co Ltd v A D Motor Co (Kilburn) Ltd* [1963] 2 All ER 396.

[21]   *Royscot Trust Ltd v Rogerson* [1991] 2 QB 297, CA.

[22]   *Branwhite v Worcester Works Finance Ltd* [1969] 1 AC 552.

arrangement is that as the term requires repurchase of the goods by the retailer the goods have to be available. This may not be very easy if the vehicle has been lost or destroyed or if it has been fraudulently disposed of by the hirer.

It seems that unnecessary delay on the part of the finance company will prevent them from exercising this type of provision. For example, in *United Dominions Trust (Commercial) Ltd v Eagle Aircraft Services Ltd*,[23] ten months' delay was held to bar the finance company's rights.

Alternatively, the recourse agreement may take the form of a promise by the retailer to indemnify the finance company against loss in the event of default on the part of the hirer. This type of clause means that the finance company is not concerned about what has happened to the goods and may claim from the retailer the amount required to settle the agreement. If the terms of the recourse agreement specifically provide that on payment of the sum due to the finance company the goods are to be transferred to the retailer, failure to do so is a breach of contract. This would be the case even if the goods are not available through no fault of the finance company, for example if they have been destroyed or disposed of fraudulently by the hirer. In this situation the retailer will still be liable but will have a claim for damages for breach of contract which he can set off against the finance company's claim.

Recourse agreements will generally operate as an indemnity rather than a guarantee of the terms of the finance company's agreement with the hirer. This means that the retailer will probably still be liable even if the hire-purchase contract with the consumer is unenforceable for some reason. It will therefore be no answer to a claim on the indemnity that the hire-purchase agreement was illegal provided, of course, that the finance company was not aware of the illegality. This will particularly be so if there has been some bad faith on the retailer's part, for example, where a retailer and a hirer conspired together to insert false figures in the hire-purchase agreement it was held that the hire-purchase agreement was illegal but the sale to the plaintiffs, ie the finance company, was collateral to that agreement and was therefore enforceable. They were entitled to damages.[24]

---

[23]   [1968] 1 All ER 104.
[24]   *Southern Industrial Trust Ltd v Brook House Motors Ltd* (1968) 112 Sol Jo 798.

J WHO IS LIABLE IF THE CAR IS DEFECTIVE?

I Loans

In a contract for the sale of goods which is financed by an arrangement with a finance company, eg a personal loan, the consumer will have the same terms implied in his favour as in 'any other contract' for the sale of goods and these will be enforceable against the retailer.

Since the 1974 Consumer Credit Act, he also has valuable rights against the provider of the loan, if the lender was 'connected', ie had some business agreement with the supplier of the goods.

These arise under s 75 of the Act and provide that the lender is equally responsible with the supplier for any misrepresentation or breach of contract if:

(a)   the cash price of the item being supplied is more than £100 but does not exceed £30,000 (including VAT); and

(b)   the agreement itself is for credit not exceeding £25,000 made to an individual (this includes sole traders, partnerships and un-incorporated bodies); and

(c)   the lender is in the business of granting credit—this means that non-business loans, eg to a friend, are not covered; and

(d)   the loan is made by a connected lender (see above).

Section 75 has been tested in a case brought in Scotland[25] where it was held that the misrepresentation of a retailer over the condition of a used car sold to the consumer enabled him to rescind not only the contract of purchase but also the loan agreement with the finance company.

2 Hire purchase

The hirer will have the same terms implied in his favour as in a contract for the sale of goods, although he does not exercise his option to buy until the end of the period of hiring. Despite this, the owner must have good title to the goods at the moment of delivery not at the time when the option to purchase arises.

In a hire-purchase transaction the motor retailer is not in a contractual relationship with the customer. The finance house will be directly

[25]   *United Dominions Trust v Taylor* 1980 SLT 28.

responsible to the consumer for the quality of the goods supplied by virtue of the provisions of the Supply of Goods (Implied Terms) Act as amended. This responsibility is almost identical to that of the retailer except that so far as the implied condition of fitness for purpose is concerned, it is sufficient for the consumer to make that purpose known to the retailer rather than to the finance house.

Although the motor retailer, when goods are supplied on hire purchase, will not have a contract with the consumer, he may still be liable for a misrepresentation on the basis of a collateral contract the consideration for which is the consumer entering into the main contract with the finance house.[26] The finance house will also be responsible for the retailer's misrepresentation, because s 56 of the Consumer Credit Act makes the retailer in a hire-purchase transaction an agent of the finance house, so that any misrepresentation on its part, including a misrepresentation, for example in an advertisement, is attributable to the finance house. By virtue of the same section, finance houses are also liable for the retailer's fraud, for example where a retailer has misappropriated a deposit. The effect of s 56 is that the finance house will be bound by whatever the retailer says in the course of negotiations so if, for example, a retailer states during negotiations that a car has travelled only 10,000 miles when in fact it has done 40,000, this statement will be a representation which will involve the finance house in liability.

It should be noted that the finance house will generally have in turn a right of redress against the retailer under the terms of a recourse agreement.

K PAYMENT BY CREDIT CARD

Payment by credit card has become increasingly common, particularly for items such as petrol, servicing and repair. The use of credit cards and the relationship between the cardholder and the issuing company is subject to the Consumer Credit Act, but until recently there was no clear law on the effect of a payment by credit card on the consumer's obligation to pay for the goods or services being purchased. Does the signing of the credit card voucher mean that the buyer's obligations to pay are then discharged? This question will normally be a hypothetical one, as the credit card company will pay the seller without any problems

---

[26]   *Andrews v Hopkinson* [1957] 1 QB 229, [1956] 3 All ER 422.

arising. However, this point became crucial in a case involving Charge Card Services Ltd, a company promoted by the RMIF (formally the Motor Agents Association) and the Scottish Motor Traders' Association to operate a charge card scheme known as the Motor Agents Association Fuel Card Scheme. In this case, the charge card company became insolvent and it was held that the unpaid supplier was not entitled to call on the cardholder to pay him direct. The cardholder's signature on the voucher discharged his obligations to pay.[27]

---

[27]   *Re Charge Card Services Ltd* [1986] BCLC 316.

CHAPTER 9

Credit agreements

A TYPES OF CREDIT AGREEMENT

The types of credit agreement likely to be used for the purchase of motor vehicles are the following:

I Loans

These may be made by a finance company which the retailer has introduced to the customer or may be the result of a private agreement between the customer and his bank or other source of finance. In this situation so far as the retailer is concerned he is making a sale of the goods for cash. The usual Sale of Goods Act terms would be implied into the contract as to title, satisfactory quality, fitness for purpose, and meeting any description applied to them (see Chapter 7, above). The Consumer Credit Act 1974 makes an important distinction between loans made by a 'connected' lender, eg a finance company introduced by the retailer, and other loans made by an 'unconnected' source. From the customer's point of view, this distinction gives him important additional protection where he has a loan from a connected lender and the goods prove to be defective. This was dealt with in more detail in the previous chapter.

2 Credit sale

This is similar to the above, as the legal ownership of the goods is transferred immediately to the buyer, although payment of the purchase price is made by five or more instalments. The repayment of the money is not secured by the goods that are being sold.

3 Hire-purchase agreements

This is an agreement for the hire of goods generally from a finance company to whom the retailer has sold them although it may also be from the retailer himself. The customer is given an option to purchase goods at the end of the hiring period. If the retailer himself is offering hire-purchase terms then he will remain the seller of the goods for the purposes of the Sale of Goods Act legislation. If the finance is provided by a finance company then they will become the owners of the goods and will enter into the contract direct with the consumer.

4 Conditional sale agreements

This is an agreement for the sale of goods where the passing of full legal ownership to the buyer is delayed until payment of the price or performance of some other condition. Again this type of contract may be offered by the retailer himself or he may introduce a finance company.

The Consumer Credit Act applies to the form of all regulated consumer credit and consumer hire agreements and is fundamental to the 'truth in lending' concept and to giving the consumer adequate opportunity to withdraw from the contract if he has second thoughts.

B THE FORM OF THE REGULATED AGREEMENT

An agreement caught by the Act will not be enforceable against the hirer or buyer unless the agreement is properly executed. This means it must be:
(a)   signed by the hirer or buyer and by or on behalf of all the other parties to the agreement; and
(b)   the requirements of the Act as to formalities, form and content of the agreement are complied with.[1]

---
[1]   Consumer Credit Act 1974, s 60.

I Requirements of the Act

Signature

The agreement must be signed by the hirer or buyer personally even if it is signed on behalf of the other parties by an authorised agent. The signature has to be placed on the agreement in the signature box which includes words drawing the attention of the consumer to the nature of the transaction, eg 'This is a hire purchase agreement regulated by the Consumer Credit Act 1974. Sign it only if you want to be legally bound by its terms.'

Below the space for the hirer's signature it must state: 'The goods will not become your property until you have made all the payments. You must not sell them before then.'

Content

The agreement must contain the information prescribed in the Regulations.[2] This is briefly:

(a) a descriptive heading showing the nature of the agreement, eg Hire Purchase Agreement regulated by the Consumer Credit Act 1974;

(b) the name and address of each party to the agreement;

(c) financial details;

(d) other information about the terms of agreement, eg the description of the goods, provisions for payments, cancellation rights if applicable etc; and

(e) statements about the protection of the consumer and remedies available under the 1974 Act.

The information required in each case will vary according to the type of agreement. Following the Government's recent review of the Consumer Credit Act, amendments to the present Regulations have been laid before Parliament introducing changes which will apply to all agreements entered into on or after 31 May 2005.[3] These include additional measures affecting legibility and the prominence and layout of information in the agreement, further information to be given about the term of the agreement and the total charge for credit, payment allocation,

---

[2] Consumer Credit (Agreement) Regulations 1983, SI 1983/1553 amended by SI 1984/1600 and SI 1988/2047.

[3] Consumer Credit (Agreements) (Amendment) Regulations 2004, SI 2004/1482.

charges, and examples of early settlement figures. In addition, there will be a requirement for a separate consent indicator to be completed by the debtor where he is also purchasing an optional contract of insurance which will be finance by the main or subsidiary credit agreement. In addition, where there are no cancellation rights in an agreement, this fact will have to be stated.

Legibility

The lettering of the agreement must be easily legible, and of a colour easily distinguished from the colour of the paper. All the provisions must be shown together, and the annual percentage rate (APR) must be given the same prominence as the cash price or any other rate quoted.

Copies

The Act requires various copies of the agreement to be supplied to the hirer or buyer. The copies that are required depend on when the agreement is to be 'executed', ie signed not only by the consumer but also by the owner or creditor.

Where the agreement is unexecuted, the creditor or owner must supply the debtor or hirer with a copy of the unexecuted agreement and any other documents referred to in it must be given to him, either on the spot if it is presented to him personally for signature, or where it is sent to him for signature, within seven days.

2 Failure to comply

Failure to comply with the provisions regarding signature, contents of the agreement and other formalities required by the legislation will mean that the agreement will be treated as 'improperly executed'. The effect of this will be that the agreement will be unenforceable unless the court makes an enforcement order.

This principle has recently caused some difficulties to the accident car hire business, most notably following the decision of the House of Lords in *Dimond v Lovell*.[4] This is dealt with in more detail in Chapter 12.

---

[4]   [2002] 1 AC 384, [2000] 2 All ER 897.

3 Duty to supply information

The debtor under a regulated agreement is entitled to request certain information from the creditor provided the request is in writing and the prescribed fee is paid. There are restrictions on the frequency of such requests.

The creditor must respond within twelve days giving details of the transaction including the money still owing.

The creditor under a regulated agreement is entitled to information as to the whereabouts of the goods. This must be supplied by the debtor within seven days of receiving the request.

4 Rights to withdraw or cancel

Withdrawal

In accordance with his common law rights, the customer may withdraw from the finance transaction at any time before his 'offer' to the finance company has been accepted. Where the prospective agreement is a regulated one, the customer's rights are confirmed by the Consumer Credit Act.[5] His withdrawal may be at any time before acceptance, and in effect also before execution of the agreement by the finance company, as the regulated agreement will not come into force until it has been executed. No special form of words is required, and the withdrawal may be made orally or in writing, and may be communicated not only to the finance company but also the retailer who has acted as credit broker, and anyone else acting as an agent for the customer. Once the customer has withdrawn, he will have the same rights as if the agreement were cancellable (see below). This will include the cancellation of any 'linked transaction' (eg the contract with the retailer), and the customer will be entitled to recover any money paid, such as a deposit.

Cancellation

The right to cancel a regulated consumer credit agreement is comparable with, although not identical to, the old 'cooling off' period permitted under the hire-purchase legislation.

---

5   Section 57, which came into force on 19 May 1985.

The right to cancel will not apply in a number of instances if, for example:

(a)   the debtor signed the agreement at trade premises at which business is carried on by the creditor, owner of the goods, or any party to a linked transaction or negotiator; and

(b)   there were no oral representations made to the consumer in his presence.

The time limit for cancellation is laid down in the Act and will start to run when the agreement is signed by the debtor or hirer. If, as is the normal case, the agreement is not concluded by the debtor's signature, the creditor or owner must send a copy of the executed agreement containing a notice of cancellation rights, and the debtor or hirer then has until the end of the fifth day following receipt within which to serve notice of cancellation. If the debtor's signature concludes the agreement, he must be sent a separate notice of cancellation by post, and will again have five days within which to cancel.

Effect of cancellation

On service of notice of cancellation, the debtor is entitled to repayment of any sums paid (eg the deposit) and recovery of any goods given in part exchange, and, until this has been done, the debtor has a lien on the goods received by him under the cancelled agreement.

If the part exchanged goods are not returned within 10 days, the debtor is entitled to recover a sum equal to the part exchange allowance.

Cancellation of distance sale contracts

From 31 October 2004, all credit agreements concluded at a distance with consumers will be subject to a cancellation period of 14 days from the date the contract was concluded. There will also be a requirement that consumers are made aware that they have this right.[6]

5 Early settlement and termination

Any time before the final payment falls due the debtor or hirer may give notice that he wishes to discharge his obligations under the agreement.

---

[6]   The Financial Services (Distance Marketing) Regulations 2004, SI 2004/2095.

When he does this he must pay the sums due under the agreement less any rebate allowed under s 95 of the Act.[7] The debtor also has a right to find out, on making a written request, what figure he needs to pay in order to settle early.

In addition to the rights to settle early, the debtor has the right to terminate the agreement before the final payment becomes due. If the agreement contains an acceleration clause this effectively restricts the debtor's rights however. For example, in *Wadham Stringer Finance Ltd v Meaney*,[8] an accelerated payment clause was held to be valid, which meant that the buyer under a conditional sale agreement was held liable to pay all the payments due under an agreement which she terminated having only paid the initial deposit.

If a debtor has paid at least 50% of the total due under a hire purchase or credit sale contract, he is permitted to hand back the goods and have no further liability in respect of the outstanding balance.[9]

6 Restrictions on enforcement

The Act places restrictions on the rights of the creditor to enforce the contractual terms of a credit agreement. For example, seven days' notice is needed before action can be taken except where there is a breach of the agreement, to:

(a)   demand earlier payment;

(b)   recover possession of goods;

treat any rights of the debtor as terminated, restricted or deferred. The form of notice required and of the notice to be given in case of default must be in the prescribed form.[10] In the case of a regulated hire purchase or conditional sale agreement, the goods will become 'protected' goods once the debtor has paid one third or more of the total price of the goods, and not only must notice be given, but court action will also be needed to recover possession of the goods.

---

[7]   Consumer Credit (Rebate on Early Settlement) Regulations 1983, SI 1983/1562.

[8]   [1980] 3 All ER 789.

[9]   Consumer Credit Act 1974, ss 99–100. At the time of preparing the fifth edition, the Government has published a consultation on Voluntary Termination of Hire Purchase and Conditional Sale Agreements URN 04/1557

[10]   Consumer Credit (Enforcement, Default and Termination Notices) Regulations 1983, SI 1983/1561.

C TERMS CONTROL

In common with many other categories of goods up until 1982, where a new or secondhand motor vehicle which came within certain specified definitions was sold under a hire-purchase, conditional sale, or credit sale agreement, legislation as to the period of the agreement and the minimum deposit to be paid applied. This was under an entirely separate piece of legislation[11] which operated quite independently from the Hire Purchase and Consumer Credit Acts. These controls have now been abolished.[12]

---

[11]   Emergency Laws (Re-enactments and Repeals) Act 1964.
[12]   Control of Hiring Hire Purchase and Credit Sale Agreements (Revocation) Order 1982, SI 1982/1034.

CHAPTER 10

The manufacturer's responsibility

As we have already seen, the motor retailer in common with all other retailers of goods, has to accept liability for the quality of the goods he sells: they have to be of satisfactory quality, fit for purpose and in accordance with any description applied to them, and also fulfil any express terms of the sale contract, or he will find himself faced with claims from the customer for damages for breach of contract.

He cannot use as a defence the fact that a faulty car was due to a mistake made at the factory, nor that he was completely unaware that it was defective.

That this should be so may seem unfair to the retailer—it apparently also comes as a surprise to the consumer. Various surveys have shown that a large proportion of consumers mistakenly believe that it is the manufacturer who is liable in law to compensate them for any loss or damage caused by faulty goods.

The fact that this cannot be so as the law stands at present is because of the rules relating to 'privity' of contract. This means in effect, that a contract can only be enforced by the parties to it. Because the contract for the sale of a motor car to a consumer is with the retailer, the consumer cannot sue the manufacturer direct if the car is satisfactory—there is no contract between them.

However, the manufacturer does not escape entirely without liability for the quality of the goods he puts on the market. He may be liable:
(a)   to the retailer under the contract of sale to him;
(b)   to the consumer if he was negligent in some way;

(c)   to the consumer if he fails to comply with the terms of a warranty or guarantee which he offers.

A THE MANUFACTURER'S LIABILITY TO THE RETAILER

The manufacturer who supplies motor vehicles to his franchised dealers is entering into a contract for the sale of goods which will be subject to the same implied terms of satisfactory quality, fitness for purpose and compliance with description as the dealer contracts with his customers.

The dealer will therefore have a valid claim against the manufacturer for a vehicle which is unsatisfactory or which breaks one of the other express or implied terms of the contract. His damage from the breach of contract will be the compensation he has had to pay the retail customer, and so the claim is passed back down the line.

In practice, if legal action has been brought, the dealer will probably be advised by his solicitor to join his supplier in the action as a 'third party'—all the claims will then be heard together.

I Exclusions of liability

As we have seen, the retailer is not able to exclude his liabilities under the Sale of Goods Act to supply goods which are satisfactory, fit for purpose and meeting the description applied to them, when he is selling to anyone buying as a 'consumer'. When he sells to someone buying in the course of a business, any exclusion clause will be subject to a 'reasonableness' test (see Chapter 7), and the retailer is in a similar position so far as his supplier is concerned. Whether he buys direct from the manufacturer or from a wholesaler, or another dealer, he is buying in the course of a business.

The terms of the contract, eg a dealership agreement, may well contain a clause which seeks to limit or reduce altogether the liability of the supplier for the quality of the goods. This type of clause will be subject to the test of reasonableness set out in the Unfair Contract Terms Act. In other words, in any dispute the court will look at the terms of the contract, and the surrounding circumstances, and decide whether in those circumstances it is reasonable for the seller to rely on an exclusion clause.

The Act sets out guidelines as to the 'reasonableness' test.[1] These are:

(a)   the relative bargaining strengths of the parties and any available alternative sources of supply;

(b)   any inducement received by the buyer to accept a contract in those terms, and whether he had the opportunity to buy similar goods elsewhere without accepting the clause;

(c)   whether the buyer knew or ought to have known about the term;

(d)   where the clause excludes or restricts liability if a particular condition is not complied with, whether it was reasonable at the time of the contract to expect that compliance with that condition would be practicable, eg if an exclusion is to operate if the dealer fails to carry out a PDI check;

(e)   whether the goods were manufactured, processed or adapted to the special order of the customer.

There have so far been no reported cases on the 'reasonableness' test when applied to vehicle manufacturer's agreements with their dealers in relation to quality issues. In some cases where such agreements contain exclusion clauses the manufacturers have indicated that they would not seek to rely on them in any dispute.

It seems reasonable to suppose, applying the guidelines above, that the courts would not be very sympathetic to a manufacturer who tried to use an exclusion clause in a situation where a dealer was liable to a customer for defects in a car. It is possible that the situation might be different if, for example, the dealer had contributed to his loss, for example, by failing to comply with the terms of his dealer agreement requiring him to carry out a pre-delivery check of the vehicle, and it is shown that the pre-delivery check would have revealed the fault.

B THE MANUFACTURER'S LIABILITY TO THE CUSTOMER

I Negligence

The rule is that where in a particular set of circumstances it can be seen that there is a duty of care owed by one person to another, then the breach of that duty of care which causes damage to another person will give rise to a claim for damages.

---

[1]   Unfair Contract Terms Act 1977, Sch 2.

This principle was established in a case which was decided by the House of Lords in 1932, *Donoghue v Stevenson*.[2] The facts of the case were that Mrs Donaghue visited a cafe in Paisley with a friend who had purchased a bottle of ginger beer for her. After drinking some of it Mrs Donaghue had discovered a decomposing snail in the bottle which she had not previously seen because of the opacity of the glass bottle. Not surprisingly, she became ill. She claimed damages from Mr Stevenson who was the manufacturer of the ginger beer in question on the basis that he had injured her by his negligence in putting his product on the market which was likely to cause harm.

As we have already seen, she could not sue the manufacturer for breach of contract because she had no contract with him; the contract of sale was with the retailer. The question was whether the manufacturer of a product owed any duty of care to the ultimate consumer.

The House of Lords ruled that there is a duty to take reasonable care to avoid acts or omissions which you can reasonably foresee will be likely to injure your 'neighbour'. Your 'neighbour' in this context is anyone who should reasonably have been in your mind as being likely to be affected as a result of your actions.

This principle means that the manufacturer of any product is today liable for injury or physical damage caused by defects in his products provided that certain requirements are met:

(a)   that the defect in the product is one that may result in injury to the consumer's life or property;

(b)   that the defect existed at the time the manufacturer parted with possession of it;

(c)   the defect must not be one that the manufacturer could have reasonably expected the consumer or some third party to notice and correct before it could do harm; and

(d)   the existence of the defect must be attributable to lack of reasonable care on the part of the manufacturer.

This last point gives rise to a lot of difficulties as far as consumers are concerned because it means that if a manufacturer can show that he has exercised a standard of reasonable care the consumer will not be able to recover damages even though he has been injured by some defect in the product. For example, in the case of *Daniels v White Ltd and Tarbard*[3]

---

[2]   [1932] AC 562, [1932] All ER Rep 1, HL.
[3]   [1938] 4 All ER 258.

two consumers were injured when they drank lemonade contaminated by acid. The purchaser of the lemonade was able to recover damages from the seller because of the breach of the implied terms of fitness for purpose and merchantable quality, but the other who was not a party to the contract had to take action against the manufacturer. The manufacturer successfully pleaded that since he had taken reasonable steps to stop the lemonade bottles being contaminated, he had not been negligent. The second consumer was therefore not able to obtain compensation. This case has been much criticised and it is very likely that if it were to be heard today the result would go the other way, but nevertheless, it does illustrate the difficulties that can face the consumer who has to try to prove negligence by a manufacturer. Another problem may be to prove who has been negligent.

For example, a consumer bought a car with a Triplex toughened safety glass screen. About a year after purchase for no apparent reason the screen shattered injuring the occupants. It was held that the consumer had not proved that the screen broke due to negligence on the part of the component manufacturer. Its breaking may have been due to a strain imposed in the fitting of the windscreen rather than a defect in its manufacture.[4]

Modern motor industry cases

More recent cases involving motor vehicles suggest that the courts are actually quite ready to find that manufacturers have been negligent. In *Walton v British Leyland UK Ltd*,[5] the plaintiffs were passengers in an Austin Allegro car which was involved in an accident because the rear nearside wheel came off while the car was travelling on the M1 at 50–60 mph. The plaintiffs brought an action against not only British Leyland over the alleged defective design of the Allegro but also against the selling dealer and against the dealer who had carried out certain repair and servicing work on the car since it had been purchased. It was held that British Leyland had been negligent because when they had identified that there was a problem with the stub axle of the car they had chosen to issue service bulletins to their dealers warning them of the possible dangers rather than to recall the cars which were affected. British Leyland had to pay the whole of the damages

4   *Evans v Triplex Safety Glass Co Ltd* [1936] 1 All ER 283.
5   [1980] Product Liability International 156.

being claimed by the plaintiffs and the two dealerships involved who had carried out work on the car were exonerated from any blame (on the subject of recalls see also Chapter 12).

It is generally alleged that this type of claim against the manufacturer is fairly rare as it is very difficult for a consumer to prove negligence because he will not normally have access to the type of technical information that is required. It is obviously difficult to assess how many cases are dropped for this sort of reason. However, as the *Walton* case shows it is not unheard of, and in another case[6] it was held that the manufacturers of a trailer-towing coupling which was advertised as foolproof and needing no maintenance, were liable for negligence when the coupling failed causing a serious accident. It was found that the design of the coupling was such that it was potentially defective. The facts of the case were: a trailer towing coupling was advertised as 'foolproof' and needing no maintenance. It was supplied by retailers who fitted it to a Land Rover they were selling to a customer. After fitting the coupling was damaged due to a defect in design. The retailers subsequently serviced and repaired the vehicle but did not attend to the coupling or warn the customer about its condition, and the owner continued to use it in that state.

The coupling failed and caused a serious accident. It was held that the manufacturers were liable as to 75 per cent of the claim because of the faulty design and the owner 25 per cent because he continued to use the vehicle with the defective coupling fitted to it. The retailer was in turn held by the Court of Appeal to be liable to the owner under the contract of sale, and had to indemnify him in respect of the 25 per cent. This was later overturned by the House of Lords. It is particularly relevant to note in passing that the retailer of the part who had to indemnify the owner, was himself unable to pass on liability to his supplier as he was not able to identify him.

In December 1986, the Court of Appeal held in *Winward v TVR Engineering Ltd,* that the defendants, who were manufacturers of specialist motor cars, were liable in negligence for the failure of a ferrule in a carburettor which caused a fire. The engine incorporating the carburettor had been supplied to them by the Ford Motor Company, who in turn had bought the carburettor from a third party. The court decided that TVR's failure to spot the potential problem in design of the carbu-

---

6   *Lambert v Lewis* [1982] AC 225, 268, [1981] 1 All ER 1185, HL.

rettor amounted to negligence. This decision appears to take the concept of negligence very close to strict liability, now introduced in the UK as a result of an EC Directive.

In *Carroll v Fearon*,[7] the Court of Appeal held that it was not necessary in order to prove that a manufacturer had been negligent to show that any individual or group of workers had been negligent. It had been proved that a tyre had disintegrated because of an identified fault in manufacture, and that if the manufacturing process had worked as intended the fault would not have been present. The manufacturer, Dunlop, could provide no explanation for this, and were therefore liable in negligence.

2 Strict liability

Under the terms of the EC Directive on Liability for Defective Products, the UK had to introduce the concept of manufacturers' strict liability for defects in products by July 1988. The legislation to do this is contained in Part I of the Consumer Protection Act 1987 which came into force on 1 March 1988.

This Act created a completely new framework for compensating consumers who have been injured by defective products and a new set of rules have to be applied.

First of all the Act states that a producer will be liable for a defect in any of his products which cause death or injury, or damage to private property other than the defective product itself so long as the claim exceeds £275.

Thus negligence will not be an issue. The claimant has to prove only the defect and the damage and the fact that the second was caused by the first.

What is a 'defect'?

The Act states that a product is to be considered defective if the safety of the product is not such as 'persons' generally are entitled to expect. In trying to apply this very nebulous concept, the Act sets out factors

---

7   [1999] PIQR P416 (1998) Times, 26 January, CA.

which should be taken into account, for example the way in which a product is marketed, and any accompanying instructions or warnings; reasonable uses of the product: and the time the product was supplied by the producer rather than the actual date of manufacture which may have been much earlier.

It is interesting to note that in the USA, the courts have frequently taken the view that the way a product is marketed and the extent of any instructions and warnings has a key role to play in creating the consumer's expectations of the product and the issue of establishing what amounts to reasonable use. It seems producers will be well advised to consider consumer expectations when preparing advertising and promotional material, and alert to identify and warn against possible misuse of the product. The British courts have already shown their willingness in a case brought under the law of negligence to rule against a manufacturer who failed to foresee possible unusual uses of their product, where a packing case manufacturer should have foreseen the likelihood of people using the case to stand on, and was consequently liable when the plaintiff was injured when the case he was standing on gave way.[8]

Period of liability

The Act does not create indefinite liability. The injured consumer must bring an action within three years of the date on which he became aware of his right to bring such an action and, in addition, there is a ten year cut off for liability from the date of supply of the product, although there is still the possibility that after that time a consumer could sue the producer in negligence for damages arising from a hidden defect. The Act is not retrospective and so products supplied before 1 March 1988 are not subject to strict liability. In the unreported case of *Relph v Yamaha Motor Company Ltd*,[9] a claim under the Act for injuries caused by alleged defects in an All-Terrain Vehicle imported into the UK in May or June 1988, but which left the only 'producer' in 1985, it was held that the Act did not apply.

[8]   *Hill v James Crowe (Cases) Ltd* [1978] 1 All ER 812.

[9]   *Relph v Yamaha Motor Co Ltd, Yamaha Motor Co USA and Burtonwood Development Ltd* (4 July 1996, unreported), QBD. An alternative claim in negligence also failed because the claimant had failed to follow instructions and warnings.

Level of liability

There is no overall ceiling on the producers' liability for damages, so it will be up to individual manufacturers to decide what level of insurance they wish to take out.

What is a product?

The definition is drawn very widely so that it can include components in a finished product, items in kit form for assembly by the consumer or someone else, and also raw materials and processed raw materials, as the processing may itself have given rise to a defect.

Who is to be liable?

Many products will comprise components and raw materials supplied by a variety of manufacturers or 'producers'. Liability is imposed throughout the supply chain to include both the supplier of raw materials and the manufacturers of a defective component and the finished product may be liable, as may the importer into the EC. In addition, anyone representing himself as the producer by putting his own trade name or mark on the goods, and the retailer will be liable unless they can identify their own source of supply within a reasonable time of being asked to do so. Although the Act will not allow the use of exclusions from liability so far as consumers are concerned, it does not affect the terms of the contracts between producers. It will therefore be important for indemnity provisions in contracts to be looked at very closely in the context of product liability.

The Act provides (s 2(5)) that where two or more people are liable for damage covered by the Act, then liability will be joint and several. This means that all or any of the producers can be sued for the whole of the damage. The obvious tendency will be for claimants to pursue the producer who appears best able to meet the claim.

Defences

Although the Act is described as introducing 'strict' liability, there will in fact be some defences available to the producer. He will be able to avoid liability if he can show the defect in the product was due to compliance with a regulation, or if the product was not supplied by him or not supplied in the course of a business, or that it was not defective at the time of supply. A further, crucially important, defence for component producers will be to show that the defect in his product was due to a defect in the design of the final product or in specifications given by its manufacturer. Finally, the 'development risk' shows that the state of technical knowledge in the relevant product areas was such that the defect could not have been discovered at the time the product was produced. Although a great deal of fuss has been made about the inclusion of this defence, it seems very unlikely that it could be successfully used very often.

It should be noted that although the Act does not cover goods supplied other than in the course of a business this does not exclude liability for goods given away (for example as promotional items) which underlines the need to ensure that adequate records are kept of the supplier.

The Directive permits a defence where the producer shows that the state of scientific or technical knowledge 'was not such as to enable the existence of the defect to be discovered'. The Act relieves the producer of liability if scientific or technical knowledge at the relevant time was such that 'a producer of products of the same description as the product in question' could not have been expected to discover the defect.

The Act's wording appears to be materially more favourable to producers than the Directive's which should prevail in any court proceedings.

Another way in which the producer's liability may be reduced will be if the damage to the consumer was caused by his own fault as well as the defect in the product. This provision highlights the need for clear warnings and instructions to be given with products.

At the time of writing there appear to have been very few reported cases under Part I of the Act, and none affecting the motor industry. It therefore seems reasonable to assume that any claims that do arise are being settled. A report by the National Consumer Council in 1995[10] highlighted the fact that the legislation appears to be under-used, and identified a number of factors which may be relevant including funding problems, lack of awareness of the legislation, and insurers making

---

[10]   Unsafe Products—How the Consumer Protection Act works for Consumers' National Consumer Council PD 45/D4/95.

secrecy a condition of settlement. The NCC reports anecdotal evidence of a few relevant cases including: inadequate wing mirrors on a truck; lap set belts; a glass panel in a caravan; and bicycle wheels

3 The manufacturer's warranty

Manufacturers' warranties used to come in for a great deal of justifiable criticism from the consumer lobby.

All too often, impressive gothic script and legal jargon was used to conceal the fact that, far from giving the consumer anything, the warranty actually took away what rights he already had under the Sale of Goods Act, and left him with no or greatly reduced redress if anything went wrong.

These days, that is all a thing of the past. A manufacturer's warranty now cannot:

(a)   affect the consumer's right of redress against the retailer under the Sale of Goods Act for breach of any of the implied terms; or

(b)   exclude the manufacturer's liability for death or injury arising from his negligence.

In other words, it can only add to the consumer's rights and cannot be drafted in such a way that it takes anything away. In the case of *Rogers v Parish of Scarborough* (see Chapter 7), the Court of Appeal rejected an argument that the vehicle was not made unmerchantable by defects which he could have put right free of charge under the manufacturer's warranty, on the basis that the warranty could only add to the buyer's rights, and could not substitute for them—it lasts only for a limited period and does not compensate the buyer for loss and inconvenience.

The legal status of a manufacturer's warranty

As we have already seen, the manufacturer is not a party to the contract of sale with the consumer and the consumer's right of redress under the contract of sale is always against the retailer.

Historically, there has always been some debate as to the extent to which a manufacturer's warranty or guarantee might be legally enforceable by the end consumer. For example, it has been argued that there is a 'collateral' contract when the manufacturer offers the consumer a guarantee with his product, with the consideration for which is the sale contract with the dealer. This would mean that a manufacturer would probably be held to be liable on the specific promises in his warranty and failure to comply with its terms would entitle the consumer to bring a legal action against him, and effectively takes on the liability under the Sale of Goods Act to supply goods which are of satisfactory quality and fit for purpose. It has been held,[11] for example, that the importer of a car whose warranty guaranteed that the car was of 'faultless material and workmanship' was liable directly for defects in the vehicle. In other words there was an express warranty that the car was of faultless material and workmanship and when it obviously fell short of that description, the importers were directly liable to the consumer for breach of that warranty.

In other cases it was easier to argue the existence of a direct contract. For example, where the consumer paid the manufacturer for additional warranty benefits, for example an extra twelve months cover, it seemed that a binding contract could easily be established.[12] Now however, as a result of the implementation of the European Directive on Consumer Guarantees and Related Rights[13] and implemented in the UK by the Sale and Supply of Goods to Consumers Regulations, where a free guarantee or warranty is offered to a consumer, this will become legally enforceable as if it were a contract with the guarantor coming into effect at the time the goods are delivered. If the guarantor is the vehicle manufacturer, then this opens up another possible course of action for the dissatisfied consumer who will be able to sue the manufacturer direct if, for example, a vehicle has not been rectified in accordance with the terms of the warranty. Presumably in such a case the remedies available to the consumer would be those set out in the Regulations. For non-consumers, the previous legal position is not changed.[14]

---

[11] *Ward & Armistead Ltd v Bridgland Anca Garage (Worthing) Ltd* (1976) unreported, QBD.

[12] For a recent case where it was held that a contract arose between a consumer and the provider of a 'guarantee' based on a notice displayed on the premises of a tour operator, see *Bowerman v Association of British Travel Agents Ltd* (1995) Times, 24 November, CA.

[13] 1999/44/EC.

[14] The Sale and Supply of Goods to Consumers Regulations 2002, SI 2002/3045.

Contents of a manufacturer's warranty

What may be said in a manufacturer's warranty is affected by:

(a) legislation, ie the Unfair Contract Terms Act 1977 and the Consumer Transactions (Restrictions on Statements) Order 1976,[15] as amended, and the Sale and Supply of Goods to Consumers Regulations 2002.

(b) relevant industry codes of practice;

(c) recommendations produced by the Office of Fair Trading.

Legislation

The effect of legislation on the content of the warranty may be summed up as follows:

(a) the manufacturer may not use a term in his warranty to exclude his liability for loss or damage whilst in consumer use arising from a defect caused by his negligence[16] or death or injury resulting from negligence;[17]

(b) the manufacturer may not use a clause which limits or excludes the customer's rights against the retailer if the goods turn out to be defective. It is also a criminal offence to have such an exclusion in a warranty or guarantee;[18]

(c) the manufacturer must include a statement in his warranty or guarantee that it does not alter any of the customer rights against the retailer.[19] The motor industry abounds with examples of exclusions from warranties: tyres and windscreens on new cars; cars used for rallying; accessories used outside the UK; consumers having to pay the cost of transporting a product back to the manufacturer. The extent to which these provisions are affected by the Unfair Contract Terms Act is unclear. If the warranty is, as has already been discussed, a form of contract between the manufacturer and the customer, it is subject to the Unfair Contract Terms Act. It is not a contract for the sale of goods, and would therefore seem to be caught by s 3 of the Act which applies to situations where one of the contracting parties

---

15 SI 1976/1813, as amended by SI 1978/127.
16 Unfair Contract Terms Act 1977, s 5(1).
17 Unfair Contract Terms Act 1977, s 2.
18 Unfair Contract Terms Act 1977, s 2.
19 Unfair Contract Terms Act 1977, s 2.

deals as a consumer or on the other's written standard terms of business. It provides that any clause which seeks to limit or exclude liability for breach of contract, or which provides for one party to provide substantially less than what was reasonably expected of him, or to do nothing at all, will be subject to a reasonableness test.

In practice of course the consumer can ignore the warranty if he gets into difficulties of this sort, and press his claim with the retailer under the Sale of Goods Act.

(d) In addition, from 31 March 2003 the following rules will apply to free guarantees given to consumers (individuals buying goods for purposes outside their trade profession or business)[20]:

 (i) the terms of a consumer guarantee will be those set out in the guarantee and any associated advertising;

 (ii) the consumer guarantee must set out in plain intelligible language the contents of the guarantee and the essential particulars necessary for making claims under the guarantee, notably the duration and territorial scope of the guarantee as well as the name and address of the guarantor.

 (iii) the consumer guarantee must be made available to the consumer in writing or other durable form on request;

 (iv) where consumer goods are offered with a guarantee in the UK, the guarantee must be written in English.

The codes of practice

In addition to this control by statute of the contents of warranties, the New Car Code also makes various promises to the consumer about new car warranties, for example :

'3.1 You will continue to benefit from the manufacturer's new car warranty whilst the car is serviced to the manufacturer's recommendations, even if this service is carried out by an independent service/repair outlet.

3.4 Where repair work is required under the new car warranty it may be carried out by any dealer in the manufacturer's network anywhere in Europe.

---

[20] Sale and Supply of Goods to Consumers Regulations 2002, SI 2002/3045.

3.5   The transfer of the unexpired portion of any new car warranty to a subsequent owner is permitted.

3.6   In the event that your car is off the road for an extended period for rectification of warranty faults, we will consider extension of the warranty period'.

From the legal point of view it is clear that there is no direct responsibility on the manufacturer to provide the customer, for example, with alternative transport while his vehicle is off the road unless the warranty expressly made provision for that, and the Code makes it clear that this is the case. The point is also made that where a loan car is made available this will be merely as a reasonable alternative transport rather than an exact replacement for the car which is off the road.

OFT recommendations

In June 1986 the Office of Fair Trading produced a report on Consumer Guarantees following an earlier Discussion Document setting out their views.

The Report contains a number of recommendations directed not only to those who offer guarantees but also to consumers. They therefore apply to retailers and extended warranty companies as well as to manufacturers.

The main recommendations of the report are:
— terminology should be standardised to avoid confusion, and the term 'consumer guarantee' should be used. The OFT intends to ensure that all guarantees in consumer transactions confer legally enforceable rights;
— documents should be clear and comprehensive and give all relevant information;
— guarantees should state that statutory consumer rights are not affected. This is already a legal requirement in relation to guarantees relating to contracts for the sale of goods or hire purchase (see above), but the OFT is considering whether a wider form of wording should be used, and would like to see more information being given than the bare minimum required by law;
— guarantees should allow free transfer to a future owner. This proposal was previously contained in OFT Guidelines on the content of guarantees, and, so far as the motor industry is concerned, is

already a feature of the Motor Industry Code of Practice as it
relates to new cars;

— guarantees should not involve the purchaser in costs which are
designed to deter claims;

— guarantees should be extended when repairs take some time.
Again, this is a point which is included in the Motor Industry
Code of Practice;

— short-term guarantees for used cars should not exclude reasonably foreseeable defects;

— long-term guarantees should not be issued unless there are satisfactory arrangements to ensure that consumers are protected
against failure of the party offering the guarantees. This really
implies that such guarantees should be insured;

— traders should ensure that insurers are properly authorised to
underwrite risks;

— peace of mind should not be oversold and guarantee terms and
conditions should be provided for inspection by consumers in
advance.

The OFT also recommended that manufacturers and retailers should
take account of other points regarded as particularly important, and said it
would consider legislation if these points were not adopted voluntarily:

— guarantees should not be offered which are not intended to be
legally binding;

— guarantees should give consumers more information about their
statutory rights, and this should include cases involving work and
materials, supply of services and hire;

— guarantees should be fully transferable;

— guarantees lasting for more than one year should not be issued
unless they either form a direct contract of insurance between the
consumer and an authorised insurer, or have some other form of
protection scheme possibly operated on an industry basis;

— guarantees which purport to offer complete protection against
failure should not contain exclusions or over-restrictive conditions.

In addition to the points directed to those offering guarantees, the OFT
addresses advice to the consumer, for example encouraging consumers
to ask to see copies of guarantee terms before entering into the contract;
to beware of exclusions; and to remember that guarantees are not
designed to cover products against wear and tear or accidental damage.

CHAPTER 11

Contracts for the repair and servicing of motor vehicles

A INTRODUCTION

Since the last edition of this book was prepared, motor vehicle repair and servicing contracts excluding vehicle recovery services, car body/crash repairs, provision of the MOT test and the sale of warranties, have come under scrutiny by the Office of Fair Trading. As a result, in August 2000, a report[1] was published which indicated that the number of complaints received by trading standards had more than doubled in the 15 years since the sector had previously been scrutinised by the OFT, and that action was needed to deal with this situation. The key recommendations in this report were:

- A task force should be established to address training deficiencies, quality control, consider improved systems for redress and to propose schemes to promote better consumer awareness and understanding.

- Manufacturers should make better information available to consumers about servicing requirements, including information contained in the owner's handbook.

- Written fixed-price quotations should be provided wherever possible before work commences. Mechanisms must be in place to authorise additional work. All costs must be clearly stated in the invoice.

- The industry needs to make a greater investment in training at all levels.

- Local authorities need to ensure best practice is followed in discharging their enforcement duties in this sector.

[1] Car Servicing and Repairs – The Report of the Director General's inquiry into car servicing and repairs OFT 307.

Against this background it is perhaps surprising that while general trading legislation such as the Trade Descriptions Act and the rules on misleading pricing apply equally to the supply of services as to the supply of goods[2], the service and repair contract itself with the consumer was governed only by the common law up until 1982, and many of the rules which will affect the civil rights and liabilities of the parties are applied still as a matter of common law. At present, however, the OFT seems content to pursue other initiatives rather than propose further legislative control of the sector.

B DUTIES OF THE REPAIRER

Since 1982 the Supply of Goods and Services Act has applied to contracts for repair and servicing, as well as covering contracts for the supply of goods other than by way of sale, for example hiring contracts which are dealt with in the next chapter. This is not to say that before 1982 there were no legal rules relating to contracts of this type, but it was the common law which applied. It is these common law rules that have formed the basis of the legislation.

There are three main terms which will be implied into contracts for the supply of a service:
(a)   where the supplier of the service is acting in the course of a business, there is an implied term that he will carry out the service with reasonable care and skill;[3]
(b)   where there is no provision in the contract as to the time for performance of the service, there is an implied term that the supplier will carry out the service within a reasonable time;[4]
(c)   where there is no provision in the contract as to the charge to be made for the service, the Act provides that there will be an implied term that a reasonable charge should be paid.

I Liability for workmanship

The repairer must do the work which he has agreed to take on with reasonable care and skill, and he must also employ competent staff to

[2]   See Chapters 3 and 4.
[3]   Section 13.
[4]   Section 14.

do the work. If the work is unsatisfactory, the customer may be able to refuse to pay altogether, or may be able to pay a reduced price to allow for compensation. The appropriate level of redress will depend very much on the facts of the case, and what value if any the customer got out of the work that had been carried out. If the repair fails, can the customer get the car fixed elsewhere without giving the repairer the opportunity to examine it? It seems that this would not prevent the customer recovering the cost of the further repair, particularly if the vehicle broke down some distance from the original repairer. However, failure to allow the first repairer to see the vehicle may well make it more difficult for the customer to prove that the repair was unsatisfactory, and it could be argued that the customer has failed to mitigate his loss if he did not take advantage of an offer to do the repair again free.

Breach of the contract to repair does not give rise to liability for damages for distress or loss of enjoyment in the use of the car.[5]

Quality of parts

Where a garage enters into a contract to repair a customer's vehicle this will be a contract for the supply of a service, but also for the supply of the parts needed to complete the work. This is known as a contract for work and materials and is likely to be covered by the 1982 Act rather than the Sale of Goods Act. However, in practical terms this makes no difference to the issue of satisfactory quality and fitness for purpose of the parts supplied in this sort of contract. The common law originally provided, and the 1982 Act confirms, that the materials supplied must be satisfactory and reasonably fit for purpose.

If an accident occurs as a result of defective parts having been fitted then the repairer will be liable for the damage which results even though he may have been ignorant of the defect. A repairer has been held to be liable in damages for supplying defective connecting rods even though the defect was not one which was apparent at the time the parts were fitted.[6] This responsibility is in addition to his obligation under the Road Traffic Act 1988 to supply 'suitable' parts.[7]

---

[5]   *Alexander v Rolls Royce Motor Cars Ltd* [1996] RTR 95, CA.

[6]   *Myers (GH) & Co v Brent Cross Service Co* [1933] All ER Rep 9.

[7]   Section 76.

Negligence

It should also be noted that apart from the liabilities arising from the contract, the repairer will also have liability in tort if he is negligent in carrying out the work. This will be particularly relevant if the negligence has caused injury, for example to another road user or passenger in the car who was not a party to the contract of repair and who would otherwise not be able to bring an action. In *Stennett v Hancock and Peters*,[8] damages were recovered from the defendant who had been negligent in working on a vehicle wheel shortly before an accident in which part of the wheel came off and struck a pedestrian.

If the repairer is modifying a vehicle or fabricating parts to the extent of 'producing' a new 'product' he may also be liable for any defects under the Consumer Protection Act 1987, Pt I (see Chapter 10).

In the event that a fatality is caused through gross negligence it seems that a repairer may now also be vulnerable to a criminal prosecution for manslaughter.[9]

Vicarious liability

In discussing the servicing and repair of motor vehicles a frequently asked question queries whether it is the employer or the employee who is liable in civil law to pay compensation to those injured as a result of negligence in carrying out work. The relevant principle here is whether it can be said that the employer is 'vicariously liable' when his employee has been negligent. If the person who committed the tort is an employee as opposed to a self employed contractor, and he is carrying out work in the course of his employment, then the employer will be liable, even if the employee does the work in an unauthorised way. For example, in *Century Insurance v Northern Ireland Road Transport Board*,[10] an employee was delivering petrol from a tanker into the garage storage tank. The employee caused a fire by lighting a cigarette and throwing away the match. The employee was in general doing his job at the time, so express authority was not needed.

---

[8]   [1939] 2 All ER 578.
[9]   See *R v Holloway* reported at (1989) Times, 31 January.
[10]   [1942] AC 509, [1942] 1 All ER 491, HL.

2 Liability for delay

If a set date or time has been fixed for completion of the contract, failure to do the work within this time will entitle the customer to compensation for the delay. If a customer tells the repairer that 'time is of the essence' in setting the date, then failure to do the work on time will entitle the customer to treat the contract as being at an end, with no liability on his part to pay for what has already been done.

If no time or date has been set, the 'reasonable' time set by the Act will be a matter of fact in each case. If a delay is caused by the repairer being unable, for example, to obtain the necessary parts, then this will not necessarily amount to a breach of contract. In *Charnock v Liverpool Corpn*,[11] a car was taken into a garage for repair after an accident. The garage took eight weeks to carry out the repair, whereas the evidence showed that reasonably competent repairer would have taken five weeks. The Court of Appeal ruled that the work had not been done within a reasonable time.

3 Estimates and quotations

It is important that any quotation or estimate given for work to be done makes clear whether it is a firm quotation or only an approximate estimate. Once a quotation has been given, that cannot be exceeded without the customer's authority.[12] It should also be noted however that the use of the word 'estimate' alone is not enough if the intention of the parties was to treat it as a firm figure for the carrying out of the work, both parties will be bound by it. For example,[13] in a case where a document headed 'Estimate' was given by a firm of builders for work to be done, and they were asked to go ahead on this basis, they were not able to argue that no binding contract existed. When they tried to withdraw from the contract they had to compensate the customer for the difference between their estimate and the cost of his having the work done elsewhere.

The Code of Practice for the Retail Motor Industry provides that such quotations should be given in writing, and that estimates should be given in writing if requested. This goes further than the original motor

---

[11]   [1968] 3 All ER 473, [1968] 1 WLR 1498, CA.
[12]   *Forman & Co Pty Ltd v The Liddesdale* [1900] AC 190.
[13]   *Croshaw v Pritchard and Renwick* (1899) 16 TLR 45.

industry code and is no doubt introduced as a result of the recent OFT survey reported above

Where a repairer is giving a customer an estimate for work to be carried out, he should ensure that it includes the cost of any dismantling and reassembly necessary for the making of the estimate. If this has not been included, a repairer could find that having given an estimate for work to be carried out which involved, for example, stripping down the engine, and the customer then decides not to have the work done, he may not be able to recover from him the cost of dismantling and reassembly.

4 Care of customer's property

The repairer is known in law as a 'bailee' and is under a duty to take care of property belonging to customers that has been entrusted to him. Where a vehicle is lost or damaged whilst in the custody of a repairer he will be liable for all the damage sustained unless it can be shown that this was due to an inevitable accident and not to a lack of care on his part. This responsibility also covers the actions of any employees providing that they were acting within the scope of their contract of employment. This means that if, for example, an employee takes a customer's car without permission on a joy ride and damages it then the employer will not be liable unless he can be proved to have been negligent in employing that particular employee. Damage done to a vehicle whilst being road tested, however, or being moved on the garage premises would be the responsibility of the employer.

The bailee must take reasonable care of the goods throughout the time they are in his care, but it seems that this does not require the goods to be maintained.[14] The standard of care which the repairer must take of customers' vehicles is not completely unlimited. For example, it has been held that it is not a duty on the part of the garage to ensure that vehicles are always kept in a lock-up compound overnight.[15] A repairer was therefore not liable for damage sustained to a customer's car when it was stolen from the road outside their premises having been left there

---

[14] In *Nightingale v Tildsley* [1980] CLY 134 it was held that the bailee of a truck over an extensive period was not required to maintain it so that it remained in roadworthy condition.

[15] *Idnani v Elisha* [1979] RTR 488.

overnight in an immobilised state. The standard of care which is expected of the garage will depend on the particular circumstances. Matters such as the previous course of dealing, if any, between the customer and the repairer may be relevant in the court's decision as to whether the repairer acted reasonably in the way he took care of the customer's car. In another case, a garage was held liable for damage to a vehicle stolen from its car park because the car was left unlocked with the key in the dashboard and no supervision.[16]

A customer who unreasonably refuses to collect his vehicle may lose his rights altogether. A dealer had a protracted dispute with a customer over a vehicle which they had supplied, and which they had attempted unsuccessfully to repair under a separate contract. This led to the customer refusing to collect the car. The dealer removed the car from its premises and put it in a public car park, and the customer was reminded of its location on several occasions. The customer then sued for rescission of the sale contract. By the time the case came to court the car had been stolen and, when his claim for rescission failed, the undaunted customer then sued the dealer for breach of its duty of care as a bailee. This too failed – the court took the view that by failing to collect the vehicle within a reasonable time, the customer had foregone his rights under the original contract of bailment.[17]

The situation often arises where a customer will leave a car in a repairer's premises, eg outside normal working hours with the keys and a request attached to it that certain work be carried out. The repairer's liability in this situation is unclear. It may well be that if no prior arrangement had been made for the car to be left for work to be done, then no liability will rest on the repairer if it is stolen or damaged before he accepts it. For example,[18] an author was asked by the owner of a theatre to send him a synopsis of a play. The author instead sent him the whole manuscript which the theatre owner then lost. It was held that no liability arose because he had not asked the author for the whole manuscript.

This situation is similar to the one which will arise if articles in the car are lost. If the repairer is unaware that eg the customer has left an

[16]   *Cooper v Dempsey* (1961) So Jo 320, CA.
[17]   *Pedrick v Morning Star Motors Ltd* (14 February 1979, unreported), CA, discussed in Bailment, Palmer.
[18]   *Howard v Harris* (1884) 1 Cab & El 253.

expensive fur coat in the boot, it seems that, providing he was not actually negligent, he will not be liable for its loss he will be what lawyers call an 'involuntary bailee' of the coat.[19] The logical conclusion to draw seems to be that the repairer will be liable in respect of the vehicle and presumably anything that can be said to be part of it, eg the radio, but not for property of which he is unaware, and does not accept into his custody.

The original Motor Industry Code of Practice provided that every garage should make sure that they carry adequate insurance to cover their legal responsibilities to their customers for care of their possessions, and this is repeated in the new Code. In addition, the ability of the repairer to contract out of his legal liabilities is now limited by the Unfair Contract Terms Act 1977 (see below).

Where a garage accepts a vehicle for repair, it does not become the owner. The owner remains the registered keeper, and therefore liable for fixed penalty notices incurred in respect of the vehicle.[20]

5 Subcontracting

Where a repairer subcontracts work to a third party he will normally be liable for the quality of the work carried out by a subcontractor and will be liable to pay the subcontractor's bill. This will not be so however if the customer has selected the subcontractor.[21] There is no contract between the subcontractor and the owner of the vehicle and therefore the subcontractor is not able to recover the cost of the work done direct from the customer.

6 Exclusion clauses

Contractual liability

Under the Unfair Contract Terms Act 1977 notices such as 'All cars driven at customer's risk' are now only effective if the court decides that they are 'reasonable'.[22] (For the tests of 'reasonableness' see Chapter 10, above.) However, it should be noted that such notices will

---

[19] *Elvin and Powell Ltd v Plummer Roddis Ltd* (1933) 50 TLR 158.
[20] *R v Parking Adjudicator, ex p Wandsworth Council* [1998] RTR 51, CA.
[21] *Stewart v Reavell's Garage Ltd* [1952] 2 QB 545.
[22] Unfair Contract Terms Act 1977, s 3.

now be caught by the Unfair Terms in Consumer Contracts Regulations where they relate to contractual liability, and will almost certainly be regarded as unfair (see Chapter 7).

Liability for negligence

Any clause which attempts to exclude or limit liability for death or injury caused by negligence is now completely without any legal effect.[23] The repairer of a motor vehicle will therefore be liable if due to his negligence someone is killed or injured and he cannot avoid that liability. It is therefore of prime importance for the repairer to make sure that his insurance policies are adequate to cover him against this eventuality.

7 Road Traffic Acts

Apart from the potential liability for manslaughter mentioned above, the repairer may also be liable under the Road Traffic Acts if he hands back a customer's car after working on it if it is in fact unroadworthy. In *Devon County Council v DB Cars*[24], a garage was successfully prosecuted for 'supplying' an unroadworthy vehicle some two months earlier when it handed back a vehicle to its owner with an MOT certificate supplied by another garage which had carried out the test on its behalf. When carrying out the test the testing garage had failed to spot the fact that there were other faults on the vehicle. These had in fact been picked up by a third garage which had refused to issue an MOT certificate some months earlier, but the owner had not had the work carried out.

Courtesy cars

Where a courtesy loan car is supplied to a customer, it must be roadworthy and comply with all relevant safety requirements.

C LIEN

If the repairer has not been paid by the customer he will have a lien over the customer's vehicle providing that his bill relates to the

---

[23] Unfair Contract Terms Act 1977, s 2.
[24] [2001] EWHC Admin 521, [2002] Crim LR 71.

improvement or repair of the car, not for items which are simply of routine maintenance. This will mean that the repairer's lien will exist in the case of repairs carried out on a car but not where the bill relates only to servicing. Where the bill is for a mixture of improvements and maintenance there may not be a valid lien unless it can be shown that the two elements of the job can be separated. If they are costed separately on the bill, this will obviously help to establish separation. This seems a distinction which is difficult to justify, but nevertheless has been maintained by the courts even in recent cases.[25] There must be express or implied authority for the work to be carried out by the retailer in order for him to have a valid lien. This will normally not present any problems, if the customer owns the vehicle. If, however, he is not the owner, eg because it is hired or is on hire purchase, difficulties may arise. For example, in a case where a hirer whose HP agreement was void refused to pay for work done by a retailer it was held that there was no lien.[26] This authority for the work to be done may be implied by the undertaking which is contained in most hire-purchase agreements for the hirer to keep the property in repair,[27] by trade usage or from the fact that the goods are delivered by the employee of the owner with whom the workman is accustomed to deal. A subcontractor will also have a lien because he can assume that the contractor has the authority to subcontract.

It is unclear whether such a right of lien arises when a trader recovers a vehicle, for example from the scene of an accident, and then stores it. Recently, recovery operators have been trying to establish that a lien for recovery and storage charges does exist.

In a recent case in which the recovery operator removed a vehicle from the highway, at the request of the police, and refused to release it to the owner because his charges for the recovery and storage had not been paid, the county court ordered that the plaintiff customer, who had issued a summons for the delivery of the vehicle to him, could not have it by a summary procedure because the defendant recovery operator had raised issues in his defence which merited a formal hearing. As a result the plaintiff abandoned the action and paid an agreed sum to the recovery operator to obtain his vehicle. The actual legal position is therefore still unclear and, even if the county court had given judgment after hearing the evidence, it would not have produced a precedent to

---

[25]   *Re Southern Livestock Producers Ltd* [1963] 3 All ER 801.
[26]   *Bowmaker Ltd v Wycombe Motors Ltd* [1946] 2 All ER 113.
[27]   *Green v All Motors Ltd* [1917] 1 KB 625.

guide others in the future, but encouraged by this limited success another similar case is being brought and supported by the Association of Vehicle Recovery Operators.

In order for the retailer to rely on his lien it is essential that he retains possession of the car. In *Hatton v Car Maintenance Co Ltd*,[28] where a company who by agreement with the owner of a motor car maintained the car and provided a driver but allowed the owner to take the car out when she liked, they were held to have no lien on the car for money due under the agreement. If the retailer lets the customer take the car without having paid a bill for work done and then has the car in his possession again on a later occasion for work where the bill is paid, he will have lost his lien in respect of the earlier bill and will not be able to hold the car once the second bill has been paid.

I Enforcing the lien

At common law there is no right to sell goods subject to a lien. The bailee can only retain the goods until he has been paid. However, there is a statutory power to sell goods subject to a lien which is conferred by the Tort (Interference with Goods) Act on the bailees of goods accepted for repair or other treatment.

2 Selling uncollected goods

The Torts (Interference with Goods) Act 1977 gives the bailee of goods two powers, one to impose an obligation on the owner to take delivery of the goods, and two, to take steps to sell the goods.

The power to impose an obligation to collect the goods is implemented by the bailee by giving notice in writing either by delivering it to the bailor or by leaving it at his proper address or by post. The notice has to:

(a)   specify the name and address of the bailee and give sufficient particulars of the goods and the address or place where they are held; and

(b)   state that the goods are ready for delivery to the bailor or where combined with the notice terminating the contract of bailment will be ready for delivery when the contract is terminated; and

---

[28]   [1915] 1 Ch 621.

(c)   specify the amount, if any, which is payable by the bailor to the
       bailee in respect of the goods and which became due before the
       giving of the notice.

A notice of intention to sell the goods must:
(a)   specify the name and address of the bailee and give sufficient
       particulars of the goods and the address or place where they are
       held; and
(b)   specify the date on or after which the bailee proposes to sell the
       goods; and
(c)   specify the amount if any which is payable by the bailor to the
       bailee in respect of the goods and which became due before the
       giving of the notice.

The period between the giving of the notice and the date specified for
the exercising of the power of sale has to be such as will give the bailor
a reasonable opportunity of taking delivery of the goods but if any
amount is payable in respect of the goods by the bailor to the bailee and
which became due before the giving of the notice the period of notice
must not be less than three months. The notice is to be in writing and
shall be sent by post in a registered letter or by recorded delivery.

The bailee may not however exercise his right to serve a notice or sell
the goods if at the time he has notice that, because of a dispute concerning the goods, the bailor is questioning or refusing to pay all or any part
of what the bailee claims to be due in respect of the goods.[29]

3 Effect of sale by bailee

The bailee who has exercised a power of sale under the Act is liable
to account to the bailor for the proceeds of sale less any costs of the
sale and he will be expected to have adopted the best method of sale
reasonably available in the circumstances. Providing this has been
done any sum which was due to the bailee before he gave notice of
intention to sell the goods, can be deducted from the proceeds of
sale.

Providing the steps outlined above have been followed the sale made
under the Act will give a good title to the new purchaser as against the
bailor of the goods. Where, however, the bailor did not actually own the

---

[29]   Torts (Interference with Goods) Act 1977, Sch 1, Pt II, para 7.

goods a sale under this section of the Act will not give the purchaser a good title against the true owner or against a person claiming under the true owner, for example, a subsequent purchaser. If there is some doubt about the true ownership of the car, the bailee would be better advised to use s 13 of the Act. That section provides that where the bailee of goods is able to satisfy the court that he is entitled to sell the goods under s 12 of the Act, the court may:

(a)   authorise the sale of the goods subject to specific terms and conditions; and

(b)   may authorise the bailee to deduct from the proceeds of sale any costs of sale and any amount due from the bailor to the bailee in respect of the goods; and

(c)   may direct the payment into court of the net proceeds of sale any amounts deducted under para (b) to be held to the credit of the bailor.

A court order authorising a sale under s 13 will be conclusive as against the bailor of the bailee's entitlement to sell the goods and gives a good title to the purchaser against the bailor.[30] The retailer will need to check with HPI to find out whether any HP agreement is registered before exercising his right of sale.

4 Extinguishment of lien

The tender by the debtor of the money due to the bailee will bring the lien to an end as will loss of possession on the part of the bailee. Loss of possession on a temporary basis in consideration for an agreement to return the goods may, however, result in the lien being retained. For example in *Albemarle Supply Co Ltd v Hind & Co*,[31] the bailee allowed taxicabs to be taken out daily to ply for hire. It was held in that case that the lien still existed.

D INSURANCE REGULATION

From 14 January 2005, vehicle repairers who help customers to buy insurance-based products, or who help customers make claims under insurance policies will be regulated by the Financial Services Agency

---

[30]   See App 5 for form of Application for Court Order.
[31]   [1928] 1 KB 307, CA.

(FSA).[32] This means that it will be illegal to continue such activities unless the repairer is authorised by the FSA, or is an appointed representative of a company which is itself authorised, and that businesses carrying out these activities must ensure that FSA requirements in carrying out these activities are met.

The full extent to which vehicle repairers' activities will require FSA authorisation is not yet entirely clear, and is likely to vary from business to business, and some repairers may not require it all. Activities that will not require the repairer to be regulated, if incidental to the repair of cars, are:

- the display of motor insurance, credit hire or post accident insurance leaflets
- the provision of information to help a customer complete an application for motor insurance
- the provision of information to help the customer complete an accident claim form
- transferring a policyholder's cover from his own vehicle to a courtesy car provided by a repairer or other supplier, provided the policyholder is not acquiring new rights.

Carrying out work for insurance companies

Where a repairer is carrying out work on the instructions of an insurance company, he is in effect acting on behalf of the insurer when dealing with the customer. This is not likely to fall within the scope of the regulation as he is not acting as an agent for the customer. However, completing an application form for insurance for a customer would be regulated, as would completing an accident claim form for a customer, or helping to negotiate a settlement with an insurer or advising a customer whether to take out a particular insurance policy.

Courtesy cars

Selling insurance cover for a courtesy car, or insurance excess cover, is not likely to be a regulated activity provided the customer does not become a policyholder in their own right.

---

[32]   The Financial Services and Markets Act 2000 (Regulated Activities) (Amendment) (No2) Order 2003, SI 2003/1476.

Effect of regulation

The broad effects of regulation are to ensure that advice relating to the sales process is adequate to the customer's needs; that advice is given in understandable format; that consumers are treated fairly particularly in respect of inducements and cancellation periods; that consumers get key product information at the right time; that claims handling procedures are in place to deal with claims promptly and fairly; and that there is a training and competency regime for individuals selling and managing insurance contracts.

Carrying out regulated activities while not authorised and failure to comply with the requirements of the Act [33] is a criminal offence punishable by up to 6 months imprisonment, and fines of up to £5000 on a summary conviction, and on indictment up to two years' imprisonment and/or a fine. There is a statutory defence available of all reasonable precautions and due diligence.

---

[33] The Financial Services and Markets Act 2000, s 23.

CHAPTER 12

Other contracts with customers

A HIRING CONTRACTS

Until 1982, the content of contracts of hire was not covered by any statutory controls and the legal rules about them were dealt with entirely by common law rules. This situation changed with the introduction of the provisions of the Consumer Credit Act relating to regulated consumer hire agreements on 19 May 1985 and the passing of the Supply of Goods and Services Act in 1982.

A regulated consumer hire agreement is any agreement:
— under which goods are hired, leased, rented or bailed to an individual. An individual will include a sole trader or partnership as well as the private hirer;
— which can last for more than three months;
— which does not require payments of more than £25,000 in total;
— which is not an exempt agreement.

I Contents of a consumer hire agreement

In order for a regulated consumer hire agreement to be enforceable without the necessity of a court order, the agreement must be in writing, signed by both parties and comply with requirements as to legibility.

The first page of the agreement must have as a heading the words 'Hire Agreement regulated by the Consumer Credit Act 1974'. The agreement must then set out the names and postal addresses of the owner and the hirer, a description of any security provided by the hirer, details of any default charges that the hirer will be required to pay if he breaches the agreement, financial and other related details, and statements about the forms of protection and remedies available to the hirer.

The regulations also set out detailed requirements for the wording of the signature box, and legibility, on similar lines to that required for other regulated consumer credit agreements.[1]

2 Copies of agreement

The general rule is that one copy of the agreement must be given to the hirer when he is given the agreement for signature. Unless the agreement has at that point already been signed by the owner in advance, there must then be sent to the hirer a second copy of the agreement within seven days. If the second copy is not required because it has already been signed by the owner, then a notice of the right to cancel must be sent to the hirer within seven days.

3 The right to cancel

The Act provides that certain regulated hire contracts will be cancellable. This right will apply where:
— during the pre-contract negotiations a representation is made to the hirer by the owner or his representative about the goods or the agreement under which they are to be hired; and
— the agreement is signed by the hirer off trade premises.

The hirer will then have five days after receipt of the second statutory copy of the agreement within which to communicate his wish to cancel.

After cancellation, the hirer must return the goods hired to him or keep them safe and unused until collection. He will however have a lien over the goods if the owner owes him any money until he has been paid. The owner must return any payments made and also any property given by the hirer as security or in part exchange or, if this is not practical, must pay the hirer their value.

---

[1] These requirements will be amended in line with those for consumer credit agreements with effect from 31 May 2005 by the Consumer Credit (Agreements) (Amendment) Regulations 2004, SI 2004/1482.

4 Right of hirer to terminate contract

In addition to the provisions of the agreement regarding termination, the hirer will be entitled to terminate a regulated consumer hire agreement by giving notice provided the total annual rentals do not exceed £900, and the goods are not hired for business purposes. The notice given must as a minimum be the shorter of either the period stated in the agreement, or the length of the shortest interval between the payments, or three months. This may only be done, however, where at least 18 months will have expired by the end of the notice period, unless the agreement itself allows for termination earlier.

5 Owners' rights if hirer defaults

The rights of the owner to take action under the hire agreement in the event of default by the hirer will now be affected by the Consumer Credit Act if it is a regulated consumer hire agreement.

If the hirer defaults on payment or is in breach of any other terms of the agreement, the owner must send a default notice giving at least seven days' notice before he can take any action to:

— terminate the agreement;
— demand earlier payment of any sum;
— recover possession of any goods;
— treat any right of the customer as terminated, restricted or deferred; or
— enforce any security.

The regulations set out the form of a default notice which must include a clear and unambiguous statement of the action which the owner of the goods intends to take.

If the customer fails to remedy the default specified in the notice, the owner cannot enter onto premises to recover the goods, and therefore unless they are given up voluntarily by the hirer he will have to obtain a court order to recover them.

6 Terms implied into a contract of hire

Apart from the provisions of the Consumer Credit Act, the common law has traditionally applied to the provisions of the contract in relation to the quality of the goods hired.

These are now statutorily implied into the contract by the Supply of Goods and Services Act 1982.

The Act covers not only contracts of direct hire from the owner (or bailor) to the hirer (or bailee), but also in cases where the goods are sold to a finance house by the retailer, the finance house then entering into the contract of hire with the customer. It will, however, only cover cases where there is in fact a contract in existence, so it will not cover cases where goods, for example a replacement motor vehicle, are lent free of charge.

Title

The terms implied into these contracts by the 1982 Act are:

(a) that the bailor of the goods has the right to transfer the goods under a hiring agreement or that he will have that right at the time the goods are to be handed over;

(b) that the bailee will be able to enjoy 'quiet possession' of the goods for the period of the hiring contract. This means that the bailee will be entitled to keep the goods for the contract period without interference except where the goods are subject to some sort of charge which was disclosed to the bailee before the contract was made.[2] It should be noted that these provisions do not affect the rights of the bailor to repossess the goods under the terms of the contract, although if the contract is a regulated consumer hire agreement, it will be covered by the Consumer Credit Act requiring a court order to be obtained before repossession.

Description

Where the goods are being hired by description there is an implied condition that the goods will meet the description.

This provision repeats the old common law rules. In one case, a customer inspected a car which he wished to hire, and found it in good condition. When it was delivered a few weeks later its condition had deteriorated so much that the court held that the customer was entitled to reject the vehicle because it no longer conformed to its description.

2   *Karsales (Harrow) Ltd v Wallis* [1956] 2 All ER 866, [1956] 1 WLR 936, CA.

Quality

(a)   Where the bailor is acting in the course of a business there is
      an implied term that the goods will be of satisfactory quality.
      This condition is similar to the one implied into contracts for
      the sale of goods and excludes defects which have been specif-
      ically drawn to the hirer's attention, or where he has examined
      the goods, as regards the defects he should have seen.

(b)   Where the bailor is acting in the course of a business, and the
      hirer makes known to him either expressly or by implication the
      purpose for which the goods are being hired, there is an implied
      condition that the goods will be fit for that purpose. It should be
      noted that this will also apply if the contract is going to be one of
      finance leasing where the goods will be sold first to a finance
      company, where the negotiations are in fact being carried out by a
      credit broker.

(c)   Where the goods are hired by sample there is an implied condi-
      tion that the goods will correspond with the sample.

The effect of these rules is that motor vehicles hired out to consumers
must comply with the same standards of satisfactory quality and fitness
for purpose as motor vehicles which are the subject of a contract of sale.
Although exclusions of liability in this type of contract will not be caught
by the provisions applying to contracts for the sale of goods (see Chapter
7, above), the provisions of the Unfair Contract Terms Act 1977 will apply
to hiring contracts and will have the effect of making any exclusion of liability in a hiring contract subject to a reasonableness test[3] by the courts. It
seems unlikely that a court would allow an exclusion clause in a hiring
contract to stand up against a consumer in circumstances where, if he had
bought the goods outright under a contract of sale, the retailer would have
been liable for a breach of satisfactory quality or fitness for the purpose.

7 Obligations of the bailee

The Act does not cover the obligations of the customer who hires the
goods, therefore it seems that the old common law rules will continue
to apply, although these will be subject, in the case of regulated consumer hire agreements, to the controls imposed by the Consumer Credit
Act 1974 (see above).

---

[3]   See ch 10, above for details of the 'reasonableness' test.

The hirer has to take reasonable care of the vehicle and will not be liable for loss or injury unless caused by his negligence or that of his employees. This liability, however, may be affected by the contract terms. For example, a car hire contract made the hirer responsible for accident damage repairs, stating that insurance was in force. In fact no valid insurance policy existed and it was held that the owner of the car could not recover from the hirer for accidental damage.[4] Similarly in another case,[5] a car hirer was held not to be liable for an accident when he hit a tree to avoid a cat. It was held that this accident was not due to his act or default but was an inevitable accident.

The hirer is not responsible for fair wear and tear unless there is an express term in the contract, nor is he under any duty to do repairs or incur expenses, except those which follow naturally from the performance of his obligation to take reasonable care of the vehicle. If he has repairs done outside his obligation it is doubtful whether he can recover the cost even if the repairs were necessary and the expenditure was reasonable. Finally, the hirer is obliged to return the vehicle at the expiration of the agreed term.[6]

8 Deferred payment car hire schemes

The growth in popularity of schemes where a car owner, whose car has been damaged through the fault of someone else, can hire a car but not have to pay for it until the conclusion of a successful claim against the other driver, has lead in recent years to a considerable amount of litigation as insurers have tried to restrict their liability for the ensuing costs.

There have been a variety of legal challenges, and a number of reported cases. The first challenge of significance came in 1993[7] when the House of Lords had to consider whether this type of arrangement was illegal on the basis that such agreements contravened the ancient law of

---

4   *Moons Motors Ltd v Kiuan Wou* [1952] 2 Lloyd's Rep 80, CA.
5   *Ritchie's Car Hire Ltd v Bailey* (1958) 108 L Jo 348.
6   'This car wash is used entirely at owner's risk' challenged under the Unfair Terms in Consumer Contracts Regulations 1994, Sch 3, para 1(b) (see ch 7): OFT Unfair Contract Terms Bulletin Issue No 1.
7   *Giles v Thompson* [1994] 1 AC 142.

champerty. This mediaeval concept was aimed at preventing the rich agreeing to fund the legal action of the less well off in return for a share of the damages. Their Lordships decided that as there was no profit made from the litigation, only from hiring cars, such agreements were not champertous or against the public interest, and insurers would have to pay out. This decision undoubtedly encouraged the growth of this type of arrangement, and further legal challenges followed. One of the most significant was *Dimond v Lovell*[8], another House of Lords' case. In this instance, insurers argued that the agreements were regulated by the Consumer Credit Act, either as consumer hire agreements, or as consumer credit agreements (because payment was deferred). If this argument was right, then any hire agreement which did not comply with the requirements of the Consumer Credit Act would be unenforceable. The House of Lords decided that the agreement in this case was not a regulated consumer hire agreement because it was not capable of lasting for more than three months, but agreed that it was a regulated consumer credit agreement. The agreement should therefore have met the requirements of the Consumer Credit Act as to its form and content[9], and was unenforceable.

9 Courtesy cars

Where a garage lends a car to a customer while his own is off the road being repaired, it is important that the arrangement is formalised as a hiring agreement, and that it includes an indemnity signed by the customer which complies with road traffic legislation in order for the garage to avoid car parking fines issued in respect of the vehicle. Under the Road Traffic Offenders Act 1988[10], the owner of a vehicle not the driver is liable for a penalty charge notice issued in respect of it. However, provided that the hire contract contains a statement of liability on the part of the driver, and other specified details, the owners of hire cars are protected from fixed penalty offences if they are engaged in hiring vehicles under a hiring agreement in the course of a business[11].

---

[8]   [2002] 1 AC 384, [2000] 2 WLR 1121, HL.
[9]   See Chapter 9.
[10]   Section 66. Similar provisions apply to parking offences committed in London.
[11]   Road Traffic (Owner Liability) Regulations 1975, SI 1975/324.

B CAR WASHES

The provision of a car wash facility forms a contract for the supply of a service. If the car wash fails to wash satisfactorily, or if it damages a customer's car, then the operator of the car wash will be liable unless the customer failed to observe an instruction as to its proper use, for example by failing to lower a radio aerial.

The Unfair Contract Terms Act 1977 will apply to this type of contract, therefore any exclusion clause along the lines of 'No liability will be accepted for any loss or damage' will be subject to a 'reasonableness' test.[12] The Unfair Terms in Consumer Contracts Regulations (see Chapter 7) will also now apply and the Office of Fair Trading have requested the removal of such notices.

C PROVISION OF OTHER FACILITIES

The provision of other facilities for use by customers where no payment is made, eg airlines, distilled water, probably does not constitute a contract as there is no 'consideration'. However, if there were some defect in the equipment which caused injury, then if it could be shown that the proprietor had been negligent in some way, eg in allowing the facilities to be used in a defective condition, he will be liable for the damage caused. Similarly, he might also be held liable for damage or injuries caused by customer misuse if he failed to give adequate warnings, eg that airlines on the forecourt should not be used for inflating airbeds.

D GARAGING AND PARKING

The motor trader who garages customers' cars or provides car parking facilities will be in the same position as the repairer[13] of a vehicle. He will be in law a 'bailee' and will be bound to take reasonable care, and will be liable if it is damaged through his negligence.

---

[12] See ch 10, above, for details of 'reasonableness'.
[13] See ch 11, above.

CHAPTER 13

Safety matters

It has often been said that the motor car is one of the most potentially dangerous products on general sale to consumers. The requirements of road safety, as well as the need to control the impact of the motor car on the environment through control matters such as of noise and exhaust emissions are therefore a major factor in the legislation affecting the construction and use of motor vehicles. Earlier chapters considered the civil liability of the retailer (Chapter 7) and the manufacturer (Chapter 10) for defects in the product. This chapter concerns the way in which criminal sanctions may apply in respect of vehicles and parts which are unsafe or do not conform to specific legislative requirements.

A NATIONAL REGULATIONS

The main controls over the construction and use of motor vehicles are to be found in the Road Traffic Acts and the construction and use and lighting regulations which are made under those Acts.

1 Construction and Use Regulations

The Construction and Use Regulations[1] are made under the provisions of s 41 of the Road Traffic Act 1988.[2] Section 42 provides that a person who:

---

[1]   SI 1986/1078.
[2]   As amended by the Road Traffic Act 1991.

(a)   contravenes or fails to comply with any regulations under s 41; or

(b)   who uses on a road a motor vehicle or trailer which does not comply with any such regulations or causes or permits a vehicle to be so used,

is guilty of an offence.

It should be noted that the effect of this provision is to make the owner of a vehicle equally responsible for its continued compliance with the construction and use requirements.

The owner or user of a vehicle must not use it on the road in a manner which involves a danger of injury to any person. This includes the condition of the vehicle, its accessories or equipment, the purpose for which it is used, the number of passengers or manner in which they are carried and the weight of distribution of the load and the way in which it is secured.[3]

In addition, there are to be specific offences relating to the breach of requirements as to tyres, steering, brakes and weights of goods and passenger vehicles.[4]

2 Fitting of parts subsequent to sale

Despite the extensive regulations governing the construction and use of motor vehicles, there is no comparable control over spare parts.

There are no regulations specifying design or performance. All the regulations apply to parts fitted as original equipment to vehicles. However, as construction and use regulations do specify that vehicles should be kept in accordance with the construction and use requirements, it may well be that the sale of certain types of spare parts for cars, if not an offence on the part of the retailer, may well be an offence on the part of the customer who buys them for fitting to his car. In addition the selling retailer is bound by the Road Traffic Act 1988, s 76 to supply parts which are suitable for their use. It is an offence to offer to sell, supply or fit, or actually to sell, supply or fit any part which is unsuitable, ie which will cause a vehicle not to comply with the construction and use requirements. It is also an offence under the Act to

---

[3]   Section 40A.
[4]   Sections 41A and 41B.

sell or offer for sale safety equipment for children to be used in motor vehicles which does not comply with regulations made under s 15(A) of the Act.[5]

There are also indirect controls over certain spare parts which are required to be 'E' marked[6] throughout the life of the vehicle. The effect of this requirement is to make the fitting of any other type of part illegal.

3 National and EC type approval

Since 1 August 1978 all motor vehicles sold for use on the road in Great Britain must comply with the national type approval requirements. These requirements are that in the case of a vehicle manufactured in the UK, a type approval certificate must be obtained in respect of each type of vehicle which the manufacturer is making. He must satisfy certain conformity of production requirements laid down by the Department of Transport and in theory must provide a Certificate of Conformity to the effect that each vehicle conforming to that type which has been approved corresponds to the original Type Approval Certificate. In practice a separate piece of paper comprising a Certificate of Conformity is not required and the manufacturer indicates by giving the approval number on the V55 registration document that that vehicle does conform. So far as cars that are imported from abroad are concerned, the requirement is that an individual approval certificate known as a Minister's Approval Certificate, be applied for each vehicle entering the UK.

It should be noted that the requirement is that the vehicle should correspond with the Type Approval Certificate at the time that it is submitted for first registration. Once registration has taken place it does not matter that the car's specification is altered even in a fundamental way so far as the type approval regulations are concerned. This means that there is no control over conversions carried out on type approved vehicles, and it is in theory possible for a type approved vehicle to be radically changed in specification once it reaches the first retail customer. However, as many of the type approval requirements are identical to those in the construction and use regulations the effect is that there is some continuing requirement that the vehicle should comply.

[5]　Motor Vehicles (Safety Equipment for Children) Act 1991.
[6]　See p 176, below.

EC type approval has now replaced the existing national system for vehicles made in the European Community. First registration is obtained on production of evidence that an EC certificate of conformity or a Minister's Approval certificate has been issued in respect of the vehicle.[7]

Single Vehicle Approval

Special arrangements have been made to deal with the approval of single vehicles, personal imports and low volume vehicles. The rules were last updated in 2001.[8] They apply to passenger vehicles and dual-purpose vehicles constructed to carry no more than eight passengers excluding the driver, some three-wheeled vehicles with a maximum unladen weight of more than 410kg, light goods vehicles maximum gross weight not exceeding 3,500 kg, and certain other goods vehicles with a design gross weight not exceeding 5,500 kg.[9]

4 British Standards

British Standards do not normally have legal effect. Their intention is to provide a voluntary framework of compliance with standards of design and to act as a marketing aid and an aid to exporters in overseas countries. However, there are instances in relation to motor vehicles where a particular British Standard is called up or referred to in a construction and use regulation, for example, seats with integral seat belt anchorages, methods of measurement of noise emitted by motor vehicles, and safety glass must all conform with specific British Standards.

In these cases, non-compliance with the relevant British Standard will be a breach of the construction and use regulations. It is an offence under the Trade Descriptions Act 1968 to indicate that goods conform to a BS or other approval standard (see below), if they do not in fact conform.

---

[7] Motor Vehicles (EC Type Approval) Regulations 1998, SI 1998/2051.

[8] Motor Vehicles (Approval) Regulations 2001, SI 2001/25.

[9] A manufacturer refusing to supply type approval information, or who demands excessive fees for producing a certificate of conformity may fall foul of Article 86 of the Treaty of Rome by abusing his dominant position in respect of that information. See *British Leyland plc v EC Commission*: 226/84 [1986] ECR 3263.

B INTERNATIONAL REGULATIONS

It is no longer possible for the UK to operate in isolation from the international scene when making regulations affecting the construction and use of vehicles. As a member both the ECE (the Economic Commission for Europe) and the EEC, the UK has obligations towards the international community to work towards the harmonisation of technical regulations affecting motor vehicles.

I ECE regulations

The UK became a member of the United Nations Economic Commission for Europe in 1958. Ever since then, when an agreement was reached covering the adoption of 'Uniform Conditions of Approval and Reciprocal Recognition of Approval for Motor Vehicle Equipment and Parts', the ECE has progressively harmonised vehicle regulations throughout Europe. A most important point about the ECE regulations is that they are voluntary, not mandatory. They may be either 'accepted' or 'adopted' by the individual ECE members. 'Acceptance' means that manufacturers may have tests carried out and approvals issued by the country of origin, on a voluntary basis. 'Adoption' means that the ECE regulation is incorporated in national legislation and therefore becomes mandatory.

When an ECE regulation has been adopted, the vehicle is required to be marked with the 'E' mark indicating the country of origin where the approval was given, and the ECE regulation with which the vehicle conforms. Where a regulation has been merely 'accepted' 'E' marks will be applied on a voluntary basis.

The 'E' mark is of importance to the retailer of motor vehicles because it is specifically provided by the Road Traffic Act 1988[10] that such an approval mark is a trade description. If therefore a vehicle is sold bearing an 'E' mark which it no longer conforms with, the retailer who is selling the vehicle, in theory commits an offence under the Act, subject of course to the usual defences. This is particularly relevant if a second hand car is being sold which has been modified, eg by having a new steering wheel fitted.

---

[10] Section 80 and see ch 4, above.

2 EC Directives

European Directives which lay down construction requirements for vehicles will require that complying vehicles bear an 'e' mark. These may be an alternative to an 'E' mark or an approved British Standard.

Type Approval

From January 1998, EC Type Approval applies to all 'light passenger vehicles' subject to certain specified exclusions (see above).

C VEHICLE RECALLS

There is currently no statutory requirement in English law for manufacturers to recall their vehicles if they discover a defect in design or manufacture. There are, however, obvious legal constraints which will make a prudent manufacturer consider very carefully whether or not he should institute a vehicle recall if he discovers a problem with one of his vehicles.

First, if he knows of a defect and fails to institute a recall he may be held liable to a consumer who is injured by the defect because of his negligence. Negligence may arise at the design or the manufacture stage or if, after having discovered the existence of a defect in design or manufacture where the manufacturer does not take what the court considers to be adequate action to protect the consumers who have bought the vehicle. This was illustrated in the case involving the Allegro car,[11] when the manufacturer (British Leyland) were found by the court to have been negligent in not instituting a recall campaign once they became aware of the potential problem with the cars. With the introduction of strict liability (see Chapter 10) this becomes a less important consideration in terms of 'fault' reduction, but remains equally valid from the point of view of limiting the number of potential claims which may arise from a defect.

Second, the fact that a defective vehicle is being sold and used on the roads by customers obviously opens the way to claims against retailers under their contract of sale and so back to the manufacturer down the chain of contracts.

[11] See ch 10, above; *Walton v British Leyland (UK) Ltd* [1980] PLI 156.

Third, the Consumer Protection Act 1987, Pt II enables the Secretary of State to prohibit the sale of any particular goods which are 'unsafe'. Prohibition of sale is not, of course, the same thing as a vehicle recall but so far as the vehicle manufacturer is concerned it is surely even more damaging. With this legal background the Department of Transport decided in 1978 to establish a code of practice concerning the recall of motor vehicles. This was to be a voluntary code but would be all the more effective knowing of the potential powers that existed under the consumer safety legislation. The code is now monitored by the Vehicle Inspectorate.

1 The Code of Practice on Vehicle Safety Defects

The first Code was announced in July 1979; it was revised in 1992 and the current version was issued in 2004. It concerns cases where vehicle manufacturers concessionaires or official/independent importers (defined in the Code as 'suppliers') become aware of the existence of safety defects in vehicles and components that have been fitted as original equipment that are available for supply in the UK. It covers passenger cars, commercial vehicles, passenger service vehicles two- and three-wheeled motor cycles, quadracycles, commercial trailers, motor homes/caravans, private trailers and components fitted as original equipment.

'Safety defect' is defined as 'a feature of design or construction liable to cause significant risk of personal injury or death'.

The Code covers cases where evidence indicates the existence of a safety defect in units which appears to be common to a number of units and where the units are available for supply in the UK. It is the responsibility of the supplier to decide whether evidence of a safety defect amounts to a case which is notifiable under the terms of the Code. As soon as a supplier has concluded that there is evidence of a safety defect which requires remedial action he must notify the Vehicle and Operators Service Agency (VOSA) indicating:
(a)   the nature of the defect and estimated number of units involved;
(b)   the nature of the safety hazard involved; and
(c)   the action planned at that time to remedy the defect.

In cases where the defect appears to stem from a fault in a component produced by another supplier, the other supplier must also be notified and VOSA advised accordingly.

When a supplier has made a decision to recall he has to take all reasonable steps to notify the owners or registered keepers of the affected vehicles. The supplier is permitted by the Code to use any method at his disposal to notify and may either contact the owner direct or through his franchised dealer network. If no response is received from the owner to the first communication the manufacturer or the franchised dealer must send a further letter by recorded delivery. The supplier may request the Driver and Vehicle Licensing Agency to obtain details of the name and address of the owner or registered keeper shown on the records there or to address and despatch a letter from the manufacturer to the owner or registered keeper.

Reporting of information

Vehicle manufacturers are required to notify VOSA at three-monthly intervals until the recall action is complete or it is mutually agreed that the campaign be closed as any remaining unactioned vehicles are unlikely to be traced. VOSA reserves the right to publish at any time any information which it receives where this seems to be necessary in the public interest. Before doing this, however, it must consult with the supplier , and must not disclose publicly information on matters of commercial confidence unless there appear to be overriding safety considerations. VOSA publishes a regular summary of the information on action taken on cases notified under the code including response rates.

VOSA may also seek information from a supplier on its own initiative about safety defects that have been brought to its attention. In this instance the supplier must pass all relevant information available to VOSA and cooperate in establishing whether a defect is present. While the prime responsibility for action rests with the supplier, VOSA may offer views and make recommendations.

2 Customer's failure to respond to a recall campaign

The code of practice recognises that not all customers will respond to the first contact from the manufacturer or his franchised dealer and that this may involve a second contact. Even when this has been done there will still be cases when the customer does not respond to the campaign. The question can then arise as to what will happen if a customer, whose vehicle was not taken in for remedial treatment, is subsequently involved in an accident caused by the safety defect which causes him damage and injury. If the customer deliberately chooses to ignore a recall campaign despite receiving the appropriate communications from the manufacturer or the franchised dealer, then it seems that any subsequent accident caused by the defect must be contributed to by his own negligence and he will be unlikely to be able to recover the full amount of any damage from the manufacturer, whether he makes a claim in negligence or based on strict liability under the Consumer Protection Act 1987, Pt I (see Chapter 10). The (former) Ministry of Transport has remarked that 'owners who choose not to respond to a recall notice are a potential hazard not only to themselves, but to other road users'.

If, however, the lack of response to the campaign has been due, for example, to an administrative error or if the correct registered keeper or owner's name is not for some reason recorded at the Driver and Vehicle Licensing Agency then the position is not so straightforward. Similarly, if a vehicle has not been taken to a franchised dealer for the necessary work to be done because of some delay on the part of the owner who fully intends to respond, or perhaps where the dealer is not able to take the vehicle in because he does not have an adequate supply of parts necessary to carry out the work, the fact that the manufacturer has instituted a recall campaign in accordance with the Code because this cannot in itself affect the manufacturer's legal responsibility to his customers, particularly in respect of strict liability. In a claim based on negligence however, compliance with the code of practice, however, may well be evidence which will support a manufacturer's contention that he was not negligent and that he had discharged his duty of care towards his customer.

D SUPPLY OF UNROADWORTHY VEHICLES

The Road Traffic Act 1988 (as amended by the Road Traffic Act 1991) provides[12] that it is an offence to supply a motor vehicle or trailer in an unroadworthy condition. This means where use on the roads would be unlawful because of a failure to comply with requirements as to brakes, steering gear or tyres, or as to construction, weight or equipment, or

---

[12]   Section 75(1).

maintenance of parts or accessories, or its condition would involve the danger of injury to any person. Two recent cases have considered the meaning of the word 'supply', first in the context of the Trade Descriptions Act 1968[13], the second *Devon County Council v DB Cars*[14] in the context of the Road Traffic Acts. In both cases the court came to the view that the return of a vehicle to its owner could amount to a 'supply'. In the *DB Cars* case, a repairer committed an offence when an unroadworthy vehicle was handed back to the owner with an MOT certificate issued by another garage. It is also an offence to alter a vehicle so that it does not conform with construction requirements, or so that it involves a danger of injury to any person.[15]

There is a defence if the supplier proves that the vehicle was to be exported, or where the seller believed the vehicle would not be used on the road at all, or before it was repaired. An important amendment to this defence in the 1991 Act provides that where a vehicle is supplied by a trader he will not be able to rely on this defence unless he can prove that he took all reasonable steps to ensure that any prospective purchaser would be aware that use on the road would be unlawful. Similarly, where the vehicle is offered for sale he must prove that reasonable steps were taken to ensure that the person to whom the vehicle was offered was aware of the fact that it was unroadworthy.

The contract of sale will not be invalidated simply because of an offence under this section, but the customer will of course have his rights in respect of satisfactory quality and fitness for purpose (see Chapter 7).

Parts

It is an offence for any person to fit, permit or cause the fitting of a part which causes the vehicle to pose a danger or to contravene construction and use requirements, or to sell or supply such a part. Similar defences apply as those that relate to unroadworthy vehicles.[16]

---

[13] *Formula One Autocentres Ltd v Birmingham City Council* [1999] RTR 195 and see Chapter 4.
[14] [2001] EWHC Admin 521, [2002] Crim LR 71 and see Chapter 11.
[15] Section 75(4)(b) and (6)(a).
[16] Section 76.

E GENERAL SAFETY REQUIREMENTS

The government had power under the Consumer Safety Act 1978 to ban the sale and supply of unsafe goods (see above). Whilst this was never used in relation to motor vehicles, some orders have been made in respect of certain equipment for motor vehicles, and used to supplement the Construction and Use Regulations.

In 1982 a regulation was passed to ban the sale of filament lamps not marked with the appropriate EEC or ECE approval mark.[17] In 1984, the sale of tyres for passenger and dual purpose vehicles not complying with the appropriate regulations was banned.[18] These Regulations have now been superseded by Regulations made under the Consumer Protection Act (see below).[19]

I Consumer Protection Act 1987, Pt II

The Consumer Protection Act 1987 contains important provisions to introduce a general duty to sell only safe goods and supplements the provisions in Part I of the Act which introduces strict manufacturers' liability for defects.[20] Part II of the Act sets up criminal sanctions against the suppliers of unsafe consumer goods. This part of the Act will be dealt with through the criminal courts, leading to a fine of £5,000 or three months' imprisonment which can be applied even if the product concerned has not killed or injured anyone.

An important exclusion from the criminal offences in the Act are motor vehicles, which are of course covered by specific regulation under the Road Traffic Acts. However, spare parts and accessories are not excluded, and suppliers of these products will be subject to the provisions of the Act as will products not caught by the definition of 'motor vehicle'. For example, in 1988 the powers were used to ban the sale of three-wheeled all-terrain vehicles,[21] which are not vehicles intended or adapted for use on the roads.[22] Similarly, the Motor Vehicle Tyres

---

17   Filament Lamps for Vehicles (Safety) Regulations 1982, SI 1982/444.

18   Motor Vehicles Tyres (Safety) Regulations 1984, SI 1984/1233.

19   The Motor Vehicle Tyres (Safety) Regulations 1994, SI 1994/3117.

20   See ch 10, above.

21   The Three-Wheeled All-Terrain Motor Vehicles (Safety) Regulations 1988, SI 1988/2122.

22   See s 185 of the Road Traffic Act 1988.

(Safety) Regulations 1994,[23] place restrictions on the supply of defective tyres.

Goods covered by the Act must be 'reasonably safe'. In deciding what is reasonable the way the goods are marketed, or marked and any instructions or warning given with the goods will all be relevant, as will any published safety standards, and any reasonable means by which the goods could have been made safer.

What is safe?

The Act defines this as meaning that there is no risk, or only a risk reduced to a minimum, associated with the goods themselves, their use, keeping or consumption; their assembly; reliance on the accuracy of any measurement or reading made by the goods; or omission or leakage from the goods or from anything else caused by the goods.

Because this part of the Act creates criminal liability, there are more defences available to the supplier of goods than in Part 1. For example, it will be a defence to show that the goods are only safe because of compliance with a regulation, and safety standards. It will also be a defence to show that there was a reasonable belief that the goods would not be used in the UK, or that at the time of supply the retailer did not have reasonable grounds for knowing that the goods were unsafe. The Act does not apply to second hand goods, ie those not supplied as new.

Enforcement

Under previous safety legislation, trading standards officers and the Secretary of State had considerable powers to require goods to be removed from sale, and to order forfeiture of unsafe goods. These provisions are repeated in the Act, as are general powers to make safety regulations covering specific goods (see for example the regulations on unsafe tyres, above).

---

[23] SI 1994/3117, and see also the Road Vehicles (Brake Linings Safety) Regulations, 1999, SI 1999/2978.

2 General Product Safety Regulations 1994

These regulations, which implement an EC Directive on General Product Safety, came into force on 3 October 1994[24]. The regulations exist side by side with Part II of the Consumer Protection Act (see above), but do not overlap because where the regulations do not apply s 10 of the Consumer Protection Act will continue to apply. The regulations do not apply where there are specific provisions in Community law governing all aspects of the safety of the product. The regulations will therefore apply to those aspects of motor vehicles not covered by specific Community requirements,[25] and on a similar basis to parts and accessories. Both new and used products are covered. The Government has issued guidelines to local authorities confirming that the regulations may be used by trading standards officers to deal with unsafe used care on dealers' premises.[26] This has subsequently been confirmed by the Divisional Court.[27]

Prohibition of unsafe consumer products

The objective of the regulations is to try to ensure that unsafe products do not get into the hands of consumers by imposing responsibilities on producers not to place unsafe goods on the market. Producers include manufacturers, those who import into Europe or put their name or brand on goods, and anyone in the supply chain whose activities affect the safety of the product. Distributors are also covered, and are required to act with due care not to supply unsafe goods and to monitor the safety of goods placed on the market, in particular by passing on safety information.

It seems therefore that the retailer will become a producer for the purposes of this legislation when, for example, a conversion of the

---

[24]   SI 1994/2328. A revised Directive 2001/95/EC has been adopted which must be implemented in member states by 15 January 2004.

[25]   A company was prosecuted under the regulations, fined £4,000 and ordered to pay costs of £2,750 in respect of the supply of a horsebox fitted with dangerously hazardous electrical installations: *R v Ascot Horseboxes International Ltd* (Redhill Magistrates' Court, 17 February 1998, unreported).

[26]   The guidance was issued by the Department of Trade & Industry in August 1998 in response to a recommendation by the Director General of Fair Trading in the report *The Sale of Used Cars* (October 1997) requiring clarification on the powers of trading standards officers entering motor traders' premises for this purpose.

[27]   *Caerphilly County Borough Council v Stripp* CO/609/00 22 March 2000.

vehicle or pre-delivery inspection is carried out, or accessories affecting safety such as a spoiler or tow bar, are fitted by him to the vehicle.

The regulations create criminal offences for contravention of these requirements for both producers (under regulation 7) and distributors (under regulation 9a). The producer will be strictly liable for his actions, but the distributor will have a defence if he can show he did not know, and could not have been expected to know, that the goods were unsafe.

Products

This is defined as a product intended for use by consumers or likely to be used by consumers, supplied in the course of a commercial activity. New and second hand goods are caught, except where a supplier tells the consumer that second hand goods are supplied for repair or reconditioning before use.

The regulation applies to any product which is not a safe product. A safe product is defined as one which under normal use does not present any risk, or only a minimum acceptable risk, taking into account the characteristics of the product; its effect on other products with which it is reasonably foreseeable it will be used; the presentation of the product including labelling, instructions and other information supplied by the producer; the categories of consumers at serious risk when using the product. The fact that other products may be safer does not automatically mean that a product will be regarded as unsafe.

Monitoring

Producers are required to monitor their products to ensure that he informs himself about risks, and can recall products if necessary. They must also provide consumers with relevant information to enable them to assess the risks inherent in a product throughout the normal or reasonably foreseeable period of use, where the risks are not immediately obvious. Distributors are also required to assist in this process and to pass on information and details of any action needed.

Defences

A defence of 'due diligence' is allowed, on a similar basis to the offences under the Trade Descriptions Act 1968 and offences under pricing legislation (see Chapters 3 and 4).

Penalties

On conviction, a fine of up to £5,000 can be imposed, and/or imprisonment for up to three months.

CHAPTER 14

Petrol

One of the features of the legislation governing the storage and sale of petrol is the very great emphasis that is laid on the sites where petrol is stored and sold, and the responsibility of the proprietor of the site to ensure that safe standards are maintained.

A LICENSING

The basis of the control of the storage and sale of petrol is the licensing system. A licence is required to keep petrol or other petroleum products,[1] except[2] where not more than four gallons, kept in not more than two vessels not exceeding two gallons each in capacity, is kept for specified uses, including use in a motor vehicle, and not for the purpose of sale. The storage container must be marked with the words 'Petroleum Spirit' and 'Highly Inflammable'.

I Conditions

The licences are granted by the appropriate local authority. Conditions may be attached to the licence as to:
(a)   the manner of storage;
(b)   the nature and situation of the premises for which the licence is being issued;

---

[1]   Petroleum (Consolidation) Act 1928, s 1.
[2]   Petroleum-Spirit (Motor Vehicles, etc) Regulations 1929, SI 1929/952, and the Petroleum-Spirit (Plastic Containers) Regulations 1982, SI 1982/630.

(c)   any goods with which the petrol is to be stored;

(d)   generally as to the safe keeping of petrol.

The local authority may impose any conditions it wishes which fall within one of these categories. There is however a right of appeal if they go beyond the Model Code of the Health and Safety Executive. Where the conditions have to be observed by employees at the site the occupier has a duty to keep the conditions posted, in such a form and position that they can be easily read by employees.

It should be noted that not only is it an offence for the occupier to fail to give notice of the licence conditions, but also an offence for any individual employee who has been given notice of them, to contravene them, or to deface or pull down the notice.

2 Period of the licence

The licence may be granted for whatever period the local authority thinks necessary and may be subject to whatever renewal provisions that the authority thinks necessary.

3 Appeals

If an application for a licence is refused by a local authority, or if it is granted on conditions to which the applicant objects, the applicant can request the local authority to give him a written certificate of the grounds on which the licence was refused, or the conditions stipulated.

The applicant then has 10 days in which to appeal to the Health and Safety Executive. A further period may be allowed by the Executive. The appeal must be made in writing, and may ask for the licence to be issued, or for the conditions to be withdrawn or modified.

The appeal must be accompanied by the certificate from the local authority. The Executive may then agree to issue the licence, or withdraw or modify the conditions, may specify the period of the licence and any provisions as to renewal. The Executive may, if they think it necessary or desirable, institute an enquiry before making any decision regarding the appeal.

4 Fees

Fees are payable to the local authority for the issue of a licence, and are prescribed by regulation.

5 Penalties

Keeping petrol without the required licence is an offence. The occupier of the premises is liable on summary conviction to a fine for every day on which the contravention occurs or continues. In addition, the petrol, and any container in which it is held, may be forfeited.

In addition, any person who contravenes the conditions of the licence commits an offence. This extends not just to the occupier of the premises, but also to individual employees. There is a fine for every day on which the contravention occurs or continues.

B TAKING DELIVERY

The conveyance of petrol by road in tankers, and the delivery to filling stations is now covered by the Carriage of Dangerous Goods by Road Regulations 1996.[3]

I General requirements

There are various general requirements on any person who is engaged in transporting, loading or unloading petrol:
(a)   all necessary precautions to prevent fire and explosion must be observed;
(b)   as far as is reasonably possible, it must be ensured that no petrol escapes into any sewer or drain;
(c)   any person on or attending a vehicle transporting petrol must refrain from smoking, and may not carry any matches or lighter;
(d)   no fire or artificial light capable of igniting inflammable vapour shall be allowed on any vehicle transporting petrol, and no explosive substance, or substance or article capable of causing a fire or explosion may be carried on such a vehicle;

---

[3]   SI 1996/2095.

(e)   a suitable and efficient fire extinguisher shall be carried in an easily accessible position on any vehicle transporting petrol.

The fuel tank of a mechanically propelled vehicle may not be filled or replenished with petrol direct from a petrol transporting vehicle covered by the regulations, and the cover of the fuel tank of a mechanically propelled vehicle must be kept securely closed except when it is being filled.

2 Storage tanks

The following regulations apply when petrol is transferred from the carrying tank of the transporter into a storage tank, and make it the responsibility of the proprietor of the licensed premises:

(a)   to ensure that the storage tank is clearly marked with a number which cannot be readily altered or defaced, and its maximum capacity and grade of petrol permitted to be stored in it;

(b)   to ensure that every dipstick other than those permanently fixed to a storage tank, and any other device used to check the quantity of petrol contained in a storage tank, is marked with the same number as the storage tank for which it is being used;

(c)   to ensure that any pipe leading to a filling point not on or immediately adjacent to the storage tank is also marked with the same number as that on the relevant storage tank;

(d)   to ensure before delivery begins, that a competent person who is not the driver or attendant on the tanker, is in charge of the storage tank for the purpose of the delivery; the person in charge of the storage tank must ensure that as far as possible no petrol overflows from the storage tank, or escapes at the filling point of the tank, or at any point between the filling point and the tank;

(e)   in addition, the competent person must not allow the delivery to start until:

   (i)   the storage tank has been checked with a dipstick or other suitable device and the test has shown that the quantity to be delivered can be safely accommodated by the tank;

   (ii)   where the delivery to the storage tank is by means of a pipe to a filling point not on or immediately adjacent to the tank itself, he has taken reasonable steps to ensure that the connecting hose through which the petrol is to be delivered is properly and securely connected to the filling point. In this

case he must also check that all the other pipes are properly
connected and in good condition;

(iii)   in any other case, that the connecting hose is properly and
securely connected to the filling point of the tank.

Once he has satisfied himself that all these points have been satisfactorily complied with, he must complete two copies of the prescribed
form showing:

(a)   the number of the storage tank;

(b)   the quantity and grade of petrol being delivered.

The person in charge of the storage tank must then sign each of the two
copies of the form in the presence of the tank driver or attendant. One
copy must then be handed to the driver or attendant.

The proprietor of the licensed premises, and the employer of the tanker
driver or attendant must then keep their copies of the certificate for a
period of not less than six months from the date of delivery.

During the delivery, both the person in charge of the storage tank, and
the tanker driver or attendant must keep a constant watch.

Where the licensee has a special licence and written agreement with the
operator of every road tanker likely to make deliveries to the premises,
it is possible for driver-controlled deliveries to be carried out. In this
instance the regulations set out further specific requirements.

3 Enforcement

The proprietor of licensed premises is obliged to give a duly authorised
officer of a local authority all reasonable facilities to check to see
whether the provisions of the regulations are being observed.

4 Penalties

Breach of the regulations is an offence punishable by a fine.

5 Warning notices

At any place where petrol is kept or sold, or offered or displayed for sale,
a label must be displayed containing in conspicuous letters the words

'Petroleum Spirit' and 'Highly Inflammable'. This notice must either be affixed to the container, or if that is impracticable, displayed nearby.

C DISPLAY OF PETROL PRICES

The failure of a minority of petrol stations to observe a voluntary code on the display of petrol prices led in 1978 to the introduction of legislation which followed fairly closely the content of the original code. The Price Marking (Petrol) Order 1980, which came into force on 1 January 1981 was consolidated into the Price Marking Order 1991.[4] This order was revoked by the Price Marking Order 1999[5], which now covers the pricing requirements for products offered for sale to consumers including petrol, and requires a trader to give details of the unit price where goods are sold from bulk. Unit prices of liquid fuel, lubricating oil, mixtures of fuel and oil, lubricating grease and anti-freeze are required to be indicated by volume.[6]

D CALIBRATION OF PETROL PUMPS

The Weights and Measures Act 1963[7] and the Measuring Equipment (Liquid Fuel and Lubricants) Regulations 1995[8] as amended prescribe the principles of construction for measuring instruments used for trade in liquid fuel and lubricants. In addition, measuring instruments are required to be tested in accordance with the Act, and stamped by an inspector.

I Testing

Every measuring instrument covered by the regulations must be tested, passed fit for trade and stamped before use. No instrument may be passed as fit for use for trade unless:

(a)   it complies with the requirements of the regulations; and

(b)   it measures and delivers fuel within the prescribed limits of error when operated at any reasonable speed (for prescribed limits of

4   SI 1991/1382.
5   Price Marking Order 1999, SI 1999/3042.
6   Price Marking Order 1999, SI 1999/3042 Annex 2 now itself revoked and replaced by SI 2004/102.
7   As amended by the Weights and Measures Act 1985.
8   SI 1995/1014 as amended by SI 1998/2218.

error see tables 1 and 2 on pp 244 and 245 below). The speed of operation for any individual delivery must be as uniform as practicable.

The person submitting equipment for testing must provide the inspector with such liquid fuel for testing as he may reasonably require.

2 Method of testing

Testing must be carried out under practical working conditions with the liquid fuel or lubricant or mixture of fuel and lubricant that the instrument is designed to deliver.

No measuring instrument may be tested unless it is complete with all parts and attachments concerned in the operations of measurement and delivery, and completely erected ready for use and installed at the place and in the permanent position where it is to be used.

Except where the measuring instrument is of a type where the delivery system remains permanently full up to the outer extremity of the discharge pipe, the inspector must ensure that the fuel has been passed through the instrument.

Before testing, if the equipment is fitted with a discharge hose, the inspector must ensure that liquid fuel has first passed through the equipment.

Any fuel withdrawn for the purpose of the test must be returned to the tank or container it was drawn from, if the proprietor does not object. Otherwise it must be placed in another receptacle chosen by the proprietor, if it is reasonably convenient.

The inspector shall, if requested to do so, give the proprietor a signed and dated statement of the quantity of fuel withdrawn and returned.

The inspector may open any locked or sealed tank or container for the purpose of his tests, and immediately after the fuel has been returned he must reseal and stamp it.

3 Stamping

The inspector's stamp must be placed on all the plugs, seals or sealing devices with which the instrument is required to be provided under the regulations.

The inspector may not stamp any instrument bearing a mark which might be mistaken for the prescribed stamp, or for an expression of approval or guarantee of accuracy by any other person.

The inspector must obliterate the stamp on any instrument which:
(a)   fails upon testing to fall within the prescribed limits of error; or
(b)   which fails to comply with any other requirement of the regulations; or
(c)   has been adjusted, altered, added to, repaired or replaced since it was last stamped, and could no longer be passed as fit for trade.

If, however, in the inspector's judgment the degree of non-compliance does not call for immediate obliteration, he may leave with the proprietor a notice calling on him to have the instrument corrected within a stated period, not exceeding twenty-eight days. If the correction has not been made within that period he must then obliterate the stamp.

Obliteration of one stamp acts as an obliteration of all the stamps on any particular instrument.

4 Continued use of unstamped equipment

The use for trade of unstamped equipment is an offence, and any transactions carried out with unstamped equipment are legally unenforceable.

The regulations however provide that:
(a)   where the stamped seal has been broken by the proprietor or his authorised agent for the purpose of adjusting the price computing device and indicator; or
(b)   the stamped seal has been broken by either the manufacturer, or regular repairer of the measuring instrument (or their authorised agent) for the purpose of adapting the instrument to measure in metric quantities and in each case, prior notice in writing complying with the regulations has been given to the inspector, the instrument may continue to be used for a period of twenty-eight days from the date of the notice in the case of a price change or five days in the case of a metric conversion.

5 Notice

The written notice required must contain the following information:
(a)   the location of, and particulars of the instrument concerned so that it can be identified;

(b)   the intended date of the alteration;

(c)   the business name and address of the manufacturer or repairer, if appropriate;

(d)   the name and address of the person giving the notification;

(e)   whether the proposed alteration relates to the price mechanism, or metric conversion.

E APPLICATION OF THE TRADE DESCRIPTIONS ACT 1968

The provisions of the Trade Descriptions Act 1968 apply to the sale of petrol as of any other goods. For example: because of supply problems, a trader obtained fuel from another source. He was summonsed for offering petrol for sale from pumps bearing the brand names of Shell Mex and BP Ltd when in fact the petrol was not the product of that company and this was therefore a false trade description. In addition, the petrol sold was a lower octane than that marked on the pump. In another case a trader has been convicted of an offence under the Act for selling 2 star petrol described as 4 star. In *Roberts v Severn Petroleum and Trading Co Ltd*, a bulk supplier delivered petrol to a retailer whose site was clearly operating as an Esso site. The petrol delivered was not Esso product. The garage owner, having been convicted of the offence of 'supplying' falsely described petrol to customers, the bulk supplier was also convicted of 'applying' a false description even though he only delivered the petrol into the Esso labelled tanks.[9]

F THE CONTRACT WITH THE CONSUMER

As in any other contract for the supply of goods, the trader has to supply petrol of the type he has contracted to sell which must be satisfactory and fit for purpose. Therefore, the sale of fuel which has become contaminated or not corresponding to the 'star' rating will be a breach of contract, actionable by the consumer.

The consumer, on the other hand, must pay for the petrol which he buys. Because of the special nature of the product, the usual rules about the ownership not passing until payment is received do not apply. As soon as the petrol is delivered into the car it has been held that because it could not be separated again from any fuel already in the tank it has

[9]   [1981] RTR 312, DC.

been allocated to that contract with the customer and the ownership has passed. The consequence that follows from this is that the customer who drives away without paying commits an offence under the Theft Act 1968.[10]

Table I
Prescribed Limits of Error Ordinarily Applicable on Testing for Quantities Above the Minimum Delivery of the Equipment

Quantity indicated	*In relation to passing as fit for use for trade, in excess or in deficiency*	
	Dynamic viscosity less than or equal to 1000 mPa.s	*Dynamic viscosity less than or equal to 1000 mPa.s*
Less than 0.1L	2mL	4mL
From 0.1L to 0.2L	2% of the quantity indicated	4% of the quantity indicated
From 0.2L to 0.4L	4mL	8mL
From 0.4L to 1L	1% of the quantity indicated	2% of the quantity indicated
From 1L to 2L	10mL	20mL
2L or more	0.5% of the quantity indicated	1% of the quantity indicated

Quantity indicated	*In relation to obliteration of the stamp*	
	Dynamic viscosity less than or equal to 1000 mPa.s	*Dynamic viscosity less than or equal to 1000 mPa.s*
Less than 0.1L	4mL in excess	8mL in excess
	2mL in deficiency	4mL in deficiency
From 0.1L to 0.2L	4% in excess	8% in excess
	2% in deficiency	4% in deficiency
From 0.2L to 0.4L	8mL in excess	16mL in excess
	4mL in deficiency	8mL in deficiency
From 0.4L to 1L	2% in excess	4% in excess
	1% in deficiency	2% in deficiency
From 1L to 2L	20mL in excess	40mL in excess
	10mL in deficiency	20 m in deficiency
2L or more	1% in excess	2% in excess
	0.5% in deficiency	1% in deficiency

---

[10]   *Edwards v Ddin* [1976] 3 All ER 705 and *R v McHugh* [1977] RTR 1, CA.

Table 2
Prescribed Limits of Error Ordinarily Applicable on Testing for Quantities Equivalent to the Minimum Delivery of the Equipment Only

Quantity indicated	*In relation to passing as fit for use for trade, in excess or in deficiency*	
	Dynamic viscosity less than or equal to 1000 mPa.s	*Dynamic viscosity less than or equal to 1000 mPa.s*
Less than 0.1L	2mL	4mL
From 0.1L to 0.2L	2% of the quantity indicated	4% of the quantity indicated
From 0.2L to 0.4L	4mL	8mL
From 0.4L to 1L	1% of the quantity indicated	2% of the quantity indicated
From 1L to 2L	10mL	20mL
2L or more	0.5% of the quantity indicated	1% of the quantity indicated

Quantity indicated	*In relation to obliteration of the stamp*	
	Dynamic viscosity less than or equal to 1000 mPa.s	*Dynamic viscosity less than or equal to 1000 mPa.s*
Less than 0.1L	4mL in excess 2mL in deficiency	8mL in excess 4mL in deficiency
From 0.1L to 0.2L	4% in excess 2% in deficiency	8% in excess 4% in deficiency
From 0.2L to 0.4L	8mL in excess 4mL in deficiency	16mL in excess 8mL in deficiency
From 0.4L to 1L	2% in excess 1% in deficiency	4% in excess 2% in deficiency
From 1L to 2L	20mL in excess 10mL in deficiency	40mL in excess 20 m in deficiency
2L or more	1% in excess 0.5% in deficiency	2% in excess 1% in deficiency

CHAPTER 15

Dealing with complaints

Even companies which make every effort to ensure the quality of the goods they are selling and the fairness of their policy towards customer relations will sometimes get complaints. Dealing with them success-fully is never easy. Getting the balance right so that customers are treated fairly and in accordance with their legal rights without turning down justified complaints or becoming a soft touch for customers who want to get something for nothing requires careful judgment. An unbal-anced decision either way can cost money. It is also essential for the manufacturer's or retailer's own protection that he and his staff are aware of the possible legal implications of complaints and the way they are handled.

The quick successful handling of complaints is, like many other things, easier to theorise about than to handle in practice. The basic essentials must be however:

(a)   efficient and well-trained customer relations and service staff;

(b)   a thorough system of record-keeping so that the full history of a complaint can be available for immediate reference at any time;

(c)   a sound grasp of the legal principles involved, and an awareness of when to seek legal advice.

A REQUIREMENTS OF THE CODES

The Office of Fair Trading quite rightly views the way in which complaints are handled as being one of the most important aspects of the relationship between an industry and its customers. From the consumer's point of view it is after all pointless to have great amounts of legislation to protect him, if at the end of the day he is still not able to get what he is legally entitled to.

I Obligations of the industry

The Codes of Practice therefore goes to some lengths to give guidance on handling complaints:

(a)   manufacturers and dealers have a responsibility to ensure that effective and immediate action is taken to settle complaints and there must be an easily identifiable arrangement for the handling of complaints, and manufacturers must cooperate with their dealer networks in handling complaints;

(b)   in the event of no settlement being reached, the consumer must be advised of this right to refer the complaint to the relevant trade association;

(c)   manufacturers and dealers must co-operate with their trade association in the investigation of a complaint;

(d)   if conciliation fails, the consumer has the right to request arbitration organised by the independent Panel of Arbitrators.

2 Obligations of the consumer

In addition, the Codes also advise the consumer as to the way he should go about making his complaint:

(a)   a complaint about the quality of goods or service should be made in the first instance to the dealer concerned;

(b)   it should be addressed to a senior executive;

(c)   if the complaint relates to a new car and it is not resolved by the dealer the consumer should take it to the manufacturer;

(d)   if no solution is reached at dealer or manufacturer level, the consumer can then refer the complaint to the relevant trade association, the RMIF, SMTA or SMMT;

(e)   the trade association must use its 'best endeavour' to settle the complaint;

(f)   if it fails, the manufacturer/dealer must agree to arbitration unless the association believes it is 'unreasonable' for the members to have to do so.

The 'effective and immediate' action to deal with complaints required by the code is not only important to consumers but is also clearly in the best interests of dealers and manufacturers because:

(a)   it helps to retain customer goodwill; and

(b)   it saves staff time, and therefore money, otherwise being spent on a complaint which will have to be settled eventually.

B LEGAL ASPECTS OF COMPLAINTS

The majority of complaints made by the customer will involve questions of legal liability:

— the car is rusting after eighteen months: is the retailer or the manufacturer liable?

— the car was serviced last week, and it now needs a major repair: does the servicing garage have to pay?

— the steering failed, causing an accident: who has to pay?

— the customer wants to cancel his order because of late delivery: is he able to?

— the customer wants a replacement car because of the problems he's had: is he entitled to it?

Fortunately, the number of customers who actually take a retailer or manufacturer to court over this type of dispute are few and far between. This is no doubt due partly to the fact that legal action is expensive and its outcome is uncertain and partly because most cases of genuine grievance are identified early enough so that they can be settled in a satisfactory way. This is really the nub of dealing with complaints. It does no one any good to let a case go to court where the customer has the law on his side.

In some cases, it may be that the law is sufficiently uncertain to warrant a complaint being treated as a 'test case', but these are comparatively rare. In other cases it will simply create adverse publicity which the media will make the most of, regardless of the actual outcome of the case. Bear in mind that a major case, say in the High Court, is likely to go on for several days. The plaintiff, ie the customer, will put his case first.

The press will seize on his evidence and use it in sensationalised form under headings such as 'Doctor's 'rogue' car' or 'solicitor 'suffered' from buying British'. The evidence from the retailer may be heard several days later, and the judgment given even later than that. There is no guarantee that even if the retailer is successful in resisting the claim, the full story will be printed, or, if it is, that potential customers will associate the two stories together. It is more likely that the first story will have done further damage both to the reputation of the individuals involved, and to the motor industry as a whole.

This is not to say of course, that there are never cases which should be allowed to go to court. What it does mean is that it is essential, that in any case which does get that far, a conscious decision has been taken by the manufacturer or trader concerned not to dispose of it in some other way.

In looking at a complaint which threatens to escalate into legal action, various aspects have to be taken into account before a decision is made.

I Considering a claim

What are the facts?

This may seem an obvious point, but it is surprising how often the facts as seen by the customer differ in some fundamental respect from the facts as seen by, eg the service manager. The first step has to be to go back over the history with the staff concerned and establish as clearly as possible what the facts are, and where, if at all, they differ from the customer's version. If the customer has an engineer's report in his favour, it will be important to judge how reliable it is, and how it might stand up in court should the worst come to the worst. Remember, that if you are dealing with a consumer customer[1], the burden of proof will be reversed and it will now be assumed that any defect arising during the first six months after delivery of the goods was present at the time of sale.[2]

What evidence do I have?

This is where properly completed job sheets and instruction cards are essential and a written record of the handling of every complaint

---

[1] For the definition of a consumer, see Chapter 7.

[2] Sale and Supply of Goods to Consumers Regulations 2002, SI 2002/3045; see Chapter 7.

received in other words a formal record system. It is no good relying on the memory of the service receptionist as to what the customer said on a busy morning three months ago—if it's down on paper it reinforces the case tremendously and could be crucial if there is a difference of opinion as to what actually happened. If there are two versions, consider how your paperwork will stand up in court, and also how reliable your witnesses are. If there is no written evidence in your support, think very carefully at this stage as to whether you should let it go on.

What does the law say?

In some cases this will not be a clear cut question to answer in others it will be obvious even to a layman. The essential point here is that it is always better to get expert advice too early rather than too late. The money it costs will be more than offset by the financial and commercial risks you will run if you have to settle after a writ has been issued. If you agree to pay the claim after issue of legal proceedings, not only will you have involved further staff time and money, but you will also be liable for the legal costs of the other side.

If the customer has gone to solicitors who are literally laying down the law to you, don't automatically assume that they are right—it has been known for a lawyer to get it wrong occasionally. It is far better at that stage to get your own solicitor to look at the case, so that he can help you with the correspondence and negotiations, and possibly take it over for you altogether. Let him get involved in the niceties of the legal argument—it can be dangerous ground. Make sure that you have given him all the information which you have about the complaint. If you hold something back which you think is unimportant, you might find too late that it was a vital point which altered the whole case. If, as a result of a case, your lawyer advises you to change some aspect of your procedure or paperwork, make sure it is done; don't simply ignore it and hope for the best.

Is the customer's claim reasonable?

This is another aspect of considering the legal aspects of the customer's claim. If you believe, or are advised, that the customer has a legally enforceable claim against you, it does not necessarily follow that he is entitled to all that he is claiming.

For example, a customer who is complaining about a series of faults in a new car may well be entitled to compensation for towing charges, the cost of alternative transport, and to have the car put right. He may not be entitled to have the car replaced if this is 'disproportionate' in terms of the cost to the seller [3] Expert advice may well be needed at this stage if not earlier, to determine just how much a reasonable offer should be.

Making an offer to settle

Where it has been decided to try to settle with a customer, it is very important to make sure that you are not going to make your position any worse. If, for example, you offer a customer £200 because of defects in a car you sold him and he turns this down, he may then try to use your offer in court as an argument proving your legal liability, and his entitlement to a larger sum.

In order to avoid this sort of problem, it is common for letters containing an offer of payment to state, eg 'this offer is made without any admission of liability on our part'. It is probably better, particularly in difficult cases, to head all the correspondence about a possible settlement 'Without Prejudice'. The effect of this is to make all the letters bearing this heading 'privileged' from production in any subsequent court hearing. In other words, anything said in those letters will remain confidential between the parties, and cannot be used by one side against the other. If a solicitor is handling the negotiations, he will normally use this formula unless there are good reasons why not.

Is there any aspect I wouldn't want published?

This is an important consideration if you are unwilling on legal grounds to settle with the customer. Bear in mind that in a legal action all documents relevant to the dispute can be ordered by the court to be produced (except 'without prejudice' correspondence see above). Try to look at your evidence and your documentation through the eyes of a possibly unsympathetic judge, and see whether you may be laying yourself open to criticism, even if legally you are in the right.

---

[3]   Sale and Supply of Goods to Consumers Regulations 2002, SI 2002/3045; and see Chapter 7.

Has the customer been offered conciliation?

Although this is a consideration not strictly relevant to the legal issues, it is a point which has to be borne in mind because the New Car Code provides that in the event of a complaint remains unresolved the manufacturer must make it clear to a consumer that he has a right to refer the complaint to the Regulations and Compliance Unit of the SMMT. The manufacturer must then give every assistance to them in investigating the complaint.

Similarly, the Code of Practice for the Retail Motor Industry gives consumers the right to have complaints referred to the RMIF or SMTA.

Have other aspects of the Code been complied with?

Although the legal enforceability of the Code is not entirely clear (see Chapter 2, above), any failure to comply with any of its specific provisions will at the best give an opportunity for adverse publicity, and at worst, action by the Office of Fair Trading.

2 Arbitration

If a complaint is not settled, the consumer may decide to bring legal action. If he has used the complaints procedure set out in the Codes and conciliation by the trade association has failed, he may request that the case be referred to an Independent Panel of Arbitrators for a low-cost, usually documents only, arbitration under the provisions of the Codes. Note that he does not have to use the arbitration scheme; he is perfectly entitled to pursue his claim through the courts if he prefers. Indeed, even if the contract with him contained an agreement to refer all disputes automatically to arbitration, this would not now be enforceable against him.[4] In addition, under the Arbitration Act 1996 a clause referring present or future disputes to arbitration will be treated as unfair under the Unfair Terms in Consumer Contracts Regulations where the value in dispute does not exceed £3000.[5].

Where a customer has requested arbitration, the member has to agree to it, except where the trade association is of the opinion that it would be

---

[4]   Consumer Arbitration Agreements Act 1988.
[5]   SI 1996/3211.

unreasonable for the member to be required to do so. There has been a great deal of discussion about the practical effect of this provision. What circumstances will make it 'unreasonable' for a member to have to agree to arbitration? It seems that there will be very few cases where this will apply. Possibly this might arise where a point of law of major importance is involved, or where personal injuries are the subject of the claim, and it would clearly be better for both parties if the case were to go to court.

Parties to an arbitration

The parties to an arbitration under the Code will usually be the selling or servicing/repairing dealer, and the customer. In cases involving a new car, under warranty or where a manufacturing defect is alleged, the arbitrator may ask that the manufacturer also be joined in as a party to a dispute.

Fees

The parties each pay a fee on a sliding scale related to the size of the claim. When the arbitrator makes his award he may return this to the successful party.

Application for arbitration

An application form must be signed by all the parties and despatched with the appropriate fees.

The arbitrator

The arbitrator is appointed from an independent panel of arbitrators. He will usually be someone with relevant experience or qualifications, eg in engineering, as well as being a lawyer.

Evidence

Evidence to the arbitrator will normally be by way of documents only. The objective of this system is that costs will be kept down, and oral evidence will normally only be given if specifically required by the arbitrator. The documentary evidence is submitted by the trade association, which must supply all the papers they consider relevant.

The arbitrator may indicate that further evidence is needed, and he may order the parties to provide him with whatever further evidence he requires. This might include the provision of a report by an independent engineer, which will then be paid for by the relevant trade association.

Technical assessors

The arbitrator is able to draw on panels of technical assessors for detailed technical advice provided by the membership of the trade association. Care is taken to ensure that the technical assessors are impartial in relation to the cases they are advising on.

Legal representation

As the objective of the scheme is to keep costs down, legal representation will not normally be allowed unless the arbitrator makes a specific direction.

Publication of the arbitration award

Publication of the award is made to the parties, and to the relevant trade association. This will normally consist of the decision only, and not the reasoning behind it.

Enforcing the award

The decision of the arbitrator is binding on both parties by virtue of the agreement to go to arbitration, and can be enforced through the courts if it is not honoured.

Appeals

There is no appeal against the award made by an arbitrator unless it can be shown that he was 'mad or bad', or that the decision was wrong in law. As the arbitrator will not normally publish the reasons for his award the effect is to preclude appeals to the courts.

Pros and cons of arbitration

From the retailer's or manufacturer's point of view the arbitration scheme does have advantages. It is private in the sense that the public has no access to the hearing, and the result will only be publicised if one of the parties chooses to do so. The fact that the same arbitrators are frequently used in motor industry cases means that there may be more consistency in their decisions than if left to, eg local county courts up and down the country. This familiarity with motor industry cases can of course also operate to a dealer or manufacturer's disadvantage, particularly if he has several cases of the same type all going to arbitration.

Against arbitration it has to be said that in some cases it may come up with what is just a solution, rather than an answer which is precisely legally correct or fair to both parties. However, it may be felt that this is one of its strongest points too—it is a way of bringing a conclusion to an otherwise intractable dispute, without the unwelcome cost and publicity involved in going into court.

The 'low cost' aspect of the arbitration really only operates from the consumer's point of view. Although the dealer or manufacturer will be saving on the legal costs which would be incurred if the case came to court, there is nevertheless a good deal of staff time involved in making sure that the documents presented to the arbitrator, and the replies given to any questions he asks, are accurate and complete.

3 The courts

If the arbitration scheme is not used, the consumer who wants to take legal action will have to take his claim through the courts. This will be by way of an action either in the High Court or the county court depending on the size of the claim.

Procedure

The rules of procedure are fairly complicated, and in recent years steps have been taken to make it easier for consumers and others who have small claims to pursue them in the county court without legal representation. In 1999, a complete new set of procedural rules came into force aimed at reducing the expense, delays and uncertainty of going to court. This is very much oriented towards the avoidance of court action, by encouraging efforts to settle, by requiring the parties to be open and to disclose documents at an early stage, to co-operate with the court, and finally by giving the courts much greater powers to manage cases. This includes allocating the case into one of three 'tracks'. The small claims track will deal with claims up to £5000, the fast track relatively simple claims between £5000 and £15000, and the multi-track for cases over £15,000 or for fast track cases taking more than one day.

The trader should not overlook the fact that the county court may also be of use to him in recovering debts from customers. Advice on the procedure to bring a claim will be available from any county court.

For either pursuing or defending any larger claims it is best to get legal advice. There is a rule which operates in both the High Court and the county court that a limited company may only be represented by a lawyer and that it cannot represent itself, eg by a director. This rule is now not always enforced in the county courts, and therefore in relation to small claims it may be worthwhile considering disposing with the services of a lawyer.

Pros and cons

The major disadvantage of court proceedings is that they are held in public. Not only the outcome of the case but also the evidence can be published, and in many cases this may be undesirable. This does not however apply to small claims arbitrations in the county courts or to the intermediate proceedings in the High Court or county court between the issue of the summons or writ, and the actual hearing of the case in open court.

Costs

The cost involved in going to court will obviously depend on various factors: the nature of the claim, whether lawyers are instructed on both sides; whether any third party is joined in eg the manufacturer in a claim relating to a new car; and the complexity of the evidence. Bear in mind though, that the general rule is that 'costs follow the event'. This means that generally the winner takes all, and the loser has to pay not only his own costs but also those of the other party as well. It should be borne in mind that an action in the High Court involves costs in quite a different financial league from the county court, and this must be a factor in deciding how to handle a particular case.

4 To litigate or not?

If litigation can be avoided with customers or with anyone else, the advice must be to avoid it. It is too long-winded, too expensive and too uncertain to be anything but a frustrating and costly experience. Sometimes it will be inevitable, however, and the question may then be, arbitration or the courts?

This decision is one which is obviously going to depend on the facts in each case, but in any case except one involving a very important point of law, or a very large claim for damages, it is very worthwhile considering the advantages of opting for arbitration.

Appendix I
Who's who and what's in consumer protection

CONSUMER ORGANISATIONS

Citizens' Advice Bureaux

The Citizens' Advice Bureaux exist to offer a service of advice on individual problems. Although the scope of their activities is wider than just advice on consumer problems, advice on this sort of matter accounts for a fair proportion of their work. They are funded by local authorities and also partially by central government.

Consumer Advice Centres

Consumer Advice Centres date from the early 1970s when it was felt there was a need to provide an advisory service to consumers to help them in getting satisfaction when they have a complaint about faulty goods or poor services, and also to give advice before they purchase goods. The centres are set up by the local authorities, and aided by grants from central government. Few now remain due to the cut-backs in public spending.

The Consumers' Association

The Consumers' Association was formed in 1957 and aims to give consumer information about products and services by testing them and publishing the results in its magazines, eg *Which?* and *Motoring Which?*. The Association is financed by members' subscriptions.

The National Consumers Council

The National Consumers Council is sponsored directly by government and its main function is to represent the consumer interest in dealings with government and industry to ensure that the consumer point of view is taken into account before policies are formulated or implemented.

ENFORCEMENT AUTHORITIES

Consumer protection departments of local authorities

The consumer protection departments of local authorities have a wide range of responsibilities in the day-to-day enforcement of consumer protection legislation, and other trading laws which affect motor traders, for example:
The Trade Descriptions Act 1968;
pricing legislation;
calibration of petrol pumps.

The Office of Fair Trading

The Office of Fair Trading was originally the staff of the Director-General of Fair Trading, a post created by the 1973 Fair Trading Act.

Now reconstituted under the Enterprise Act 2002, the OFT has wide powers in relation to monopolies, mergers, restrictive practices, competition law, consumer credit and fair trading generally. It has powers to obtain undertakings and enforcement orders under the Enterprise Act from traders which do not comply with a variety of consumer protection statutes. It also controls the issue of consumer credit licences, and monitors the Unfair Terms in Consumer Contracts Regulations 1999

Health and Safety Executive

The Health and Safety Executive was created by the Health and Safety at Work Act 1974, and has a wide range of responsibilities with regard to safety in the workplace. In particular, they have responsibilities for the issuing and control of petroleum licences.

GOVERNMENT DEPARTMENTS

Government departments with an interest in consumer protection matters within the scope of this book include:

The Department of Trade and Industry

This is the department responsible for the implementation of government policy towards consumer protection. The Minister responsible for consumer affairs is also responsible for the work of the Office of Fair Trading, and the National Consumer Council. It also sponsors the British Standards Institution.

The Department for Transport

This Department is responsible for the operation of the road traffic legislation including the construction and use of vehicles, and through the Vehicle and Operator Services Agency sponsors the SMMT Code of Practice on Vehicle Safety Defects.

Appendix 2
Guidance for Car Dealers – for consumer credit licence holders and applicants in the used and new car markets

GUIDANCE FOR CAR DEALERS
FOR CONSUMER CREDIT LICENCE HOLDERS AND APPLICANTS
IN THE USED AND NEW CAR MARKETSDECEMBER 2003

Introduction

This guidance is primarily for the use of secondhand car dealers. It is based on the OFT's experience of problems with unfair trading in this market gained through our powers under the Consumer Credit Act 1974. For most people in the UK, buying a used car is one of the most expensive purchases they make and so it is important that they are fairly treated, yet there are significant potential problems of which many people are unaware. We have therefore set out in one document the criteria we use to assess whether a used car dealer is fit to hold a consumer credit licence. By publishing these criteria we aim to encourage businesses to develop better trading practices and so reduce the amount of unfair trading experienced by the public.

Some of the practices described in this guidance also apply to the new car market, for example, failing to deal adequately with complaints and giving misleading information on prices. Where these practices apply to the new car market, you should note that we also use them to assess the fitness to hold a consumer credit licence of traders selling new cars.

Scope of the guidance

This guidance is specific to the motor trade and should be read in conjunction with the general guidance given in *Consumer credit licences – guidance for holders and applicants*[1].

This guidance is not exhaustive. Further issues which bear on your fitness to hold a licence may be dealt with in other guidance to be published in the future such as guidance on debt collection or – on an individual basis – by your local trading standards service.

In issuing this guidance we have consulted a wide range of interested parties. This guidance deals only with the acts or omissions which may affect your fitness to hold a consumer credit licence. If your acts or omissions were to constitute a criminal offence or breach a statutory duty, you might also be liable for prosecution or in some cases, action under Part 8 of the Enterprise Act 2002[2] either by us or other enforcement bodies such as trading standards.

Purpose of the guidance

The OFT has a duty under the Consumer Credit Act 1974 to ensure that applicants for licences are fit to engage in the activities for which they wish to be licensed and to monitor the continuing fitness of those to whom licences have been granted. In considering fitness we must take into account any circumstances which appear to be relevant. In particular, we will consider any evidence that an applicant or licensee, or any of their employees, agents or associates, have

- committed any offence involving fraud or other dishonesty or violence, or
- contravened any provision made by or under the Consumer Credit Act 1974 or by or under any other enactment regulating the provision of credit to individuals or other transactions with individuals, or
- practised discrimination on grounds of sex, colour, race, or ethnic origin in connection with the carrying on of any business, or
- engaged in business practices appearing to the OFT to be deceitful, oppressive or otherwise unfair or improper (whether unlawful or not).

---

[1]   To order a copy see page 12.
[2]   Prior to this Act coming into force you may face action under the Stop Now Regulations.

Where we have evidence of such practices, action can be taken to refuse or revoke the consumer credit licence of those concerned.

We also have the power to take action, where appropriate, under other legislation such as
- the Control of Misleading Advertisements Regulations 1988
- the Unfair Terms in Consumer Contracts Regulations 1999
- the Consumer Protection (Distance Selling) Regulations 2000.

The main problems identified in the secondhand car market are:
- incorrect mileage readings
- difficulty in establishing ownership
- faulty mechanical condition of vehicles, and
- poor after sales service.

None of these problems are new and they are all very serious. Clocked or stolen cars can involve substantial financial loss as can undetected mechanical faults. Where safety is compromised the risks are even greater. Every unsafe car on the road has the potential to damage the lives of its owner, passengers and other road users. The purpose of this guidance is to identify the kinds of conduct which may adversely influence the consideration of the fitness of a secondhand car dealer to hold a consumer credit licence.

Not all points listed will apply to every car dealer nor is the list exhaustive – even when read together with *Consumer credit licences – guidance for holders and applicants* (to order a copy see page 12). We decide every case on its merits and trading practices not mentioned in this guidance may be taken into account when we determine your fitness. You are expected to abide by the spirit, as well as the letter, of this guidance.

The guidance

The following guidance highlights trading practices or conduct which are specific to the secondhand car market and in some instances to the new car market as well. We consider this conduct to be relevant to a trader's fitness to hold a consumer credit licence and so we will take them into consideration when deciding whether a consumer credit licensee or an applicant for such a licence is fit to hold that licence.

Vehicle roadworthiness

Secondhand vehicles must conform to the legislation affecting their construction and use (that is, their roadworthiness under the Road Traffic Act 1988) and, where appropriate, be accompanied by a current MOT Certificate. Under the Sale of Goods Act 1979, used cars supplied by a trader must also be of satisfactory quality and fit for their purpose. Consumers should be able to buy a car which is in reasonable mechanical condition (for its age) and is safe. The following conduct will be considered to have a bearing on the fitness of a licensee or applicant:

a)   discouraging consumers from examining or having vehicles examined

b)   selling or offering to sell vehicles which are not of a satisfactory quality or fit for their purpose

c)   supplying, offering to supply or exposing for sale on your forecourt, in your showroom or other part of your premises including on the highway, an unroadworthy[3] vehicle, in contravention of section 75(1) of the Road Traffic Act 1988 and/or regulation 9 of the General Product Safety Regulations 1994

d)   altering[4] the construction, weight or equipment of a vehicle so that under the Road Traffic Act 1988, it would be unlawful to use it on the road in that condition

e)   obtaining or providing stolen or fraudulent MOT documents

f)   using terms such as 'trade sale', 'must not be driven on public roads until put into a roadworthy state' or 'awaiting preparation' in a consumer transaction.

g)   selling 'cut and shut' vehicles, that is, cars produced by welding together the front and back of two different vehicles.

False or misleading descriptions or advertising

False or misleading descriptions may be applied in a number of ways. They may be

●   made verbally over the telephone or in the course of discussions prior to the sale of the vehicle, or

---

[3]   Unroadworthy' has the meaning given to it by section 75(3) of the Road Traffic Act 1988.

[4]   This may be done by way of a faulty repair for example.

- made in writing in advertising on the car, in the showroom or in a newspaper or they may be contained in documentation provided to the prospective buyer.

The following conduct will be considered as having a bearing on the fitness of a licensee or applicant:

a)   offering to alter the mileage on a vehicle's odometer (commonly known as car clocking)

b)   altering the mileage on a vehicle's odometer contrary to section 1(1)(a) of the Trade Descriptions Act 1968. It is irrelevant that you may later disclaim the mileage as incorrect.

c)   arranging for the alteration of the mileage on a vehicle's odometer contrary to section 20 of the Trade Descriptions Act 1968. It is irrelevant that you may later disclaim the mileage as incorrect.

d)   supplying, offering to supply or having on your forecourt for sale a clocked car contrary to section 1(1)(b) of the Trade Descriptions Act 1968

e)   using a disclaimer on a clocked car which is not as bold, precise and compelling as the mileage it is to disclaim

f)   reducing in any way the effectiveness of a disclaimer

g)   failing to tell consumers the true mileage of a car when it is known to the trader or any of his employees. Where the mileage shown on the odometer is incorrect, the true mileage must be disclosed to any prospective purchaser in a manner which is as bold, precise and compelling as the incorrect mileage recorded on the odometer. The OFT takes the view that it is deceitful and/or improper to merely disclaim the mileage when the true mileage is known and in such circumstances a disclaimer would not be a defence to a criminal charge and should not be used.

h)   offering to supply mileage alteration products

i)   misrepresenting in any other way the specification or history of the vehicle, for example, providing false service histories or misrepresenting the age or specification of a grey import[5] car.

j)   failing to inform consumers when selling a grey import car that it does not meet UK or EC specifications if that is the case

k)   applying other false or misleading descriptions to a vehicle including such descriptions as 'beautiful car' to a vehicle which is mechanically unsound

l)   falsely claiming or implying that cars have been checked by motoring organisations or that checks are used which meet those standards when they do not

m) representing the business or any individual partner, employee or associate of the business as belonging to or being a member of an organisation, institute or other body, to which they do not in fact belong

n) giving misleading price indications by whatever means contrary to section 20(1) of the Consumer Protection Act 1987.

Business ownership

It is important that a buyer knows who they are entering into a contract with, so that if necessary they are able to pursue their statutory rights through the Courts. The issue of trading names may be complex and the items listed below should not be considered exhaustive. If you have a query on complying with the law as it relates to disclosing your business identity then you should contact your local trading standards service for advice.

The following conduct will be considered to have a bearing on the fitness of a licensee or applicant:

a) claiming to be a private seller when this is not the case

b) causing an advertisement to be published which did not make it clear that the car was being sold in the course of a business contrary to the Business Advertisements (Disclosure) Order 1977

c) failing to display details of the ownership of a business in the form of a notice and on business letters and order forms in compliance with the Business Names Act 1985

d) if you are a company, failing to display your company name outside every premise from which you trade in compliance with section 348 of the Companies Act 1985. Failing to display on business documentation details of the company name, the address of the registered office and the company's registration number and place of registration in accordance with sections 349 and 351 of the Companies Act 1985.

---

[5] A 'grey' import is a vehicle designed and built for sale into a country outside the EU, and imported into the UK independently of the manufacturer or his appointed agent. Because such a vehicle may not originally have been intended for sale in the UK or Europe, it is not manufactured to European specifications and may not have undergone 'European Type Approval'. This means that it may not meet a number of EU safety and environmental standards. It is also possible that the vehicle may not comply with UK/EC directive legislation.

e) failing to give written notice immediately on request of the details of the ownership of the business as required under the Business Names Act 1985

f) misrepresenting the identity of the owner of the business, the supplier of the vehicle or the business providing the finance for the transaction

Vehicle ownership

There are major hazards for consumers if they cannot be sure of ownership of a vehicle, for example, used cars may have been stolen or they may be subject to a financial charge. In nearly all such cases the dealer cannot transfer ownership of the vehicle to the buyer. It is therefore important that a car dealer has full ownership of a vehicle before selling it.

The following conduct will be considered to have a bearing on the fitness of a licensee or applicant:

a) failing to settle outstanding finance on trade-in vehicles when contracting to do so

b) supplying a vehicle on which there is a finance agreement outstanding

c) supplying a stolen or cloned[6] vehicle.

Credit

You will be expected to comply in full with the requirements of the Consumer Credit Act 1974 and any regulations or orders made under that Act. In addition, you should also take note of any further publications we may produce giving guidance on finance issues relevant to your business. However, the following conduct will be considered to have a particular bearing on the fitness of a licensee or applicant:

a) asking consumers to sign blank or incomplete credit application forms or failing to supply the necessary copies of concluded agreements

b) publishing or causing to be published advertisements which do not comply with the Consumer Credit (Advertisement) Regulations 1989

---

[6] A 'cloned vehicle' – cloaking the identity of a stolen car by replacing its number plates with those of a legitimate vehicle. It may also have the Vehicle Identification Number (VIN) changed to match the numberplate.

c) making false statements as to deposits paid by customers to increase the amount of the loan or making statements to lenders in order to increase the consumer's credit score, for example, overstating income, understating current commitments or falsely stating age

d) giving incorrect APRs

e) improper repossession of vehicles subject to finance agreements or the making of threats that vehicles will be repossessed where no legal right to repossess them exists.

General

The following will also be considered to have a bearing on the fitness of a licensee or applicant:

a) failing to deal with complaints adequately or attempting to mislead consumers about their statutory or other rights

b) failing to give adequate redress to consumers when appropriate or traders failing to honour County Court Judgments against them

c) failing to return deposits when the consumer is due a refund or if the finance company withdraws from the transaction

d) using or making restrictive statements in particular those that purport to restrict Sale of Goods Act 1979 rights, for example, the display of a 'No Refund' sign even if the statement 'this does not affect your statutory rights' is included

e) failing to notify DVLA that a car has been sold or has been transferred into the trade

f) failing to comply with pre-contract information and cancellation requirements of the Consumer Protection (Distance Selling) Regulations 2000.

Other publications in this series

Consumer credit licences – guidance for holders and applicants, April 2002

Debt management guidance, December 2001

OFT information leaflets can be ordered free of charge from:

tel 0870 60 60 321
fax 0870 60 70 321
email oft@eclogistics.co.uk
address PO Box 366, Hayes UB3 1XB

Our publications can also be downloaded and/or ordered from our website

www.oft.gov.uk

CONSUMER CREDIT LICENCES
GUIDANCE FOR HOLDERS AND APPLICANTSDECEMBER 2003

Protecting consumers – encouraging competition

If your business offers any kind of consumer credit or hire, or if you are involved in activities relating to credit or hire you must have a licence, as required by the Consumer Credit Act, 1974 ('the Act'). To find out if your type of business or activity needs a licence, see our booklet Do you need a credit licence? You can get a copy from the Consumer Credit Licensing Bureau, Craven House, 40 Uxbridge Road, Ealing, London W5 2BS, telephone 020 7211 8608.[7]

This guidance leaflet explains how we make sure that you are fit to hold a licence and describes the kind of unfair business practices that could result in you losing an existing licence. The OFT has to make sure your business trades fairly, and may refuse to grant you a licence or take your licence away if you don't. It's very important for you to understand your responsibilities. By failing to do so you could commit a criminal offence or lose the right to hold a licence.

We have tried to make this guidance as simple and jargon-free as possible but inevitably explaining the legislation can be complicated. So if in doubt, contact our helpline or ask your professional adviser to help.

Some organisations hold a group credit licence which covers such persons and activities as described in the licence. If you are covered by a group licence and wish to carry on a licensable activity which is not covered by the group licence you will need to apply for a standard licence.

---

[7]   A list of guidance booklets for traders is given on page 11.

The fitness test: making sure you are fit to hold a licence

The Act[8] says that you shall be granted a consumer credit licence if you satisfy the OFT that:

- you are a fit person to be involved in the activities the licence covers, and
- the name under which you want to be licensed is not misleading or undesirable in any other way.

Your business must meet the required standards of 'fitness' in order to be given a licence. The Act does not give an exact definition of 'fitness' but it requires the OFT to take into account any circumstances which we consider relevant[9].

Those covered by a group licence must also meet the required standards of 'fitness' in order to be covered by the group licence. You must trade honestly, lawfully and fairly with consumers. As a general guide, you will not be granted a licence unless you can show the OFT that you can be trusted to maintain this standard.

As well as your own activities, the activities of your employees, agents or associates, whether past or present, will be taken into account[10]. The term 'associates' can include many kinds of people – the Act gives a very broad definition. It could be a business associate – for example, where a broker has a continuing relationship with a lender, or frequently does business with a lender. It can also mean a spouse or partner, or someone associated with running the business.

When you apply for a licence, you must make sure that you do not supply any false or misleading information. Section 7 of the Act makes it a criminal offence to 'knowingly or recklessly' give information to the OFT that in a particular manner is 'false or misleading'. As an applicant, it is your responsibility to make sure that you provide all the information requested and check its accuracy. You must do this carefully and honestly.

If you give false or misleading information, for example, by failing to declare convictions of anyone named in the application or by failing to declare the involvement of other people in the running of the business,

---

[8]   Section 25(1).
[9]   Section 25(2) of the Act.
[10]   Section 25 of the Act.

it is extremely likely that action will be taken. You should be aware of these requirements even when you have been granted a licence.

You must keep up the same standards after you have been granted a licence. The fitness requirement continues for the duration of the licence, and the OFT will keep your fitness under review. Any relevant evidence will be considered carefully. Where necessary, a licence may be revoked or suspended, or compulsory changes may be made to it.

Protecting the interests of consumers is our top priority.

Ensuring the fitness of applicants and licence holders is of vital importance to the OFT's statutory licensing role.

Fitness – the key issues

The OFT will take into account a number of key issues when assessing and monitoring fitness. Some of the main ones are listed below.

- Any offence or conviction connected with the business.
- Any offence or conviction connected with anyone involved in running the business.
- Any evidence of discrimination on grounds of sex, colour, race or ethnic or national origin.
- Failure to comply with any of the requirements of the Act or regulations made under it. Examples include giving any false or misleading information to the OFT, as explained earlier[11], engaging in licensable activities without holding a licence[12], and failing to refund credit brokerage fees[13].
- Contravention of other consumer protection legislation such as the Trade Descriptions Act, the Consumer Protection Act and the Sale of Goods Act.
- Any consumer complaints about the business.
- Evidence of business practices that damage – or could damage – the interests of consumers.
- Information from other regulators, professional bodies, trade bodies, consumer organisations or other traders.
- Insolvency, bankruptcy or disqualification as a director.

[11] Section 7 of the Act.
[12] Section 39(1) of the Act.
[13] Section 155 of the Act.

- Unauthorised use of the OFT name or logo to suggest that the business is 'approved' by the OFT.
- Failure to comply with general or sector specific guidance on fitness to hold a consumer credit licence.

There is no need for the OFT to demonstrate that individual consumers have been harmed when taking these key issues into account. Showing that there is a real risk to consumers is enough.

What are unfair business practices?

Unfair business practices not involving convictions or breaches of legislation may also result in your licence being refused or revoked.

- No breach of criminal law or civil obligations is necessary. The OFT can take any other issues into account when considering your fitness to hold a licence.
- Business practices that do not directly involve any licensable credit activity are equally important. Many businesses requiring a licence are not primarily involved with credit. An obvious example is car dealers who primarily sell cars but require a licence to support their main business. They could lose their licence through unfair behaviour such as making false representations about cars or failing to deal properly with complaints.
- Consumer choice is an important factor in deciding whether a business practice is oppressive or unfair. We will consider the consumer's ability to go elsewhere rather than deal with your business. For example, if some of your consumers are in a particularly vulnerable position this could make it easier for you to act unfairly. You must take full account of their circumstances and behave appropriately towards them.

Each case is considered separately. We will take full account of all the relevant circumstances. Some examples of what is considered unfair are given next – **but remember, these are only examples, not a complete list**.

- Applying unreasonable pressure on consumers to sign an agreement when you are dealing with them face to face. An example would be a broker visiting consumers at their home and staying long into the evening to coerce them into signing a credit agreement.

- Not giving consumers enough time to read and consider the terms of a contract, or – where appropriate – not telling them where to obtain independent advice.
- Misrepresenting or concealing the terms of the contract.
- Making false representations to persuade them to agree more quickly – for example, by saying that the price will rise if they do not sign straightaway.
- Failure to deal with complaints fairly and promptly or not giving proper redress.

Make sure you are open and honest in all your dealings with consumers. This is the best way to ensure that you meet your responsibilities under the Act. You should also provide them with accurate and reliable information to make their decisions. Take full account of the position of each consumer, and never exploit those who are vulnerable. Keep your promises and provide a good standard of care.

Knowing when practices have been considered unfair

It is impossible to give a full list of business practices that are considered unfair for the purposes of the Act[14]. The exact circumstances will often make a difference. New products and trading methods appear all the time. Where appropriate, the OFT will publicise industry practices which we consider unfair.

Other steps may be taken to demonstrate unfair practices. Action could be taken under separate legislation – covering unfair contract terms, for example. The OFT could also issue a statement about practices drawn to our attention that we regard as unfair and will act against. The list of such practices given in the Annexe also appears on our website (www.oft.gov.uk), where it will be updated from time to time. If you are in any doubt, you should consult your local trading standards authority, or seek independent legal advice.

How we gather information

The OFT gathers information from a wide range of sources, including trading standards authorities, citizens advice bureaux, trade associations,

---

[14] This refers to section 25 of the Act.

other regulatory bodies, consumer complaints, media and others. Where appropriate, we will use this information when considering applications for licences or when monitoring the fitness of those already licensed. Trading standards authorities are one of the main sources. We obtain information from them when licence applications are received and after licences have been issued. We would encourage you to establish a good working relationship with your local trading standards authority, as this could be very helpful to you should problems arise in the future.

How information on fitness is considered

We look carefully at any relevant information when considering applications for licences, or monitoring the fitness of those with licences. If the evidence raises sufficient doubts, an OFT adjudicator will decide whether to issue a notice letting you know that we are considering whether to refuse or revoke your licence.

Further information about the adjudication process can be found in the leaflet – *Licensing – your right to make representations*. This is downloadable from our website www.oft.gov.uk

Other important information

Business names

If your business trades under one or more names, you must specify all the names in the licence and only use those names in carrying out your consumer credit business. It is a criminal offence to use any other name. The OFT will not issue licences in names that we consider to be misleading or otherwise undesirable.

Variation of a licence

If you hold a licence and you wish to change the trading name or the categories covered, you must apply to the OFT. You must not carry out any business covered by this variation in your licence until it has been granted.

Notifying changes

You must inform the OFT of any changes relating to the licence during its lifetime. These would include any changes of address and new or retiring partners or directors. You must tell us about changes within 21 working days after the date of change. If you do not do this you will be committing a criminal offence.

Transferring a licence

A licence cannot be transferred or assigned to another person or business.

Annexe

All licence holders must ensure that they adhere to relevant

legislation and sector specific guidance issued by the OFT.

Now available (October 2003) are guidance documents
- on debt management
- on debt collection
- for car dealers.

To order copies go to our website www.oft.gov.uk or call our mailing house on 0870 60 60 321.

Below is a general list of practices that are considered unfair, according to subject (please note this list is not exhaustive).

Credit brokerage services and fees

- Failing to return fees in excess of £5 when a consumer does not take up a loan or enter into an agreement within six months of an introduction to a lender, for whatever reasons, contrary to section 155 of the Consumer Credit Act 1974.
- Inducing consumers to enter into agreements for mortgage arrangements where the licensee knew or ought to have known that the outcome of the loan application was uncertain.
- Purporting, notwithstanding the provisions of section 155 and 173(1) of the Consumer Credit Act, to set terms as to when fees paid as commission would become refundable, in stating that such

fees were non-returnable and/or that the consumer would only be entitled to a refund of a proportion of the original fee.

Consumer credit agreements

- Requiring consumers to enter into credit agreements in a manner not meeting the requirements of proper execution as prescribed by section 61(1)(a)-(c) of the Consumer Credit Act 1974.
- Using false or misleading statements in order to induce consumers to enter into a contract, by way of misleading advertising relating to finance.
- Inducing consumers to enter into contracts for the purchase of goods by making false statements about the description and availability of goods.
- Misleading price indications, contrary to section 20(1) of the Consumer Protection Act 1987.

Consumer goods and services

- Inducing consumers to enter into contracts for the provision of services by knowingly, recklessly or negligently making false statements as to the nature of those services.
- Failure to carry out work as agreed, or with reasonable care and skill.
- Failing to perform contractual obligations with consumers, and failing, when in breach of contract, to give a refund, pay damages, or to provide the goods or services as agreed.
- Failing to give consumers any or any adequate redress when in breach of any other legal duty owed to them.
- Failure to meet the requirements of the Sale of Goods Act 1979.
- Applying false trade descriptions to goods, contrary to section 1(1)(a) of the Trade Descriptions Act 1968.
- Selling of unroadworthy vehicles, contrary to section 75(5) of the Road Traffic Act 1988.

Responsibilities under the Company Directors Disqualification Act 1986

- Directly or indirectly taking part in the management of a company without leave of the court, contrary to section 1(1) of the Company Directors Disqualification Act 1986.

Business Advertisements (Disclosure) Order 1977

- Causing an advertisement to be published which did not make it clear that the goods were being sold in the course of a business, contrary to the Business Advertisements (Disclosure) Order 1977.

Handling money in the course of business administration

- Inappropriate or improper dealing with money held in trust for clients.
- Misappropriating business funds without having regard to the interests of creditors.

Companies Act 1985

- Failing to ensure that accounts are prepared and delivered for filing to the Registrar of Companies in accordance with sections 227, 241 and 242 of the Companies Act 1985.
- Failing to ensure that annual returns were delivered for filing with the Registrar of Companies in accordance with sections 363 and 365 of the Companies Act 1985.
- Failure to ensure that the accounting records of a company are sufficient to comply with section 221 of the Companies Act 1985.

Credit repair

- Providing self-help information in kit form encouraging consumers to lie to the Courts so as to set County Court judgments aside, in order to improve credit ratings and thus to obtain loans.
- Publishing advertisements promising to remove negative information from credit reference files even if they are accurate and timely.
- Obtaining up-front fees for services, and failing to refund fees where services are not provided.
- Providing worthless 'money back' guarantees as follow-up literature to consumers in order to induce consumers to proceed with credit repair services.

Non-status lending

- Inducing consumers to borrow on excessive or oppressive terms against the security of their homes without regard to their ability *to repay the loan.*
- Offers of inappropriate and sometimes catastrophic loans, whilst failing to assess the consumer's ability to repay.
- Making only limited or no enquiries about consumers' income before offering loans.
- Marketing or targeting loans explicitly at consumers in debt.
- Failure of the broker to act in the best interests of the borrower; a preoccupation with the value of the security rather than the borrower's credit-worthiness ('equity lending').
- Imposing substantial brokerage or other advance fees, and failure to explain that such fees could be charged and deducted from the loan.
- Imposing very high interest rates, and increasing interest rates when a loan is in arrears, sometimes in breach of section 93 of the Consumer Credit Act.
- Illegal canvassing of agreements in consumers' homes.
- Irregular documentation including failure to give, or misquoting interest rates and APRs.
- Improper tying-in of insurance.
- Falsifying information as to borrower's income or other aspects of their financial status in order to secure the loan.
- Misrepresentation as to the form, nature, purpose or long-term implications of loan agreements.
- Unacceptably high-pressure selling techniques.

Guidance booklets for traders

Other booklets about the consumer credit licensing regime

Credit advertising, Consumer Credit Act 1974, Advertisement Regulations 1989, October 2003

Credit charges and APR – how to calculate the total charge for credit and the annual percentage rate of charge, July 2002

Regulated and exempt agreements, Consumer Credit Act 1974, June 2003

Matters arising during the lifetime of an agreement, Consumer Credit Act 1974, January 2001

Non-cancellable agreements, Consumer Credit Act 1974, June 2003

Cancellable agreements, Consumer Credit Act 1974, June 2003

Hire agreements, Consumer Credit Act 1974, January 2001

Sector specific guidance

Debt management guidance, December 2001

Guidance for car dealers, January 2003

Debt collection guidance, July 2003

Other booklets that might be of interest

The estate agency guide – what you need to know if you are engaged in estate agency, Estate Agents Act 1979, August 2003

Misleading advertisements, Briefing, December 1994, October 2000

For a full list of OFT publications visit our website at www.oft.gov.uk

OFT publications can be obtained, free of charge, from the following address:

Office of Fair Trading,
PO Box 366, Hayes UB3 1XB
Tel. 0870 60 60 321

Appendix 3
The motor industry codes of practice

CODE OF PRACTICE FOR THE RETAIL MOTOR INDUSTRY (OFFICE OF FAIR TRADING STAGE ONE APPROVAL 2004)

A Code of Practice, drawn up by the Retail Motor Industry Federation and the Scottish Motor Trade Association in consultation with the Office of Fair Trading ('OFT').

Introduction

This Code of Practice ('the Code') is based upon the code that was originally drawn up in 1976 by the Society of Motor Manufacturers and Traders ('SMMT'), the Retail Motor Industry Federation ('RMI') (formerly Motor Agents Association) and the Scottish Motor Trade Association ('SMTA') in consultation with the Director General of Fair Trading. It has been revised and improved by the RMI and the SMTA ('trade associations') in consultation with the OFT and governs the conduct of dealers or repairers in relation to the supply of new and used cars, fuel, parts and accessories and car servicing and repair. It embodies principles which have been observed by the majority of the retail motor industry for many years. The principles set out are not intended to interpret, qualify or supplant the law of the land and are not intended to be applied to business sales.

A condition of membership of the RMI or the SMTA is the acceptance of this Code in its entirety. Consumers who feel dissatisfied with the treatment they have received from members will be able to submit their grievance to the conciliation and advisory service operated by the relevant trade association.

It should not be overlooked that consumers also have their part to play. It is only by cooperating fully with those who make, sell and service cars that consumers can get the maximum benefit from their purchases. In particular, by maintaining their cars in accordance with the manufacturer's instructions; by observing any warnings given in the handbook; and by giving as much information as possible to anyone servicing or repairing it, they can ensure that they get the best possible use out of their cars and any problems are reduced to a minimum.

Throughout the Code: The term 'manufacturer' shall include concessionaire or importer. The term 'Dealer' shall include retail dealer or distributor or supplier of goods or services, whether or not franchised by a manufacturer. The term 'car' shall include a mechanically propelled vehicle except a vehicle – i) constructed in such a way that it is primarily suited for transporting goods of any sort, or ii) of a type which is not commonly used as a private vehicle and is not suitable for use as a private vehicle; unless such vehicles detailed in i) and ii) above are sold as business to consumer transactions.

References to the singular shall include references to the plural and vice versa.

I General

1.1 Members of the RMI or the SMTA ('Members') must be aware of and comply with the terms of this Code and all applicable laws and regulations that relate to consumers. Members must ensure that their staff shall comply with the spirit as well as the letter of this Code and such laws and regulations relating to consumers including, but not limited to, those relating to Sale of Goods, Supply of Services, Unfair Contract Terms, Trade Descriptions and Consumer Protection. Those Members who engage in credit brokerage must comply with the provisions of the Consumer Credit Act and follow the relevant guidance issued by the OFT.

1.2 Members will deal with consumers fairly, courteously and in accordance with good business practice. This shall include, but not be limited to, the avoidance of high pressure selling, sensitive treatment of vulnerable consumers, full written information to be provided to consumers on request and the provision of clear and accurate information on the availability and price of linked goods such as routine servicing, extended warranties etc.

1.3 Order forms and any other pre-contractual information are intended to help both parties to the contract by clarifying the terms and conditions on which business is to be done. Such terms and conditions must be fair and reasonable and, as with all documents, be set out clearly, in plain English and legible. Order forms must include statements covering the circumstances under which the order can be cancelled (including where delivery is delayed), deposits and pre-payments can be refunded fully and speedily in the event that the Member is unable to deliver the promised goods/services and delivery/completion dates. Members must ensure that an appropriate protection mechanism is in place such as a separate bank account to protect consumers' deposits and pre-payments in case the Member goes into receivership or suffers a similar event. Where delays in delivery subsequently prove unavoidable, consumers must be given as much advance notice as possible. Consumers can then negotiate alternative delivery/completion arrangements if they wish to do so.

1.4 Members will ensure appropriate processes are in place which ensure quality checks on work as specified in the RMI/SMTA compliance regime issued to Members from time to time.

1.5 Members will have in place a written training policy to ensure that staff are competent to complete the work that they undertake.

2 Warranties

2.1 Warranties are a simple and straightforward way for consumers to have faults that are covered by the warranty appearing within a certain period, or before the new or used car has done a certain mileage, corrected at little or no cost to consumers. It is important to note, however, that consumers still have a right to redress against the seller of a car even while the car is under a manufacturer's or other warranty. 2.2 Warranties are governed by the Sale and Supply of Goods to Consumers Regulations 2002. Members are required to ensure that the warranty sets out in plain English the contents of the warranty and the details for making a claim. The warranty must not purport to take away or diminish any rights which consumers would otherwise enjoy in law. The document must also include a statement advising consumers that the warranty is in addition to their statutory or common law rights.

2.3 The key elements of warranties and, if applicable, any free extensions to warranties must be drawn to the attention of consumers. This includes details of what is and is not covered and the geographical scope of the warranties.

2.4 Any relevant document published by the warranty provider must be handed over. The consumer must be advised of what type of warranty is being provided, for example, manufacturer's, free extended manufacturer's/dealer's, insurance backed used car or member's own warranty. The consumer must be informed of the identity of the warranty provider and the address to which claims may be directed. The different types of warranty and any significant differences between them should be explained to consumers as appropriate.

2.5 The consumer must be informed when there are limitations on where the car can be serviced in order to maintain the warranty, and where there are no such restrictions on the garage that can be used, conditions that need to be followed for the warranty to remain valid.

2.6 Members will give advice to consumers as to who they should address a claim if they have a problem regarding defective parts and accessories not covered by the manufacturer's warranty.

2.7 Members will ensure that warranty work is carried out promptly and that completion dates are made clear to consumers before any work has commenced.

3 New Car Sales

3.1 Members are reminded that in sales of goods to consumers they are responsible under the Sale of Goods Act 1979 for ensuring that the goods are of satisfactory quality and fit for the purpose for which they are required. Statements whether oral or in writing which are in apparent conflict with this principle must be avoided.

3.2 Where Members are required by the manufacturer to carry out a Pre-Delivery Inspection ('PDI'), the Member shall carry out such PDI properly and in accordance with the manufacturer's recommendations.

Where PDI check lists are provided by the manufacturer, the Member shall provide a copy of the properly completed check list to consumers.

3.3 The car must be delivered in a condition which is to the manufacturer's standard. Each car must conform fully to all legislation affecting its construction, use and maintenance. This paragraph does not affect any legal responsibilities which may be placed on manufacturers and users to ensure this.

3.4 The benefit and limitations of any treatment over and above that already provided by the manufacturer which is recommended by the Member in order to inhibit the growth of rust or other corrosion must be explained to consumers.

3.5 Order forms must contain details of all charges additional to the car price so that consumers may understand clearly the total price they have to pay to put the car on the road.

3.6 Members must ensure that the manufacturer's handbook relating to the model of car being sold is available to consumers at the time of sale of the car and for a reasonable length of time thereafter.

4 Used Car Sales

4.1 Used cars sold to consumers must conform to legislation affecting the construction and use of cars and should, where appropriate, be accompanied by a current Department for Transport Test (MOT) Certificate.

4.2 Members must bear in mind that sales of used cars are subject to the Sale of Goods Act 1979 and attention is specifically drawn to the conditions of satisfactory quality and fitness for purpose. If, however, defects are specifically brought to the attention of consumers or consumers examine the car before a contract is made there is no condition of satisfactory quality as regards those specific defects or ones that examination ought to reveal. Members should therefore reveal defects on an approved checklist (see 4.5 below). The format of the checklist is determined and/or approved by the RMI or SMTA as appropriate. Members should provide reasonable facilities to enable prospective consumers or their nominees to carry out an examination of the car prior to sale, in order that any defects which ought to be revealed at the time of sale are made known to both parties.

4.3 If a printed guarantee or warranty is not used, then any specific promises which the Member is willing to make in relation to the used car should be set out in writing and be in plain and intelligible language.

4.4 Used cars must be offered for sale in a roadworthy condition. The Member will carry out a pre-sales inspection in accordance with a checklist approved by the RMI or SMTA. The checklist must be completed and either prominently displayed on the car or shown to a prospective purchaser of the car before it is sold. A copy of the checklist shall be given to the purchaser on completion of the sale.

4.5 All descriptions, whether used in advertisements or in negotiations regarding the sale of used cars should be honest, truthful and not misleading. Terms which are likely to be misunderstood by consumers or which are not capable of exact definition must be avoided.

4.6 Relevant written information provided by previous owners regarding the history of cars must be passed on to consumers. This may include service records, repair invoices, inspection reports, handbooks and warranties, as applicable.

4.7 Reasonable steps will be taken to verify the recorded mileage of a used car and Members will use reasonable endeavors to obtain a signed statement from the previous owner as to the car's mileage. Members must pass on any known facts about an odometer reading to prospective consumers.

4.8 Unless the Member is satisfied that the quoted mileage of a used car is accurate, such mileage must not be quoted in advertisements, discussions or negotiations or in any documents related to the supply of the used car. Where cars' mileage cannot be verified, consumers will be informed. The law requires that any disclaimer used must be as bold, precise and compelling as the car's mileage reading itself and as effectively brought to the prospective consumer's attention.

4.9 Finance on Part Exchanges Members are obliged to make reasonable efforts to ensure they give good title (eg by obtaining a statement from a finance checking house) by checking and discharging existing finance on cars they sell. Also, whenever possible, Members will check whether any outstanding recalls exist on a car.

5 Replacement Parts, Accessories and Fuel

5.1 Members must bear in mind that in sales of goods to consumers they are responsible under the Sale of Goods Act 1979 that the goods are of satisfactory quality and fit for the purpose for which they are required. Statements, whether oral or in writing, in apparent conflict with this principal must be avoided.

5.2 Without prejudice to the general obligation to always give clear indications of price as detailed in Clause 7.5 below, whenever goods are offered for sale and an extra charge is payable for certain non-cash forms of payment (credit cards etc) a clear indication of cash price must be available to consumers.

5.3 All descriptions, whether used in advertisements or in negotiations regarding the sale of replacement parts, accessories and fuel should be honest, truthful and not misleading. Terms must not be used in advertisements if they are likely to be misunderstood by consumers or if they are not capable of exact definition.

5.4 With offers of promotions any restrictions which are attached to sales other than cash sales must be clearly stated.

5.5 A Member must not display any notices or make any statements which might mislead consumers about their legal rights in relation to the purchase of faulty goods.

6 Repairs and Servicing (excluding work carried out under a Car Manufacturer's warranty)

6.1 Members must bear in mind that when supplying parts or accessories in connection with repairs or servicing work for consumers, they have a similar responsibility to that which exists under a contract for the sale of goods to ensure that the goods are of satisfactory quality and fit for the purpose for which they are required and that work is performed with reasonable care and skill. Members shall not accept work for which they, or their sub-contractors, do not have the requisite expertise or equipment.

6.2 Members will provide at least an estimate of the cost of labour and materials for repairs and servicing. A firm quotation will be offered wherever possible. It must be made clear to consumers whether an estimate or quotation is being made. All estimates and quotations shall be inclusive of VAT. Quotations must always be in writing identifying the Member. If requested, estimates will be in writing. It should be remembered that an estimate is a considered approximation of the likely cost involved whereas a quotation constitutes a firm price for which the work will be done. If a charge is to be made for the estimate or quotation this must be made known to consumers before their instructions are accepted. Any dismantling costs which are necessary to arrive at such estimates or quotations must be notified to consumers in advance on the clear understanding whether or not dismantling costs are to be charged on an estimate or quotation which is refused. If, during the progress of any work, it appears that the estimate will be exceeded by a significant amount, then consumers must be notified and asked for permission to continue with the work.

6.3 Parts replaced during service or repair will be offered to consumers unless a warranty claim is involved or unless the parts have to be submitted to the supplier because replacement parts are being supplied on an exchange basis.

6.4 Invoices must be clearly written or typed and give full details of the work carried out and materials used. The amount and rate of VAT must be clearly indicated. Dates and recorded mileages must always be noted where applicable.

6.5 Members must exercise adequate care in protecting consumers' property while it is in their custody, and must not seek by disclaimers to avoid their legal liability for damage or loss. Members must carry adequate insurance to cover their legal liability and should strongly advise consumers to remove any items of value not related to the car.

6.6 Repairs must be guaranteed against failure due to workmanship for a specific mileage or time period which must be stated on the invoice together with a statement confirming that any such guarantee does not affect consumer's existing legal rights.

6.7 Members must notify consumers of any methods of payment that are not accepted before the work is accepted.

6.8 When it is necessary to sub-contract work, the Member will be responsible for the quality of the sub-contractors' work. Any estimate given to consumers must include the subcontracted work and in the event of any increase in charge for the work, the principles in paragraph 6.2 must apply.

6.9 Members must make it clear whether or not servicing will be carried out in accordance with the appropriate manufacturer's recommended service schedule.

6.10 The Member must advise consumers of any material defects which become apparent while any servicing or repair work is being carried out.

7 Advertising

7.1 All advertising by Members must comply with the British Codes of Advertising and Sales Promotion, or any other code of advertising or regulations that may be relevant (eg Independent Television Commission (ITC), Radio Authority or Independent Committee for the Supervision of Standards of Telephone Information Services (ICSTIS), Control of Misleading Advertisement Regulations).

7.2 Advertisements must not contain any references to guarantees or warranties which would take away or diminish any rights of consumers nor should they be worded as to be understood by consumers as doing so.

7.3 Advertisements must not contain the words 'guarantee' or 'warranty' unless the full terms of such undertakings as well as the remedial action open to consumers are either clearly set out in the advertisement or are available to consumers in writing at the point of sale or with the product.

7.4 Claims and descriptions in advertisements should not be misleading. In particular any comparison with other models of different manufacturers should conform to all legal requirements governing comparative advertising including being based on a similar set of criteria and not being presented in such a way as to confuse or mislead consumers.

7.5 A price quoted must be a price at which consumers can buy the goods. Members must therefore quote prices for cars, whether in advertisements or in showrooms, inclusive of the price of any extras known to be fitted to the car together with the appropriate VAT and Car Tax.

7.6 In the description of used cars, terms likely to be misunderstood by consumers or which are not capable of exact definition must be avoided. For example, if the word 'reconditioned' is used, the nature of the reconditioning must be carefully explained.

7.7 In the description of a used car, any year must be either: (a) the year of first use or (b) the year of the first registration, or (c) the last year that the car complied with the manufacturer's specification of a model sold as new during that calendar year, whichever is the earliest.

7.8 Where an advertisement quotes the price of one model in any model range but depicts another, the actual price of that other model must also be shown.

7.9 Where a manufacturer advertises a rust-proofing process, information about the process and its limitations must be made freely available.

8 Handling Complaints

8.1 Members must ensure that effective and immediate action is taken with a view to achieving a just and prompt settlement of a complaint. To this end there will be, from the point of view of consumers, an easily identifiable and accessible procedure for the reception and handling of complaints. This must include details of how to complain, who to complain to, reasonable timescales for dealing with the complaint and details of the conciliation and independent arbitration procedures. This procedure must be understood by all relevant staff. A written complaint must be acknowledged within seven days and a substantive response sent within twenty one days of receipt. The same time scales will apply to the RMI and SMTA when dealing with written complaints from consumers.

8.2 When complaints are raised through a third party (eg the Automobile Association, the Royal Automobile Club, the Trading Standards services or a Citizens Advice Bureau), full cooperation must be given to that body although, if appropriate under the circumstances, reasonable efforts should be made to re-establish direct communication with complaining consumers and to reach a satisfactory settlement.

8.3 In the event that a complaint is not resolved, Members must make it clear to consumers that they have a right to refer the complaint to the appropriate trade association for conciliation.

8.4 Members will give assistance to the trade association concerned while it is investigating a complaint.

8.5 Where conciliation has failed to resolve a dispute the RMI and the SMTA have agreed to co-operate in the operation of low cost independent arbitration agreements which will be through an Independent Panel of Arbitrators. Details of the arbitration arrangements are set out in the Appendix to this Code. Consumers must always be advised that they have the option of taking a claim to the Courts.

8.6 The award of the arbitrator is enforceable in law on all parties.

9 Monitoring and Disciplinary Procedure

9.1 Members are obliged to fully cooperate and comply with the RMI's National Conciliation Service and Arbitration procedure and this monitoring and disciplinary procedure and the compliance arrangements detailed within this section of the Code.

9.2 As subscribers to the Code, Members must ensure by the clear display of appropriate logos, pamphlets or other means as determined by the trade associations that consumers are informed of Members' adherence to the Code and basic details of the Code. Copies of the full Code shall be made available to consumers on request.

9.3 The RMI and SMTA shall ensure Members' compliance with the Code by implementing an effective compliance regime as determined from time to time by the RMI and SMTA in conjunction with an independent Scrutiny Committee. The compliance regime shall, for example, contain elements such as periodic visits to Members' premises, mystery shopping exercises, analysis of consumer complaints and consumer survey programmes.

9.4 Incidences of minor non-compliance will prompt appropriate advice. More serious incidences will result in a written warning detailing what corrective action must be taken and by when. If appropriate, such serious incidences shall also result in a follow up compliance visit or mystery shop, the cost of which shall be born by the Member. A very serious breach or persistent minor breaches of the Code will result in a Member being called before an Independent Disciplinary Committee which may, if it sees fit, expel the Member from participation in the Code and membership of the appropriate trade association. The Member has the right to be accompanied and/or represented at the hearing. There is a right of appeal. In the event of expulsion, the Member may not re-apply for membership before two years has elapsed and the cause of the expulsion been properly addressed.

9.5 The Independent Disciplinary Committee shall comprise five people drawn from a pool of at least ten. It shall be independently chaired and include two independent and two other members from within the retail motor industry. Any appeals will be heard by three members from the pool that were not involved in the initial hearing and will comprise of an independent chair and one other independent member and a member from within the motor industry.

9.6 The independent Scrutiny Committee shall oversee the monitoring activities of the trade associations and make recommendations as it sees fit. It shall also produce an annual report on its findings which it shall make available to the trade associations for inclusion in their respective annual reports and to the OFT.

9.7 Members must maintain a record of consumer complaints relating to any of the provisions of the Code and must take action based on this information to improve their service to consumers. Complaint records must be kept on file for a minimum period of 12 months after resolution and made available to the appropriate trade association on request.

9.8 The RMI and the SMTA will analyse the consumer complaints received under the Code and matters referred to them for conciliation or arbitration. The results of the analysis will be made available to the Scrutiny Committee to assist it with its duties referred to in 9.5 above.

9.9 In the event that a Member is prosecuted or becomes aware of the likelihood that it will be prosecuted as a result of a matter connected with its business activities, the Member must immediately notify the RMI or SMTA as appropriate and provide relevant details.

Appendix: Complaints and Arbitration

1 Consumers who have a complaint about the quality of the goods or service to their cars should in the first place and at the earliest opportunity refer it to the Member concerned.

2 The complaint, preferably in writing, should he addressed to a senior executive, a director, a partner, the proprietor or an executive especially nominated to deal with complaints. The Member must acknowledge

receipt of the complaint within seven days and send a substantive response within twenty one days of receipt of the complaint.

3 If the complaint relates to warranty on a new car and the Member is unable to resolve the matter, consumers must have the situation properly explained to them and be referred to the manufacturer concerned.

4 If attempts to reach a satisfactory conclusion fail, consumers have a right to refer their complaint to the Member's appropriate trade association. Any such complaint must be in writing.

(a)   if the complaint lies against a Member who is situated in any part of the United Kingdom except Scotland the address is: **The National Conciliation Service, Retail Motor Industry Federation Ltd, 9 North Street, Rugby CV21 2AB.**

(b)   if the complaint lies against a Member who is situated in Scotland, the address is: **Consumer Complaints Service, Scottish Motor Trade Association Ltd, Palmerston House, 10 The Loan, South Queensferry, EH30 9NS.**

5 All complaints referred to the appropriate trade association within a reasonable time of the cause for complaint arising will be considered.

6 If the trade association is unable to resolve a complaint, the Member will agree to go to arbitration. Consumers must be informed how the arbitration procedure works, that the result is binding on both parties and that they will need to enter into a binding arbitration arrangement. Consumers must be advised that they do not have to follow this procedure and are free to pursue their rights through the Courts if they prefer.

7 Parties to arbitration will be asked to pay any applicable registration fee. When the Arbitrator makes his/her award, he/she will determine whether the registration fee should be returned to the successful party.

8 The parties will also be asked to sign an application for arbitration which will be sent, together with the registration fee, to: **The Independent Panel of Arbitrators, c/o Retail Motor Industry Federation Ltd, 9 North Street, Rugby CV21 2AB.**

9 In order to keep costs as low as possible, the arbitration will normally rely solely on documents. In these cases, none of the parties to the dispute may be present nor may they be represented by any other person.

10 The relevant trade association will submit to the Independent Panel of Arbitrators all the documentary evidence in its possession that it considers relevant to the case. The Independent Panel of Arbitrators will advise the parties to the dispute of the written evidence they have available on which it will base its judgment and invite the parties to submit any further evidence which it considers relevant.

11 The Chairman of the Independent Panel of Arbitrators will appoint a single arbitrator ('the Arbitrator') and will make all the necessary arrangements for the arbitration to be conducted as speedily as possible.

12 If appropriate under the circumstances, the Arbitrator may conduct an oral arbitration hearing and the parties may then attend to present their evidence. Legal representation may only be employed if the Arbitrator so directs.

13 The Arbitrator has the power to direct any party to provide him/her and the other party(ies) any additional documents or information he/she considers to be relevant to the matter under dispute.

14 The award of the Arbitrator will be published in writing to the parties to the dispute and to the relevant trade association.

15 The award of the Arbitrator is binding on the parties and enforceable in the Courts.

Retail Motor Industry Federation Ltd, 201 Great Portland Street, London W1W 5AB.

The Scottish Motor Trade Association Ltd, Palmerston House, 10 The Loan, South Queensferry, EH30 9NS.

SMMT NEW CAR CODE OF PRACTICE

Introduction

The SMMT New Car Code of Practice ('the Code') confirms promises made by vehicle manufacturers (our members) in the provision of new cars and the cover provided by manufacturer's warranty. This consumer code sets out standards that members will comply with regarding new car sales, car manufacturer's warranties, availability of replacement parts, advertising and complaints handling.

It is a duty laid on members that they will accept the Code in its entirety and ensure that their staff are aware of their legal responsibilities as well as their responsibilities under the Code. A consumer who feels dissatisfied with any item covered by this Code is able to submit their grievance to the conciliation and advisory service operated by SMMT Regulation and Compliance Unit. A detailed procedure explaining how to do this appears in the Appendix of this Code.

The principles set out in this Code are not intended to interpret, qualify or supplement the law, and are not intended to be applied to non-consumer sales.

It must be remembered that the consumer also has a part to play, by co-operating fully with those who make, sell and maintain cars, maintaining the car in accordance with the manufacturer's instructions and observing any warnings given in the handbook any major problems should be avoided. Guidance is included within each section under the heading 'We would advise you to'.

The relationship between manufacturer and consumer

It is important to remember the relationship between vehicle manufacturer and consumer, which the following flowchart details below:

Definitions

Throughout the code: The term **member** describes vehicle manufacturers within SMMT membership which have agreed to adhere to this Code. The term **manufacturer** is taken to include official importer. The term **dealer** describes only retailers of new cars and/or distributors of new parts and/or suppliers of car services who in each case are parties authorised by the relevant manufacturer. The term **car** is taken to include light and medium commercial vehicles and derivatives. The term **consumer** describes the owner/end user of any car as described above and includes the requirements of any vulnerable consumer; for which members will have in place satisfactory provision for attending to their needs. The term **new car warranty** is taken to include the manufacturers warranty and any extension offered free with the vehicle.

I Advertising

Our advertising promise

'It is our intention to use advertising as a means of promotion only'

What our promise means to you

1.1 Our advertisements, promotions or any other publications, whether in writing or otherwise, will not contain any items which are likely to mislead you or be misunderstood.

1.2 Our advertisements, promotions or any other publications will comply with the requirements of Acts of Parliament and Government regulation along with the codes, regulations and rulings of the relevant organisations or associations.

1.3 Any comparison made within our advertisements with other models of different manufacturers will be based upon a similar set of criteria which will not confuse or mislead the consumer.

1.4 Where our advertisements quote the price of one model in any model range but depict another, the actual price of that other model will also be clearly shown.

1.5 In principle, a price quoted should be the 'on the road' price at which you can buy the goods, in accordance with the **SMMT Guide to New Car Price Advertising** (developed in consultation with the Office of Fair Trading).

1.6 The words 'guarantee' or 'warranty' within any of our advertisements will not be used unless the full terms of that warranty are set out clearly within the advertisement or are available at point of sale. Furthermore, any reference to a warranty or guarantee will not be made if they diminish your consumer rights, or appear to do so.

1.7 Where a rust/corrosion-proofing process is advertised, information about the process and its limitations will be made freely available.

1.8 In the unlikely event that any member is convicted of an offence relating to advertisements for a new car, then that member will be deemed to be in breach of this Code.

We would advise you to

- Read our advertisements carefully and in full. If an advertisement is not clear to you, clarify it before you commit yourself to any transaction.
- Check the specification and appearance of the car you are ordering matches your requirements, as many features are often optional or substitutable extras.
- Check with your dealer that you have the latest sales brochure.
- Ensure that the car you are considering purchasing is fit for the purpose, or in other words, suits your requirements. Therefore, statements whether oral or written which conflict, or apparently conflict, with this principle should be questioned.
- Inform your dealer of any special needs relating to the car, as they cannot advise as to the suitability of a car for any particular purpose if you do not explain that purpose.

Relevant legislation

Where applicable to the member, we observe the requirements of all legislation and regulatory requirements, including:

Advertising Standards Authority (Committee of Advertising Practice) Control of Misleading Advertisements Regulations 1988 Trade Descriptions Act 1968 Ofcom (TV/radio advertising)

2 Your New Car

Our new car promise

'Once you have ordered your new car, it is our responsibility to ensure that the car supplied to the retailer is manufactured to a high quality standard which will meet with your expectations'

What our promise means to you

2.1 When you take delivery of your new car you will be made aware of the after-sales service provisions available.

2.2 You will receive a copy of the manufacturer's handbook relating to your new car, replacement copies of which will be available for a reasonable period thereafter.

2.3 All of our documents supplied for new cars purchased in the UK will be written in plain and intelligible English.

We would advise you to

- Be aware of who any deposit is being paid to and its security, along with the cancellation terms.
- Ensure that any order form used contains all charges additional to the car price in order to fully understand the total cost of your purchase.
- Check that the specification matches your order at the handover and the dealer has fulfilled their requirement to supply you with a car of satisfactory quality.
- Ensure that the dealer provides you with a detailed handover of your new car which should form part of the delivery of a new car.

Relevant legislation

Where applicable to the car manufacture, we observe the requirements of all legislation and regulatory requirements, including:

Sale of Goods Act 1979 (sections 14, 35), Supply of Goods and Services Act 1982 (sections 4, 9, 11D and 18 (3) as amended by – Sale and Supply of Goods Act 1994 Sale and Supply of Goods to Consumers Regulations 2002 (Regulation 15) Consumer Protection (Distance Selling) Regulations 2000 Conformity with all legislation affecting a car's construction & use

3 Manufacturers' New Car Warranties

Our warranty promise

'We will supply a manufacturer's new car warranty with every new car purchased, which will provide you with cover in the event that you experience problems with your new car resulting from a manufacturing defect'

What our promise means to you

3.1 You will continue to benefit from the manufacturer's new car warranty whilst the car is serviced to the manufacturer's recommendations, even if this service is carried out by an independent service/repair outlet.

3.2 The manufacturer's new car warranty document, which will be written clearly in plain and intelligible English, will be supplied to you on delivery of your new car. This document will also include claim procedures and contact information.

3.3 The terms of the new car warranty will be clear and written in plain and intelligible English, including items specifically included in or excluded from its provisions and the geographical coverage of the warranty provided.

3.4 Where repair work is required under the new car warranty it may be carried out by any dealer in the manufacturer's network anywhere in Europe. A repairer who is not part of the manufacturer's network may not carry out repair work under the new car warranty, which may be invalidated if this happens.

3.5 The transfer of the unexpired portion of any new car warranty to a subsequent owner is permitted.

3.6 In the event that your car is off the road for an extended period for rectification of warranty faults, we will consider the extension of the new car warranty period.

3.7 Where a loan car is made available, this will be as reasonable alternative transport rather than an exact replacement of the car that is being repaired. There is no automatic right to a loan car or contribution towards hiring charges while a car is undergoing warranty rectification work.

We would advise you to

- Remember, a manufacturer's new car warranty is a simple and straightforward method allowing any faults of manufacture to be corrected at no cost to the consumer, without the necessity of pursuing legal remedies against the seller.
- Understand the terms of the new car warranty, including the servicing criteria, specifically the service intervals in terms of mileage and time periods.

- If your car has been serviced by an independent service/repair out-let make sure you keep records of work completed including receipts of servicing/repair.
- Ensure that the service/repair is completed according to the manu-facturer's requirements, if you take your car to an independent service/repair outlet. In general terms warranty repair work will only be covered at no cost to you as long as it is undertaken by a franchised/authorised outlet.

Relevant legislation

Where applicable to the member, we observe the requirements of all legislation and regulatory requirements, including the following:

The warranty is in addition to and must not affect the consumer's reme-dies against the seller under legislation listed in the previous section 'Your New Car'. It must include a statement which makes this clear to the consumer.

4 Replacement Parts and Accessories

Our parts promise

'To enable the routine maintenance and warranty rectification work to be completed effectively we will ensure that our spare parts are readily available to our authorised networks'

What our promise means to you

4.1 Where our parts are supplied to our authorised networks they will be of a satisfactory quality and fit for the purpose for which parts of that type are normally used.

4.2 With offers of promotions, any restrictions which are attached to sales will be clearly stated.

4.3 We will ensure that spare parts are available from the time a new model is launched, throughout its production and for a reasonable period thereafter.

We would advise you to

● Ensure the replacement parts and accessories fitted to your car meet with the vehicle manufacturer's specifications and requirements.

Relevant legislation

Where applicable to the car manufacture, we observe the requirements of all legislation and regulatory requirements, including:

Sale of Goods Act 1979 (sections 14, 35), Supply of Goods and Services Act 1982 (sections 4, 9 and 11D and 13, 18(3)) as amended by Sale and Supply of Goods Act 1994 Sale and Supply of Goods to Consumers Regulations 2002 (Regulation 15) Consumer Protection (Distance Selling Regulations) 2000 Conformity with all legislation affecting a car's construction & use

'In the event that you feel that we have failed on any of our promises, we would refer you to the Code monitoring body: the SMMT Regulation and Compliance Unit. Their role is to ensure that we are acting responsibly and fulfilling our obligations under this Code. The following sections of this Code detail how this function operates.'

SMMT Guidance – Handling Complaints

Step one

It is a member company's responsibility to ensure effective, immediate action is taken in order that a just settlement of a complaint is achieved. From the consumer perspective an easily identifiable and accessible arrangement for the reception and handling of complaints must be available. Every assistance must be provided by manufacturers to their dealer networks in the handling of complaints.

Step two

In the event that a complaint remains unresolved at both dealer and manufacturer level, it is the manufacturer's obligation to make clear to the consumer their right to refer the complaint to the Regulation and Compliance Unit of SMMT.

Conciliation

The Regulation and Compliance Unit is responsible for the operation of an impartial conciliation service. Each conciliation case will be assessed and investigated from both a technical and legal perspective. The Regulation and Compliance Unit will advise both member and consumer on a remedy as appropriate. Manufacturers will give every assistance to the Regulation and Compliance Unit while investigating a complaint.

Arbitration

If a satisfactory resolution cannot be achieved through conciliation, the Regulation and Compliance Unit have agreed the operation of a low cost arbitration service organised by the Independent Panel of Arbitrators. Details of the arbitration arrangements are set out in the appendix.

Consumers must always be advised that they have the option of taking a claim to the Courts. The award of the arbitrator is enforceable in law on all parties

Code awareness

Members will ensure consumers are aware of their adherence to the SMMT New Car Code of Practice by displaying appropriate symbols.

Complaints

Members will maintain an analysis of complaints relating to any of the provisions of the SMMT New Car Code of Practice.

Reports

The Regulation and Compliance Unit will analyse complaints regarding the Code or other matters referred for conciliation or arbitration. The results of this analysis will be published within the SMMT Annual Review.

Any trends or issues identified, or raised in consultation with advisory bodies, which could potentially lead to consumer detriment will be considered for inclusion when the Code is reviewed.

Additionally the Regulation and Compliance Unit will meet with members and issue consumer surveys to assess member code compliance on a regular basis. Consumer surveys will also be available within the 'Brief Guide to the Code', available from consumer organisations, members and the Regulation and Compliance Unit.

SMMT Guidance – Monitoring

Appendix

Complaints, Conciliation and Arbitration

A consumer, or intermediary, who has a complaint about the quality of the goods supplied should, in the first instance, refer the matter to the selling dealer.

The complaint, preferably in writing, should be addressed to a senior executive, director, or the proprietor of the selling dealer. Members will co-operate with local consumer advisors or intermediaries where necessary.

If the complaint relates to warranty on a new car and the dealer is unable to resolve the matter, take the complaint directly to the consumer relations department of the manufacturer concerned. As stated in section 3.2, the warranty document supplied with your new car will detail the claims procedure and relevant contact information.

Any letters will receive a reply from the manufacturer within 10 working days of receipt. If attempts to reach a satisfactory solution fail, refer the complaint to the SMMT Regulation and Compliance Unit. Any such complaint must be in writing or emailed via the SMMT website.

New Car Code Conciliation Service PO Box 44755 London SWIX 7WU. www.smmt.co.uk

In the first instance the Regulation and Compliance Unit has a direct consumer advice line **0870 751 8270**   All written enquiries referred to the Regulation and Compliance Unit within a reasonable time of the cause for complaint arising will be considered. A written response will be received by the consumer within 7 working days of receipt and within reasonable timescales, determined by the nature of the investigation, thereafter.

If conciliation does not resolve the complaint to the satisfaction of the consumer, members will agree to independent arbitration if the consumer so wishes.

The parties will be required to sign an application for arbitration which will be sent, together with the registration fee, to: **The Independent Panel of Arbitrators, c/o Retail Motor Industry Federation, 9 North Street, Rugby CV21 2AB**

As the arbitration service is designed to be low cost to allow it to be accessible, any hearing will normally rely on documents only. None of the parties to the dispute may be present or be represented by another person.

The Regulation and Compliance Unit will submit to the Independent Panel of Arbitrators all documentary evidence in its possession. The Independent Panel of Arbitrators (which is unconnected to SMMT and members) will advise the parties to submit any further evidence which it considers relevant as necessary.

The Chairman of the Independent Panel of Arbitrators will appoint a single Arbitrator and make arrangements for the arbitration to be conducted.

The Arbitrator has the right to conduct an oral arbitration, in which case parties may attend to present their evidence. Legal representation may only be employed if the Arbitrator so directs. The Arbitrator has the power to direct any party to provide any additional document or information considered relevant.

The award of the Arbitrator will be published in writing to all parties involved in the dispute. The award of the Arbitrator is enforceable in the Courts by any party.

Dispute Resolution and Disciplinary Action

The Society of Motor Manufacturers and Traders Ltd and members acknowledge the joint responsibility to the Code.

If you find yourself in dispute with an SMMT member who appears to be in breach of the Code, the Regulation and Compliance Unit will investigate the matter and the SMMT member is obliged to give every assistance while doing so through the conciliation service attached to the Code. It is our intention to review and resolve any breach of the Code in a speedy fashion with as little disruption to the consumer as possible.

In certain complex cases this is not always possible as it can take some time to gather all the information necessary to come to a decision and a satisfactory outcome in line with the terms and conditions of the Code and conciliation service.

Disciplinary Action

In cases where a member does not correct a breach of the Code or is seen to be in serious or persistent breach of the Code, there is an independent panel which will convene to address a problem of this nature; The Independent Compliance Assessment Panel (ICAP). ICAP is independent of the sector. Its authority over members reflects the serious nature with which SMMT view non–compliance. It is the responsibility of the Regulation and Compliance Unit to acknowledge when a member has breached the Code in a manner that requires more than conciliation or arbitration.

ICAP has the authority to instigate an independent investigation, with which the member is required to assist fully. Depending on the outcome of any investigation, the Panel can impose a varied selection of sanctions upon a member, ranging from education and monitoring, through to financial penalties and ultimately expulsion from the Code regime.

If a financial penalty is imposed on a member, the penalty sum is donated to the motor industry charity BEN.

It must be remembered that disciplinary action in this respect is different to any individual case that may be accepted through the conciliation service. However a number of similar conciliation cases regarding the same member could instigate disciplinary action.

The outcome of any ICAP investigation will be published in the SMMT Annual Review, which we are required to supply to the Office of Fair Trading for monitoring purposes.

Appendix 4
Code of Practice on Vehicle Safety Defects 2004

INTRODUCTION

This code of practice on vehicle safety defects (thereby after referred to as the 'code'), has been developed by;

- Vehicle and Operator Services Agency (VOSA) representing the Secretary of State for Transport
- The Society of Motor Manufacturers and Traders Limited (SMMT)
- The Motor Cycle Industry Association Limited (MCI)
- Commercial Trailer Association (CTA)
- Association of trailer Manufacturers (ATM)
- The National Caravan Council (NCC)
- Independent Commercial Importers
- British Independent Motor Trade Association (BIMTA)
- Motor Factors Association (MFA)
- Retail Motor Industry Federation (RMIF)
- British Rubber manufacturers association Ltd (BRMA)
- Trailer and Towing Association (TTA)

INTRODUCTION

This code concerns cases where manufacturers, concessionaires or official/independent Importers become aware of the existence of safety defects (as defined below) in units that are available for supply in the UK.

The Code deals with information provision to VOSA and the owner/ registered keeper in respect of passenger cars, commercial vehicles, passenger service vehicles, two and three wheeled motorcycles, quadracyles, commercial trailers, motor homes/caravans, private trailers and components fitted as original equipment.

This Code does not cover components or tyres and wheels supplied to the automotive aftermarket.

DEFINITION

Safety Defect – **is a feature of design or construction liable to cause significant risk of personal injury or death.**

Supplier – **is taken to mean vehicle or component manufacturer, official/ independent importer or concessionaire.**

Unit – **describes the affected part or vehicle**

CASES COVERED BY THE CODE

a   where evidence indicates the existence of a safety defect in the unit; and

b   the defect appears to be common to a number of units; and

c   units are available for supply in the UK

It will be a matter of VOSA/ Supplier judgement to decide whether the number of vehicles affected is sufficient to justify invoking the Code. A fixed numerical limit can not be specified as the decision will take account of the degree of seriousness of any possible hazard involved.

RECALL ARRANGEMENTS WITH INDIVIDUAL MANUFACTURERS

VOSA will require a supplier to notify it of the names of a recall co-ordinator and deputy with safety recall campaign responsibility.

CASES AFFECTING COMPONENTS

Safety defects covered by the Code include those relating to components bought by suppliers from other (component) manufacturers and (component) suppliers, sold with the vehicle as original equipment.

NOTIFICATION OF VOSA

Primary responsibility is that of the supplier to notify VOSA as soon as safety defect evidence requiring remedial action amounts to a case under the terms of the Code.

The manufacturer shall at that stage indicate:
- the nature of the defect and estimate number of units involved;
- the nature of the safety hazard involved
- action planned at that time to remedy the defect

In cases where the defect appears to stem from a fault in a component produced by another supplier, that other supplier will also be notified and VOSA advised accordingly.

The supplier will also inform VOSA of all subsequent decisions on remedial action. This includes cases in which component manufacturers are involved, unless in the circumstances of the case it is agreed between the vehicle supplier and the appropriate component manufacturer for all remedial action to become the responsibility of the component manufacturer, in which case the latter shall keep VOSA informed.

INITIATIVES BY VOSA IN PARTICULAR CASES

VOSA may wish to seek information from a supplier or component manufacturer of safety defects that have been brought to their attention. In these cases, the supplier will pass all relevant information available, and cooperate with VOSA in establishing whether a defect is present.

The primary responsibility for deciding on remedial action lies with the manufacturer, but VOSA may, at its discretion, offer views and make recommendations on the measures proposed.

NOTIFICATION OF VEHICLE OWNERS

The supplier will take all reasonable action to contact affected owners/registered keepers and recall their vehicles for inspection and, if necessary, rectify components or assemblies the supplier believes are safety defective.

In consultation with VOSA the supplier will send communication, in layman's terms, to the owner/registered keeper, directly or through the franchised dealer network explaining the nature of the defect and its safety significance. VOSA are to be given the opportunity to comment on the content of this letter prior to instigating a campaign.

If the supplier or franchised dealer receives no response from the owner/ registered keeper then further communication will be sent.

If requested, the DVLA will furnish the supplier with names and addresses of the owner/registered keepers shown on their record, in accordance with existing procedures. Alternatively DVLA can address and dispatch letters from the supplier to the owner/registered keeper.

Vehicle suppliers will notify VOSA of the response rate at three monthly intervals, until the recall action is complete or it is mutually agreed that the campaign be closed for reporting purposes.

PUBLICATION OF INFORMATION ON VEHICLE DEPECTS BY VOSA

VOSA reserves the right, under Ministerial authority, to publish at any time information of public interest. Before doing so, VOSA will consult the supplier, and where appropriate the component manufacturer concerned. VOSA will not disclose publicly information on matters of commercial confidence unless there appear to be overriding safety considerations. Subject to this proviso, VOSA will also make public at regular intervals, summary information on action taken on cases notified under the Code. It will normally divert to a supplier more specific requests on particular cases.

IMPORTED VEHICLES

In the case of a recall affecting units imported by an independent importer, that importer shall bear the responsibilities specified in this code.

If the independent importer is not available to undertake this obligation, then VOSA will contact the manufacturer of the affected units.

This Code will also apply to personally imported vehicles, insofar as the manufacturer or concessionaire is able to identify the vehicle's presence in the UK.

EXPORTED VEHICLES

The Code does not cover exported vehicles. Measures to be taken in relation to these will depend upon the legal and administrative arrangements prevailing in the country of import. However, the sponsors of the Code are prepared to participate in any international discussions designed to harmonise arrangements governing notification of defects and related remedial action.

FURTHER INFORMATION

This Code of practice is drawn up as a consequence of the implementation of the General Product Safety Directive 2002 and is not intended to interpret, qualify or supplement English Law.

You retain your rights under the General Product Safety Directive and a copy can be viewed

Any further information is obtainable by contacting VOSA via the details provided below.

This code of practice is produced in tandem with the VOSA Guide to Recalls and acknowledged within the Europe Recall Guide.

For Further Information Contact:

Vehicle Safety Branch
Vehicle and Operator Services Agency
Vehicle Inspectorate Division
Berkeley House
Croydon StreetBristol
BS5 ODA

Tel: 0117–9543300

www.vosa.gov.uk

Appendix 4A
VBRA Consumer Code of Practice

INTRODUCTION TO THE VBRA CONSUMER CODE OF PRACTICE

The VBRA is the UK's lead body for the Vehicle Bodybuilding and Vehicle Body Repair Industry.

It sets and monitors its members' industry operating standards in order to ensure that customers who choose to use a VBRA member will have confidence and assurance that in their choice they will be provided with high standards of service and repairs. VBRA members are also required to comply with current legislative and environmental requirements together with the VBRA Consumer Code of Practice that guides all parties to ensuring a satisfactory outcome in the provision of services and repairs.

VBRA members recognize that customers may find themselves in difficult and unfamiliar circumstances when requiring advice and or the provision of services or repairs for their vehicles. It is also recognized that it can be even more stressful and inconvenient for customers should the vehicle have been damaged or involved in a road traffic accident.

The Code incorporates information and procedures that have been established to assist the motoring public in selecting a business with complete confidence that is able to offer, as a matter of course, all the necessary information and assistance and to be able to provide the necessary levels of service and repairs.

The information and assistance available also includes advice on the procedures and options that may be taken in the event of vehicle damage and that may require an insurance claim.

The information and the procedures set out in the Code are intended to help avoid any misunderstandings between the customer and the business. By ensuring all parties are clear as to what is required and what is to be carried out and the costs involved, this prior to any work being undertaken, will help avoid any customer dissatisfaction.

To further enhance customer confidence, in the unlikely event of some query or dissatisfaction that cannot settled locally, there is incorporated within the VBRA Consumer Code an easily accessible Conciliation and Arbitration scheme for bringing them to a satisfactory conclusion.

The Code's administration, operating standards and monitoring are regulated by procedures established by the VBRA Ltd.

AIMS OF THE CODE

1. To uphold and maintain the best interests of the general motoring public by ensuring a regulated free and open market between VBRA members.
2. To reflect issues which are important to customers.
3. To ensure there is clear pre-contractual information readily available regarding the terms and conditions on which the services and/or repairs are undertaken, including pricing, payment and warranty.
4. In the event of any form of query or dissatisfaction that there is an easily accessible procedure to ensure that these are addressed and resolved in the most speedy and cost effective manner.
5. To ensure that VBRA members comply with current legislation and environmental requirements.
6. To enhance the reputation of the industry sector in the eyes of the motoring public by ensuring compliance of the consumer Code by all VBRA member businesses.

CUSTOMER CHOICE

The motoring public, when faced with making a choice of where to obtain services or repairs for their motoring needs, may have difficulty in identifying and locating a business which they can trust to carry out their requirements in a professional, cost effective manner.

To assist the motoring public in making a free and fully informed choice all VBRA members are obliged to comply with the consumer Code of Practice. To identify and locate VBRA members look for the distinctive logo on their premises or documentation, which only VBRA members are authorized to display. The location of all members can be found on the VBRA web site www.vbra.co.uk under 'Find Member' on the Home page.

THE VBRA CONSUMER CODE OF PRACTICE

VBRA members are required to comply with the operational policies and procedures of the Code including those identified below.

These procedures have been developed to safeguard and enhance customer confidence and satisfaction.

The contents of the Code are not a limiting factor and VBRA members may exceed those included in the Code.

The VBRA Code of Practice

1. The Code

A Copy / text of the Code is available from VBRA members and can also be obtained from the VBRA web site www.vbra.co.uk.

2. Code Awareness

The management and relevant staff of VBRA members are aware of their responsibilities regarding the operation of the Code.

3. Estimates and quotations

The customer should be offered and if required be provided with a written estimate or quotation for the services or work that is agreed to be carried out.

The estimate/quotation should include the cost of labour / parts / materials and VAT where applicable should be shown, together with any other costs for which the customer will be responsible.

*Where investigative or diagnostic work is required before a final esti-
mate/quotation can be established a financial limit as to this diagnosis
work should be agreed and set before any further expense is incurred.*

*The customer's agreement should be obtained prior to any further costs
are incurred.*

If there is a cost for the production of an estimate / quotation this
should be made known to the customer and their agreement obtained
prior to its completion.

The difference between an estimate and quotation should be explained
to the customer.

Definition of an estimate:

An estimate is the anticipated cost for the work requested. In the event
of further work or parts required being identified an estimate may be
increased to cover these costs. However as soon as any reason is found
for an increase to the estimate, which is above a nominal amount, the
customer should be informed as to the reasons and the costs involved.
The customers' agreement must be obtained prior to further costs being
incurred.

Definition of a quotation:

A quotation is an all-inclusive fixed cost for carrying out the work as
described and may not be increased.

4. Payment

The methods and terms of payment that are available should be advised
prior to any work being undertaken.

In the event of any pre-payments or deposits being required, the
business will have a procedure in place for the handling and security of
any pre-payment to ensure that in the event of non-supply of services or
goods the pre- paid money is safeguarded and can be returned. The
details of this procedure are available on request from the repairer
company.

5. Parts used

Where parts are required to be fitted the customer should be provided with a clear explanation for the need for replacement. If other than new and original manufacturers main structural parts, panels or mechanical items, are to be fitted, the customer should be advised as to the reason(s) for their use and the customer's authorization obtained.

6. Displaced parts

The customer should be advised that if required any displaced parts can be made available for inspection or return with the exception of those parts required for exchange or warranty.

The returning of any parts / materials should comply with the current disposal of waste regulations.

7. The final invoice

The final invoice and associated documents should have a clear explanation of the work carried out.

It should also include the description of the parts and materials used and include VAT if applicable, invoice date, mileage and reference to the terms of warranty.

8. Warranties

Terms of warranties are displayed in customer facing areas and on other documentation. A copy of the warranty and information on how to proceed in the event of any warranty work being required available on request.

However the warranty in respect of workmanship, parts and materials will not detract from customer rights under the supply of Goods and Services Act 1982.

Workmanship

The warranty in respect of workmanship shall be for a period of not less than 24 months or 24,000 miles use whichever occurs first from the date of repair.

The recommended procedure to overcome any fault is to exchange or repair any defective part that needs replacement by reason of defective material or workmanship during repair.

Parts and Materials

The warranty in respect of parts and materials will be not less than those of the manufacturer of the parts or materials.

The period of warranty shall be extended to compensate for any prolonged period that the vehicle may be off the road for rectification of faults or further work that may be required as a result of previous work being defective.

The period of the warranty remaining can be transferred to subsequent owners. This applies only to the work actually carried out by the repairer and which is detailed on the original invoice.

Vehicle manufacturers anti perforation warranty

Where a period of the vehicle manufacturer's anti-perforation warranty still exists, the repairer will observe the same terms and conditions as those of the V.M. on those areas of the vehicle that the work has been carried out for the remaining period of the vehicle manufacturer's full warranty, while observing the same conditions on the repaired area as those of the V.M.

If any member attaches any specific terms and conditions to the anti perforation or rust warranty these should be brought to the attention of the customer before acceptance of the work.

Any work that is required to be carried out under warranty should be referred to the original repairer.

In an event such as that of a business closure, where the warranty work cannot be carried out by the original repairer, the relevant details should be passed directly to the VBRA who will make the necessary arrangements.

Exclusions

Any exclusion from the warranty will be brought to the customer's attention and recorded at the time of repair. This may be due to the nature of the repair and or the condition of the vehicle.

Limitations

No claim will be met under the warranty if the vehicle has been:
- Used for competitions, racing or record attempts or otherwise than for private or commercial use of the owner or other users with his / her permission.
- Normal wear and tear, damage, neglect, corrosion.
- Improper use or failure to use or maintain in accordance with the manufacturer's recommendations, or abused in any way.
- Any damage caused in a subsequent accident or non-associated fault.

9. Completion delivery times / dates

When the work required has been established and agreed, a completion time / date will be given. If it is found that this time / date, for whatever reason, cannot be achieved the customer will immediately be contacted and advised.

10. Vehicle Accident Damage / Insurance Claim

In the event of a vehicle incurring accident damage, that may involve an insurance claim, the policyholder should be advised as to the procedures and options that are available to them and to ensure their vehicle is reinstated in a professional manner.

These options may include:
- Customers right to select a repairer of their own choice.
- Procedure for an insurance claim made under the policyholders own insurance.
- Procedure for 'no fault' accidents, where the driver of the vehicle was not at fault in causing the accident / damage.
- Advices for paying or recovering other costs involved in the claim such as insurance policy excess, no claims bonus, betterment, VAT.

11. Contractual Terms and Conditions

The terms and conditions under which the company undertakes to provide services or repairs must be clear and fair and made available to
customer before they agree to services or work being carried out and
also displayed in customer facing areas.

12. Cancellation of repair agreement

The customer may cancel the repair agreement at any time preferably in
writing. However the customer would be liable for any costs that had
already been accrued by the repairer. These costs may include the labour
for work carried out up to the time / date of cancellation, parts ordered /
obtained / used that cannot be cancelled, returned or resold and / or the
handling charge for their return and any other direct costs that have been
incurred in carrying out the original agreement. In any case the repairer
is under a duty to minimize the customers loss. A reasonable amount of
time will be allowed for the removal of the vehicle from the site, after
which a daily storage charge may be levied. Unless the company gives
their permission allowing the vehicle to be removed from the site any
costs incurred should be paid prior to the vehicle being released.

13. Care of customers vehicles and possessions

Reasonable care will be taken of customers' vehicles and possessions
while in the care of the repairer. If the vehicle is to remain with the
repairer for any length of time the customer should be encouraged and
given every opportunity to collect all such possessions.

Repairers must not avoid their responsibility by the use of disclaimers,
and will be adequately insured to cover such legal liabilities.

14. Customer confidence and satisfaction

The Company is dedicated to achieving high levels of customer confidence and satisfaction.

Therefore resolving any customer misunderstanding or dissatisfaction
regarding the level of service and the quality of the work carried out is
a major priority.

To this end the Company will appoint a 'named' customer relations person with authority and responsibility to resolve any customer query or dissatisfaction. The name of this is person will be displayed in a customer facing area.

If satisfaction has not been obtained through contact with other management or staff, the named person should be contacted and provided with the information that will enable them to investigate the situation.

To reduce the possibility of any misunderstanding or confusion, it is recommended that the customer should record their concerns providing details of the vehicle, the work and date the work or services were provided and the specific reasons for dissatisfaction together with details of any previous contacts that have been made in an attempt to resolve the problem.

They should respond within 5 working days outlining the course of action they propose to achieve a satisfactory resolution.

If preferred the customer may complete a 'Customer Satisfaction' card and returned to the customer relations manager. This will provide an easy and positive means of recording any dissatisfaction. These cards are freely available in customer facing areas.

If after exhausting the above procedure the dissatisfaction has not been resolved the customer can refer it to the Conciliation and Arbitration service.

(See Conciliation and Arbitration Process)

If a customer refers a complaint to a Trading Standards Officer, Consumer Advice Centre, Citizens Advice Bureau or any other similar recognized organization or body VBRA members should positively cooperate with that body providing the necessary information and to give assistance to ensure a speedy resolution.

15. Customer Satisfaction Survey Cards

Customer satisfaction survey cards are made available to help the organization to continuously monitor and improve their operation. It is important that customers help by completing and returning these highlighting both the good and not so good experiences that were encountered while obtaining the services required.

16. Advertising

All claims, descriptions and advertisements should be honest and truthful and should comply with the letter and spirit of the Code and standards set by the relevant advertising regulatory body.

17. The VBRA member will act according to the letter of the Code and in the spirit in which it has been produced.

18. Executive Information and Control

The VBRA will maintain an analysis of any complaints where the Association provided an expert opinion and also those referred for Conciliation and Arbitration.

The association will publish results of such analisis annually.

19. Enforcement

The Code is mandatory on VBRA members.

The VBRA Constitution contains provision for the enforcement of the Code by the Association's Board of Management and by the National Builders and Repairer Councils. In the event of a member not delivering the standards set out in the Code the penalties that may be imposed include a reprimand and / or fine or termination of VBRA membership. The Constitution provides that any penalty imposed and the reasons shall be published in the VBRA's journal 'BODY'

The Conciliation and Arbitration Process

The Conciliation Service

The Conciliation Service, which is an independent department of the VBRA, is available for any member of the general public or a member of the Association to use to help settle any dispute. There is no charge for the customer to use the conciliation procedure.

Where there is cause for complaint the first step should be for the customer to use the repairer's own internal complaints procedure as described in Section 14. This should, in the vast majority of cases, achieve a quick and satisfactory conclusion.

However small minorities of complaints are not resolved. Some misunderstanding or a breakdown in communication may have caused them.

To address such a circumstance the VBRA has set in place an independent Conciliation and Arbitration service. The repairer may suggest this service to the customer and the customer has the option of agreeing to proceed or not. However if the customer chooses to use the Conciliation and Arbitration service the repairer MUST agree that this option be progressed.

The services of the VBRA are also available to assist other bodies such as Trading Standards Officers, Consumer Advice Centers, Citizens Advice and motoring organizations where a member of the VBRA is involved.

Details of any dispute should be made within the warranty period of the repair, preferably in writing. In exceptional circumstances, such as where the fault did not become apparent within the warranty period, consideration will be given outside this time or mileage. This term will not adversely affect consumer rights.

How to use the Conciliation Service

1) The customer or member should contact the VBRA secretariat. Contact details can be found in this document.

2) An information form will be sent to the customer on which details of the complaint can be recorded. The completed form together with any other supporting evidence should be returned to the VBRA.

3) Based on the information provided it may be considered appropriate to appoint an independent expert in order to achieve a settlement. If so one would be appointed. The outcome of the inspection will be issued and copied to all the parties and copied to the Association. The cost of this service is paid for by the VBRA.

4) If at the conciliation stage a satisfactory resolution cannot be achieved, the customer can request the dispute be referred to the Arbitration Service.

5) If the customer requests the dispute to go to arbitration, the member must also agree to this request.

Arbitration

The VBRA Arbitration scheme offers to all parties an inexpensive means of resolving disputes.

A copy of the procedure and an explanation of any costs that may be involved are available from the VBRA. The Arbitrator's findings are binding on all parties.

Using the Arbitration Service

1) If the customer requests that the case should be processed by the arbrtration scheme the VBRA will transfer the relevant files to the National Conciliation Service.

2) The National Conciliation Service will make contact with the customer and proceed with the arbitration process.

3) Neither the complainant nor the repairer member has the right to appear or to be represented at the arbitration hearing unless the appointed Arbitrator requests it.

4) After considering all the relevant evidence, reports and documents, the Arbitrator will make known his/her decision in writing and copies will be provided to both parties and the VBRA. The Arbitrator's decision, including directions regarding costs, is legally binding and enforceable by law on all the parties.

Appendix 5
Disposal of uncollected goods forms

IN THE COUNTY COURT

IN THE MATTER OF THE TORTS (INTERFERENCE WITH GOODS) ACT 1977

BETWEEN:

Applicant

and

Respondent

TAKE NOTICE that the above named Applicant intends to apply to the Judge/registrar of this Court at on the day of 19 for an Order that the Applicant shall be at liberty to sell the Respondent's motor vehicle registered number at the best price obtainable under prevailing circumstances and to pay into Court to the credit of the respondent the proceeds of such sale less the sum due to the Applicant from the Respondent and after deducting the costs, charges and expenses of and incidental to the sale of the vehicle incurred by the Applicant, pursuant to section 13 of the Torts (Interference with Goods) Act 1977.

And such further order as may be just including costs.

Dated day of 19

(Signature)

To: The Registrar of the Court and to the Applicant

Name and address of Solicitors for the Applicant, or the Applicant

NOTICE THAT GOODS ARE READY FOR RE-DELIVERY

I   of

hereby give you notice that the undermentioned goods held at
                          are ready for re-delivery.

The sum which I claim to be due to me in respect of the goods is set out below.

Description of goods   *Sum claimed*

If you fail to pay the said sum, and to take delivery of the goods, or give directions as to their delivery, they may be sold under the provisions of the Torts (Interference with Goods) Act 1977.

Dated the   day of   19

To: Signed:

NOTICE OF BAILEE'S INTENTION TO SELL GOODS

I   of

hereby give you notice of my intention to sell the goods described below, held at   . The sale will take place on

19   . The sum which I claim to be due to me in relation to the goods is as shown below.

Description of goods   *Sum claimed*

If you fail to pay the said sum and to take delivery of the goods or give directions as to their delivery before   they may be sold under the provisions of the Torts (Interference with Goods) Act 1979.

To: Signed:

Appendix 6
Code of practice for traders on price indications

The Consumer Protection Act

1. The Consumer Protection Act 1987 makes it a criminal offence to give consumers a misleading price indication about goods, services, accommodation (including the sale of new homes) or facilities. It applies however you give the price indication – whether in a TV or press advertisement, in a catalogue or leaflet, on notices, price tickets or shelf-edge marking in stores, or if you give it orally, for example on the telephone. The term 'price indication' includes price comparisons as well as indications of a single price.

2. This code of practice is approved under section 25 of the Act which gives the Secretary of State power to approve codes of practice to give practical guidance to traders. It is addressed to traders and sets out what is good practice to follow in giving price indications in a wide range of different circumstances, so as to avoid giving misleading price indications. But the Act does not require you to do so as this code tells you. You may still give price indications which do not accord with this code, provided they are not misleading. 'Misleading' is defined in section 21 of the Act.

The definition covers indications about any conditions attached to a price, about what you expect to happen to a price in future and what you say in price comparisons, as well as indications about the actual price the consumer will have to pay. It also applies in the same way to any indications you give about the way in which a price will be calculated.

Price comparisons

3. If you want to make price comparisons, you should do so only if you can show that they are accurate and valid. Indications which give only the price of the product are unlikely to be misleading if they are accurate and cover the total charge you will make. Comparisons with prices which you can show have been or are being charged for the same or similar goods, services, accommodation or facilities and have applied for a reasonable period are also unlikely to be misleading. Guidance on these matters is contained in this code.

Enforcement

4. Enforcement of the Consumer Protection Act 1987 is the responsibility of officers of the local weights and measures authority (in Northern Ireland, the Department of Economic Development) – usually called Trading Standards Officers. If a Trading Standards Officer has reasonable grounds to suspect that you have given a misleading price indication, the Act gives the Officer power to require you to produce any records relating to your business and to seize and detain goods or records which the Officer has reasonable grounds for believing may be required as evidence in court proceedings.

5. It may only be practicable for Trading Standards Officers to obtain from you the information necessary to carry out their duties under the Act. In these circumstances the Officer may seek information and assistance about both the claim and the supporting evidence from you. Be prepared to co-operate with Trading Standards Officers and respond to reasonable requests for information and assistance. The Act makes it an offence to obstruct a Trading Standards Officer intentionally or to fail (without good cause) to give any assistance or information the Officer may reasonably require to carry out duties under the Act.

Court proceedings

6. If you are taken to court for giving a misleading price indication, the court can take into account whether or not you have followed the code.

If you have done as the code advises, that will not be an absolute defence but it will tend to show that you have not committed an offence. Similar if you have done something the code advises against doing it may tend to show that the price indication was misleading. If you do something which is not covered by the code, your price indication will need to be judged only against the terms of the general offence. The Act provides for a defence of due diligence, that is, that you have taken all reasonable steps to avoid committing the offence of giving a misleading price indication, but failure to follow the code of practice may make it difficult to show this.

Regulations

7. The Act also provides power to make regulations about price indications and you should ensure that your price indications comply with any such regulations. There are none at present.

Other legislation

8. This code deals only with the requirements of Part III of the Consumer Protection Act 1987. In some sectors there will be other relevant legislation. For example, price indications about credit terms must comply with the Consumer Credit Act 1974 and the regulations made under it, as well as with the Consumer Protection Act 1987.

Definitions

In this code:
Accommodation includes hotel and other holiday accommodation and new homes for sale freehold or on a lease of over 21 years but does not include rented homes.
Consumer means anyone who might want the goods, services, accommodation or facilities, other than for business use.
Price means both the total amount the consumer will have to pay to get the goods, services, accommodation or facilities and any method which has been or will be used to calculate that amount.
Price comparison means any indication given to consumers that the price at which something is offered to consumers is less than or equal to someone other price.

Product means goods, services, accommodation and facilities (but not credit facilities, except where otherwise specified).

Services and Facilities means any services or facilities whatever (including credit, banking and insurance services, purchase or sale of foreign currency, supply of electricity, off-street car parking and caravan sites) except those provided by a person who is an authorised person or appointed representative under the Financial Services Act 1986 in the course of an investment business, services provided by an employee to his employer and facilities for a caravan which is the occupier's main or only home.

Shop means any shop, store, stall or other place (including a vehicle or the consumer's home) at which goods, services, accommodation or facilities are offered to consumers.

Trader means anyone (retailers, manufacturers, agents, service providers and others) who is acting in the course of a business.

PART I   PRICE COMPARISONS

1.1 Price comparisons generally

1.1.1. Always make the meaning of price indications clear. Do not leave consumers to guess whether or not a price comparison is being made. If no price comparison is intended, do not use words or phrases which, in their normal, everyday use and in the context in which they are used, are likely to give your customers the impression that a price comparison is being made.

1.1.2. Price comparisons should always state the higher price as well as the price you intend to charge for the product (goods, services, accommodation or facilities). Do not make statements like 'sale price £5' or 'reduced to £39' without quoting the higher price to which they refer.

1.1.3. It should be clear what sort of price the higher price is. For example, comparisons with something described by words like 'regular price', 'usual price' or 'normal price' should say whose regular, usual or normal price it is (eg 'our normal price'). Description like 'reduced from' and crossed out higher prices should be used only if they refer to your own previous price. Words should not be used in price indications other than with their normal everyday meanings.

1.1.4. Do not use initials or abbreviations to describe the higher price in a comparison, except for the initials 'RRP' to describe a recommended retail price or the abbreviation 'man.rec. price' to describe a manufacturer's recommended price (see paragraph 1.6.2 below).

1.1.5. Follow the part of the code (sections 1.2 to 1.6 as appropriate) which applies to the type of comparison you intend to make.

1.2 Comparisons with the trader's own previous price

General

1.2.1. In any comparison between your present selling price and another price at which you have in the past offered the product, you should state the previous price as well as the new lower price.

1.2.2. In any comparison with your own previous price:
(a)   the previous price should be the last price at which the product was available to consumers in the previous 6 months;
(b)   the product should have been available to consumers at that price for at least 28 consecutive days in the previous 6 months; and
(c)   the previous price should have applied (as above) for that period at the same shop where the reduced price is now being offered.

The 28 days at (b) above may include bank holidays, Sundays or other days of religious observance when the shop was closed; and up to 4 days when, for reasons beyond your control, the product was not available for supply. The product must not have been offered at a different price between that 28 day period and the day when the reduced price is first offered.

1.2.3. If the previous price in a comparison does not meet one or more of the conditions set out in paragraph 1.2.2. above:
(i)   the comparison should be fair and meaningful; and
(ii)   give a clear and positive explanation of the period for which and the circumstances in which that higher price applied.

For example 'these goods were on sale here at the higher price from 1 February to 26 February' or 'these goods were on sale at the higher price in 10 of our 95 stores only'. Display the explanation clearly, and as prominently as the price indication. You should not use general disclaimers saying for example that the higher prices used in comparisons have not necessarily applied for 28 consecutive days.

Food, drink and perishable goods

1.2.4. For any food and drink, you need not give a positive explanation if the previous price in a comparison has not applied for 28 consecutive days, provided it was the last price at which the goods were on sale in the previous 6 months and applied in the same shop where the reduced price is now being offered. This also applies to non-food perishables, if they have a shelf-life of less than 6 weeks.

Catalogue and Mail order traders

1.2.5. Where products are sold only through a catalogue, advertisements or leaflet, any comparison with a previous price should be with the price in your own last catalogue, advertisement or leaflet. If you sell the same products both in shops and through catalogues etc, the previous price should be the last price at which you offered the product. You should also follow the guidance in paragraphs 1.2.2(a) and (b). If you price comparison does not meet these conditions, you should follow the guidance in paragraph 1.2.3.

Making a series of reductions

1.2.6. If you advertise a price reduction and then want to reduce the price further during the same sale or special offer period, the intervening price (or prices) need not have applied for 28 days. In these circumstances unless you use a positive explanation (paragraph 1.2.3.):

the highest price in the series must have applied for 28 consecutive days in the last 6 months at the same shop: and
you must show the highest price, the intervening price(s) and the current selling price (eg '£40, £20, £10, £5').

1.3 Introductory offers, after-sale or after-promotion prices

Introduction offers

1.3.1. Do not call a promotion an introductory offer unless you intend to continue to offer the product for sale after the offer period is over and to do so at a higher price.

1.3.2. Do not allow an offer to run on so long that it becomes misleading to describe it as an introductory or other special offer. What is a reasonable period will depend on the circumstances (but, depending on the shelf-life on the product, it is likely to be a matter of weeks, not months). An offer is unlikely to be misleading if you state the date the offer will end and keep to it. If you then extend the offer will period, make it clear that you have done so.

Quoting a future price

1.3.3. If you indicate an after-sale or after-promotion price, do so only if you are certain that, subject only to circumstances beyond your control, you will continue to offer identical products at that price for at least 28 days in the 3 months after the end of the offer period or after the offer stocks run out.

1.3.4. If you decide to quote a future price, write what you mean in full. Do not use initials to describe it (eg 'ASP', 'APP'). The description should be clearly and prominently displayed, with the price indication.

1.4 Comparisons with prices related to different circumstances

1.4.1. This section covers comparisons with prices:
(a)   for different quantities (eg '15p each, 4 for 50p');
(b)   for goods in a different conditions (eg 'seconds £20, when perfect £30');
(c)   for a different availability (eg 'price £50, price when ordered specially £60');
(d)   for goods in a totally different state (eg 'price in kit form £50, price ready-assembled £70'); or
(e)   for special groups of people (eg 'senior citizens' price £2.50, others £5').

General

1.4.2. Do not make such comparisons unless the product is available in the different quantity, conditions etc at the price you quote. Make clear to consumers the different circumstances which apply and show them prominently with the price indication. Do not use initials (eg 'RAP' for 'ready-assembled price') to describe the different circumstances, but write what you mean in full.

'When perfect' comparisons

1.4.3. If you do not have the perfect goods on sale in the same shop:
(a) follow section 1.2 if the 'when perfect' price is your own previous price for the goods;
(b) follow section 1.5 if the 'when perfect' price is another trader's price; or
(c) follow section 1.6 if the 'when perfect' price is one recommended by the manufacturer or supplier.

Goods in a different state

1.4.4. Only make comparisons with goods in a totally different state if:
(a) a reasonable proportion (say a third (by quantity)) of your stock of those goods is readily available for sale to consumers in that different state (for example, ready assembled) at the quoted price and from the shop where the price comparison is made; or
(b) another trader is offering those goods in that state at the quoted price and you follow section 1.5 below.

Prices for special groups of people

1.4.5. If you want to compare different prices which you charge to different groups of people (eg one price for existing customers and another for new customers, or one price for people who are members of a named organisation (other than the trader) and another for those who are not), do not use words like 'our normal' or 'our regular' to describe the higher price, unless it applies to at least half your customers.

1.5 Comparisons with another trader's prices

1.5.1. Only compare your prices with another trader's price if:
(a) you know that his price which you quote is accurate and up-to-date;

(b)   you give the name of the other trader clearly and prominently, with the price comparison;

(c)   you identify the shop where the other trader's price applies, if that other trader is a retailer; and

(d)   the other trader's price which you quote applies to the same products – or to substantially similar products and you state any differences clearly.

1.5.2. Do not make statements like 'if you can buy this product elsewhere for less, we will refund the difference' about your 'own brand' products which other traders do not stock, unless your offer will also apply to other traders' equivalent goods. If there are any conditions attached to the offer (eg it only applies to goods on sale in the same town) you should show them clearly and prominently, with the statement.

1.6 Comparisons with 'Recommended Retail Price' or similar

General

1.6.1. This section covers comparisons with recommended retail prices, manufacturers' recommended price, suggested retail prices, suppliers' suggested retail prices and similar descriptions. It also covers prices given to co-operative and voluntary group organisations by their wholesalers or headquarters organisations.

1.6.2. Do not use initials or abbreviations to describe the higher price in a comparison unless:

(a)   you see the initials 'RRP' to describe a recommended retail price; or

(b)   you use the abbreviation 'man. rec. price' to describe a manufacturer's recommended price.

Write all other descriptions out in full and show them clearly and prominently with the price indication.

1.6.3. Do not use a recommended price in a comparison unless:

(a)   it has been recommended to you by the manufacturer or supplier as a price at which the product might be sold to consumers;

(b)   you deal with the manufacturer or supplier on normal commercial terms. (This will generally be the case for members of co-opera-

tive or voluntary group organisations in relation to their wholesalers or headquarter organisations); and

(c)   the price is not significantly higher than prices at which the product is generally sold at the time you first make that comparison.

1.7 Pre-printed prices

1.7.1. Make sure you pass on to consumers any reduction stated
on the manufacturer's packaging (eg 'flash packs' such as '10p off
RRP').

1.7.2. You are making a price comparison if goods have a clearly visible price already printed on the packaging which is higher than the
price you will charge for them. Such pre-printed prices are, in effect,
recommended prices (except for retailers' own label goods) and you
should follow paragraphs 1.6.4. You need not state that the price is a
recommended price.

1.8 References to value or worth

1.8.1. Do not compare your prices with an amount described only as
'worth' or 'value'.

1.8.2. Do not present general advertising slogans which refer to 'value'
or 'worth' in a way which is likely to be seen by consumers as a price
comparison.

1.9 Sales or special events

1.9.1. If you have bought in items specially for a sale, and you make
this clear, you should not quote a higher price when indicating that they
are special purchases. Otherwise, your price indications for individual
items in the sale which are reduced should comply with section 1.1 of
the code and whichever of sections 1.2 to 1.6 applies to the type of
comparison you are making.

1.9.2. If you just have a general notice saying, for example, that all
products are at 'half marked price', the marked price on the individual
items should be your own previous price and you should follow section
1.2 of the code.

1.9.3. Do not use general notices saying, eg 'up to 50% off' unless the maximum reduction quoted applies at least 10% (by quantity) of the range of products on offer.

1.10 Free offers

1.10.1. Make clear to consumers, at the time of the offer for sale, exactly what they will have to buy to get the 'free offer'.

1.10.2. If you give any indication of the monetary value of the 'free offer', and that sum is not your own present price for the product, follow whichever of sections 1.2 to 1.6 covers the type of price it is.

1.10.3. If there are any conditions attached to the 'free offer', give at least the main points of those conditions with the price indication and make clear to consumers where, before they are committed to buy, they can get full details of the conditions.

1.10.4. Do not claim that an offer is free if:
(a) you have imposed additional charges that you would not normally make;
(b) you have inflated the price of any product the consumer must buy or the incidental charges (for example, postage) the consumer must pay to get the 'free offer', or
(c) you will reduce the price to the consumers who do not take it up.

PART 2 ACTUAL PRICE TO CONSUMER

2.1 Indicating two different prices

2.1.1. The Consumer Protection Act makes it an offence to indicate a price for goods or services which is lower than the one that actually applies, showing one price in an advertisement, window display, shelf marking or on the item itself, and then charging a higher price at the point of sale or checkout.

2.2 Incomplete information and non-optional extras

2.2.1. Make clear in your price indications the full price consumers will have to pay for the product. Some examples of how to do so in particular circumstances are set out below.

Limited availability of product

2.2.2. Where the price you are quoting for products only applies to a limited number of, say, orders, sizes or colours, you should make this clear in your price indication (eg 'available in other colours or sizes at additional cost').

Prices relating to differing forms of products

2.2.3. If the price you are quoting for particular products does not apply to the products in the form they are displayed or advertised, say so clearly in your price indication. For example, advertisements for self-assembly furniture and the like should make it clear that the price refers to a kit of parts.

Postage, packing and delivery charges

2.2.4. If you sell by mail order, make clear any additional charges for postage, packing and delivery on the order form or similar document, so that consumers are fully aware of them before being committed to buying. Where you cannot determine these charges in advance, show clearly on the order form how they will be calculated (eg 'Post Office rates apply'), or the place in the catalogue etc where the information is given.

2.2.5. If you sell goods from a shop and offer a delivery service for certain items, make it clear whether there are any separate delivery charges (eg for delivery outside a particular area) and what those charges are, before the consumer is committed to buying.

VALUE ADDED TAX

(i) Price indications to consumers

2.2.6. All price indications you give to private consumers, by whatever means, should include VAT.

(ii) Price indications to business customers

2.2.7. Prices may be indicated exclusive of VAT in shops where or advertisements from which most of your business is with business customers. If you also carry out business with private consumers at those shops or from those advertisements you should make clear that the prices exclude VAT and:

(i)   display VAT-inclusive prices with equal prominence, or

(ii) display prominent statements that on top of the quoted price customers will also have to pay VAT at 15% (or the current rate).

(iii) Professional fees

2.2.8. Where you indicate a price (including estimates) for a professional fee, make clear what it covers. The price should generally include VAT. In cases where the fee is based on an as-yet-unknown sum of money (for example, the sale price of a house), either:

(i)   quote a fee which includes VAT; or

(ii) make it clear that in addition to your fee the consumer would have to pay VAT at the current rate (eg 'fee of 1.5% of purchase price, plus VAT at 15%').

Make sure that whichever method you choose is used for both estimates and final bills.

(iv) Building work

2.2.9. In estimates for building work, either include VAT in the price indication or indicate with equal prominence the amount or rate of VAT payable in addition to your basic figure. If you give a separate amount for VAT, make it clear that if any provisional sums in estimates vary then the amount of VAT payable would also vary.

SERVICE, COVER AND MINIMUM CHARGES IN HOTELS, RESTAURANTS AND SIMILAR ESTABLISHMENTS

2.2.10. If your customers in hotels, restaurants or similar places must pay a non-optional extra charge, eg a 'service charge':

(i)   incorporate the charge within fully inclusive prices wherever practicable; and

(ii) display the fact clearly on any price list or priced menu, whether displayed inside or outside (eg by using statements like 'all prices include service').

Do not include suggested optional sums, whether for service or any other item, in the bill presented to the customer.

2.2.11. It will not be practical to include some non-optional extra charges in a quoted price; for instance, if you make a flat charge per person or per table in a restaurant (often referred to as a 'cover charge') or a minimum charge. In such cases the charge should be shown as prominently as other prices on any list or menu, whether displayed inside or outside.

HOLIDAYS AND TRAVEL PRICES

2.2.12. If you offer a variety of prices to give consumers a choice, (for example, paying more or less for a holiday depending on the time of year or the standard of accommodation), make clear in your brochure— or any other price indication—what the basic price is and what it covers. Give details of any optional additional charges and what those charges cover, or of the place where this information can be found, clearly and close to the basic price.

2.2.13. Any non-optional extra charges which are for fixed amounts should be included in the basic price and not shown as additions, unless they are only payable by some consumers. In that case you should specify, near to the details of the basic price, either what the amounts are and the circumstances in which they are payable, or where in the brochure etc the information is given.

2.2.14. Details of non-optional extra charges which may vary, (such as holiday insurance) or of where in the brochure etc the information is given should be made clear to consumers near to the basic price.

2.2.15. If you reserve the right to increase the prices after consumers have made their bookings, state this clearly with all indications of prices, and include prominently in your brochure full information on the circumstances in which a surcharge is payable.

TICKET PRICES

2.2.16. If you sell tickets, whether for sporting events, cinema, theatre etc and your prices are higher than the regular price that wold be charged to the public at the box office, ie higher than the 'face value', you should make clear in any price indication what the 'face value' of the ticket is.

CALL-OUT CHARGES

2.2.17. If you make a minimum call-out charge or other flat-rate charge (for example, for plumbing, gas or electrical appliance repairs etc carried out in consumers' homes) ensure that the consumer is made aware of the charges and whether the actual price may be higher (eg if work takes longer than a specific time) before being committed to using your services.

CREDIT FACILITIES

2.2.18. Price indications about consumer credit should comply with the relevant requirements of regulations under the Consumer Credit Act 1974 governing the form and content of advertisements.

INSURANCE

2.2.19. Where actual premium rates for a particular consumer or the availability of insurance cover depend on an individual assessment, this should be made clear when any indication of the premium or the method or determining it is given to consumers.

PART 3   PRICE INDICATIONS WHICH BECOME MISLEADING AFTER THEY HAVE BEEN GIVEN

3.1. General

3.1.1. The Consumer Protection Act makes it an offence to give a price indication which, although correct at the time, becomes misleading after you have given it, if:
  (i) consumers could reasonably be expected still to be relying on it; and
  (ii) you do not take reasonably steps to prevent them doing so.

Clearly it will not be necessary or even possible in many instances to inform all those who may have been given the misleading price indication. However, you should always make sure consumers are given the correct information before they are committed to buying a product and be prepared to cancel any transaction which a consumer has entered into the basis of a price indication which has become misleading.

3.1.2. Do not give price indications which you know or intend will only apply for a limited period, without making this fact clear in the advertisement or price indication.

3.1.3. The following paragraphs set out what you should do in some particular circumstances.

3.2. Newspaper and magazine advertisements

3.2.1. If the advertisement does not say otherwise, the price indication should apply for a reasonable period (as a general guide, at least 7 days or until the next issue of the newspaper or magazine in which the advertisement was published, whichever is longer). If the price indication becomes misleading within this period make sure consumers are given the correct information before they are committed to buying the product.

3.3. Mail order advertisements, catalogues and leaflets

3.3.1. Paragraph 3.2.1. above also applies to the time for which price indications in mail order advertisements and in regularly published catalogues or brochures should apply. If a price indication becomes misleading within this period, make the correct price indication clear to anyone who orders the product to which it relates. Do so before the consumer is committed to buying the product and, wherever practicable, before the goods are sent to the consumer.

3.4. Selling through agents

Holiday brochures and travel agents

3.4.1. Surcharges are covered in paragraph 2.2.15. If a price indication becomes misleading for any other reason, tour operators who sell direct to consumers should follow paragraph 3.3.1 above; and tour operators who sell through travel agents should follow paragraphs 3.4.2 and 3.4.3 below.

3.4.2. If a price indication become misleading while your brochure is still current, make this clear to the travel agents to whom you distributed the brochures. Be prepared to cancel any holiday bookings consumers have made on the basis of a misleading price indication.

3.4.3. In the circumstances set out in paragraph 3.4.2, travel agents should ensure that the correct price indication is made clear to consumers before they make a booking.

Insurance and independent intermediaries

3.4.4. Insurers who sell their products through agents or independent intermediaries should take all reasonable steps to ensure that all such agents who are known to hold information on the insurer's premium rates and terms of the cover provided are told clearly of any changes in those rates or terms.

3.4.5. Agents, independent intermediaries and providers of quotation systems should ensure that they act on changes notified to them by an insurer.

3.5. Changes in the rate of Value Added Tax

3.5.1. If your price indications become misleading because of a change in the general rate of VAT, or other taxes paid at point of sale, make the correct price indication clear to any consumers who order products. Do so before the consumer is committed to buying the product and, wherever practicable, before the goods are sent to the consumer.

PART 4   SALE OF NEW HOMES

4.1. A 'new home' is any building, or part of a building to be used only as a private dwelling which is either:
(i)   a newly-built house or flat; or
(ii)   a newly-converted existing building which has not previously been used in that form as a private home.

4.2. The Consumer Protection Act and this code apply to new homes which are either for sale freehold or covered by a long lease, ie with more than 21 years to run. In this context the term 'trader' covers not only a business vendor, such as a developer, but also an estate agent acting on behalf of such a vendor.

4.3. You should follow the relevant provision of Part 1 of the code if:
- (i)   you want to make a comparison between the price at which you offer new homes for sale and any other price;
- (ii) you offer an inclusive price for new homes which also covers such items as furnishings, domestic appliances and insurance and you compare their value with, for example, High Street prices for similar items.

4.4. Part 2 of the code gives details of the provisions you should follow if:
- (i)   the new houses you are selling, or any goods or services which apply to them, are only available in limited numbers or range;
- (ii) the sale price you give does not apply to the houses as displayed; or
- (iii) there are additional non-optional charges payable.

Index

Acceptance   73–74
  counter-offer, and   73–74
  silence, and   74
  uncertainty about terms   74
Advertisements   25–35
  businesses, by   33–34
  comparative   34–35
  consumer credit   34
  contract, and   28
  CO_2 emissions information   31–33
   application of 2001
    Regulations   32
   dealers, responsibility of   33
   importers, responsibility of   33
   manufacturers, responsibility
    of   33
   offences   33
   statutory provisions   32
  fuel consumption   31–33
   application of 2001
    Regulations   32
   dealers, responsibility of   33
   importers, responsibility of   33
   manufacturers, responsibility
    of   33
   offences   33
   statutory provisions   32
  legal controls   28–35

Advertisements—*continued*
  misleading   34–35
  offer   29
  powers of Director General
   of Fair Trading   25–26
  representations in   28–29
  statutory requirements   25
  Trade Descriptions Act   30–31
  trade descriptions, and   58–59
  voluntary controls   25, 26–28
   British Codes of
    Advertising Sales
    Promotion and
    Direct Marketing   26–27
   New Car Code of Practice   27–28
After sales service
  competition law, and   95
  parties to contract   77
An available market
  meaning   111–112
Arbitration   252–255
  advantages   255
  appeals   254–255
  application for   253
  arbitrator   253
   award enforcing   254
   publication   254
  disadvantages   255

Arbitration—*continued*
evidence 253–254
fees 253
legal representation 254
low cost 255
parties to 253
technical assessors 254
Auctions
offer, and 72

Bailee. *See also* Hiring contracts
repairer, as 202–204
sale by, effect of 208–209
sales by 120
Breach of statutory duty
seller's liability 152
'BSI approved'
trade descriptions 60
Businesses
advertising by 33–34

Car washes 219
Cash payment
money laundering, and 113
Citizens' Advice Bureaux 259
Clocking
liability for 57
Code of Practice for the Retail
Motor Industry 283–296
accessories 289
advertising 291–292
arbitration 294–296
complaints 294–296
disciplinary procedure 293–294
fuel 289
general provisions 284–285
handling complaints 292–293
introductions 283–284
monitoring 293–294
new car sales 286–287
repairs 289–291
replacement parts 289
servicing 289–291
used car sales 287–288
warranties 285–286

Code of practice for traders
on price indications 317–334
actual price to consumer 327–331
after-promotion prices 322–323
after-sale prices 322–323
call-out charges 331
Consumer Protection
Act 317–318
credit facilities 331
comparisons with another
trader's prices 324–325
comparisons with prices
related to different
circumstances 323–324
comparisons with
'recommended retail
price' 325–326
comparisons with trader's
own previous price 321
court proceedings 318–319
definitions 319–320
enforcement 318
free offers 327
holidays 330
incomplete information 327–328
indicating two different
prices 327
insurance 331
introductory offers 322–323
legislation other than At
of 1987 319
new homes, sale of 333–334
non-optional extras 327–328
pre-paid prices 326
price comparisons 318, 320–327
price indications which
become misleading
after they have been
given 331–333
references to value or
worth 326
regulations 319
sales 326–327
service charges 329–330

Code of practice for traders
    on price indications—*contined*
    special events   326–327
    ticket prices   330–331
    travel prices   330
    value added tax   328–329
Code of Practice on Vehicle
    Safety Defects 2004   309–313
    cases covered by   310
    components   310
    definition   310
    exported vehicles   313
    further information   313
    imported vehicles   312
    initiatives by VOSA in
        particular cases   311
    introduction   309–310
    notification of vehicle owners
        311–312
    notification of VOSA   311
    publication of information on
        vehicle defects by VOSA   312
    recall arrangements   310
Codes of Practice   14–23, 283–308
    advantages   17–18
    benefits to motorist   22
    consumer sales, and   19–20
    disciplinary procedures   22–23
    effect   18
    general statements   21
    impact of   21–22
    legal effect   19–21
    monitoring   22–23
    motor industry   18–19
    operation of   21
    restatement of legal rules   20
Companies
    parties to contract   76
Compensation orders
    trade descriptions, and   57
Competition Act 1998   90–91
Competition law   89–96
    Competition Act 1998   90–91
    Enterprise Act 2002   91

Competition law—*continued*
    Fair Trading Act 1973   89–90
        controls on sales of spare
            parts   89–90
    national legislation   89–91
    Restrictive Trade Practices
        Act 1976   90
    Treaty of Rome   91–96
        See also Treaty of Rome
Competition policy   9
Complaints   246–257
    arbitration. *See* Arbitration
    Codes, requirements of   246–248
        obligations of consumer   247–248
        obligations of industry   247
    considering a claim   249–252
        compliance with Code   252
        conciliation   252
        evidence   249–250
        facts   249
        law   250
        offer to settle   251
        publicity   251
        reasonableness   250–251
    courts, and   255–257
        advantages   256
        avoiding litigation   257
        costs   256
        disadvantages   256
        procedure   255–256
    dealing with   246–259
    handling, essentials of   246
    legal aspects   248–257
    number of   2
Condition of vehicle
    statements about
        trade descriptions, and   62
Conditions
    meaning   83
Conditions of sale   4–6
    exclusion clauses   4–5
Consideration   74–75
    release of debt, and   75

Construction and Use
   Regulations   220–221
Consumer
   meaning   37, 98–99
Consumer Advice Centres   259
Consumer credit   8
   advertisements   34
Consumer Credit Act 1974   157
   advertisements   162–166.
      See also Consumer
      credit advertisements
   agreements covered by   157–158
   licensing   158–162
      applications for standard
         licence   160
      duty to notify changes   160
      motor trade, and   160–162
      types of licence   158–159
      unlicensed activities   160
      who needs licence   159–160
   total charge for credit   162
Consumer credit
   advertisements   162–166
   application of Act of 1974   163
   APR   165
   general information   164
   'interest free'   165–166
   'no deposit'   166
   requirements   163–166
   restricted statements   165–166
   restructured use of words   164
   'weekly equivalent'   166
   specified key information
      about cost of loan   165
   "truth in lending"   162
Consumer hire agreement.
   See Hiring contracts
Consumer organisations   259–260
Consumer protection   259–261
   development of   3–10
      motor trade, and   1–13
   functioning of   10–13
Consumer safety   7–8
Consumer transactions
   meaning   127

Consumers' Association   259
Consumers, remedies for   146–150
   full refund   149
   manufacturer's warranty,
      relevance of   149–150
   partial refund   149
   powers of court   149
   repair of goods   147–149
   replacement of goods   147–149
   retailer's warranty,
      relevance of   149–150
   reversal of burden of proof   147
Contract   70–88
   acceptance   73–74
   consideration   74–75
   distance selling. *See* Distance
      selling contracts
   elements   71
   forming   71–75
   fraud, and   78
   illegal   78
   intention to enter into legal
      relations   75
   mistake   78–80.
      See also Mistake
   offer   71–73
      See also Offer
   parties to. *See* Parties to contract
   subject matter   78
   terms   80–83
      See also Terms of Contract
   unenforceable   78–80
CO_2 emissions information
   advertisements, and
      See Advertisements
Counter-offer
   acceptance, and   73–74
Country of origin
   trade descriptions   62
Courtesy cars   205, 210
   hiring contracts, and   218
Credit card
   payment by   171–172
Criminal law
   appropriate, whether   13

Criminal liability
  seller, and   150–151
'Current MOT certificate'
  trade descriptions, and   60
Customers' remedies   140–150
  consumers   146–150
    See also Consumers,
      remedies for
  damages   145–146
    See also Damages
  rejection   141–144

Damages   145–146
  consequential losses   145–146
  misrepresentation, for   105–106
  meaning   187–188
Delivery problems   106–112
  charges   107
  customer's failure to take
    delivery   108–109
  delivery, meaning   106
  failure to deliver within
    time agreed   107–108
  specific goods   107
  unpaid seller   109–112
    See also Unpaid seller
  what has to be delivered   107
Department for Transport   261
Deposits   103–105
  consumer customers   104–105
  non-consumer customers   104
Director General of Fair Trading   14
'Director's car'
  trade descriptions   64
Disclaimers
  odometers. *See* Odometers
Disposal of uncollected goods
  forms   315–316
Distance selling contracts   83–88
  enforcement   87–88
  'organised process'   83–84
  performing   87
  right to cancel   85–87
  consequences of
    cancellation   86–87

Distance selling contracts—*continued*
  exceptions   86
  scope of Regulations   83–84, 85

Enforcement authorities   260
Enforcement orders   14–16
  procedure   15–16
Enterprise Act 2002   91
Estoppel
  seller's right to sell, and   115–116
Exclusion clauses   4–5
Exclusive distribution   9–10
Extended warranties   153–155
  Financial Services Agency,
    and   155
  insurance, as   154
  unfairness of terms   154–155

Facilities
  provision for no payment   219
Fair trading   14–23
Fair Trading Act 1973   89–90
  controls on sales of spare
    parts   89–90
False
  meaning   52
Financing the sale   156–172
  canvassing   167
  Consumer Credit Act 1974   157
    See also Consumer
      Credit Act 1974
  credit card   171–172
  liability where car
    defective   170–171
    hire purchase   170–171
    loans   170
  pre-contract information   166–167
    distance selling, and   167
  retailer and finance
    company   167–169
    recourse agreements   168–169
    retailer as agent of
      finance company   168
    terms of contract   167
  sources of credit   156

Finance for purpose 138–140
  cars 139
  secondhand cars 140
  statutory provision 138
Fraud
  contract, and 78
Fuel consumption
  advertisements, and. *See*
    Advertisements

Garaging
  contract 219
General safety requirements 230–234
  Consumer Protection Act
    1987, Pt II 230–231
  enforcement 23
  safe, meaning 231
  General Product Safety
    Regulations 1994 232–234
  defences 234
  monitoring 233
  penalties 234
  products 233
  prohibition of unsafe
    consumer products 232–233
Guidance for car dealers
  consumer credit licence holders
    and applicants 263–281
  Business Advertisements
    (Disclosure) Order
    1977 279
  business names 276
  business ownership 268–269
  Companies Act 1985 279
  consideration of information
    on fitness 276
  consumer credit
    agreements 278
  consumer goods and
    services 278
  credit 269–270
  credit brokerage services
    and fees 277–278

Guidance for car dealers—*continued*
  credit repair 279
  encouraging competition 271
  false or misleading
    descriptions or
    advertising 266–268
  fitness-key issues 273–274
  fitness of licensee or
    applicant 270
  fitness test 272–273
  gathering information 275–276
  guidance booklets for
    traders 280–281
  handling money in
    course of business
    administration 279
  knowing when practices
    have been considered
    unfair 275
  non-status lending 280
  notifying changes 277
  protecting consumers 271
  purpose 264–265
  responsibilities under
    Company Directors
    Disqualification Act
    1986 278
  roadworthiness 266
  scope 264
  transferring licence 277
  variation of licence 276
  vehicle ownership 269

Handbooks
  trade descriptions, and 59–60
Health and Safety Executive 260
Hire purchase
  liability where car
    defective 170–171
Hire Purchase Information
  Ltd 119
Hire-purchase sales
  terms of contract 82–83

Hiring contracts | 212–218
  consumer hire agreement | 212
  contents | 212–213
  copies of agreement | 213
  courtesy cars | 218
  deferred payment
    schemes | 217–218
  implied terms | 214–216
    description | 215
    quality | 216
    title | 215
  owners' rights if hirer
    defaults | 214
  right of hirer to terminate
    contract | 214
  right to cancel | 213

Identity
  mistake as to | 79–80
In the course of a trade or
  business
  meaning | 49–50
Insurance regulation
  repairs, and | 209–211
  servicing, and | 209–211
Intention to enter into legal
  relations | 75

Licensed vehicles
  seller's right to sell, and | 119–120
Licensing, control of | 16–17
Lien 205–209
  repairer, of | 205–209
    effect of sale by bailee | 208–209
    enforcing | 207
    extinguishment | 209
    selling uncollected
      goods | 207–208
Loans
  liability where car defective | 170
Local authorities
  consumer protection
    departments | 260

Mail order transactions | 45

Married women
  parties to contract | 77
Manufacturer's liability to
  customer | 183–196
  negligence | 183–187
    duty of care | 183–185
    modern motor industry
      cases | 185–187
  strict liability | 187–191
    defect, meaning | 187–188
    defences | 189–191
    design defect | 190
    'development risk' | 190
    level of | 189
    period of | 188
    product, meaning | 189
    who is liable | 189
Manufacturer's
  responsibility | 181–196
  customers, liability to | 183–196
    See also Manufacturer's
      liability to customer
  privity of contract, and | 181
  retailer, liability to | 182–183
    exclusions of liability | 182–183
Manufacturer's warranty | 191–196
  codes of practice | 194–195
  contents | 193
  collateral contract, as | 192
  effect | 191
  legal status | 191
  legislation | 193–194
  New Car Code | 194–195
  OFT recommendations | 195–196
Mercantile agents
  sales by | 114–115
Merchantability | 129–134
  new cars | 130–133
    minor faults | 130–133
    rectification at low cost | 132
    serious faults | 130
    teething troubles | 131
  used cars | 133–134
    price, relevance of | 134
    safety | 133

Merchantable quality
  meaning 129
Minors
  parties in contract 76–77
Misdescription of goods 6
Misleading
  meaning 38
Misleading price indications 36–41
  Code of Practice for Retailers on Price Indications 39–40
  consumer, meaning 37
  defences 40
  misleading, meaning 38
  price, meaning 37
  regulations 40–41
  who can commit offence 37
Misrepresentation
  damages for 105–106
Mistake 78–80
  contract, and 78–80
  documents mistakenly signed 80
  identity 79–80
Money laundering 113
MOT certificate
  trade descriptions, and 60
Motor industry
  codes of practice for 18–19
  development of consumer protection, and 1–13
  service standards 1
  trade descriptions. *See* Trade descriptions

National Consumer Council 260
Negligence
  duties of repairer, and 200
  manufacturer, and. *See* Manufacturer's liability to consumer
  seller's liability, and 151–152
Negotiating sale 97–106
  deposits 103–105
    See also Deposits

Negotiating sale—*continued*
  order form 98–103
    See also Order form
  part-exchange 103
  statements made during 98
'New car' 63–64
  delivery mileage 64
  merchantability 130–133
    See also Merchantibility
  mint condition 64
  previous retail sale 63
  trade descriptions 63–64
  year of manufacture 64
New Car Code
  disciplinary proceedings 22–23
New passenger car
  meaning 32

Odometers 65–68
  disclaimer 66–68
    inadequate 67
    rules for use 67–68
  replacement 65–66
  trade descriptions 65–68
  zeroing 65
Offer 71–73
  auctions 72
  conditional 73
  meaning 29–30
  self-service displays 72–73
Office of Fair Trading 14, 260
  recommendations as to manufacturer's warranties 195–196
  repair and servicing contracts, and 197
'One lady owner' 64
Order form 98–103
  clear and intelligible language 100
  consumer 98–99
  examples of motor industry terms challenged as unfair 101–103

Order form—*continued*
  scope of regulations 99–100
  unfairness consequences
    of 100–101
Origin marking 68–69
'Over 40 mpg'
  trade descriptions 61

Parking
  contract 219
Part-exchange
  terms 103
Parties to contract 76–77
  agents 77
  limited companies 76
  married women 77
  minors 76–77
Paying for goods 112–113
  cash 112–113
Petrol 235–245
  consumer, contract with 243–245
  display of prices 240
  licensing 235–237
    appeals 236
    conditions 235–236
    fees 237
    penalties 237
    period of licence 236
  prescribed limits of error
    ordinarily applicable on
    testing for quantities above
    minimum delivery of
    equipment 244
  prescribed limits of error
    ordinarily applicable on
    testing for quantities
    equivalent to minimum
    delivery of equipment
    only 245
  pumps, calibration 240–243
    continued use of unstamped
      equipment 242
    notice 242–243

Petrol—*continued*
  pumps, calibration—*continued*
    method of testing 241
    stamping 241
    testing 240–241
  taking delivery 237–240
    enforcement 239
    general requirements 237–238
    penalties 239
    storage tanks 238–239
    warning notices 239–240
  Trade Descriptions Act
    1968 243
Price
  meaning 37
Price marking 41–43
  indicating selling price 41–42
  Price Marking Order 2004 41
    application 42–43
    defences 43
    penalties 43
    unit prices 42
    VAT 42
Pricing 35–43
  misleading price
    indications 36–41
    See also Misleading
      price indications
  resale price maintenance 35–36
Private purchase
  meaning 118–119
Privity of contract
  manufacturer's responsibility,
    and 181
Product
  meaning 189
Product liability 10
Prosecution 13

Quality of goods 123–140
  buying in course of
    business 126–128
  consumer sales 125–126, 127

Quality of goods—*continued*
  exclusion clauses   128–129
    prosecutions   128–129
  implied terms   125–129
  merchantable quality   129
    See also Merchantability
  non-consumer sales   125–129
  sale in course of business   125
  satisfactory quality   129, 134–138
    See also Satisfactory
      quality
  unclear law   124

Reasonable precautions
  meaning   55–56
Recklessly
  meaning   53
Recourse agreements   168–169
Rejection of goods   141–144
  acceptance, and   141–144
  non-consumer buyers'
    rights   144
  reasonable time   141–144
Remedies
  customers, of. *See* Customers'
    remedies
Repair and servicing   197–211
  care of customer's property
    202–204
    articles in car lost   203–204
    bailee   202–204
    customer leaving car in
      repairer's premises   203
    customer refusing to collect
      vehicle   203
  contracts for   197–211
  courtesy cars   205
  delay, liability for   201
  duties of repairer   198–200
    implied terms   198
    liability for delay   201
    negligence   200
    quality of parts   199
    vicarious liability   200

Repair and servicing—*continued*
  duties of repairer—*continued*
    workmanship, liability
      for   198–200
  estimates   201–202
  exclusion clauses   204–205
    contractual liability   204–205
    negligence, liability for   205
  insurance regulation   209–211
    carrying out work for
      insurance companies   210
    courtesy cars   210
    effect   211
    Financial Services Agency   210
  lien   205–209
    See also Lien
  Office of Fair Trading, and   197
  quotations   201–202
  Road Traffic Acts   205
  subcontracting   204
Representations
  advertisements, in   28–29
Resale price maintenance   35–36
Restrictive Trade Practices
  Act 1976   90

Safe
  meaning   231
Safety   220–234
  British Standards   223
  Construction and Use
    Regulations   220–221
  EC Directives   225
    type approval   225
  ECE regulations   224
  fitting of parts subsequent
    to sale   221–222
  international regulations   224–225
  national regulations   220–223
  type approval   222–223
    single vehicle approval   223
  vehicle recalls   225–228
    See also Vehicle recalls
Sale by description   122–123
  words with special meaning   123

Sales literature
  trade descriptions, and   58–59
Sales promotion   24–25
  American courts   25
  UK courts   24
Satisfactory quality   134–138
Services
  false statements about. *See* Trade
    descriptions
SMMT Guidance-Handling
    complaints   303–305
SMMT Guidance-
    Monitoring   305–306
SMMT New Car Code of
    Practice   296–308
  accessories   302–303
  advertising   298–299
  definitions   297
  disciplinary action   307–308
  dispute resolution   307–308
  manufacturers' new car
    warranties   300–302
  new car promise   299–300
  relationship between
    manufacturer and
    consumer   297
  replacement parts   302–303
Spare parts
  competition law, and   95–96
  controls on sales   89–90
Self-service displays
  offer, and   72–73
Seller's right to sell   113–122
  bailee   120
  estoppel, and   115–116
  exceptions   114–120
  implied term   113–114
  leased vehicles   119–120
  mercantile agents   114–115
  no right to sell, effect   120–121
  private purchaser   118–119
  sale of motor vehicle
    subject to outstanding
    credit agreements   117–119

Seller's right to sell—*continued*
  sale of motor vehicle subject to
    outstanding credit
    agreements—*continued*
    Hire Purchase Information
      Ltd   119
    sales by buyer in possession   117
    sales by seller in possession 117
    seller limiting responsibility 122
    voidable title   116
Selling goods
  additional liability of
    retailer   97–155,
  breach of statutory duty   152
  consumer transactions   137–138
  criminal liability   150–151
  durability   136
  inspection by buyer   136
  negligence   151–152
  negotiating   97–106
    See also Negotiating sale
  non-contractual civil
    liability   151–152
  reasonableness   136
  statutory provision   135
  strict liability under
    Consumer Protection
    Act 1987, Pt I   152
Servicing   197–211
    See also Repair and
    Servicing
Shop
  meaning   44
Spare parts
  quality of   199
  unroadworthy vehicles, and   229
Statutory approval marks
  trade descriptions   60–61
Strict liability
  Consumer Protection Act
    1987, Pt. I, under
    seller's liability   152
  manufacturer, and. *See*
    Manufacturer's liability to
    customer

Sunday trading   44–45
    large shops   44
    offences   45
    restrictions   44–45
    shops   44
Supply of goods and services   8–9
Super complaints   16

Terms of contract   80–83
    conditions   83
    express   81–82
    express representations   81–82
    hire-purchase sales   82–83
    implied   83
    warranties   83
Trade descriptions   46–69
    Act of 1968   46–58
        'another person'   56
        defences   55–57
        due care and diligence   56–57
        mistake   55
        penalties   57
        reasonable precautions   55–56
        scope   46–47
        time limits   58
    advertisements   58–59
    'any person'   48
    application   50–51
    BS1 approved   60
    compensation orders   57
    country of origin   62
    current MOT certificate   60
    'director's car'   64
    false, meaning   52
    goods, of   47–48
    handbooks   59–60
    in the course of a trade or
        business   49–50
    motor vehicles   58–68
    'new car'   63–64
    notices   43
    odometers   65–68
        See also Odometers
    offence committed, when   48
    'one lady owner'   64

Trade descriptions—*continued*
    oral statements   52
    origin marking   68–69
    'over 40 mpg'   61
    partners   49
    persons liable   48–49
    recorded mileage, statement
        of   51
    sales literature   58–59
    seller   49
    services, false statements
        about   52–55
        free goods   53
        future promise   54
        proof of guilty knowledge
            or recklessness   52–55
        'recklessly'   53
    statements about condition of
        vehicle   62
    statutory approval marks   60–61
    supply of goods, in relation
        to   51
    Trade Descriptions Act 1968   44
    2002 model   61–62
    type approval   60–61
    vehicle specification   65
Trade Descriptions Act
    advertisements, and   30–31
Trade or business
    meaning   34
Trading stamps   43–44
    offences   44
Trading standards officers
    role of   11–12
    powers   12–13
Treaty of Rome   91–96
    Article 81   91–92
    block exemptions   92–93
        after sales service   95
        sales   94
        scope   93
        spare parts   95–96
        type approval   95
    competition law, and   91–96

2002 model
    trade descriptions   61–62
Type approval   222–223
    competition law, and   95
    EC Directives   225
    trade descriptions   60–61

Unfair trading practices   6–7
Unpaid seller   109–112
    'an avoidable market' 111–112
    assessment of damages   110
    damages for non-acceptance   110
    meaning   109
    suing for price   109–110
Unroadworthy vehicles   228–229
    parts   229
    supply   228–229
Used cars
    fitness for purpose   139
    merchantability   133–134

VAT
    price markings, and   42
Vehicle recalls   225–228
    Code of Practice on Vehicle
        Safety Defects   226–227
        reporting of information 227

Vehicle recalls—*continued*
    customer's failure to
      respond to
        campaign   227–228
    legal constraints   225
Vehicle specification
    trade descriptions   65
Vicarious liability
    duties of repairer, and   200
Voidable title
    sale under   116

Warranties
    meaning   83
Warranty
    extended   153–155
        See also Extended
        warranties
    manufacturer's. *See*
        Manufacturer's
        warranty
    remedies of consumer,
      and   141–150
    retailers'   152–153
      contract of sale, and   153
Words with special meaning 123